D1826972

S
T
U
D
Y

T
E
X
T

CIM

PROFESSIONAL DIPLOMA IN MARKETING

PAPER 6

MARKETING PLANNING

In this July 2008 edition

- A **user-friendly format** for easy navigation
- Regular **fast forward** summaries emphasising the key points in each chapter
- Recent examples of marketing practice
- Fully revised for recent exams and developments
- A full **index**

FOR EXAMS IN DECEMBER 2008 AND JUNE 2009

LEARNING MEDIA

Fourth edition July 2008

ISBN 9780 7517 4867 3
(previous edition 9780 7517 4172 8)

British Library Cataloguing-in-Publication Data
A catalogue record for this book
is available from the British Library

Published by

BPP Learning Media Ltd
BPP House, Aldine Place
London W12 8AA

www.bpp.com/learningmedia

Printed in the United Kingdom

We are grateful to the Chartered Institute of Marketing
for permission to reproduce in this text the syllabus,
tutor's guidance notes and past examination
questions. We are also grateful to Karen Beamish of
Stone Consulting for preparing the assignment based
assessment learning material.

Contents

The BPP Study Text

Aims of this Study Text

> To provide you with the knowledge and understanding, skills and application techniques that you need if you are to be successful in your exams

This Study Text has been written around the **Marketing Planning** syllabus.

- It is **comprehensive**. It covers the syllabus content. No more, no less.

- It is targeted to the **exam**. We have taken account of the pilot paper, guidance the examiner has given and the assessment methodology.

> To allow you to study in the way that best suits your learning style and the time you have available, by following your personal Study Plan (see below)

You may be studying at home on your own until the date of the exam, or you may be attending a full-time course. You may like to (and have time to) read every word, or you may prefer to (or only have time to) skim-read and devote the remainder of your time to question practice. Wherever you fall in the spectrum, you will find the BPP Study Text meets your needs in designing and following your personal Study Plan.

> To tie in with the other components of the BPP Effective Study Package to ensure you have the best possible chance of passing the exam

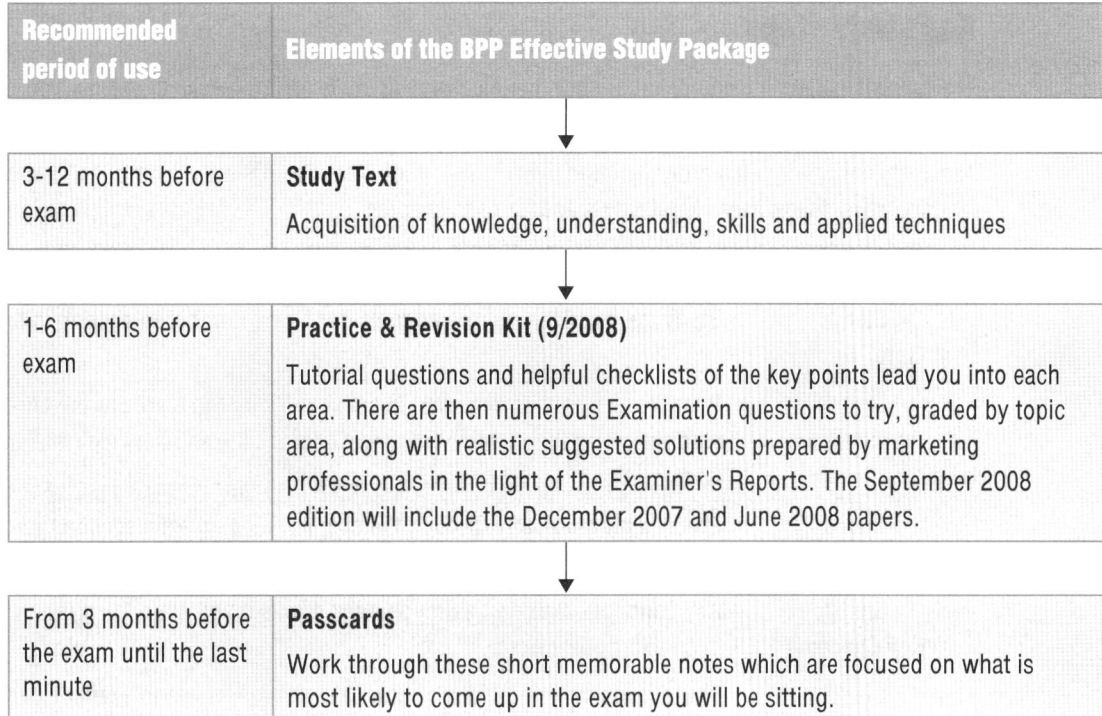

Recommended period of use	Elements of the BPP Effective Study Package
3-12 months before exam	**Study Text** Acquisition of knowledge, understanding, skills and applied techniques
1-6 months before exam	**Practice & Revision Kit (9/2008)** Tutorial questions and helpful checklists of the key points lead you into each area. There are then numerous Examination questions to try, graded by topic area, along with realistic suggested solutions prepared by marketing professionals in the light of the Examiner's Reports. The September 2008 edition will include the December 2007 and June 2008 papers.
From 3 months before the exam until the last minute	**Passcards** Work through these short memorable notes which are focused on what is most likely to come up in the exam you will be sitting.

Settling down to study

By this stage in your career you may be a very experienced learner and taker of exams. But have you ever thought about *how* you learn? Let's have a quick look at the key elements required for effective learning. You can then identify your learning style and go on to design your own approach to how you are going to study this text – your personal Study Plan.

Key element of learning	Using the BPP Study Text
Motivation	You can rely on the comprehensiveness and technical quality of BPP. You've chosen the right Study Text – so you're in pole position to pass your exam!
Clear objectives and standards	Do you want to be a prizewinner or simply achieve a moderate pass? Decide.
Feedback	Follow through the examples in this text and do the Action Programme and the Quick Quizzes. Evaluate your efforts critically – how are you doing?
Study Plan	You need to be honest about your progress to yourself – don't be over-confident, but don't be negative either. Make your Study Plan (see below) and try to stick to it. Focus on the short-term objectives – completing two chapters a night, say – but beware of losing sight of your study objectives.
Practice	Use the Quick Quizzes and Chapter Roundups to refresh your memory regularly after you have completed your initial study of each chapter.

These introductory pages let you see exactly what you are up against. However you study, you should:

- **Read through the syllabus** – this will help you to identify areas you have already covered, perhaps at a lower level of detail, and areas that are totally new to you

- **Study the examination paper section**, where we show you the format of the exam (how many and what kind of questions and so on)

Key study steps

The following steps are, in our experience, the ideal way to study for professional exams. You can of course adapt it for your particular learning style (see below).

Tackle the chapters in the order you find them in the Study Text. Taking into account your individual learning style, follow these key study steps for each chapter.

Key study steps	Activity
Step 1 **Chapter Topic list**	Study the list. Each numbered topic denotes a **numbered section** in the chapter.
Step 2 **Introduction**	Read it through. It is designed to show you **why the topics in the chapter need to be studied** – how they lead on from previous topics, and how they lead into subsequent ones.
Step 3 **Explanations**	Proceed **methodically** through the chapter, reading each section thoroughly and making sure you understand.
Step 4 **Key Concepts**	**Key concepts** can often earn you **easy marks** if you state them clearly and correctly in an appropriate exam.
Step 5 **Exam Tips**	These give you a good idea of how the examiner tends to examine certain topics – pinpointing **easy marks** and highlighting **pitfalls**.
Step 6 **Note taking**	Take **brief notes** if you wish, avoiding the temptation to copy out too much.
Step 7 **Marketing at Work**	Study each one, and try if you can to add flesh to them from your **own experience** – they are designed to show how the topics you are studying come alive (and often come unstuck) in the **real world**. You can also update yourself on these companies by going on to the Internet.
Step 8 **Action Programme**	Make a very good attempt at each one in each chapter. These are designed to put your **knowledge into practice** in much the same way as you will be required to do in the exam. Check the answer at the end of the chapter in the **Action Programme review**, and make sure you understand the reasons why yours may be different.
Step 9 **Chapter Roundup**	Check through it very carefully, to make sure you have grasped the **major points** it is highlighting
Step 10 **Quick Quiz**	When you are happy that you have covered the chapter, use the **Quick Quiz** to check your recall of the topics covered. The answers are in the paragraphs in the chapter that we refer you to.
Step 11 **Illustrative question(s)**	Either at this point, or later when you are thinking about revising, make a full attempt at the **illustrative questions**. You can find these at the end of the Study Text, along with the **Answers** so you can see how you did.

Developing your personal Study Plan

Preparing a Study Plan (and sticking closely to it) is one of the key elements in learning success.

First you need to be aware of your style of learning. There are four typical learning styles. Consider yourself in the light of the following descriptions. and work out which you fit most closely. You can then plan to follow the key study steps in the sequence suggested.

Learning styles	Characteristics	Sequence of key study steps in the BPP Study Text
Theorist	Seeks to understand principles before applying them in practice	1, 2, 3, 7, 4, 5, 8, 9, 10, 11 (6 continuous)
Reflector	Seeks to observe phenomena, thinks about them and then chooses to act	
Activist	Prefers to deal with practical, active problems; does not have much patience with theory	1, 2, 8 (read through), 7, 4, 5, 9, 3, 8 (full attempt), 10, 11 (6 continuous)
Pragmatist	Prefers to study only if a direct link to practical problems can be seen; not interested in theory for its own sake	8 (read through), 2, 4, 5, 7, 9, 1, 3, 8 (full attempt), 10, 11 (6 continuous)

Next you should complete the following checklist.

Am I motivated? (a) [ ]

Do I have an objective and a standard that I want to achieve? (b) [ ]

Am I a theorist, a reflector, an activist or a pragmatist? (c) [ ]

How much time do I have available per week, given: (d) [ ]

- The standard I have set myself

- The time I need to set aside later for work on the Practice and Revision Kit

- The other exam(s) I am sitting, and (of course)

- Practical matters such as work, travel, exercise, sleep and social life?

Now:

- Take the time you have available per week for this Study Text (d), and multiply it by the number of weeks available to give (e) (e) [ ]

- Divide (e) by the number of chapters to give (f) (f) [ ]

- Set about studying each chapter in the time represented by (f), following the key study steps in the order suggested by your particular learning style

This is your personal **Study Plan**.

Short of time?

Whatever your objectives, standards or style, you may find you simply do not have the time available to follow all the key study steps for each chapter, however you adapt them for your particular learning style. If this is the case, follow the Skim Study technique below (the icons in the Study Text will help you to do this).

Skim Study technique

Study the chapters in the order you find them in the Study Text. For each chapter, follow the key study steps 1–2, and then skim-read through step 3, Jump to step 9 and then go back to steps 4–5. Follow through step 7, and prepare outline Answers to the Action Programme (step 8). Try the Quick Quiz (step 10), following up any items you can't answer, then do a plan for the illustrative question (step 11), comparing it against our answers. You should probably still follow step 6 (note-taking).

Moving on...

However you study, when you are ready to embark on the practice and revision phase of the BPP Effective Study Package, you should still refer back to this Study Text:

- As a source of **reference** (you should find the list of key concepts and the index particularly helpful for this)

- As a **refresher** (the Chapter Roundups and Quick Quizzes help you here)

A note on pronouns

On occasions in this Study Text, 'he' is used for 'he or she', 'him' for 'him or her' and so forth. Whilst we try to avoid this practice it is sometimes necessary for reasons of style. No prejudice or stereotyping according to sex is intended or assumed.

Syllabus

Aims and objectives

The *Marketing Planning* module provides the essential knowledge and understanding for Stage 2 in the creation and use of operational marketing plans and the marketing process. It aims to provide participants with an understanding of the differences in the internal organisational and external contexts within which operational marketing planning and marketing are carried out and the different models of marketing used to meet these contingencies. The module aims in particular to ensure that the knowledge and understanding can be applied in the practical construction of appropriate and realistic marketing plans.

Learning outcomes

Participants will be able to:

- Explain the role of the marketing plan within the context of the organisation's strategy and culture and the broader marketing environment (ethics, social responsibility, legal frameworks, sustainability)

- Conduct a marketing audit considering appropriate internal and external factors

- Develop marketing objectives and plans at an operational level appropriate to the internal and external environment

- Develop the role of branding and positioning within the marketing plan

- Integrate marketing mix tools to achieve effective implementation of plans

- Select an appropriate co-ordinated marketing mix incorporating appropriate stakeholder relationships for a particular marketing context

- Set and justify budgets for marketing plans and mix decisions

- Define and use appropriate measurements to evaluate the effectiveness of marketing plans and activities

- Make recommendations for changes and innovations to marketing processes based on an understanding of the organisational context and an evaluation of past marketing activities

Knowledge and skill requirements

Element 1: The marketing plan in its organisational and wider marketing context (15%)		Covered in Chapter
1.1	Describe the roles of marketing and the nature of relationships with other functions in organisations operating in a range of different industries and contexts.	1
1.2	Explain the synergistic planning process – analysis, planning, implementation and control.	2
1.3	List and describe the components of the marketing plan.	2
1.4	Evaluate the role of the marketing plan in relation to the organisation's philosophy or business definition.	2
1.5	Assess the potential impact of wider macro-environmental forces relating to the role of culture, ethical approach, social responsibility, legal frameworks and sustainability.	1

Element 2: Marketing planning & budgeting (20%)		Covered in Chapter
2.1	Explain the constituents of the macro environmental and micro environmental marketing audit.	3
2.2	Assess the external marketing environment for an organisation through a PESTEL audit.	3
2.3	Assess the internal marketing environment for an organisation through an internal audit.	3
2.4	Critically appraise processes and techniques used for auditing the marketing environments.	3
2.5	Explain the role of marketing information and research in conducting and analysing the marketing audit.	3
2.6	Evaluate the relationship between corporate objectives, business objectives and marketing objectives at an operational level.	4
2.7	Explain the concept of the planning gap and its impact on operational decisions.	4
2.8	Determine segmentation, targeting and positioning within the marketing plan.	4
2.9	Determine and evaluate marketing budgets for mix decisions included in the marketing plan.	4
2.10	Describe methods for evaluating and controlling the marketing mix.	4

Element 3: The extended marketing mix and related tools (50%)		Covered in Chapter
3.1	Explain the role of strategy development in relation to developing market share and growth.	4
3.2	Explain how strategy formulation and decisions relating to the selection of markets impact at an operational level on the planning and implementation of an integrated marketing mix.	4
3.3	Explain the role of branding and its impact on the marketing mix decisions.	6
3.4	Describe methods for maintaining and managing the brand.	6

Element 3: The extended marketing mix and related tools (50%)		Covered in Chapter
3.5	Explain how a product or service portfolio is developed to achieve marketing objectives.	6
3.6	Explain the new product development process (including innovative, replacement, re-launched and imitative products) and the role of innovation.	6
3.7	Explain pricing frameworks available to, and used by, organisations for decision-making.	7
3.8	Describe how pricing is developed as an integrated part of the marketing mix.	7
3.9	Determine the channels of distribution and logistics to be used by an organisation and develop a plan for channel support.	7
3.10	Explain how the marketing communications mix is coordinated with the marketing mix as part of a marketing plan.	5
3.11	Explain the importance of customer relationships to the organisation and how they can be developed and supported by the marketing mix.	8
3.12	Describe how a plan is developed for the human element of the service encounter, including staff at different levels of the organisation.	8
3.13	Explain how the physical evidence element of the integrated marketing mix is developed.	8
3.14	Explain how a plan covering the process or the systems of delivery for a service is developed.	8

Element 4: Marketing in different contexts (15%)		Covered in Chapter
4.1	Explain how marketing plans and activities vary in organisations that operate in an international context and develop an appropriate marketing mix.	9
4.2	Develop a marketing plan and select an appropriate marketing mix for an organisation operating in any context such as FMCG, business-to-business (supply chain), large or capital project-based, services, voluntary and not-for-profit, sales support (eg SMES).	10,11
4.3	Explain how marketing plans and activities vary in organisations that operate in a virtual market place and develop an appropriate marketing mix.	8
4.4	Determine an effective extended marketing mix in relation to design and delivery of service encounters (SERVQUAL).	8

Related skills for marketers

There is only so much that a syllabus can include. The syllabus itself is designed to cover the knowledge and skills highlighted by research as core to professional marketers in organisations. However, marketing is performed in an organisational context so there are other broader business and organisational skills that marketing professionals should also posses. The 'key skills for marketers' are therefore an essential part of armoury of the 'complete marketer' in today's organisations. They have been identified from research carried out in organisations where marketers are working.

'Key skills for marketers' are areas of knowledge and competency common to business professionals. They fall outside the CIM's syllabus, providing underpinning knowledge and skills. As such they will be treated as systemic to all marketing activities, rather than subjects treated independently in their turn. While it is not intended that the key skills are formally taught as part of programmes, it is expected that tutors will encourage participants to demonstrate the application of relevant key skills through activities, assignments and discussions during learning.

Using ICT and the Internet

Planning and using different sources to search for and select information; explore, develop and exchange information and derive new information; and present information including text, numbers and images.

Using financial information and metrics

Planning and interpreting information from different sources; carrying out calculations; and presenting and justifying findings.

Presenting information

Contributing to discussions; making a presentation; reading and synthesising information and writing different types of document.

Improving own learning and performance

Agreeing targets and planning how these will be met; using plans to meet targets; and reviewing progress.

Working with others

Planning work and agreeing objectives, responsibilities and working arrangements; seeking to establish and maintain co-operative working relationships; and reviewing work and agreeing ways of future collaborative work.

Problem solving

Exploring problems, comparing different ways of solving them and selecting options; planning and implementing options; and applying agreed methods for checking problems have been solved.

Applying business law

Identifying, applying and checking compliance with relevant law when undertaking marketing activities.

Assessment

CIM will normally offer two forms of assessment for this module from which centres or participants may choose: written examination and continuous assessment. CIM may also recognise, or make joint awards for, modules at an equivalent level undertaken with other professional marketing bodies and educational institutions.

Marketing journals

In addition to reading core and supplementary textbooks participants will be expected to acquire a knowledge and understanding of developments in contemporary marketing theory, practice and issues. The most appropriate sources of information for this include specialist magazines eg *Marketing, Marketing Week, Campaign and Revolution*; dedicated CIM publications eg *Marketing Business*; and business magazines and newspapers eg *The Economist, Management Today, Business Week, The Financial Times*, and the business pages and supplements of the quality press. A flavour of developments in academic marketing can be derived from the key marketing journals including:

Admap
European Journal of Marketing
Journal of the Academy of Marketing Science
Journal of Consumer Behaviour: An International Research Review
Journal of Consumer Research
Marketing Intelligence and Planning
Journal of Marketing
Journal of Marketing Management

The CIM's Magic Formula

The Magic Formula is a tool used by the CIM to help both examiners write exam and assignment questions and you to more easily interpret what you are being asked to write about. It is useful for helping you to check that you are using an appropriate balance between theory and practice for your particular level of qualification.

Contrary to the title, there is nothing mystical about the Magic Formula and simply by knowing it (or even mentioning it in an assessment) will not automatically secure a pass. What it does do however is to help you to check that you are presenting your answers in an appropriate format, including enough marketing theory and applying it to a real marketing context or issue. After passing the Professional Certificate in Marketing, if you continue to study for higher level CIM qualifications, you would be expected to evaluate more and apply a more demanding range of marketing decisions. As such the Magic Formula is weighted with an even greater emphasis on evaluation and application as you move to the Professional Diploma and Postgraduate CIM levels.

Websites

The Chartered Institute of Marketing

www.cim.co.uk	CIM website with information and access to learning support for participants.
www.cimeducator.com	Direct access to information and support materials for all levels of CIM qualification
www.cim.co.uk/tutors	Access for Tutors
www.shapetheagenda.com	Quarterly agenda paper from CIM

Publications on line

www.ft.com	Extensive research resources across all industry sectors, with links to more specialist reports. (Charges may apply)
www.thetimes.co.uk	One of the best online versions of a quality newspaper.
www.economist.com	Useful links, and easily-searched archives of articles from back issues of the magazine.
www.mad.co.uk	Marketing Week magazine online.
www.brandrepublic.com	Marketing magazine online.
www.westburn.co.uk	Journal of Marketing Management online, the official Journal of the Academy of Marketing and Marketing Review.
http://smr.mit.edu/smr/	Free abstracts from Sloan Management Review articles
www.hbsp.harvard.edu	Free abstracts from Harvard Business Review articles
www.ecommercetimes.com	Daily enews on the latest ebusiness developments
www.cim.co.uk/knowledgehub	3000 full text journals titles are available to members via the Knowledge Hub – includes the range of titles above - embargoes may apply.
www.cim.co.uk/cuttingedge	Weekly round up of marketing news (available to CIM members) plus list of awards and forthcoming marketing events.

Sources of useful information

www.1to1.com	The Peppers and Rogers One-to-One Marketing site which contains useful information about the tools and techniques of relationship marketing
www.balancetime.com	The Productivity Institute provides free articles, a time management email newsletter, and other resources to improve personal productivity
www.bbc.co.uk	The Learning Zone at BBC Education contains extensive educational resources, including the video, CD Rom, ability to watch TV programmes such as the News online, at your convenience, after they have been screened
www.busreslab.com	Useful specimen online questionnaires to measure customer satisfaction levels and tips on effective Internet marketing research
www.lifelonglearning.co.uk	Encourages and promotes Lifelong Learning through press releases, free articles, useful links and progress reports on the development of the University for Industry (UFI)
www.marketresearch.org.uk	The Market Research Society. Contains useful material on the nature of research, choosing an agency, ethical standards and codes of conduct for research practice
www.nielsen-netratings.com	Details the current levels of banner advertising activity, including the creative content of the ten most popular banners each week (within Top Rankings area)

Sources of useful information

www.open.ac.uk	Some good Open University videos available for a broad range of subjects
www.direct.gov.uk	Gateway to a wide range of UK government information
www.srg.co.uk	The Self Renewal Group – provides useful tips on managing your time, leading others, managing human resources, motivating others etc
www.statistics.gov.uk	Detailed information on a variety of consumer demographics from the Government Statistics Office
www.durlacher.com	The latest research on business use of the Internet, often with extensive free reports
www.cyberatlas.com	Regular updates on the latest Internet developments from a business perspective
http://ecommerce.vanderbilt.edu	eLab is a corporate sponsored research centre at the Owen Graduate School of Management, Vanderbilt University
www.kpmg.co.uk www.ey.com/uk www.pwcglobal.com	The major consultancy company websites contain useful research reports, often free of charge
http://web.mit.edu	Massachusetts Institute of Technology site has extensive research resources
www.adassoc.org.uk	Advertising Association
www.dma.org.uk	The Direct Marketing Association
www.theidm.co.uk	Institute of Direct Marketing
www.export.org.uk	Institute of Export
www.bl.uk	The British Library, with one of the most extensive book collections in the world
www.managers.org.uk	Chartered Management Institute
www.cipd.co.uk	Chartered Institute of Personnel and Development
www.emerald-library.com	Article abstracts on a range of business topics (fees apply)
www.w3.org	An organisation responsible for defining worldwide standards for the Internet

Case studies

Case studies

www.1800flowers.com	Flower and gift delivery service that allows customers to specify key dates when they request the firm to send them a reminder, together with an invitation to send a gift
www.amazon.co.uk	Classic example of how Internet technology can be harnessed to provide innovative customer service
www.broadvision.com	Broadvision specialises in customer 'personalisation' software. The site contains many useful case studies showing how communicating through the Internet allow you to find out more about your customers
www.doubleclick.net	DoubleClick offers advertisers the ability to target their advertisements on the web through sourcing of specific interest groups, ad display only at certain times of the day, or at particular geographic locations, or on certain types of hardware
www.facetime.com	Good example of a site that overcomes the impersonal nature of the Internet by allowing the establishment of real time links with a customer service representative
www.hotcoupons.com	Site visitors can key in their postcode to receive local promotions, and advertisers can post their offers on the site using a specially designed software package
www.superbrands.org	Access to case studies on international brands

The exam paper

Assessment methods and format of the paper

		Number of marks
Part A:	Compulsory question	50
Part B:	Two questions from a choice of four (25 marks each)	50
		100

Analysis of past papers

December 2007

Part A (compulsory question worth 50 marks)

1   Successful family-owned 'country club' hotel is assessing its options.

    (a)   Environmental challenges; SWOT; choice of strategic options

    (b)   Business expansion

    (c)   Budgeting methods

Part B (two questions to be chosen from four, 25 marks each)

2   B2B marketing plan

3   International product positioning

4   Planning gap and pricing objectives

5   Virtual markets and new media

June 2007

Part A (compulsory question worth 50 marks)

1   Male grooming is a growth market, with fragrance products being an important aspect. Traditional sales channels are being threatened by supermarkets and online retailers.

    (a)   Marketing audit – internal and external factors, SWOT – for online fragrance retailer

    (b)   Two year marketing plan (including budget) aimed at increasing market share

Part B (two questions to be chosen from four, 25 marks each)

2   Branding in FMCG markets; application of product life cycle to marketing mix considerations

3   Importance of customer relationships; plan for overcoming staff problems to improve service

4   New product development

5   Models to use in a marketing audit; role of marketing information and research in the audit

December 2006

Part A (compulsory question worth 50 marks)

1 The UK music industry is embracing the new technology associated with downloading music from the Internet, to turn digital music into a profitable business and drive the industry forward.

    (a)   Environmental scanning and its importance for marketing planners

    (b)   Macro, micro and SWOT analysis

    (c)   Recommendations and justification of marketing strategy to ensure growth

Part B (two questions to be chosen from four, 25 marks each)

2 Product life cycle and BCG – uses and weaknesses

3 B2B marketing communications mix for product launch; use of technology

4 Segmentation, targeting and positioning strategy; impact of strategic decisions upon planning and implementation

5 Marketing plan for a school; methods for evaluating and controlling a marketing plan

June 2006

Part A (compulsory question worth 50 marks)

1 City Cruises is seeking to cement its position as a market leader by opening up new business avenues and more effectively utilising its spare capacity throughout the year.

    (a)   Micro environment analysis

    (b)   Business growth strategy

    (c)   Differentiation for competitive advantage

Part B (two questions to be chosen from four, 25 marks each)

2 Virtual marketing vs traditional marketing mix

3 International marketing and branding

4 Pricing policy and external market influences

5 Social and ethical considerations in marketing plans; evaluating effectiveness and methods for setting the budget

December 2005

Part A (compulsory question worth 50 marks)

1 UK regional airport seeking to revive its business performance.

    (a)   External marketing audit

    (b)   Marketing communications mix

    (c)   Internal marketing and improved service quality

Part B (two questions to be chosen from four, 25 marks each)

2 Product development strategy to expand FMCG sales; role of the brand and marketing mix

3 Devising a marketing budget for the marketing plan; evaluation and control of marketing plan

4 Different pricing frameworks for international market segments; channels of distribution and channel support

5 Synergistic marketing planning process; analysis tools for marketing audit

June 2005

Part A (compulsory question worth 50 marks)

1   Mobile phone market - challenges faced by dominant players.

    (a)   ODMs and other environmental challenges

    (b)   Challenges faced by market leader as a result of industry changes – impact upon marketing tools

    (c)   Suggested branding strategy

Part B (two questions to be chosen from four, 25 marks each)

2   Marketing budget for marketing plan; evaluation and control of marketing plan

3   New product development and innovation; marketing mix for new product

4   Service quality; internal marketing; marketing mix for attracting international customers

5   Gap analysis in marketing planning; distribution channels

December 2004

Part A (compulsory question worth 50 marks)

1   The case study scenario is based on an Italian fashion brand that would like to increase its market share for jeans.

    (a)   Development of a marketing plan. Micro and macro-environmental forces.

    (b)   Co-ordination of marketing communications mix objectives with the marketing mix.

    (c)   Comparison with marketing mix with an international market of the candidates choice.

    (d)   Methods of developing a marketing budget

Part B (answer two questions, 25 marks each)

2   *Fashion jewellery manufacturer*

    (a)   Market penetration strategy. Impact of macro-environmental forces on marketing decisions

    (b)   Brand development and adaptation of marketing mix

3   *Low price airline*

    (a)   SERVQUAL and other models. Improving customer loyalty, service quality and customer satisfaction

    (b)   Role of internal marketing and its importance for service companies

4   *College of education*

    (a)   Concept of the 'planning gap'

    (b)   Ways of closing a planning gap from an operational and strategic perspective

5   *A small company*

    (a)   Marketing planning constraints

    (b)   Measurements to evaluate effectiveness of marketing plans and activities

June 2004

Part A (compulsory question worth 50 marks)

1   You are marketing consultant to Beijing Olympic Organising Committee for 2006 Olympic Games.

    (a)   Macro-environmental influences on marketing plan
    (b)   Role of brand and its importance in attracting sponsorship
    (c)   Service quality and extended marketing mix

Part B (two questions 25 marks each)

2   Marketing plan for a small business looking for funds

3   Marketing audit, including macro-environmental factors, segmentation, targeting and positioning

4   Market penetration strategy, including pricing, in a recessionary environment

5   Reviving and repositioning a consumer product

December 2003

Part A (compulsory question worth 50 marks)

1   The case study setting relates to the coffee shop market, with a focus on Starbucks and its attempts to grow its brand worldwide and attract new customers.

    (a)   Challenges in the marketing environment; ole of informant in an external audit
    (b)   Expansion of the business – growth strategy
    (c)   Recommended extended marketing mix for the brand and the chosen growth strategies

Part B (two questions to be chosen from four, 25 marks each)

2   Marketing budgets – influences; approaches to setting; evaluation and control
3   Product branding and pricing strategy; marketing communications mix
4   Stakeholder relationships and the international context for a non-for profit service organisation
5   Innovation and new product development for an international market

Analysis of Pilot paper

Part A (compulsory question worth 50 marks)

1   The case study setting relates to a bicycle manufacturer with several well known brands, including a newly acquired mountain bike brand.

   (a)   Components of a marketing plan for the new brand
   (b)   Challenges in the marketing environment
   (c)   Analysis of growth strategies
   (d)   Marketing mix for a new range of mountain bike clothing

Part B (two questions from four, 25 marks each)

2   Gap analysis; segmentation and targeting; lifestyle and benefits segmentation variables in the drinks market

3   Innovation; new product development; branding of new products

4   Forecasting techniques; pricing strategy: external factors, marginal analysis and breakeven analysis

5   Service quality in a university: perceptions and internal marketing; marketing mix for international students

---

The Pilot paper and BPP's suggested answer plans are reproduced at the back of the Study Text.

Guide to the Assignment Route

- Aims and objectives of this guide
- Introduction
- Assignment Route, structure and process
- Preparing for assignments: general guide
- Presentation
- Time management
- Tips for writing assignments
- Writing reports
- Resources to support Assignment Based Assessment

Aims and objectives of this Guide to the Assignment Route

- To understand the scope and structure of the Assignment Route process
- To consider the benefits of learning through the Assignment Route
- To assist students in preparation of their assignments
- To consider the range of communication options available to students
- To look at the range of potential assignment areas that assignments may challenge
- To examine the purpose and benefits of reflective practice
- To assist with time-management within the assignment process

Introduction

At time of writing, there are over 80 CIM Approved Study Centres that offer the Assignment Route option as an alternative to examinations. This change in direction and flexibility in assessment was externally driven by industry, students and tutors alike, all of whom wanted a test of practical skills as well as a knowledge-based approach to learning.

At Stage 2, all modules are available via this Assignment Route. The Assignment Route is however optional, and examinations are still available. This will of course depend upon the nature of delivery within your chosen Study Centre.

Clearly, all of the Stage 2 subject areas lend themselves to assignment-based learning, due to their practical nature. The assignments that you will undertake provide you with an opportunity to be **creative in approach and in presentation.** They enable you to give a true demonstration of your marketing ability in a way that perhaps might be inhibited in a traditional examination situation.

The Assignment Route offers you considerable scope to produce work that provides existing and future **employers** with **evidence** of your **ability.** It offers you a **portfolio** of evidence which demonstrates your abilities and your willingness to develop continually your knowledge and skills. It will also, ultimately, help you frame your continuing professional development in the future.

It does not matter what type of organisation you are from, large or small, as you will find substantial benefit in this approach to learning. In some cases, students have made their own organisation central to their assessment and produced work to support their organisation's activities, resulting in subsequent recognition and promotion: a success story for this approach.

So, using your own organisation can be beneficial (especially if your employer sponsors you). However, it is equally valid to use a different organisation, as long as you are familiar enough with it to base your assignments on it. This is particularly useful if you are between jobs, taking time out, returning to employment or studying at university or college.

To take the Assignment Route option, you are required to register with a CIM Accredited Study Centre (ie a college, university, or distance learning provider). **Currently you would be unable to take the assignment route option as an independent learner**. If in doubt you should contact the CIM Education Division, the awarding body, who will provide you with a list of local Accredited Centres offering the Assignment Route.

Structure and process

The **assignments** that you will undertake during your studies are normally set **by CIM centrally** and not usually by the study centre. All assignments are validated to ensure a structured, consistent, approach. This standardised approach to assessment enables external organisations to interpret the results on a consistent basis.

Each module at Stage 2 has one assignment, with four separate elements within it. This is broken down as follows.

- The **Core Section** is compulsory and worth 40% of your total mark.

- The **Elective Section** has four options, from which you must complete **two**. Each of these options is worth 25% of your total mark. Please note here that it is likely that in some Study Centres the option may be chosen for you. This is common practice and is done in order to maximise resources and support provided to students.

- The **Reflective Statement** is also compulsory. It is worth 10%. It should reflect what you feel about your learning experience during the module and how that learning has helped you in your career both now and in the future.

The purpose of each assignment is to enable you to demonstrate your ability to research, analyse and problem-solve in a range of different situations. You will be expected to approach your assignment work from a professional marketer's perspective, addressing the assignment brief directly, and undertaking the tasks required. Each assignment will relate directly to the syllabus module and will be applied against the content of the syllabus.

All of the assignments clearly indicate the links with the syllabus and the assignment weighting (ie the contribution each assignment makes to your overall marks).

Once your assignments have been completed, they will be marked by your accredited centre, and then **moderated** by a CIM External Moderator. When all the assignments have been marked, they are sent to CIM for further moderation. After this, all marks are forwarded to you by CIM (not your centre) in the form of an examination result. Your **centre** will be able to you provide you with some written feedback on overall performance, but **will not** provide you with any detailed mark breakdown.

Preparing for Assignments: general guide

The whole purpose of this guide is to assist you in presenting your assessment professionally, both in terms of presentation skills and overall content. In many of the assignments, marks are awarded for presentation and coherence. It might therefore be helpful to consider how best to present your assignment. Here you should consider issues of detail, protocol and the range of communications that could be called upon within the assignment.

Presentation of the Assignment

You should always ensure that you prepare two copies of your assignment, keeping a soft copy on disc. On occasions assignments go missing, or second copies are required by CIM.

- Each assignment should be clearly marked up with your name, your study centre, your CIM Student registration number and ultimately at the end of the assignment a word count. The assignment should also be word-processed.

- The assignment presentation format should directly meet the requirements of the assignment brief, (ie reports and presentations are the most called for communication formats). You **must** ensure that you assignment does not appear to be an extended essay. If it does, you will lose marks.

- The word limit will be included in the assignment brief. These are specified by CIM and must be adhered to.

- Appendices should clearly link to the assignment and can be attached as supporting documentation at the end of the report. However failure to reference them by number (eg Appendix 1) within the report and also marked up on the Appendix itself will lose you marks. Only use an Appendix if it is essential and clearly adds value to the overall assignment. The Appendix is not a waste bin for all the materials you have come across in your research, or a way of making your assignment seem somewhat heavier and more impressive than it is.

Time management for Assignments

One of the biggest challenges we all seem to face day-to-day is that of managing time. When studying, that challenge seems to grow increasingly difficult, requiring a balance between work, home, family, social life and study life. It is therefore of pivotal importance to your own success for you to plan wisely the limited amount of time you have available.

Step 1   **Find out how much time you have**

Ensure that you are fully aware of how long your module lasts, and the final deadline. If you are studying a module from September to December, it is likely that you will have only 10-12 weeks in which to complete your assignments. This means that you will be preparing assignment work continuously throughout the course.

Step 2   **Plan your time**

Essentially you need to **work backwards** from the final deadline, submission date, and schedule your work around the possible time lines. Clearly if you have only 10-12 weeks available to complete three assignments, you will need to allocate a block of hours in the final stages of the module to ensure that all of your assignments are in on time. This will be critical as all assignments will be sent to CIM by a set day. Late submissions will not be accepted and no extensions will be awarded. Students who do not submit will be treated as a 'no show' and will have to resubmit for the next period and undertake an alternative assignment.

Step 3   **Set priorities**

You should set priorities on a daily and weekly basis (not just for study, but for your life). There is no doubt that this mode of study needs commitment (and some sacrifices in the short term). When your achievements are recognised by colleagues, peers, friends and family, it will all feel worthwhile.

Step 4   **Analyse activities and allocate time to them**

Consider the **range** of activities that you will need to undertake in order to complete the assignment and the **time** each might take. Remember, too, there will be a delay in asking for information and receiving it.

- Preparing terms of reference for the assignment, to include the following.

  1. A short title

  2. A brief outline of the assignment purpose and outcome

  3. Methodology – what methods you intend to use to carry out the required tasks

  4. Indication of any difficulties that have arisen in the duration of the assignment

  5. Time schedule

  6. Confidentiality – if the assignment includes confidential information ensure that this is clearly marked up and indicated on the assignment

  7. Literature and desk research undertaken

This should be achieved in one side of A4 paper.

- A literature search in order to undertake the necessary background reading and underpinning information that might support your assignment

- Writing letters and memos asking for information either internally or externally

- Designing questionnaires

- Undertaking surveys

- Analysis of data from questionnaires

- Secondary data search

- Preparation of first draft report

Always build in time to spare, to deal with the unexpected. This may reduce the pressure that you are faced with in meeting significant deadlines.

Warning!

The same principles apply to a student with 30 weeks to do the work. However, a word of warning is needed. Do not fall into the trap of leaving all of your work to the last minute. If you miss out important information or fail to reflect upon your work adequately or successfully you will be penalised for both. Therefore, time management is important whatever the duration of the course.

Tips for writing Assignments

Everybody has a personal style, flair and tone when it comes to writing. However, no matter what your approach, you must ensure your assignment meets the **requirements of the brief** and so is comprehensible, coherent and cohesive in approach.

Think of preparing an assignment as preparing for an examination. Ultimately, the work you are undertaking results in an examination grade. Successful achievement of all four modules in a level results in a qualification.

There are a number of positive steps that you can undertake in order to ensure that you make the best of your assignment presentation in order to maximise the marks available.

Step 1   **Work to the brief**

Ensure that you identify exactly what the assignment asks you to do.

- If it asks you to be a marketing manager, then immediately assume that role.

- If it asks you to prepare a report, then present a report, not an essay or a letter.

- Furthermore, if it asks for 2,500 words, then do not present 1,000 or 4,000 unless it is clearly justified, agreed with your tutor and a valid piece of work.

Identify whether the report should be **formal or informal**; who it should be **addressed to**; its **overall purpose** and its **potential use** and outcome. Understanding this will ensure that your assignment meets fully the requirements of the brief and addresses the key issues included within it.

Step 2   **Addressing the tasks**

It is of pivotal importance that you address **each** of the tasks within the assignment. **Many students fail to do this** and often overlook one of the tasks or indeed part of the tasks.

Many of the assignments will have two or three tasks, some will have even more. You should establish quite early on, which of the tasks:

- Require you to collect information
- Provides you with the framework of the assignment, i.e. the communication method.

Possible tasks will include the following.

- *Compare and contrast.* Take two different organisations and compare them side by side and consider the differences ie the **contrasts** between the two.

- *Carry out primary or secondary research.* Collect information to support your assignment and your subsequent decisions

- *Prepare a plan.* Some assignments will ask you to prepare a plan for an event or for a marketing activity – if so provide a step-by-step approach, a rationale, a time-line, make sure it is measurable and achievable. Make sure your actions are very specific and clearly explained. (Make sure your plan is SMART.)

- *Analyse a situation.* This will require you to collect information, consider its content and present an overall understanding of the situation as it exists. This might include looking at internal and external factors and how the current situation evolved.

- *Make recommendations.* The more advanced your get in your studies, the more likely it is that you will be required to make recommendations. Firstly **considering and evaluating your options** and then making justifiable **recommendations**, based on them.

- *Justify decisions.* You may be required to justify your decision or recommendations. This will require you to explain fully how you have arrived at as a result and to show why, supported by relevant information. In other words, you should not make decisions in a vacuum; as a marketer your decisions should always be informed by context.

- *Prepare a presentation.* This speaks for itself. If you are required to prepare a presentation, ensure that you do so, preparing clearly defined PowerPoint or

overhead slides that are not too crowded and that clearly express the points you are required to make.

- *Evaluate performance.* It is very likely that you will be asked to evaluate a campaign, a plan or even an event. You will therefore need to consider its strengths and weaknesses, why it succeeded or failed, the issues that have affected it, what can you learn from it and, importantly, how can you improve performance or sustain it in the future.

All of these points are likely requests included within a task. Ensure that you identify them clearly and address them as required.

Step 3   Information Search

Many students fail to realise the importance of collecting information to **support** and **underpin** their assignment work. However, it is vital that you demonstrate to your centre and to the CIM your ability to **establish information needs**, obtain **relevant information** and **utilise it sensibly** in order to arrive at appropriate decisions.

You should establish the nature of the information required, follow up possible sources, time involved in obtaining the information, gaps in information and the need for information.

Consider these factors very carefully. CIM are very keen that students are **seen** to collect information, **expand** their mind and consider the **breadth** and **depth** of the situation. In your *Personal Development Portfolio*, you have the opportunity to complete a **Resource Log**, to illustrate how you have expanded your knowledge to aid your personal development. You can record your additional reading and research in that log, and show how it has helped you with your portfolio and assignment work.

Step 4   Develop an Assignment Plan

Your **assignment** needs to be structured and coherent, addressing the brief and presenting the facts as required by the tasks. The only way you can successfully achieve this is by **planning the structure** of your Assignment in advance.

Earlier on in this unit, we looked at identifying your tasks and, working backwards from the release date, in order to manage time successfully. The structure and coherence of your assignment needs to be planned with similar signs.

In planning out the Assignment, you should plan to include **all the relevant information as requested** and also you should plan for the use of models, diagrams and appendices where necessary.

Your plan should cover your:

- Introduction
- Content
- Main body of the assignment
- Summary
- Conclusions and recommendations where appropriate

Step 5   Prepare Draft Assignment

It is good practice to always produce a **first draft** of a report. You should use it to ensure that you have met the aims and objectives, assignment brief and tasks related to the actual assignment. A draft document provides you with scope for improvements, and enables you to check for accuracy, spelling, punctuation and use of English.

Step 6   **Prepare Final Document**

In the section headed 'Presentation of the Assignment' in this unit, there are a number of components that should always be in place at the beginning of the assignment documentation, including **labelling** of the assignment, **word counts**, **appendices** numbering and presentation method. Ensure that you **adhere to the guidelines presented**, or alternatively those suggested by your Study Centre.

Writing reports

Students often ask 'what do they mean by a report?' or 'what should the report format include?'.

There are a number of approaches to reports, formal or informal: some report formats are company specific and designed for internal use, rather than external reporting.

For Continuous Assessment process, you should stay with traditional formats.

Below is a suggested layout of a Management Report Document that might assist you when presenting your assignments.

- A *Title Page* includes the title of the report, the author of the report and the receiver of the report

- *Acknowledgements* – this should highlight any help, support, or external information received and any extraordinary co-operation of individuals or organisations

- *Contents page* provides a clearly structured pathway of the contents of the report – page by page.

- *Executive summary* – a brief insight into purpose, nature and outcome of the report, in order that the outcome of the report can be quickly established

- *Main body of the report divided into sections, which are clearly labelled.* Suggested labelling would be on a numbered basis eg:

  - 1.0   Introduction
  - 1.1   Situation Analysis
  - 1.1.1 External Analysis
  - 1.1.2 Internal Analysis

- *Conclusions* – draw the report to a conclusion, highlighting key points of importance, that will impact upon any recommendations that might be made

- *Recommendations* – clearly outline potential options and then recommendations. Where appropriate justify recommendations in order to substantiate your decision

- *Appendices* – ensure that you only use appendices that add value to the report. Ensure that they are numbered and referenced on a numbered basis within the text. If you are not going to reference it within the text, then it should not be there

- *Bibliography* – whilst in a business environment a bibliography might not be necessary, for an **assignment-based report it is vital**. It provides an indication of the level of research, reading and collecting of relevant information that has taken place in order to fulfil the requirements of the assignment task. Where possible, and where relevant, you could provide academic references within the text, which should of course then provide the basis of your bibliography. References should realistically be listed alphabetically and in the following sequence

  - Author's name and edition of the text
  - Date of publication
  - Title and sub-title (where relevant)
  - Edition 1st, 2nd etc

–   Place of publication
–   Publisher
–   Series and individual volume number where appropriate.

Resources to support Assignment Based Assessment

The aim of this guidance is to present you with a range of questions and issues that you should consider, based upon the assignment themes. The detail to support the questions can be found within your BPP Study Text and the 'Core Reading' recommended by CIM.

Additionally you will find useful support information within the CIM Student website www.cim.co.uk -: www.cimvirtualinstitute.com, where you can access a wide range of marketing information and case studies. You can also build your own workspace within the website so that you can quickly and easily access information specific to your professional study requirements. Other websites you might find useful for some of your assignment work include www.wnim.com - (What's New in Marketing) and also www.connectedinmarketing.com – another CIM website.

Other websites include:

www.mad.com	– Marketing Week
www.ft.com	– Financial Times
www.thetimes.com	– The Times newspaper
www.theeconomist.com	– The Economist magazine
www.marketing.haynet.com	– Marketing magazine
www.ecommercetimes.com	– Daily news on e-business developments
www.open.gov.uk	– Gateway to a wide range of UK government information
www.adassoc.org.uk	– The Advertising Association
www.marketresearch.org.uk	– The Marketing Research Society
www.amazon.com	– Online Book Shop
www.1800flowers.com	– Flower and delivery gift service
www.childreninneed.com	– Charitable organisation
www.comicrelief.com	– Charitable organisation
www.samaritans.org.uk	– Charitable organisation

Part A
The marketing plan in context

The marketing context

Syllabus content – knowledge and skills requirements

- 1.1: The roles of marketing and the nature of relationships with other functions in organisations operating in a range of different industries and contexts
- 1.5: The potential impact of wider macro-environmental forces relating to the role of culture, ethical approach, social responsibility, legal frameworks and sustainability

Introduction

This chapter sets the activity known as marketing in its wider organisational and societal context. Within an organisation, the marketing concept, marketing techniques and marketing staff have a major role as integrators. They tend to draw together the disparate activities of other functions.

In Section 2 we examine the way the wider environmental setting impacts on marketing activity. Organisations find it increasingly important to safeguard their reputations. Their activities must conform both to the demands of the law and to accepted norms of ethical and socially responsible behaviour. This is particularly important in the wake of the major scandals of business ethics that have occurred in the first years of the 21st Century.

Sections 3, 4, 5, and 6 build on these wide-ranging, introductory discussions and fill in some of the detail of how marketing relates to the rest of the organisation.

1 The roles of marketing

FAST FORWARD

Marketing is a key function in a contemporary business.

Key concept

Marketing is the management process responsible for identifying, anticipating and satisfying customer requirements profitably. (CIM)

There are many other definitions that expand on the CIM's own definition. Here is what Dibb *et al* (2001) have to say:

Marketing consists of individual and organisational activities that facilitate and expedite satisfying exchange relationships in a dynamic environment through the creation, distribution, promotion and pricing of goods, services and ideas.

This is a more detailed definition and identifies some specific activities.

FAST FORWARD

Marketing as an **activity** differs from marketing as a **concept**. A market orientation can prevail outside the marketing department.

The related term **'marketing concept'** is fundamental to the modern approach to marketing. Kotler (1991) says this:

The marketing concept holds that the key to achieving organisational goals lies in determining the needs and wants of target markets and delivering the desired satisfactions more efficiently and effectively than the competition.

 Marketing at Work

Application

Needs are basic human requirements such as food, clothing, shelter, exercise, etc. Some people might be able to satisfy their needs for exercise by going for a run in a public park.

Wants refer to needs directed to specific objectives that might satisfy the need, For example, people might want to meet their needs for exercise by joining an exclusive country club to play golf.

The marketing manager of an exclusive country club may carry out various marketing activities to transform the needs of people for exercise into wants to play golf at a country club.

Kotler (1991) also uses the word **demand** which refers to the wants being backed up by an ability to pay, ie can the potential customer afford the membership fees to join an exclusive country club?

It is necessary for us to strike a clear distinction between marketing as an **activity**, and marketing as a **concept** of how an organisation should go about its business.

1.1 Models of marketing

There are four key models of marketing:

- The **sales support** model of marketing is essentially reactive and includes such activities as telesales and organising exhibitions.
- The **marketing communications** model of marketing is more proactive, promoting organisations, products and services at a tactical level.
- The **operational marketing** model of marketing includes a co-ordinated range of marketing activities, from marketing research, through brand management and corporate communications to customer relationship management.
- The **strategic marketing** model requires marketing to contribute to corporate strategy.

(a) **Sales support**: the emphasis in this role is essentially reactive: marketing supports the direct sales force. It may include activities such as telesales or telemarketing, responding to inquiries, co-ordinating diaries, customer database management, organising exhibitions or other sales promotions, and administering agents. These activities usually come under a sales and marketing director or manager. This form of marketing is common in SMEs and some organisations operating in a B2B context.

(b) **Marketing communications**: the emphasis in this role is more proactive: marketing promotes the organisation and its product or service at a tactical level, either to customers (pull) or to channel members (push). It typically includes activities such as providing brochures and catalogues to support the sales force. Some B2C organisations may use marketing to perform the selling role using direct marketing techniques, and to manage campaigns based on a mix of media to raise awareness, generate leads and even take orders. In B2B markets, larger organisations may have marketing communications departments and specialists to make efficient use of marketing expenditures and to co-ordinate communications between business units.

(c) **Operational marketing**: the emphasis in this role is for marketing to support the organisation with a co-ordinated range of marketing activities including marketing research, brand management, product development and management, corporate and marketing communications and customer relationship management. Planning is also usually performed in this role.

(d) **Strategic marketing**: the emphasis in this role is on marketing to contribute to the creation of competitive strategy. As such, it is practised in customer-focused and larger organisations. In a large or diversified organisation, it may also be responsible for the co-ordination of several marketing departments.

The strategic marketing model, and sometimes even the operational marketing model, are likely to be found in organisations with a strong market or customer orientation, or with separate marketing departments in business units that require central co-ordination.

In organisations with a weak customer orientation (typically a production, sales, product or technology orientation), the role of marketing is likely to be manifested in terms of sales support or marketing communications.

Operational marketing activities. This includes a variety of activities as illustrated in the CIM's Statement of Marketing Practice. It includes:

- Research and analysis
- Contributing to strategy and marketing planning
- Managing brands
- Implementing marketing programmes
- Measuring effectiveness
- Managing marketing teams

1.1.1 The role of operational marketing

(a)   The primary role of operational marketing is to support the organisation's business or corporate objectives and strategies. Marketers at this level may also have an input to business strategy and influence the culture of the organisation to ensure that both have a strong customer focus. The role usually entails the planning and implementation of marketing strategies. These activities are usually carried out by a marketing manager and staff, often within a department called 'marketing'.

(b)   In terms of planning, operational marketing involves making decisions about marketing resource utilisation, as well as the selection of the most appropriate marketing tools. Available tools include brands, innovation, customer relationships and service, alliances, channels and communications, and, increasingly, price.

(c)   Marketing works not in isolation but closely with other functions in the business, including management, sales, product development engineers and HR. This has important consequences for the levels of business skill and knowledge that marketers are expected to use, as well as their basic technical marketing skills.

(d)   Operational marketing supports the organisation's specific competitive position, which has been developed at the strategic planning stage.

1.2 Marketing and other functions

The role and relationships of the marketing function within any business depends on a variety of practical factors particular to that business. These factors may include the corporate culture, the size of the business, the nature of the industry (manufacturing, service, agriculture, mining, public service etc), the position of its products and services in relation the product or service life cycle, the nature of the product or service and the expectations of its customers and potential customers.

Some businesses are fragmented, and the functions operate independently. Other businesses are more integrated and operations have a high degree of co-ordination. Generally the marketing function must work closely with other departments to implement the marketing concept. However, marketers should be aware that other functions also have valid and valuable roles to fulfil in delivering customer satisfaction and implementing the corporate strategy. Here are some examples.

(a)   The **finance department** is responsible for raising the working capital that permits the granting of favourable credit terms to customers.

(b)   The **HR department** is responsible for recruiting and training the customer service personnel, delivery staff and service engineers who operate at the **customer interface** and help to build the organisation's image and reputation.

(c)   **Purchasing managers** control much of the process by which a given level of quality and reliability is incorporated into products.

Customers are not interested in how a business is structured into different functions. Hence marketers should work together with other functions in the business to provide customers with a seamless service.

Action Programme 1

Suggest another role that supports the marketing concept for each of the departments above.

Marketing at Work

A company sells electrical equipment such as fridges, washing machines, stoves and televisions. It has 50 stores spread over the country working from local retail parks.

Purchasing is done on a centralised basis and a large proportion of the goods are sourced from countries such as China, Korea, Germany and Italy. Each store or outlet places an internal orders for supplies.

There is a centralised HR department which develops recruitment practices and training standards and programmes. However, actual recruitment and training is done locally at each outlet.

The company also believes in developing innovative financing arrangements to help customers to buy its products. A popular arrangement is hire purchase schemes with 0% finance for the first 6 months.

The marketing function needs to work closely with other functions to ensure that the customer experiences a seamless offering. In practice, this may require significant discussion and internal negotiation until the needs of each function can be mutually met.

- **Finance**

  The company must have enough working capital to carry its customers through the interest free period. The paperwork must be easy to deal with so that the customer does not feel intimidated by entering into a contract to buy a piece of equipment.

  The marketing function might like 0% financing to be an ongoing sales offer, whereas the finance function might prefer a limited period. Marketing must liaise with finance to develop a business solution that satisfies the needs of the customer and the company.

- **Purchasing**

  The systems must be sufficiently sophisticated and efficient to ensure that stock-outs do not arise and also that customers receive their deliveries within the promised period.

  Marketing might prefer a delivery time of 3 days, but purchasing might be more comfortable with a delivery period of 7 days

  Again, marketing and purchasing must discuss and agree on a viable and sustainable policy.

- **Human resources**

  Marketing also needs to liaise with HR on person and pay specifications so that the company hires the appropriate sorts of employees at the appropriate pay rates.

  Marketing needs to clarify the types of skills staff should have such as selling, customer care and effective communication.

Action Programme 2   Application

The Dougall family lives in a small countryside village in Scotland where there is very little public transport available. The Dougall family consists of father, mother, daughter (aged 15), son (aged 12), daughter (aged 6) and a baby daughter (aged 3).

The father works as a shoe shop manager in a nearby town which is approximately 10 miles away. The mother has a part time job at the local bakery. The three eldest children are at school. There is a child carer who looks after the 3 year old during the day when mother is working at the bakery.

Mr and Mrs Dougall are considering acquiring a motor vehicle. Discuss how the manager of a motor dealer might assess Mr and Mrs Dougall in terms of needs, wants and demand.

1.3 Marketing activities

The basic marketing mix offers us a useful framework within which to discuss the relationship of marketing activities to other organisational functions. The marketing mix activities themselves will be covered more comprehensively in Part C of this Study Text.

1.3.1 Product

(a)   **Product development and enhancement** of physical products is usually carried out in conjunction with R&D and production. These often involve technically minded people who may have different attitudes and approaches when perceiving and solving problems. With regard to service marketing, there may be other kinds of technicality. For example, if a firm of solicitors wishes to provide independent financial advice, the very demanding regulatory regime governing such services is likely to be a key consideration in the marketing of the new service.

(b)   **Packaging** refers to 'all the activities of designing and producing the container for a product'. (Kotler, 2003). Packaging serves various purposes and involves several considerations.

   (i)   **Protection** of product eg sturdy boxes for breakable products

   (ii)   **Preservation** of the product eg plastic bags to keep bread and cakes fresh and hygienic

   (iii) **Security** of product eg small digital camera memory cards packaged in large plastic packs to deter shoplifters

   (iv)   **Convenience**. Packaging is designed to facilitate storage by supplier or customer, as well as convenience of use eg different types of nozzles on drinks and sauce containers

   (v)   **Branding** eg the Coca-Cola bottle is a huge source of promotion for the company

   (vi)   **Profitability** eg larger sized nozzles on tubes and bottles encourage more use. Larger sized cans or bottles usually encourage greater consumption.

1.3.2 Place

Distribution decisions address the question of 'where do our customers want to receive their goods or services?' This is an aspect where there has been significant change and development, and there is now much more scope for market decision making, especially with the advent of e-commerce.

In the retail sector, trends in store location should be taken into account. Sellers of bulky goods such as electrical goods and furniture are relocating from town centres to suburban retail parks, where parking is easier. On the other hand, supermarket chains are taking over smaller local operators, with a view to growing their sales by serving the town shopper.

 Marketing at Work   Application

In the UK, the big supermarket chains Tesco and Sainsbury have reached saturation growth in terms of large out-of-town and suburban retail stores. To enhance sales growth, both of these chains have acquired smaller chains and independent shops in town and city centres and converted them into small retail convenience outlets. Tesco is branded Tesco Express at such outlets whereas Sainsbury have called theirs Sainsbury Local.

Place decisions may also influence an organisation's globalisation strategy. If clients and/or customers have overseas locations it may be beneficial to set up distribution facilities locally. The presence of overseas facilities enables the organisation to extend its **market coverage** and **global reach**.

It is important to understand the structure of the distribution channel and the role of the players within it. A key concept is **channel captaincy**, which refers to the organisations that hold the most power within a channel and can drive changes in it. In the past, for example, food manufacturers controlled the retail food industry as they were fewer in number, and bigger in size, than the supermarkets and other independent retailers. Supermarkets have since become bigger and more successful, and can usually dictate terms to manufacturers and other suppliers.

Marketers are likely to be involved in activities such as outlet planning, supply chain management, and route to market decisions. They may be involved in order-processing, warehousing, logistics, stockholding and control, transport operations, delivery tracking and IT systems development. They may also be involved in export operations and the use of shipping and forwarding skills.

1.3.3 Promotion

Promotion is, of course, the focus of a great deal of marketing attention and might, with justification, be regarded as the marketing specialist's home turf. Nevertheless, it does not take place in a vacuum. It must not promise what cannot be delivered, it must work within budget (particularly where sales promotion is concerned) and individual aspects of promotion must not undermine the overall corporate image.

It is important to remember the product or service's Unique Selling Proposition (USP) or Basic Consumer Benefit (BCB) and ensure that the **message** is in **alignment** with these. The medium of communication must then match the message. Promotional tools include advertisements, press releases, sales promotions, in-store demonstrations, exhibitions, trade fairs and public relations.

1.3.4 Price

Cost is a major consideration in price-setting and here the marketer must utilise the expertise of the management accountant. Also associated with this aspect of the mix is the whole topic of terms of sale: expert advice is necessary if maximum protection is to be obtained against the customer who does not or cannot pay.

Factors influencing price include costs, competition, customer expectations and business objectives.

2 Marketing and society   6/06

Ethics is about right and wrong. An organisation exercises **social responsibility** when its acts respect the general public interest. Ethics and law are not the same. Strategies for social responsibility may be **proactive**, **reactive**, **defensive** or seek **accommodation**.

Key concept | **Ethics** is the study of right and wrong actions.

2.1 The nature of ethics

In simple terms, ethics is concerned with right and wrong and how conduct should be judged as to be good or bad. Ethics is about how we should live our lives and, in particular, how we should behave towards other people. They are the moral principles which guide thinking, decision making and action. It is therefore relevant to all forms of human activity. Business ethics is not really separate or different from ideas that apply in the general context of human life. Professionals of all specialisations should be aware of the general principles of ethics and be capable of applying them in their everyday work.

Social responsibility requires that organisations do not act in a way which harms the general public or is socially irresponsible. **Marketing ethics** relate to morality rather than society's interests, and affect customers rather than society at large. Marketing ethics concern marketing decisions, whereas social responsibility is about corporate decisions. However, because corporate decisions subsume marketing decisions the **terms marketing ethics and social responsibility are often used interchangeably**.

2.2 The well-being of individuals and society

Critics of marketing argue that it is dedicated to selling some products which are potentially damaging to the health and well-being of the **individual** or the **society** in which consumers live. Examples include tobacco, alcohol, automobiles, detergents and even electronic goods such as computers and video recorders. It has been argued that even seemingly beneficial, or at least harmless, products such as soft drinks, sunglasses or agricultural fertiliser, can be damaging. In traditional societies, new products can disrupt social order by introducing new aspirations, or changing a long established way of life.

 Marketing at Work   Application

Diageo (*www.diageo.com*) sees social responsibility as an important aspect of its activities. This is manifested in the following principles that the company has expressed with regard to social responsibility.

- Good business sense
- Proud of what we do
- Highest standards of advertising and marketing
- Employees as ambassadors
- We want our consumers to make informed choices
- Social responsibility advertising

How should the marketer react to these issues? There appears to be a clear conflict: what is profitable for a business organisation may not be in the interest of the customer, or the society within which the transaction is taking place.

2.3 Ethics and the law

Ethics deal with personal moral principles and values, but laws are the rules that can actually be enforced in court. Behaviour which is not subject to legal penalties may still be unethical.

Different cultures view marketing practices differently. While the idea of **intellectual property** is widely accepted in Europe and the USA, in other parts of the world ethical standards are quite different. Unauthorised use of copyrights, trademarks and patents is widespread in countries such as Taiwan, Mexico and Korea. According to a US trade official, the Korean view is that ' ... the thoughts of one man should benefit all', and this general value means that, in spite of legal formalities, few infringements of copyright are punished.

2.4 Ethics in marketing

2.4.1 Product issues

Ethical issues relating to products usually revolve around **safety**, **quality**, and **value** and frequently arise from failure to provide adequate **information** to the customer. This may range from omission of uncomfortable facts in product literature to deliberate deception. A typical problem arises when a product specification is changed to reduce cost. Clearly, it is essential to ensure that product function is not compromised in any important way, but a decision must be taken as to just what emphasis, if any, it is necessary to place on the changes. Another, more serious, problem occurs when product safety is compromised. **Product recall** may become necessary.

Marketing at Work — Application

When the French company Perrier, now owned by the Swiss multinational Nestlé, discovered that its mineral water was in danger of contamination, they immediately withdrew all supplies, suffering huge losses. By acting ethically, the company's reputation was enhanced. Coca Cola dithered in a similar situation, played down the issue, denied liability and suffered a huge blow to its image.

2.4.2 Promotion issues

Ethical considerations are particularly relevant to **promotional practices**. Advertising and personal selling are areas in which the temptation to select, exaggerate, slant, conceal, distort and falsify information is potentially very great. Questionable practices here are likely to create **cynicism in the customer** and ultimately preclude any trust or respect. It was because so many companies were acting unethically with regard to marketing communications that the Trade Descriptions Act 1968 came into being.

Also relevant to this area is the problem of **corrupt selling practices**. It is widely accepted that a small gift such as a mouse mat or a diary is a useful way of keeping a supplier's name in front of an industrial purchaser. Most business people would condemn the payment of substantial bribes to purchasing officers to induce them to favour a particular supplier. But where does the dividing line lie between these two extremes?

(a) **Extortion**. Government officials in some countries have been known to threaten companies with the complete closure of their local operations unless suitable payments are made.

(b) **Bribery**. Payments may be made to obtain services to which a company is not legally entitled. There are some fine distinctions to be drawn. If they are used to acquire public works contracts political contributions are bribery. In the UK, political contributions are supposed to be made at arm's length, and not to benefit the contributor with specific political favours.

(c)   **Grease money**. Multinational companies are sometimes unable to obtain services to which they are legally entitled because of deliberate stalling by local officials. Cash payments to the right people may then be enough to 'oil the wheels'.

(d)   **Gifts**. In some cultures (such as Japan) gifts are regarded as an essential part of civilised negotiation, even in circumstances where to Western eyes they might appear ethically dubious. Managers operating in such a culture may feel at liberty to adopt the local custom.

2.4.3 Pricing issues

There are several pricing practices that have attracted criticism. Not all can be described as improper, however.

(a)   **Active collusion** among suppliers to **fix prices** is illegal in most countries, but the existence of a more or less fixed market price does not necessarily imply that collusion is taking place. A tendency to compete in areas other than price is a natural feature of oligopoly markets.

(b)   **Predatory pricing** is an issue when newcomers attempt to break into a market. Established suppliers utilise their cash reserves and economies of scale to sell at prices the newcomer cannot match. Withdrawal from the market follows.

(c)   **Failure to disclose the full price** associated with a purchase has been rightly criticised as unethical. However, it must be recognised that there are occasions when it is impossible to compute the eventual full price, as when cost escalation is accepted by both parties to a contract. The measure of propriety is whether there is any **intention to deceive**.

(d)   The UK popular press have attempted to create a climate of opinion in which very large suppliers of consumer products are condemned if they ever raise prices or, indeed, if they make profits that are large in absolute terms. The former effect has been seen in the case of petrol suppliers, when they raise prices in response to tightening of supply, and the latter in the case of Tesco's record profits of billions of pounds. In fact, Tesco's turnover is such that the record profit actually represented a very modest margin.

2.4.4 Place issues

Where long and complex distribution channels are used there is potential for disputes and conflicts of interest. Even where relationships of trust have been built up over long periods of time, business pressures can lead to hard decisions and a perception by distributors that they have been treated unfairly. Here are some examples of conduct by manufacturers that distributors could reasonably complain of.

- Requiring high levels of stock holding by intermediaries
- Manipulating discount structures to the detriment of distributors
- Ending distribution agreements at short notice
- Dealing direct with end users

2.5 Ethical codes

It is now common for businesses to specify their ethical standards. Some have even published a formal declaration of their principles and rules of conduct. This would typically cover payments to government officials or political parties, relations with customers or suppliers, conflicts of interest, and accuracy of records.

Ethical standards may cause individuals to act against the organisation of which they are a part. More often, **business people are likely to adhere to moral principles which are 'utilitarian', weighing the costs and benefits of the consequences of behaviour. When benefits exceed costs, the behaviour can be said to be ethical**. This the philosophical position upon which capitalism rests, and is often cited to justify behaviour which appears to have socially unpleasant consequences. For example, food production regimes which appear inhumane are often justified by the claim that they produce cheaper food for the majority of the population.

The American Marketing Association has produced a statement of the code of ethics to which it expects members to adhere.

Code of Ethics

Members of the American Marketing Association (AMA) are committed to ethical professional conduct. They have joined together in subscribing to this Code of Ethics embracing the following topics.

Responsibilities of the Marketer

Marketers must accept responsibility for the consequence of their activities and make every effort to ensure that their decisions, recommendations, and actions function to identify, serve, and satisfy all relevant publics: customers, organisations and society.

Marketers' professional conduct must be guided by

1   The basic rule of professional ethics: not knowingly to do harm.

2   The adherence to all applicable laws and regulations.

3   The accurate representation of their education, training and experience.

4   The active support, practice and promotion of this Code of Ethics.

Honesty and Fairness

Marketers shall uphold and advance the integrity, honor and dignity of the marketing profession

1   Being honest in serving consumers, clients, employees, suppliers, distributors and the public.

2   Not knowingly participating in conflict of interest without prior notice to all parties involved.

3   Establishing equitable fee schedules including the payment or receipt of usual, customary and/or legal compensation or marketing exchanges.

Rights and Duties of Parties in the Marketing Exchange Process

Participants in the marketing exchange process should be able to expect

1   Products and services offered are safe and fit for their intended uses.

2   Communications about offered products and services are not deceptive.

3   All parties intend to discharge their obligations, financial and otherwise, in good faith.

4   Appropriate internal methods exist for equitable adjustment and/or redress of grievances concerning purchases.

It is understood that the above would include, but is not limited to, the following responsibilities of the marketer.

In the area of product development and management

- Disclosure of all substantial risks associated with product or service usage.

- Identification of any product component substitution that might materially change the product or impact on the buyer's purchase decision.

- Identification of extra-cost added features.

In the area of promotions
• Avoidance of false and misleading advertising.
• Rejection of high pressure manipulation, or misleading sales tactics.
• Avoidance of sales promotions that use deception or manipulation

In the area of distribution
• Not manipulating the availability of a product for purpose of exploitation.
• Not using coercion in the marketing channel.
• Not exerting undue influence over the resellers choice to handle the product.

In the area of pricing
• Not engaging in price fixing.
• Not practising predatory pricing.
• Disclosing the full price associated with any purchase

In the area of marketing research
• Prohibiting selling or fund raising under the guise of conducting research.
• Maintaining research integrity by avoiding misrepresentation and omission of pertinent research data.
• Treating outside clients and suppliers fairly.

Organisational relationships
Marketers should be aware of how their behaviour may influence or impact on the behaviour of others in organisational relationships. They should not demand, encourage or apply coercion to obtain unethical behaviour in their relationships with others, such as employees, suppliers or customers.
1   Apply confidentiality and anonymity in professional relationships with regard to privileged information.
2   Meet their obligations and responsibilities in contracts and mutual agreements in a timely manner.
3   Avoid taking the work of others, in whole, or in part, and represent this work as their own or directly benefit from it without compensation or consent of the originator or owner.
4   Avoid manipulation to take advantage of situations to maximise personal welfare in a way that unfairly deprives or damages the organisation or others.
Any AMA members found to be in violation of any provision of this Code of Ethics may have his or her Association membership suspended or revoked.

(Reprinted by permission of *The American Marketing Association*)

 Action Programme 3   Application/evaluation

A UK chemical products company turning over £10 million a year makes extensive sales to Company X in a country that has exchange control restrictions, and has good relations with its executives. The CEO of the Company X contacts the MD of the UK company and asks for help with a problem. In this industry a great deal of business is done at the annual trade fair in Hanover: a company that fails to send a strong sales team to this event is likely to find itself being rapidly overtaken by competitors. Company X finds it very difficult to do this since the local currency is non-convertible and it cannot obtain sufficient foreign currency from the state banking system to pay its team's expenses.

The CEO of Company X proposes that the UK company should over-invoice its deliveries (invoicing is in US dollars). There will be no difficulty in obtaining the dollars from the bank to pay the inflated invoices since they will appear to represent purchases of essential materials. The UK company will then deposit its excess receipts in a bank account in the UK. Company X will then draw on the account to pay its trade fair expenses.

What should the UK CEO do?

2.6 Social responsibility

There is a growing feeling that the concerns of the community ought to be the concerns of business, since businesses exist within society, and depend on it for continued existence. Business therefore has a moral obligation to assist in the solution of those problems which it causes. Businesses and businessmen are also socially prominent, and must be seen to be taking a lead in addressing the problems of society. Enlightened self-interest is probably beneficial to business.

In the long term, concern over the damage which may result from business activity will safeguard the interests of the business itself. In the short term, responsibility is a very valuable addition to the public relations activities within a company. As pressure for legislation grows, self-regulation can take the heat out of potentially disadvantageous campaigns.

More and more, it is being realised that it is necessary for organisations to develop a sense of responsibility for the consequences of their actions within society at large, rather than simply setting out to provide consumer satisfactions. **Social responsibility involves accepting that the organisation is part of society and, as such, will be accountable to that society for the consequences of the actions which it takes**. Three concepts of social responsibility are **profit responsibility**, **stakeholder responsibility** and **societal responsibility**.

 Marketing at Work   Application

Pepsico

'The PepsiCo family of companies cares about the health of the people who enjoy our products. As a company that provides hundreds of convenient food and beverage products that rejuvenate millions of consumers around the world every day, we are committed to offering the widest possible spectrum of great tasting food and beverage choices.

'We also recognize that consumers have an increasing need and desire for foods and beverages that make it easier and more enjoyable for them to lead healthy lives. We believe that we are ideally positioned to meet that need, and we intend to lead the way.

'Specially, we are committed to:

- Providing a spectrum of good choices
- Reaching consumers broadly
- Applying the best available science
- Promoting healthy kids lifestyles'

www.pepsico.com – accessed 8 April 2008

2.6.1 Profit responsibility

Profit responsibility argues that companies exist to maximise profits for their proprietors. Milton Friedman asserts:

> 'There is one and only one social responsibility of business: to use its resources and engage in activities designed to increase its profits so long as it stays within the rules of the game – which is to say, engages in open and free competition without deception or fraud.'

Thus, drug companies which retain sole rights to the manufacture of treatments for dangerous diseases are obeying this principle. The argument is that intervention, to provide products at affordable prices, will undermine the motivation of poorer groups to be self-sufficient, or to improve their lot. Proponents of this view argue that unless the market is allowed to exercise its disciplines, groups who are artificially cushioned will become victims of a 'dependency culture', with far worse consequences for society at large.

2.6.2 Stakeholder responsibility

Stakeholder responsibility arises from criticisms of profit responsibility, concentrating on the **obligations of the organisation to those who can affect achievement of its objectives**, for example, customers, employees, suppliers and distributors.

2.6.3 Societal responsibility

Societal responsibility focuses on the responsibilities of the organisation **towards the general public**. In particular, this includes a responsible approach to environmental issues and concerns about employment. A socially responsible posture can be promoted by an organisation via **cause related marketing**, when charitable contributions are tied directly to the sales revenues from one of its products.

2.7 The social audit

Socially responsible ideas may be converted into actions through plans developed in the course of a social audit. Companies develop, implement and evaluate their social responsibility through a social audit, which assesses their objectives, strategies and performance in terms of this dimension. Marketing and social responsibility programmes may be integrated.

Action Programme 4   Application

What do you think a social audit might involve?

In the USA, social audits on environmental issues have increased since the **Exxon Valdez** catastrophe in which millions of gallons of crude oil were released into Alaskan waters. The **Valdez principles** were drafted by the Coalition for Environmentally Responsible Economics to focus attention on environmental concerns and corporate responsibility. They encourage companies to behave responsibly towards the environment.

(a)   Eliminate pollutants, minimise hazardous wastes and conserve non-renewable resources

(b)   Market environmentally safe products and services

(c)   Prepare for accidents and restore damaged environments

(d)   Provide protection for employees who report environmental hazards

(e)   Appoint an environmentalist to their board of directors, name an executive for environmental affairs, and develop an environmental audit of their global operations, which is to be made publicly available

2.8 Strategies for social responsibility

An organisation can adopt one of **four types of strategy** for dealing with social responsibility issues.

2.9 Proactive strategy

A **proactive strategy** implies taking action before there is any outside pressure to do so and without the need for government or other regulatory intervention. A company which discovers a fault in a product and recalls the product without being forced to, before any injury or damage is caused, acts in a proactive way.

2.10 Reactive strategy

A **reactive strategy** involves allowing a situation to continue unresolved until the public, government or consumer groups find out about it. The company might already know about the problem. When challenged, it will deny responsibility, while at the same time attempting to resolve the problem. In this way, it seeks to minimise any detrimental impact.

2.11 Defensive strategy

A **defensive strategy** involves minimising or attempting to avoid additional obligations arising from a particular problem. There are several defence tactics.

- Legal manoeuvring
- Obtaining support from trade unions
- Lobbying government

2.12 Adopting an accommodation strategy

An **accommodation strategy** involves acknowledging responsibility for actions, probably when one of the following circumstances pertain.

- (a) There is encouragement from special interest groups
- (b) There is a perception that a failure to act will result in government intervention

The essence of the strategy is action to **forestall** more harmful pressure.

This approach sits somewhere between a proactive and a reactive strategy.

Marketing at Work   Application

McDonald's developed a nutrition-centred advertising campaign, and a salads range, in an attempt to appease nutritionists and dieticians who have pressed for detailed nutritional information to be provided on fast food packaging. Action before the pressure arose would have been proactive; action after government intervention in response to the pressure would have been reactive.

3 Sales-led, marketing-led and product-led organisations

FAST FORWARD

An organisation may be **sales** oriented, **product** oriented or **marketing** oriented. All the key functional departments will have a different emphasis, depending on which orientation is present.

Key concept

A **sales-led organisation** is one where the selling function is dominant. It is typically found where capacity exceeds demand and where the organisational aim is to sell what it makes rather than what the market wants.

A sales-led orientation tends to follow a period when the organisation concentrated on increasing its production capacity without necessarily improving its products. When the decline stage of the product life cycle begins, the organisation finds itself 'over-planted' and emphasis switches to selling. Unfortunately, some organisations adopt the hard-sell approach, where products or services are pushed onto prospects irrespective of their real needs. This is likely to build up considerable resentment (as occurred in the holiday market with timeshares and, it is claimed, in the insurance market with PEPs).

The sales led approach in usually more suited to **unsought goods and services**, such as insurance, double glazed windows and encyclopaedias. Here the potential customers may be prone to inertia or resistance to buying and need to be coaxed into making purchasing decisions.

Typical promotional tools used by a sales-led organisation include doorstep selling, telesales approaches and direct mail. The ethos that underpins a sales-driven organisation can be described as '**profitability through sales volume**'.

Key concept

A **market-led organisation** is one which first of all determines what customers want and then sets about providing goods or services which meet customers' wants and needs, at the right price, at the right time, at the right place and communicates effectively with these customers. The organisation will do this in a way consistent with achieving its own objectives.

The market-led organisation is therefore characterised by an emphasis on marketing research to identify customers and potential customers needs. Decisions on the marketing mix are based on relevant and up-to-date data, gathered from customers and potential customers.

When a company becomes marketing-oriented, a number of changes take place.

(a) Long-term orientation changes to market-led

(b) Planning focuses on the changing needs of the market

    (i) Developing the right **products**
    (ii) Using the right **channels**
    (iii) Providing the right level of **service**
    (iv) Formulating the right **marketing strategy** to meet the customer's changing needs

3.1 Marketing-led and sales-led organisations compared

Market-led companies tend to have a highly customer focused culture, and are organised to be sensitive to changing customer needs. Business practices and organisational values are orientated to a 'sense and respond' approach, rather than being governed by strict policies and procedures.

The ethos that underpins a market-led organisation can be described as '**Profitability through customer satisfaction**'.

The respective emphases within sales and marketing oriented companies can be depicted as follows.

Department	Sales orientation	Marketing orientation
Sales	Short-term sales	Long-term profits
	Sales most important	Customer satisfaction most important
	One department	Whole organisation
Purchasing	Narrow product line	Broad product line
	Standard parts	Non-standard parts
Finance	Hard and fast budgets	Flexible budgets
	Price to cover costs	Market-oriented pricing
Accounting	Standard transactions	Special terms and discounts
Manufacturing	Long runs	Short runs
	Few models	Many models
	Standard orders	Custom orders
	Long production lead times	Short production lead times

Theodore Levitt in a key paper *Marketing Myopia* explained the differences between selling and marketing as follows.

> 'Selling focuses on the needs of the seller; marketing on the needs of the buyer. Selling is preoccupied with the seller's need to convert his product into cash; marketing with the idea of satisfying the needs of the customer by means of the product and the whole cluster of things associated with creating, delivering and finally consuming it.'

3.2 Product-led organisations

There is also a third type of organisation: the **product-led organisation**.

Key concept

A **product-led organisation** is one which concentrates on the product itself and tends to de-emphasise other elements of the marketing mix. It takes the view that if the product is right it will sell itself.

The product-led approach is usually associated with high technology businesses, or small businesses set up to exploit a new invention. Product-led organisations can develop 'marketing myopia' to the extent that they forget the customers' needs. However, low technology or even no technology businesses might also operate in a product-led way.

3.3 The development of marketing departments

Although every organisation is different, common structural patterns appear. The position occupied currently by marketing evolved from sales departments. Traditionally, all dealings with a market would have been the responsibility of a sales director. As a marketing-oriented approach developed, a marketing director, a marketing director might appear in parallel to the sales director, with the structure of operations increasingly designed around the customer.

The adoption of a marketing philosophy by a business leads inevitably to involvement of the marketing function in other business activities. Our section on 'internal markets' later deals with this issue in more detail.

4 Organising marketing activities

FAST FORWARD There is a range of possible organisation **structures**. The position and prominence of marketing will, to some extent, depend on the structure.

There is no single best way to organise a department. The format chosen will depend on the nature of the existing organisational structure, patterns of management and the spread of the firm's product and geographical interests. However it is organised, every marketing department must take responsibility for four key areas and can be organised along such bases.

- **Functions** (promotion, pricing)
- **Geographical** areas (domestic, EU, international)
- **Products** (research, development, support, innovations)
- **Markets** (personal, corporate)

4.1 Functional organisation

The department organised by function is typically headed by a marketing director who is responsible for the overall co-ordination of the marketing effort. A number of functional specialists such as a market research manager and a sales manager will be found in the second tier of management and they take responsibility for all activities in their functional specialism across all products and markets. This is a very simple format and is relatively straightforward in administrative terms. It also allows individuals to develop their particular specialisms, at the same time imposing a burden on the marketing director who will be required to co-ordinate activities to ensure the development of a coherent marketing mix.

Functional organisation

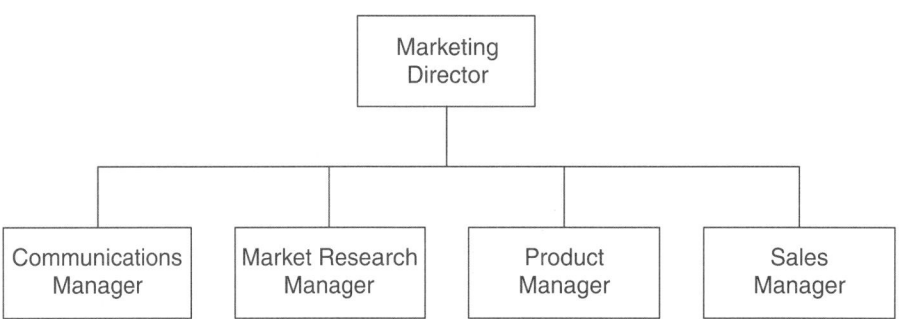

With a limited range of products, the burden on the marketing director is unlikely to be severe. As the organisation's range of products and markets expands, however, this arrangement will tend to be less efficient. There is always the danger that a particular product or market may be neglected because it is only one of a great variety being handled by a specific functional manager.

4.2 Geographical organisation

A simple geographical organisation for a marketing department is an extension of the functional organisation. Responsibility for some or all functional activities is devolved to a multi-functional office at regional level, through a national manager. This structure would probably be more common in firms operating internationally where the various functional activities would be required for each national market.

An FMCG manufacturing company, for example, may supply multiple grocery chains that are organised regionally, and therefore develop regional sales managers to link up with customers such as regional store managers. Where sales promotion activities are needed quickly in response to competition, there may be a case for regional promotions managers to decide and implement these in conjunction with regional sales managers.

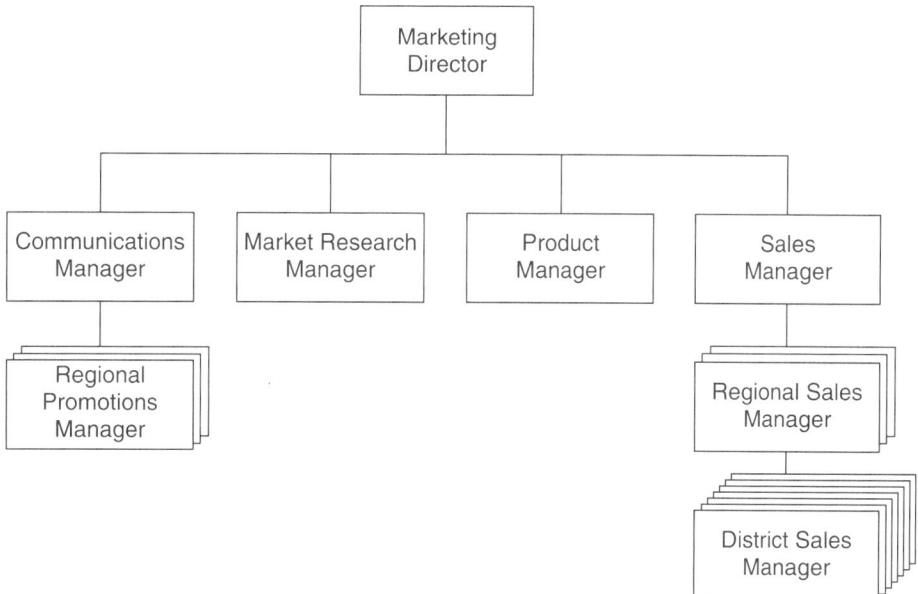

Geographical organisation

4.3 Product-based organisation

This involves adding an additional tier of management which supplements the activities of functional managers. **Product managers take responsibility for specific products or groups of products**. This type of approach is likely to be particularly appropriate for organisations with either very diverse products or with a large range of products.

Product management

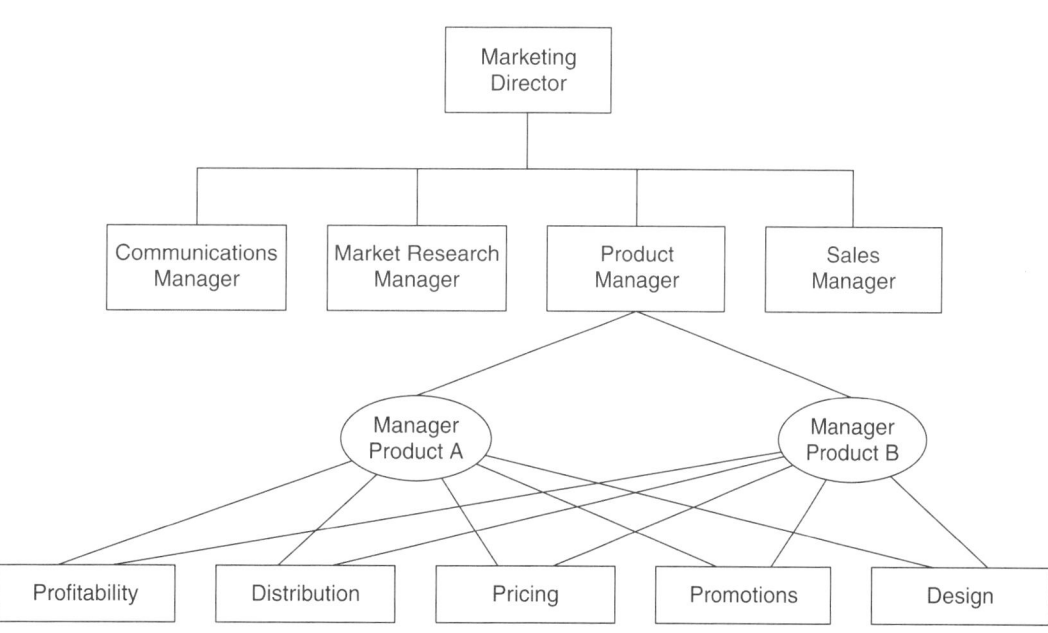

The individual product manager is responsible for developing plans to suit specific products, and ensuring that products remain competitive, drawing on the experience and guidance of functional managers. This allows the individual product managers to build up considerable experience and understanding of particular product groups, which is invaluable within a rapidly changing competitive environment. Very often the title **brand manager** rather than product manager will be used.

The product-based approach is becoming increasingly important, because the benefits of having managers with particular responsibility for specific product groups outweigh the costs associated with any loss of functional specialisation. Where the product group is large enough, the product manager may draw on the assistance provided by a product team, with individuals in that team concentrating on relevant functional specialisms.

4.4 Organisation by customer type (market management)

In a variant on the product management structure, instead of individual managers taking responsibility for particular products **they take responsibility for particular markets**. The advantage of this approach lies in an organisation offering a variety of products into particular markets. The understanding of the product here is perceived to be slightly less important than the understanding of the market.

In the case of **services**, market management would be consistent with the need to develop relationships with customers, since the individual marketing manager would be in a position to understand the needs of particular groups, and to draw on the organisation's product range to meet those needs. Individual market managers would also be able to draw on the skills and experiences of functional specialists as and when required. In contrast to the product management approach, market managers are likely to be well versed in the needs of their specific markets, but may be short on knowledge of a large and varied product range.

Where the buying motives and the buying behaviour of groups of customers differ radically from those of other groups, there is a case for organising marketing by customer type – often to the extent that each type will have its own dedicated marketing mix, its own dedicated marketing team and sometimes even a dedicated salesforce.

 Marketing at Work   Application

A large pharmaceutical product manufacturing company could be organised in this way. There might, for example, be separate marketing teams for hospitals and GPs, farmers, retail outlets and veterinary surgeons respectively. If there were many hospitals, GPs or retail outlets, each of these markets or customer groups could be serviced by a salesforce organised regionally. Conversely, there may be relatively few farmers and veterinary surgeons and so salesforces for each of these types of customers might be organised nationally.

Clearly, buying motives and selling approach would be different in each of the markets. The organisation could promote drugs to GPs as being effective with minimal side effects. In store promotions could be used with pharmacies while farmers buying commodity chemicals in bulk would be mostly interested in price.

 Action Programme 5   Application/evaluation

What would be the characteristics of a market-based approach to organising marketing departments in a banking environment?

4.5 Cross functional teams

This is one of the more modern ways of working. According to Robbins and Coutler (2002), a cross-functional work team is a 'type of work team that is a hybrid grouping of individuals who are experts in various specialties and who work together on various tasks'. People work together on a flexible and interdisciplinary basis.

Hallmark Cards is a major business in the greetings cards market. It operates on a cross functional team basis where writers, artists and production experts work together on product innovation and delivering an effective customer service.

4.6 Inter-departmental relationships

The harmony and effectiveness of inter-departmental working is likely to vary from one organisation to the next. It usually depends on a variety of factors such as corporate culture, structure and work practices. Some businesses have achieved a high degree of integration, whereas others are highly fragmented and the departments operate independently.

In practice, customers have very little interest on how a company is organised internally, provided the service is satisfactory. The overall criteria of whether an organisation is structured appropriately depends on whether it maximises customer satisfaction.

5 Gaining commitment

5.1 Marketing planning – barriers

Not all businesses use a formal marketing planning approach. Many businesses survive and some seem to prosper by processes such as 'muddling through' and 'freewheeling opportunism'.

Even in quite large and successful organisations, including some that claim to be market or customer oriented, the marketing planning process is of limited effectiveness. There are a number of reasons for this: these are sometimes called barriers to marketing planning or barriers to implementation. McDonald (2002) discusses these problems in some detail.

(a) **Weak support from the top**. Much of the planning process depends on internal information. Where this is controlled by heads of functional departments, those department heads must co-operate with marketing. There needs to be support from the top in this.

(b) **Poorly managed introduction**. Marketing planning must be introduced with care. The purpose and nature of the concept must be communicated and training must be provided in the necessary techniques. Management support must be obtained at all levels.

(c) **Lack of line management support**. Marketing planning will fail if there is hostility, lack of skill or lack of information among line managers. These can arise as a result of poor structure or processes, or for cultural reasons such as the absence of a marketing orientation.

(d) **Simplistic forecasting**. Line managers are accustomed to forecasting in numerical terms for budgetary purposes; they tend to do it by extrapolating current conditions. They are less used to exploring underlying causes and exploring key issues such as strengths and weaknesses.

(e) **Too much detail**. A linked problem is that even where a planning process exists, it is often unable to produce effective summaries. The result is huge and indigestible volumes of data. These are not only useless for planning, they also have a demotivating effect.

(f) **The annual ritual**. When the marketing planning process fails to deliver results, managers see it as a chore to be completed as soon as possible and with as little effort as possible.

5.1.1 Successful marketing planning

- A bureaucratic approach must be avoided.
- All functions must contribute to the process.
- The chief executive and top management must give their support.
- The planning process must be integrated with operations.

6 Internal marketing   Pilot paper, 6/05, 12/05

FAST FORWARD

Internal marketing has a range of meanings, but the most useful relates to the promotion of a high level of **customer awareness** throughout the **organisation**, using marketing communication techniques to change culture and deliver training.

The term **internal marketing** has been used in a variety of ways. It has, for instance, been adopted in the field of **quality management** where the concept of the internal customer is used to motivate staff towards achieving quality objectives. **In its most common usage, internal marketing means the promotion of a marketing orientation throughout the organisation** and, in particular, creating customer awareness among staff who are not primarily concerned with selling. Hotel housekeeping staff, for instance, may rarely be seen by the guests, but their work makes a major contribution to guest perceptions.

The achievement of a widespread marketing orientation may involve **major changes in working practices and organisational culture**. The successful management of organisational change depends to a great extent upon successful communication (a major marketing activity). 'Internal marketing' has therefore come to mean the communication aspect of any programme of change and, even more simply, **the presentation by management to staff of any information at all**.

6.1 Internal marketing as part of marketing management

If we concentrate on the use of the term to mean the use of marketing approaches and techniques to gain the support and co-operation of other departments and managers for the marketing plan, we will see that a number of challenges may exist. The first is that we may well be looking at a **major cultural shift**. Even in businesses which have highly skilled and motivated sales teams, **there may be areas of the organisation whose culture, aims and practices have nothing to do with customer satisfaction**.

Marketing at Work   Application

Engineering is a good example. The old nationalised industries like British Railways and Post Office Telecommunications saw engineering effectiveness as their major goal, with customer service nowhere. These nationalised industries were hidebound by tightly drawn job descriptions and task demarcations. The concepts of **flexible rostering** and **teamworking** were introduced with some difficulty.

6.1.1 Organisational change

(a)   Measuring activities against contribution to customer satisfaction means that some areas of the organisation are likely to shrink. The process of **delayering** may be necessary to streamline the organisation, make it more flexible and bring the personnel much closer to the customer. Many middle managers have company-facing jobs doing administrative and scheduling tasks that in reality require little supervision if the relevant employees are properly empowered to get on with the job. A **Total Quality approach** can also lead to staff

BPP
LEARNING MEDIA

reductions: if the organisation succeeds in improving initial quality, the need for people to handle complaints, claims and rework is much diminished.

(b) At the same time as these changes are being made, front-line sales and marketing capability will probably have to be enhanced. This is likely to involve more than just an increase in numbers. New working practices are likely to be introduced, including working in cross-functional teams. In particular, the natural partner of delayering is **empowerment**. Front line staff will take greater responsibility for delivering customer satisfaction and will be given the necessary authority to do so. Relationship marketing databases and staff will be installed and key account managers appointed.

Such restructuring of the organisation has important human resources management (HRM) implications.

Contemporary business practice is to set up a Human Resources (HR) model which is aligned with the overall business strategy. An HR model provides a coherent framework covering all aspects of HR management, so that the organisation selects, develops and rewards the appropriate people to ensure that its mission, strategy and objectives are delivered.

Sometimes, a lot of management effort is devoted to setting up policies, procedures and plans but insufficient attention is paid to people, their attitudes, skills and behaviours. The importance of developing top-class employees to serve the company's clients and customers can often be underestimated.

Research suggests that although the principles involved may be acknowledged by a large number of companies, **formalised internal marketing programmes in the UK are still fairly uncommon**. Initial findings make several other suggestions.

(a) Internal marketing is **implicit in other strategies** such as quality programmes and customer care initiatives, rather than standing alone as an explicit policy in its own right.

(b) Where it is practised, internal marketing tends to involve a **core of structured activities** surrounded by less rigorously defined ad hoc practices.

(c)   To operate successfully, internal marketing relies heavily on **good communication** networks.

(d)   Internal marketing is a key factor in **competitive differentiation**.

(e)   **Conflicts** between functional areas are significantly **reduced** by internal marketing.

(f)   Internal marketing depends heavily on **commitment at the highest level of management**, on general, active, widespread **co-operation**, and on the presence of an **open management style**.

6.2 The marketing mix for internal marketing

Product under the internal marketing concept is the changing nature of the job. **Price** is the balance of psychological costs and benefits involved in adopting the new orientation, plus those things which have to be given up in order to carry out the new tasks. Difficulties here relate to the problem of arriving at an accurate and adequate evaluation of psychological costs.

Many of the methods used for communication and **promotion** in external marketing may be employed to motivate employees and influence attitudes and behaviour. HRM practice is beginning to employ techniques, such as multi-media presentations and in-house publications. Presentational skills are borrowed from personal selling techniques, while incentive schemes are being employed to generate changes in employee behaviour.

Advertising is increasingly used to generate a favourable corporate image amongst employees as well as external customers.

Distribution for internal marketing means e-mails, meetings, conferences and physical means like noticeboards which can be used to announce policies and deliver training programmes.

Physical evidence refers to tangible items which facilitate delivery or communication of the product. Quality standards such as BS 5750/ISO 9000, for instance, place great emphasis on documentation. Other tangible elements might involve training sessions, which would constitute commitment to standards or policies.

Process, which refers to how a customer actually receives a product, is linked to communication and the medium of training which may be used to promote customer consciousness.

Participants are the people involved in producing and delivering the product. Those receiving the product, who may influence the customer's perceptions, are clearly important within the internal marketing process. Communications must be delivered by someone of the right level of authority. The way in which employees act is strongly influenced by fellow employees, particularly their immediate superiors.

Segmentation and marketing research can also be used in internal marketing. Employees may be grouped according to their service characteristics, needs, wants or tasks. Research will monitor the needs and wants of employees, and identify the impact of corporate policies.

6.3 Issues concerning the internal marketing concept

Even effective use of inwardly directed marketing techniques cannot solve all employee-related quality and customer satisfaction problems. Research clearly shows that actions by the human resources department, or effective programmes of human resources selection and training, are likely to be more effective than marketing based activities.

The internal marketing concept has a major role to play in making employees customer conscious.

Exam tip

Questions on internal marketing are likely to cover internal marketing in large service organisations, such as banks and accounting firms. This is significant. In 'people' businesses, internal marketing is essential to achieve a successful 'people' element in the service marketing mix. There is a question in this vein on the Pilot paper. In June and December 2005, internal marketing in the context of improved service quality was examined.

7 Integrated marketing

FAST FORWARD

Modern businesses are likely to organise themselves in an **integrated fashion** in order to provide customers with an efficient and effective service.

Integrated marketing is achieved when departments work together to satisfy the needs of customers.

Integrated marketing usually entails two levels.

(a) The marketing functions themselves – market research, promotion, customer service, planning, product management must work together.

(b) All other departments should recognise the importance of the marketing functions in enhancing customers' experiences of the company.

The following chart drawn from Kotler (2003) demonstrates the differences in priority given to customers by a traditional organisation chart, and a customer oriented organisation chart.

(a) Traditional organisation chart (b) Modern customer-oriented organisation chart

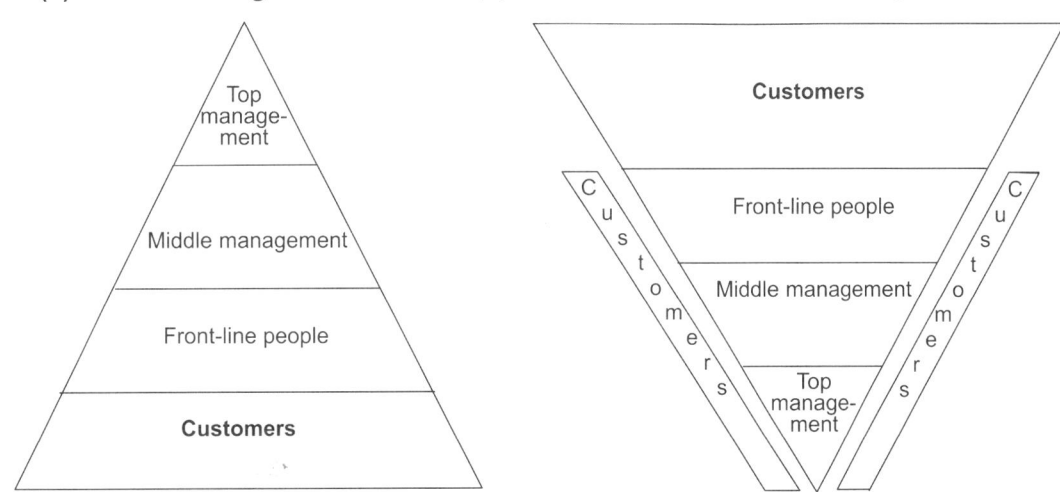

8 The boundaryless organisation

A **boundaryless organisation** facilitates cross-functional team working and a customer-focused service approach.

This is a very contemporary approach to designing an organisation. Robbins and Coutler (2002) define a boundaryless organisation as follows.

> 'An organisation whose design is not defined by, or limited to, the horizontal, vertical, or external boundaries imposed by a predefined structure'.

This approach was championed by Jack Welch, the former CEO of General Electric, when he was regenerating that organisation. He felt that boundaries were divisive.

- Vertical boundaries divided workers from managers
- Horizontal boundaries separated the various functions from each other.

The boundaryless organisation avoids inflexible structures and chains of command, preferring instead to encourage a more open and trusting environment where information and ideas flow freely. This enabled Welch and GE to introduce cross-functional team working, serve their customers better and improve the performance of the business.

Chapter Roundup

- Marketing is a key function in a contemporary business.

- Marketing as an **activity** differs from marketing as a **concept**. A market orientation can prevail outside the marketing department.

- There are four key models of marketing:

  - The **sales support** model of marketing is essentially reactive and includes such activities as telesales and organising exhibitions.

  - The **marketing communications** model of marketing is more proactive, promoting organisations, products and services at a tactical level.

  - The **operational marketing** model of marketing includes a co-ordinated range of marketing activities, from marketing research, through brand management and corporate communications to customer relationship management.

  - The **strategic marketing** model requires marketing to contribute to corporate strategy.

- **Ethics** is about right and wrong. An organisation exercises **social responsibility** when its acts respect the general public interest. Ethics and law are not the same. Strategies for social responsibility may be **proactive**, **reactive**, **defensive** or seek **accommodation**.

- An organisation may be **sales** oriented, **product** oriented or **marketing** oriented. All the key functional departments will have a different emphasis, depending on which orientation is present.

- There is a range of possible organisation **structures**. The position and prominence of marketing will, to some extent, depend on the structure.

- It will probably be necessary to overcome the barriers to planning with a programme of **internal marketing**.

- **Internal marketing** has a range of meanings but the most useful relates to the promotion of a high level of **customer awareness** throughout the **organisation** using marketing communication techniques to change culture and deliver training.

- Modern businesses are likely to organise themselves in a joined up or **integrated fashion** in order to provide customers with an efficient and effective service.

- A **boundaryless organisation** facilitates cross-functional team working and a customer focused service approach.

Quick Quiz

1   What is meant by the operational marketing model?

2   What is ethics about?

3   How does a gift differ from a bribe?

4   How does an accommodation strategy for social responsibility differ from a reactive strategy?

5   What are the characteristics of a marketing-led company?

6   What are the key distinctions between a sales-led and a marketing-led company?

7   When should marketing be organised by customer type?

8   Why do line mangers often fail to support the marketing plan?

Answers to Quick Quiz

1   Marketing supports the organisation with a co-ordinated range of marketing activities such as market research and brand management. It is more proactive than the marketing communications model, but not as significant to the strategic marketing model.

2   Right and wrong behaviour

3   Bribes are paid by companies to obtain services to which they are not entitled. In some cultures gifts are an essential part of a business relationship.

4   Under an accommodation strategy the company takes responsibility for its actions (though possibly only after encouragement) whereas under a reactive strategy it attempts to avoid responsibility.

5   An emphasis on knowing the market and the customer (both current and potential) and designing the marketing mix to provide satisfaction for customers' wants and needs.

6   By contrast with the market-led company, which makes what it can sell, the sales-led company puts a lot of effort into selling what it makes.

7   When the buying motivation and behaviour of customers varies between identifiable groups.

8   Hostility or disinterest can arise from poor structure or processes that hamper customer awareness or from cultural bias against marketing ideas.

Action Programme Review

1   (a) **Finance**: you might consider the whole field of management accounting, which is so important to any consideration of pricing; breakeven analysis; hire purchase and leasing facilities, which make it easier for customers to acquire products; and the administration of commission and rebate schemes for elements of the distribution chain.

    (b) **Human resources**: strategic human resource management supports the corporate mission by recruiting, selecting, training, rewarding and motivating and managing the performance of all the people needed.

    (c) **Purchasing**: purchasing departments are often responsible for the management of the whole inbound logistics operation, including storekeeping. It contributes to corporate image by taking a responsible approach to the interests of suppliers, particularly small ones.

2   With six people in the family, the Dougalls probably **need** a nice sized people carrier for times when the whole family is going out, eg at weekends.

    During the week, mother might possibly drop father off at work or at the local train station, then take the three eldest children to school before going off to work at the bakery.

    In terms of **wants**, they might like a nice second car so that father can have some independence and drive to work on his own.

    In terms of **demand**, they might really only be able to afford a second-hand saloon car.

3   Here are some considerations.

    • The UK company is not large and would probably be hard hit if it lost Company X's business to a competitor.

    • The proposed deal is probably illegal under Company X's local laws because it involves monetary controls, as referred to in the question.

    • A refusal to co-operate would probably cause embarrassment to the CEO.

    • The trade fair problem could be a cover story – Company X's CEO could be setting up the scheme for his own self-enrichment.

    • Does the UK company have any of its own ethical guidelines?

    • Could the UK company consults its legal advisors frame a creative but legal arrangement?

    • Will anybody lose as a result of this arrangement?

4   • Recognising society's expectations and the rationale for engaging in socially responsible activity

    • Identification of causes or programmes which are congruent with the mission of the company

    • Determination of objectives and priorities related to this programme

    • Specification of the nature and range of resources required

    • Evaluation of company involvement in such programmes past, present and future

5   In the case of banking, a market-based approach would be characterised by managers with responsibility for personal markets, large corporates and small corporates.

Now try Question 1 at the end of the Study Text

The marketing plan

Syllabus content – knowledge and skills requirements

- 1.2: The synergistic planning process – analysis, planning, implementation, control
- 1.3: Components of the marketing plan
- 1.4: Role of the marketing plan in relation to the organisation's philosophy or business definition

Introduction

You should already have a good basic knowledge of the overall marketing planning and budgeting process from your studies at Stage 1, and in particular from the syllabus for Marketing Fundamentals. In this chapter we will discuss the marketing plan in more detail and show you how it is put together.

We commence, in Section 1, with a discussion of general synergistic planning.

Exam tip

Your syllabus requires you to have an understanding of the wider applicability of the ideas underlying the techniques used in marketing planning.

In Section 2 we provide you with an outline of the contents of a marketing plan. This is intended to be brief enough that you can easily commit it to memory, so that you will have a basis to work with in the examination. Section 3 expands on the brief outline in Section 2 and discusses the content of a marketing plan in more detail.

This chapter deals with the **outcome** of the marketing planning process: the marketing plan itself. We discuss the **process** of marketing planning and the techniques used in much more detail in Chapters 3 and 4.

We conclude with a brief overview of the contribution information technology can make to the marketing planning process.

1 The synergistic planning process   12/05

FAST FORWARD

Synergistic planning is a rational process of determining future action, based upon consideration of the current situation, the desired future position and possible routes from one to the other.

Your syllabus requires you to have an understanding of the **synergistic planning process**. This term is a piece of jargon that you should not be afraid of. It is a rational technique that is not confined to marketing, or even to the world of business.

We will discuss synergistic planning under four main headings.

  (a)   Determining the **desired future position**
  (b)   Analysing the **current situation**
  (c)   Designing possible **routes** one to the other
  (d)   Deciding **what** to do and **how** to do it

1.1 The synergistic planning process

  (a)   **The desired future position**. Any process of planning must start with a clear statement of **what is to be achieved**. This process of objective setting is frequently undertaken in a very superficial manner in the real world and sometimes hardly performed at all. There may be an assumption that everybody knows what is required, or reference to long-established objectives that have lost some or all of their relevance. Only when objectives are clearly defined can courses of action be assessed, and eventual success or failure be measured.

  (b)   **The current situation**. Any plan must take into account the circumstances that will affect attainment of the objective. The first step is to establish just where the individual or organisation stands. Current circumstances will include a vast array of factors. An important aspect of the current situation is the **potential** that exists for future developments. **Strengths and weaknesses** exist now; **opportunities and threats** have potential for the future.

SWOT is a very common model for analysing the existing situation and is widely used in marketing.

(c) **Possible routes from one to the other**. Simple problems, when analysed, often suggest a single route to a satisfactory solution. The analysis of more complex problems will tend to suggest a **range of possible courses of action**. One approach is to adopt solutions that have worked in the past. Another is to seek and evaluate more innovative solutions.

(d) **Deciding what to do and how to do it**. The identification of alternative plans is usually followed by an evaluation process to determine the one which is likely to maximise the achievement of the planning objectives. This involves consideration of various factors.

- **Probability** of success
- **Resources** required
- **Acceptability** of the proposed action and its implications
- Potential **barriers** to success

After the optimal route has been selected, detailed plans need to be prepared and communicated to all the groups and individuals involved. These must be properly **integrated** to ensure that all action undertaken supports the attainment of the overall objective. **Performance measures** and **control mechanisms** must also be established.

1.2 Synergistic planning and marketing

Our description of synergistic planning above was deliberately couched in very general terms in order to emphasis its wide applicability. It is not just a marketing technique. In the rest of this chapter, we will explore synergistic planning as it is used in the marketing planning process.

Synergistic marketing planning was examined in December 2005, along with the marketing audit.

2 The purpose and content of the marketing plan

FAST FORWARD

A **marketing plan** is a specification of all aspects of an organisation's marketing intentions and activities. It is a summary document, providing a framework that permits managers and specialists to undertake the detailed work of marketing in a co-ordinated and effective fashion.

The creation of a good marketing plan is likely to be a time-consuming exercise, since it should deal with both current circumstances and plans for the future.

(a) It should be based on **detailed knowledge** of both the **target market** and the company involved.

(b) It should give sufficient detail of intentions to support the design and operation of all **marketing-related activities**.

2.1 The marketing plan and corporate strategy

It is important to remember how the marketing plan fits into overall corporate strategy. Students are often confused by the appearance of environmental analysis in the marketing planning process and assume that this means that the marketing plan is the same thing as the overall corporate strategic plan. This may be true in some highly marketing-oriented organisations, but it is not **necessarily** so.

The marketing plan and the corporate strategic plan are not the same thing. The difference is largely one of **scope:** the corporate plan has to consider **all aspects** of the organisation's business, while a marketing plan is principally about **marketing activities**. The marketing plan is aligned with the corporate plan and **supports** it.

2.2 What goes into the marketing plan?   Pilot paper

There is no standard template or list of contents for a marketing plan. Different organisations will find it appropriate to consider different things at different times in their development. We will look at one possible detailed layout for a marketing plan in Section 3. In this section we will look in general terms at what is likely to appear in most marketing plans.

2.2.1 The marketing plan – an outline

1 Situation analysis
PESTEL – SWOT – Market analysis and marketing objectives
2 Marketing strategy
Objectives – tactics – marketing mix
3 Numerical forecasts
Sales – expenses
4 Controls
Marketing organisation – performance measures

These four basic elements constitute a logical sequence of development for the basic building blocks of the marketing plan. We will look at this in more detail in Chapter 3.

Exam tips

> Ensure that you remember this basic structure. If all else fails in the examination, it should enable you to organise your thoughts and make a creditable attempt at preparing a marketing plan.
>
> The Pilot paper offers ten marks for identifying and briefly explaining the components of a marketing plan for the case study subject company.

(a)   **Situation analysis**. Any planning process should start with the collection and analysis of basic data. In the marketing context this is often called **situation analysis**. It may be appropriate for situation analysis to consider the items listed below.

       (i)   The wider environmental factors of the PESTEL model
       (ii)   Strengths, weaknesses, opportunities and threats
       (iii)   Marketing research data, including demographics data, trends, needs and growth
       (iv)   Current and planned products and services
       (v)   Critical issues

(b)   **Marketing strategy**. The statement of marketing strategy will describe in detail all the marketing concepts, practices, activities and aids that will be used. It will reiterate the marketing objectives in some form, and will probably give a detailed account of how the chosen marketing mix will be applied. This section is likely to be of considerable size.

(c)   **Numerical forecasts**. The marketing plan must include quantitative data about required resources and forecast results. Costs must be given in detail and realistic sales estimates must be provided. In particular, the cost of marketing activities must be specified.

(d)   **Controls**. Planning is worthless unless control mechanisms are established to ensure that the plan is properly executed. These may include intermediate organisational and sales milestones, the design of routine performance measures, the establishment of an appropriate marketing organisation, and the development of contingency plans.

Beard Papa

Beard Papa is a Japanese chain selling cream puffs, a type of confectionery. It has over 300 stores in Japan, Australia, Hong Kong, Singapore, Malaysia, Indonesia, Thailand, the Philippines, Taiwan, China Korea and the USA. It opened its first European outlet on London's Oxford Street, on 15 December 2006.

Competing against the US donut chain Krispy Kreme might have been considered risky. Beard Papa claims that is ingredients are fresh, and are less fatty because the pastry shells of the cream puffs are baked rather than fried.

The marketing planning exercise would refer to the product (a variety of flavours including vanilla, chocolate, green tea, pumpkin and coffee, and others products such as fondants), promotions based around it, place (where the cream puffs are sold), price (in relation to similar goods), the competition and social trends.

www.beardpapa.co.uk – accessed 8 April 2008

3 The marketing plan in detail

3.1 Executive summary

It is common practice to place an executive summary at the beginning of the marketing plan. Executive summaries are provided, as their name implies, for the convenience of senior executives who require a fast overview in order to avoid the time involved in detailed study. As a general rule, such summaries should be confined to a brief exposition of important material.

(a)   **Background information** that helps explain why particular proposals have been made or decisions taken

(b)   A description of **proposed action** with an indication of timescale

(c)   A summary of the **aims or targets** that are intended to be achieved

(d)   An assessment of any wider **implications** of the proposed action

(e)   A statement of the required investment, where appropriate

The executive summary for a marketing plan is likely to include material on the following specific matters.

- Marketing research
- Target markets and segments
- The proposed marketing mix
- Sales forecasts

3.2 Situation analysis

Situation analysis involves consideration of both the environment and internal factors. The environment can be divided into the macro-environment, consisting of the six PESTEL elements, and the micro- or market environment. Internal and environmental factors are summarised in a SWOT analysis.

(a) **The business environment**. The operation of any business implies interaction with its environment and the first stage of the detailed planning process is likely to be the collection and analysis of environmental information. For this purpose, the business environment is often split into two parts.

    (i) The **macro-environment** may be analysed into six elements.

– Political	– Technological
– Economic	– Ecological or 'green'
– Social	– Legal

Exam tip

> The acronym **PESTEL** may be used. **PEST** and **STEP** are also common, when the legal environment is included under **politics** and so-called 'green' issues are included under the **social** heading. Your syllabus uses **PESTEL**, so that is what we will use in this Study Text. A marketing plan need not include a detailed PESTEL analysis, but it should explain those aspects of it that have affected its development.

Action Programme 1

Application/evaluation

Write down one real-world factor from each of the PESTEL categories that would be of importance to the preparation of marketing plans. The factors you choose need not all be relevant to the same marketing plan.

    (i) The **micro-environment** consists of the markets in which the business operates or plans to operate. It includes current and prospective customers and existing and potential competitors. The micro-environment also includes any distribution systems used by the business. Headings such as those below may be appropriate.

– Target markets	– Products and services
– Market needs	– Competition
– Market geography	– Costs
– Market demographics	– Suppliers
– Market trends	– Critical issues
– Market forecasts	
– Market growth	

(b) **Internal analysis**. Like the overall strategic plan it is derived from, a marketing plan should reflect the characteristics of the business concerned. It will inevitably refer to current and planned products and capabilities and be designed to exploit the organisation's resources to the full. An important aspect of the internal analysis is **product-market background**, which sets the scene for those less familiar with the products and markets involved.

The environmental and internal analyses are traditionally summarised and entered into the plan under the headings of **strengths**, **weaknesses**, **opportunities** and **threats**. This **SWOT analysis** highlights aspects of the overall situation that need action by the business. The aim is to exploit strengths and opportunities, remedy areas of weakness and develop actions which minimise threats. The analysis of SWOT must be prepared honestly and objectively as it is a key foundation on which the marketing strategy is built.

3.3 Marketing strategy

FAST FORWARD

> **Marketing strategy** includes objectives and methods and may deal with such matters as gap analysis, target markets, the marketing mix and marketing research.

The marketing strategy section of the marketing plan should describe in detail the organisation's marketing objectives and methods.

(a) **Marketing objectives**. The objectives of the marketing plan are derived from the corporate plan, which is designed to support the overall corporate mission. A clear statement of marketing objectives serves a number of purposes.

(i) It provides a **focus for activity** and a sense of purpose. This should stimulate activity, particularly when overall objectives are broken down into personal targets.

(ii) It provides a **framework for co-ordination** of activity across the organisation.

(iii) IT is **fundamental to the control process**, since it defines success. Actual performance is compared with what was intended, and control action taken to correct any discrepancy.

When objectives have been considered in detail, it is possible to use them to refine a plan by means of **gap analysis**. This is discussed in detail later in this Study Text.

Objectives will relate to both market dynamics and financial results, and should be expressed in concrete form. Objectives may be set for such business parameters as those below.

- Revenue growth
- Market share
- Profitability
- Number of outlets
- Customer retention
- Brand recognition
- Marketing expenses
- Staff levels and training

(b) **Target markets**. It will be appropriate to define clearly just what the target market is. The nature of this definition will depend partly on the scale of the marketing operation envisaged. For example, a company operating nationally in a lifestyle segment might target prosperous retired people nationwide, while a locally based professional service business might target start-ups and small traders within a 20-mile radius of its base.

(c) **Products and their positioning**. Product positioning is a continuation of the process of determining the target market. Product positioning is about the way the target market perceives the product's characteristics, in relation to those of competing products.

There are two basic product positioning strategies.

(i) '**Me too**': the product is positioned to meet the competition head-on.
(ii) **Gap-filling**: the product is positioned to exploit gaps in the market.

(d) **The marketing mix**. A marketing plan will not necessarily give complete details of every component of the marketing mix. Instead, it will concentrate on those parts that are new or crucial to success. For example, a plan built around a **new or enhanced product** that will be distributed through established channels is likely to give significant product detail, and explain the aim of the new features in market terms. **Place**, on the other hand, is unlikely to receive more than a brief mention.

(e) **Marketing research**. Early marketing research should have played its part in supporting the design of the marketing plan. However, it is not confined to this phase of operations. Marketing research activities should form part of the marketing plan, so that continuing feedback may be obtained upon the degree of success achieved.

3.4 Numerical forecasts

Numerical forecasts tie down what is to be achieved and form the basis of the **control** process.

This section of the marketing plan could also be called a **budget**.

3.4.1 Typical forecast quantities

- Turnover
- Market share
- Marketing spend
- Units of sales
- Costs
- Breakeven analysis

Phasing and analysis. It will be appropriate to present numerical forecasts broken down in two ways.

(a)   **Phased by time period**. A year's total may be broken down into monthly or quarterly increments.

(b)   **Analysed by marketing characteristic**. For example, sales and expenses might be analysed by product type or by market segment.

3.4.2 Breakeven analysis

Breakeven analysis is a management accounting technique that should be of interest to marketing managers. The cumulative sales of a product reach their breakeven point when the total revenue is high enough to cover both the variable and fixed costs of producing and selling that quantity of product. The breakeven point is a vital hurdle that must be cleared if the marketing plan is to be considered successful, and a profit made on the sale of the product.

3.5 Controls

Control is vital if management is to ensure that planning targets are achieved. The control process involves three underlying components.

- Setting standards or targets
- Measuring and evaluating actual performance
- Taking corrective action

(a)   **Performance measures**. The data contained within the numerical forecasts section of the plan provides the raw material for performance measures. Mechanisms must be put in place for collecting information on actual results, so that comparisons can be made and control action taken. Overall performance is often judged by analysing two main indicators: sales and market share.

(i)   **Sales analysis** is based on the comparison of actual with budgeted turnover, but this is only the first stage. It is appropriate to delve deeper and consider the effects of differences in unit sales and selling price. Further analysis by product, region, customer and so on may be required.

(ii)   **Market share analysis**. Market share is important to overall profitability, and the attainment of a given market share is likely to be an important marketing objective. Market share should always be analysed alongside turnover, since the growth or decline of the market as a whole has implications for the achievement of both types of objective.

(b)   **Marketing organisation**. Individual responsibilities within the overall marketing plan should be given and the persons responsible named. One example of a specific responsibility is the preparation of performance reports. Other roles will include that of overall responsibility (probably discharged by the Marketing Manager or Brand Manager), management of promotional effort and management of marketing research effort.

(c)   **Implementation milestones**. Progress in implementing a programme can be monitored by the establishment of **milestones** and the dates by which they should be achieved.

Marketing at Work   Application

Examples for the launch of a new car might include:

- First delivery to show rooms
- First thousand sold
- Breakeven sales achieved

(d)   **Contingency planning**. Events in the real world very rarely go according to plan. It is necessary for planners to consider problems that might arise and make appropriate preparations to deal with them. There are several requirements.

(i)   The organisation must have the **capability to adapt** to new circumstances. This will almost certainly imply financial reserves, but may require more specific resources, such as management and productive capacity.

(ii)   There is a range of possible responses to any given contingency. The organisation should **consider its options** in advance of needing to put them into action.

(iii) A **prompt response** will normally be appropriate. Achieving this depends to some extent on having the resources and having done the planning mentioned above, but it will also depend on a kind of organisational agility. In particular, decision-making processes need to be rapid and effective.

4 Information technology and the marketing plan

FAST FORWARD

Information technology is of increasing usefulness in all stages of the marketing planning process.

Information technology (IT) is becoming increasingly useful in many aspects of marketing. These include not only applications such as market research and relationship marketing, both of which utilise large quantities of structured data, but also creative, communications aspects.

The increasing use of IT is partly a result of developments in IT systems themselves, which have made them more productive and easier to use.

(a)   Hardware and software have both fallen in price and become more powerful.

(b)   The explosive growth of the Internet has created a powerful new research and communication tool. Corporate intranets use Internet technology for publishing information internally.

(c)   Devices such as EPOS scanners and barcode readers allow rapid acquisition and manipulation of data.

(d)   Hand held devices such as mobile phones, laptop computers and personal digital assistants allow sales force people to send reports and receive information and instructions without a personal visit to the office.

4.1 Applying IT to the marketing planning process

The **Marketing Information System** (MkIS) database contains live information of importance to the marketing process. Modern relational database management systems allow rapid access to chosen aspects of this information. Such information would include both internally generated and externally generated items.

Internal information examples	External information examples
• Sales records	• Trade association information
• Customer records	• Published market information
• Marketing communications records	• Competitor information
• Market research information	• Government information
• Cost records	
• Stock records	

Exam tip

These lists show the kind of information required for the marketing audit (See Chapter 3).

4.2 IT and implementing the marketing plan

IT can be useful in four aspects of plan implementation.

(a) **Segmentation. Datamining** is a technique that reveals hidden connections between items of data. For example, one supermarket chain found that there was a link between purchases of disposable nappies and purchases of beer. Simpler techniques can be used to organise data by potential segmentation variables.

(b) **Targeting**. Analytical techniques such as sales forecasting can be used for the evaluation of promising segments.

(c) **Positioning**. Marketing communications intended to create a position can be enhanced by the use of e-mail, web sites and Internet broadcasts.

(d) **Monitoring and control**. Large volumes of feedback data can be handled by IT systems. Examples include analysis of EPOS information and its correlation with such events as sales promotions.

Chapter Roundup

- **Synergistic planning** is a rational process of determining future action based on realistic consideration of the current situation, the desired future position and possible routes from one to the other.

- A **marketing plan** is a specification of an organisation's marketing intentions and activities. It is a summary document, providing a framework that permits managers and specialists to undertake the detailed work of marketing in a co-ordinated and effective fashion.

- **Situation analysis** involves consideration of both the environment and internal factors. The environment can be divided into the macro-environment, consisting of the six PESTEL elements, and the micro- or market environment. Internal and environmental factors are summarised in a SWOT analysis.

- **Marketing strategy** includes objectives and methods and may deal with such matters as gap analysis, target markets, the marketing mix and marketing research.

- **Numerical forecasts** tie down what is to be achieved and form the basis of the **control** process.

- **Control** is vital if management is to ensure that planning targets are achieved. The control process involves three underlying components.

  - Setting standards or targets
  - Measuring and evaluating actual performance
  - Taking corrective action.

- **Information technology** is of increasing usefulness in all stages of the marketing planning process.

Quick Quiz

1. What are the four main stages of the synergistic planning process?

2. What is a marketing plan?

3. What are the main contents of a marketing plan?

4. Specify as many aspects of the micro-environment as you can.

5. Name some business parameters for which objectives may be set.

6. What are the two basic product positioning strategies?

7. Give four examples of internally generated information that might be useful for planning purposes.

Answers to Quick Quiz

1   Determining the desired future position
     Analysing the current situation
     Designing possible routes from one to the other
     Deciding what to do and how to do it

2   A specification of an organisation's marketing intentions and activities.

3   Situation analysis – marketing strategy – numerical forecasts – controls.

4
- Target markets
- Market needs
- Market geography
- Market demographics
- Market forecasts
- Costs
- Market trends
- Market growth
- Products and services
- Competition
- Suppliers
- Critical issues

5
- Revenue growth
- Market share
- Profitability
- Number of outlets
- Customer retention
- Brand recognition
- Marketing expenses

6   Gap filling and 'me too'.

7
- Sales records
- Customer records
- Marketing communications records
- Market research information
- Cost records
- Stock records

Now try Question 2 at the end of the Study Text

Part B
Marketing planning and budgeting

The marketing planning process

Syllabus content – knowledge and skills requirements

- 2.1: The constituents of the macro environmental and micro environmental marketing audit
- 2.2: The external marketing environment for an organisation through a PESTEL audit
- 2.3: The internal marketing environment for an organisation through an internal audit
- 2.4: Processes and techniques used for auditing the marketing environments
- 2.5: The role of marketing information and research in conducting and analysing the marketing audit

Introduction

In Chapter 2 we discussed the contents of the marketing plan as it would be presented to senior management or other sponsors. In this chapter and Chapter 4 we talk in much more detail about the planning **processes** that are undertaken to prepare the eventual published plan.

Marketing strategy is the theme of this chapter but we need some background before we talk about it. Marketing is an important aspect of business strategy and we will set the marketing audit within the context of corporate strategic planning. Section 1 deals with the nature of strategic planning.

The marketing planning process is then amplified in Sections 2 to 6, which deal with the marketing audit and the information that must be collected for planning to take place.

Exam tip

Be aware that terminology is sometimes used loosely. We have taken a fairly narrow approach to a definition of the marketing audit. Some people will use the term to mean a much wider strategic appraisal, really corresponding to what we have called situation analysis. There is no reason why you should not make up your own mind about this, but take care in the exam to define your terms clearly and to make your overall meaning clear.

1 The strategic planning process 6/04

FAST FORWARD

Strategic planning begins with the definition of the corporate **mission**. Strategic objectives are then set which support the mission.

Key concepts

Corporate strategy is concerned with the overall purpose and scope of the organisation in meeting the expectations of owners or major stakeholders and adding value to the different parts of the enterprise.

Strategic planning is a sequence of analytical and evaluative procedures to formulate an intended strategy, and the means of implementing it.

Marketing planning exists within the overall framework of **corporate strategic planning**. This is a process that can be broken down into several stages.

Development of the organisation's mission statement

↓

Statement of objectives

↓

Situation analysis

↓

Strategy development

↓

Specific plans

↓

Implementation

This section gives an overview of this general process before we consider the specifics of **marketing** planning.

1.1 Mission statement

Key concept

> The **mission statement** says what an organisation is aiming to achieve through the conduct of its business. The purpose is to provide the organisation with **focus** and **direction**.

The corporate mission depends on a variety of factors. Mission statements may change or evolve over time. They should be regarded as a **dynamic tool**. **Corporate history** will often influence the markets and customer groups served. A market-led business will be influenced by changing market conditions and customer tastes and behaviour.

Marketing at Work   Application

The PepsiCo mission statement

'To be the world's premier consumer products company focused on convenient foods and beverages. We seek to produce healthy financial rewards to investors as we provide opportunities for growth and enrichment to our employees, our business partners and the communities in which we operate, and in everything we do, we strive for honesty, fairness and integrity.'

Coca-Cola's mission statement

'Our mission is to create a growth strategy that allows us to bring good to the world – by refreshing people every day and inspiring them with optimism through our brands and our actions.'

http://wiki.answers.com – accessed 8 April 2008

An approach to the corporate mission is to consider the **company's product and market scope**. The mission statement then rests on customer groups, needs served and technology employed.

A mission statement should not be too limiting; it should indicate the scope of future developments. It would be insufficient for a bank to identify its mission as being 'banking' – it would be more appropriate to identify that mission as being, for example, 'meeting consumer needs for financial transactions.'

A good mission statement should be concise. It should clearly answer the classic question, 'what business are we in?' or 'what satisfactions do we aim to provide for our customers?' Financial or profit dimensions can be left out as these are contained much more specifically in the corporate objectives.

A contemporary approach to writing mission statements is to cover various key areas such as:

- Proper treatment of staff
- Customer service and satisfaction
- Environmental consciousness and social responsibility
- Product quality and innovation
- Profitability and shareholder value

Marketing at Work   Application

Here is Starbucks' mission statement which covers a range of key areas.

Starbucks mission statement

Establish Starbucks as the premier purveyor of the finest coffee in the world while maintaining our uncompromising principles as we grow.

The following six guiding principles will help us measure the appropriateness of our decisions:

- Provide a great work environment and treat each other with respect and dignity.
- Embrace diversity as an essential component in the way we do business.
- Apply the highest standards of excellence to the purchasing, roasting and delivery of our coffee.
- Develop enthusiastically satisfied customers all of the time.
- Contribute positively to our communities and our environment.
- Recognise that profitability is essential to our future success.

General Electric

Earlier, we looked at the boundaryless organisation. You might be interested in reviewing General Electric's mission statement which is based on the boundary-less approach.

GE Leaders…Always with Unyielding Integrity:

- Have a passion for excellence and hate bureaucracy
- Are open to ideas from anywhere
- Live quality…and drive cost and speed for competitive advantage
- Have the self-confidence to involve everyone and behave in a boundaryless fashion
- Create a clear, simple, reality-based vision…and communicate it to all constituencies
- Have enormous energy and the ability to energize others
- Stretch…set aggressive goals…reward progress…yet understand accountability and commitment
- See change as opportunity…not threat
- Have global brains…and build diverse and global teams

1.2 Situation analysis

Key concept

> **Situation analysis** involves a thorough study of the broad trends within the economy and society, and a comprehensive analysis of markets, consumers, competitors and the company itself.

Environmental factors will affect the mission statement and the identification of objectives, but once strategic objectives are established, a much more comprehensive analysis is necessary. This analysis is considered further in later parts of this chapter.

1.3 Strategy development

The process of strategy development links corporate level plans and market level plans. In developing strategy, most large organisations will be required to make important **resource allocation** decisions. This process of resource allocation is a key component of corporate strategy and it indicates the direction in which specific markets or products are expected to develop. It therefore provides direction for the development of **market level plans**.

1.4 Specific plans

Market specific plans express the organisation's intentions concerning **particular markets and products**. These are linked to the corporate plan through the statement of objectives and the resource allocation component in strategy development. Situation analysis at the market level can provide information on patterns of competition, consumer behaviour and market segmentation, as an input to the development of marketing objectives and market specific strategies.

Market specific variables, typically under the control of the marketing department, constitute the marketing mix: **product, price, promotion and place**. The development of the marketing mix aims to ensure that the

product is appropriate to the market in terms of its features, its image, its perceived value and its availability.

Marketing expenditure will depend on resource allocation decisions at corporate level, but any marketing plan will include, as a matter of course, a statement of the budget required and the way it is to be spent.

1.5 Implementation

Implementation consists of identifying the specific tasks to be performed, the allocation of those tasks to individuals and putting in place a system of control. The implementation procedure may also include some elements of contingency planning. The market is always evolving so even the most well formed marketing plan will need to be changed and certain planned activities may turn out to be inappropriate or ineffective.

2 Marketing planning and the marketing audit

6/04, 12/04, 12/05, 12/06, 6/07

FAST FORWARD

Marketing objectives will support and flow from the overall corporate strategic objectives.

Key concept

'The **marketing planning** process combines the organisation's overall marketing strategy with fundamental analyses of trends in the marketing environment; company strengths, weaknesses, opportunities and threats, competitive strategies; and identification of target market segments. Ultimately the process leads to the formulation of marketing programmes or marketing mixes which facilitate the implementation of the organisation's strategies and plans'. (Dibb, Simkin, Pride & Ferrell.)

In line with strategic planning, the marketing planning process includes the following stages.

(a) A general **overview**, setting the marketing function in context: a kind of 'marketing mission statement' (see Section 4).

(b) The **marketing audit**
 – external analysis (Section 5)
 – competitor and customer analysis (Section 6)
 – internal analysis (Section 7)
 – SWOT analysis (Section 8)

Exam tip

The tools to be used in a marketing audit were the subject of a question on the December 2005 paper.

(c) Defining marketing **objectives** (see Section 4)

(d) **Segmentation** and **targeting** (see Chapter 4)

(e) **Evaluation** of strategic choices (see Chapter 4)

(f) **Implementation** of the marketing mix (see Part C of the Text)

(g) **Control** and budgets (see Chapter 4)

Corporate strategic plans aim to guide the overall development of an organisation. Marketing planning is subordinate to corporate planning but makes a significant contribution to it and is concerned with many of the same issues. The corporate audit of product/market strengths and weaknesses, and much of its external environmental analysis is directly informed by the **marketing audit**.

Specific marketing strategies will be determined within the overall corporate strategy. To be effective, these plans will be interdependent with those for other functions of the organisation.

(a)   The **strategic** component of marketing planning focuses on the direction which an organisation will take in relation to a specific market, or set of markets, in order to achieve a specified set of objectives.

(b)   Marketing planning also requires an **operational** component that defines tasks and activities to be undertaken in order to implement the desired strategy. The **marketing plan** is concerned uniquely with **products** and **markets**.

2.1 The marketing audit

FAST FORWARD

A **marketing audit** must be comprehensive and objective and should be carried out regularly. It is a comprehensive review of a firm's marketing activities, covering:

- The marketing environment
- Marketing strategies
- Marketing systems

- Marketing organisation
- Marketing function
- Marketing productivity

Key concept

The **marketing audit** is a detailed analysis of marketing capacity and practice, which enables the making of marketing plans aimed at improving the company's marketing performance.

Marketing management aims to ensure the company is pursuing effective policies to promote its products, markets and distribution channels. This involves exercising strategic control of marketing, and the means to apply strategic control is known as the **marketing audit**. The diagram below shows how the marketing audit fits into the overall setting. Not only is the marketing audit an important aspect of **marketing control**, it can be used to provide much information and analysis for the **corporate planning process** by contributing to the **corporate SWOT**.

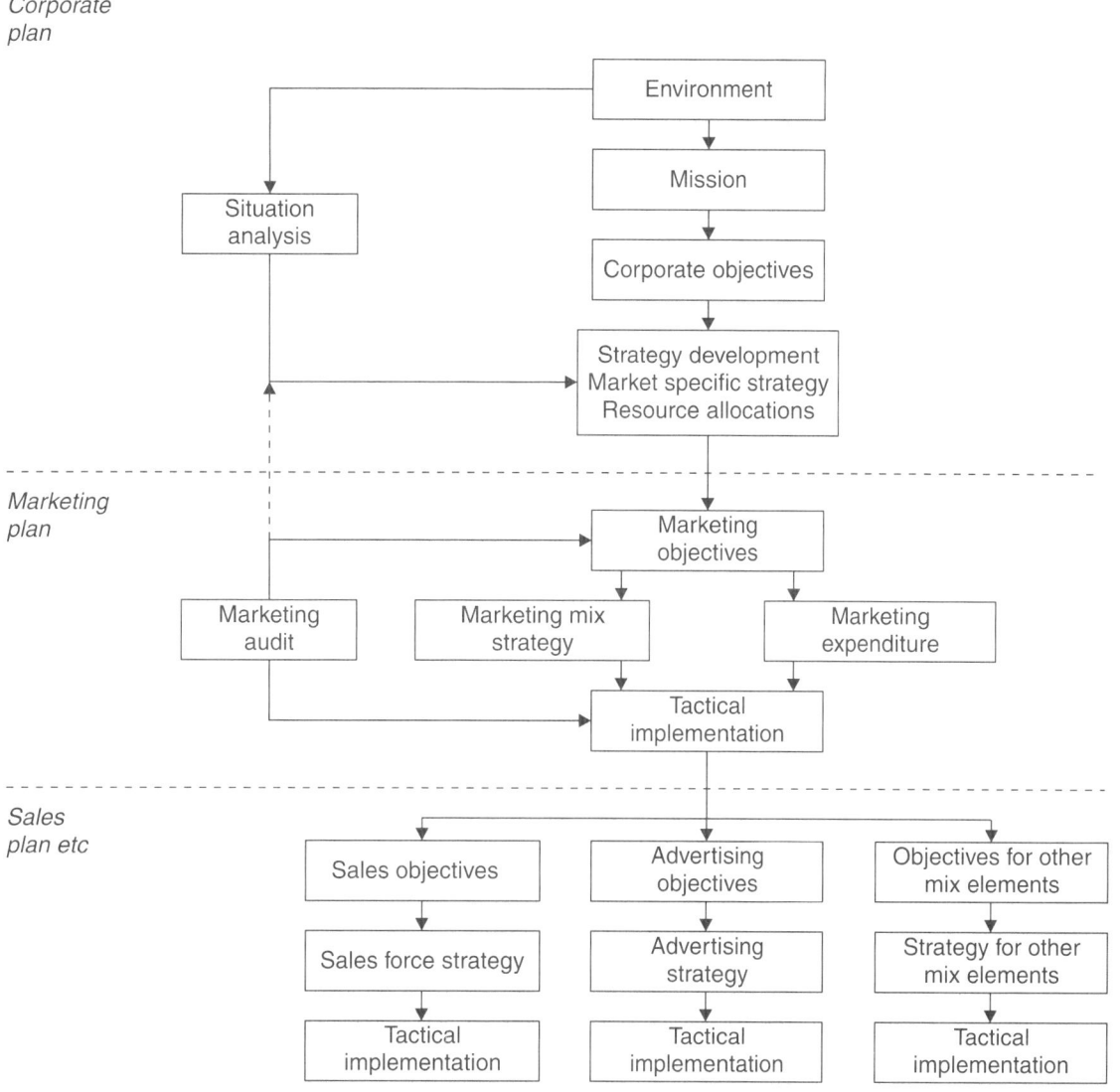

Exam tip

You may have to produce a plan, or a section of a plan, in answers to exam questions on this paper. The evaluation and control of a marketing plan in also likely to feature regularly.

2.2 Conducting a marketing audit

In order to exercise proper strategic control a marketing audit should satisfy four requirements.

(a) It should take a **comprehensive** look at every product, market, distribution channel and ingredient in the marketing mix.

(b) It should **not be restricted** to areas of apparent ineffectiveness such as an unprofitable product, a troublesome distribution channel, or low efficiency on direct selling.

(c) It should be carried out according to a set of **predetermined**, **specified procedures**.

(d) It should be conducted **regularly**.

The auditors should be independent of particular job and organisational interests.

2.3 Areas to consider in the marketing audit

- The marketing environment
- Marketing strategies
- Marketing systems
- Marketing organisation
- Marketing function
- Marketing productivity

(a) **The marketing environment**

(i) **Micro**. What are the organisation's major markets, and what is the segmentation of these markets? What are the future prospects of each market segment?

(1) Who are the customers, what is known about customer needs, intentions and behaviour?

(2) Who are the competitors, and what is their standing in the market?

(ii) **Macro**. Have there been any significant developments in the broader environment for example economic or political changes, population or social changes etc?

(b) **Marketing strategy audit**

(i) What are the organisation's marketing objectives and how do they relate to overall objectives? Are they reasonable?

(ii) Are appropriate resources being committed to marketing to enable the objectives to be achieved? Is the division of costs between products and geographic areas satisfactory?

(c) **Marketing systems**. What are the procedures for formulating marketing plans and management control of these plans? Are they satisfactory?

(d) **Marketing organisation**. Does the organisation have the structural capability to implement the plan?

(e) **Marketing functions**. A review of the effectiveness of each element of the mix (eg advertising and sales promotion activities) should be carried out.

(i) A review of sales and price levels should be made (for example supply and demand, customer attitudes, the use of temporary price reductions etc).

(ii) A review of the state of each individual product (ie its market 'health') and of the product mix as a whole should be made.

(iii) A critical analysis of the distribution system should be made, with a view to finding improvements.

(f) **Marketing productivity**. How profitable are the company's products, markets and channels of distribution? How cost-effective is the marketing programme?

Exam tip

> You may have to explain the purpose, focus and components of a marketing audit. Show how it can be made relevant to the firm, how it can be conducted, and how the results might be used.

2.3.1 Advantages of a marketing audit

- It should reduce the need for crisis management
- It should identify information needs
- A formal process forces people to think

2.4 The auditing process as a control mechanism

A **marketing audit** performs a dual role in checking both where we are, and where we have come from. In other words **marketing planning is a cyclical process**.

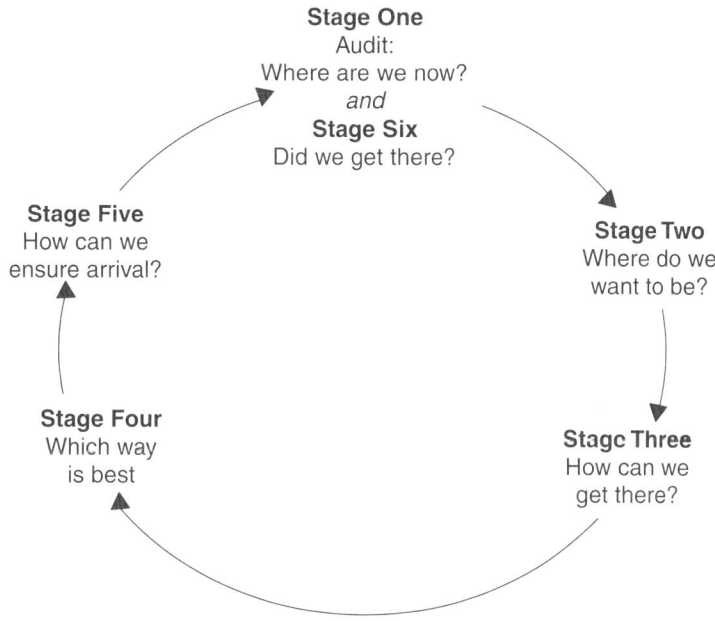

Stage One
Audit:
Where are we now?
and
Stage Six
Did we get there?

Stage Two
Where do we
want to be?

Stage Three
How can we
get there?

Stage Four
Which way
is best

Stage Five
How can we
ensure arrival?

Wilson, Gilligan, Pearson (1997)

Marketing audits will feature regularly in the examination. The Pilot paper and the December 2003 paper both focused on the information required for the marketing audit. It was also examined in December 2005.

3 Defining objectives

FAST FORWARD

The setting of **objectives** is a key part of marketing planning.

3.1 Primary objectives

Most commercial organisations will express their primary objective in financial terms. There are three main measures.

- Profitability
- Return on capital employed (ROCE) or return on investment (ROI)
- Earnings per share (EPS)

Although a company must make profits, **profit** on its own is not satisfactory as an overall long term corporate objective because it fails to allow for the size of the capital investment required to make the profit. ROCE and ROI take the level of investment into account.

Action Programme 2

Evaluation

What other drawbacks can you identify to the use of profitability as a primary objective?

3.2 Subsidiary objectives

Whatever primary objective or objectives are set, subsidiary objectives will then be developed beneath them. The diagram below illustrates this process in outline.

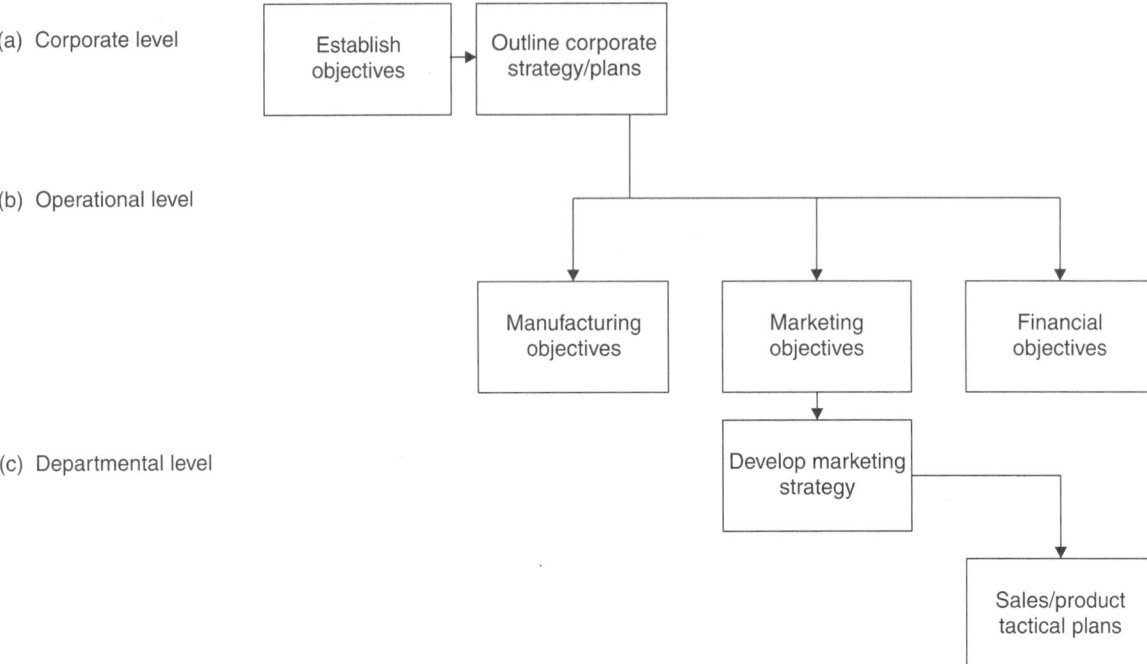

Unless an organisation is so small that it is a single unit, without functional departments, the overall objectives of the organisation must indicate different requirements for different functions. While some corporate goals cannot be stated in quantifiable terms, subsidiary objectives must be very clear cut, so that performance can be **measured**. The SMART criteria are often used to ensure that objectives are adequately stated.

(a)   **Specific**. Vague generalities must be avoided.

(b)   **Measurable**. Desired outcomes must be quantified so that clear measures of performance can be set.

(c)   **Attainable**. A 'blue sky' hope is useless for controlling performance or motivating staff.

(d)   **Results-orientated**. Objectives should be stated in terms of **outcomes** rather than **inputs**.

(e)   **Time-bounded**. A time by which the objective is to be achieved should be set.

3.3 The monitoring and revision of objectives

Successful planning requires a commitment to objectives, and so objectives should not be subject to frequent change. A planning review, in which objectives are reassessed and planning horizons reviewed, should however be held regularly, perhaps once a year.

3.4 Marketing objectives

Marketing objectives should be clear statements of where the organisation wants to be in marketing terms. They describe what the organisation expects to achieve as a result of its planned marketing actions. Remembering the SMART criteria, examples of marketing objectives might look like this:

'To increase market share from the current X% to Y% by 20XX.'
'To achieve a sales revenue of £X million at a cost of sales not exceeding 80% in 20X1.'

Objectives can be set for overall achievement as above, or for elements of the strategic plan. For example, if one of the strategies to achieve a profitable increase in sales revenue is to increase awareness of the product, then an advertising objective (a marketing sub-objective) might be: 'To increase product awareness in the target market from V% to W% in 20X1.'

When developing a strategy, a company is seeking a match with its operating environment. This may mean adjusting the company's strategy to fit into the existing market environment, although it may possibly involve attempting to change the environment to fit the company. Overall, the strategy must enable the company to meet the specific needs of its consumers and to do so more efficiently than its competitors.

Exam tip

> Questions are likely to cover marketing strategy alternatives, with a particular objective in mind (eg to grow sales) or in a particular context (decline stage of product life cycle). According to the syllabus notes, 'the setting of objectives should include an understanding of corporate objectives and strategic marketing objectives but should concentrate on the operational objectives to achieve the marketing plan'.

4 Environmental analysis – the macro-environment
Pilot paper, 12/03, 6/04, 12/06, 6/07, 12/07

FAST FORWARD 〉〉

> The wider **macro** environment may be analysed using the **PESTEL** mnemonic.

Key concept

> The **business environment** comprises all the economic, political, social, cultural, legal, technological and demographic influences acting on the markets within which the organisation operates. It encompasses influences on customers and the behaviour of competitors and suppliers in these markets. All these factors have an impact on the performance of the organisation, but cannot be controlled by management actions.

'The essence of formulating competitive strategy is relating a company to its environment … Every industry has an underlying structure or set of fundamental economic and technical characteristics … .The strategist must learn what makes the environment tick.'   Porter (1996)

The wider macro-environment may be analysed under the headings below

- Political
- Economic
- Social

- Technological
- Environmental (green)
- Legal

The mnemonic is **PESTEL**.

Exam tip

> The Pilot paper offers 15 marks for a question on environmental analysis. It will always feature in the exam in some way, often as part of the 50-mark scenario question.

4.1 The political environment

An organisation's freedom of action is constrained by what is politically acceptable. Note that this is not the same thing as 'legal'. Changes in society are reflected in the priorities of politicians and governments have many ways of bringing pressure to bear on business. They frequently use such levers as economic power, codes of conduct and statements of policy to set the ground rules for organisational life.

The government **controls** much of the economy, being the nation's largest supplier, employer, customer and investor. It also influences the **money supply**, controls the level of **interest rates** and sets **exchange rate** policy.

4.1.1 Political change

Changes in political ideology have profound implications for business.

. Application

In recent UK history, Conservative governments held the right to set interest rates. The consequences were that there were significant fluctuations in interest rates, inflation and unemployment resulting in periods of boom and recession. Whilst free enterprise was encouraged, the economic environment was not as stable as many business managers would have preferred. It was accepted wisdom that business cycles inevitably involved ups and downs.

When a Labour government was elected into office in 1997, one of their priorities was to delegate the responsibilities for setting interest rates and controlling inflation to an independent monetary policy committee within the Bank of England.

4.1.2 Political factors

- The possible impact of political change on the organisation
- The likelihood of change taking place and the possible need for contingency plans
- What needs to be done to cope with the change ('scenario planning')

4.2 The economic environment

The general state of the economy influences prospects for all businesses. Generally, economic growth produces a benign environment with healthy demand for most goods and services.

Some **economic influences**

- The rate of inflation
- Unemployment and the availability of manpower
- Interest rates
- The level and type of taxation
- The availability of credit
- Exchange rates

Action Programme 3

Application

Give examples of economic influences at an international level. Many of these are subject to the policies of national governments.

4.2.1 Economic trends – regional, national and international

The **local** economic environment affects wage rates, availability of labour, disposable income of local consumers, and the provision of business infrastructure and services.

National economic trends will affect prospects for growth, inflation, unemployment and taxation levels.

World trends have an important influence on the future of any company with plans to trade abroad, whether buying imports or selling as exporters.

4.3 The social environment

Social change involves changes in the nature, attitudes and habits of society.

(a) **Rising standards of living** may result in wider ownership of items like DVD players, dishwashers, microwave ovens, compact disc players and sailing boats.

(b) **Society's changing attitude to business** tends to increase companies' obligations and responsibilities with respect to environmental protection and ethical conduct.

(c) An increasing proportion of people are employed in clerical, supervisory or management jobs.

4.3.1 Cultural changes

Cultural variables are particularly significant for overseas marketing.

Language differences have clear marketing implications. For example, brand names have to be translated, often leading to entirely different (and sometimes embarrassing) meanings in the new language.

Cultural differences may affect business in a variety of ways.

- Design of goods
- Trading hours
- Distribution methods

4.3.2 Socio-economic groups

Marketing interest stems from the observable fact that members of particular groups have similar lifestyles, beliefs and values which affect their purchasing behaviour. Socio-economic classification involves taking factors such as occupation, education and income into account.

4.3.3 Family

Family background is a very strong influence on purchasing behaviour. Family structure is changing in most of the developed world. There are more single person and single parent households due to the increased divorce rate and population ages. The traditional nuclear family represents a relatively small proportion of all families.

4.4 The technological environment

(a) **Types of products and services**. Within consumer markets we have seen the emergence of home computers and Internet services.

(b) **The way in which products are made**. Modern automated systems of design and manufacture have revolutionised manufacturing.

(c) **The way in which services are provided**. Call centres and Internet trading have expanded widely.

(d) **The way in which markets are identified**. Database systems make it easier to analyse the market place. New types of marketing strategy, and new organisational structures, have been developed.

The effects of technological change are wide-ranging.

- Cuts in costs may afford the opportunity to reduce prices.
- The development of better quality products and services provides greater satisfaction.
- Products and services exist that did not exist before.

4.4.1 The ecological (green) environment

Public awareness of the connections between industrial production, mass consumption and environmental damage is higher than it has ever been, with information flooding out through the mass media and sometimes generating profound public reaction. Modern marketing practice needs to reflect awareness of these concerns, and is itself being changed by the issues that they raise.

4.4.2 Green concerns

The modern green movement is animated by concerns over pollution, overpopulation and the effects of massive growth on the finite resources of the earth. Green economists have tried to put together an economics based on alternative ideas.

- Monetary valuation of economic resources
- Promoting the quality of life
- Self reliance
- Mutual aid
- Personal growth
- Human rights

4.5 The impact of green issues on marketing practices

Environmental impacts on business

    (a)   **Direct**

        (i)   Changes affecting costs or resource availability
        (ii)   Impact on demand
        (iii) Effect on power balances between competitors in a market

    (b)   **Indirect**. Examples are pressure from concerned customers or staff and legislation affecting the business environment.

Sustainability requires that the company only uses resources at a rate which allows them to be replenished, and confines emissions of waste to levels which do not exceed the capacity of the environment to absorb them. **Policies based on sustainability have three aims**.

- To pursue equity in the **distribution** of resources
- To maintain the integrity of the world's **ecosystems**
- To increase the capacity of human populations for **self-reliance**

4.6 Green marketing

There are strong reasons for bringing the environment into the business equation. The green consumer is a driving force behind changes in marketing and business practices. Green consumption can be defined as the decisions related to consumer choice which involve environmentally-related beliefs, values and behaviour. There is extensive evidence that this is of growing importance to business, provided by:

- Surveys which indicate increased levels of environmental awareness and concern
- Increasing demand for, and availability of, information on environmental issues
- Value shifts from consumption to conservation
- Effective PR and marketing campaigns by environmental charities and causes

4.6.1 Segmenting the green market

Profiles of green consumers show that the force of green concern varies. Many consumers have not resolved the complex, confusing and often contradictory messages which are being sent out by various interest groups in this area. Broadly, females are more environmentally-aware than males, and families

with children are more likely to be concerned about making green consumption choices. The evidence also shows that consumers are becoming both more aware and more sophisticated in their approach.

Marketing diagnostics has developed a **typology of green consumers which identifies four main groups**.

(a) **Green activists** (5 – 15% of the population) are members or supporters of environmental organisations.

(b) **Green thinkers** (30%, including the activists) seek out green products and services, and look for new ways to care for the environment.

(c) **Green consumer base** (45 – 60%) includes anyone who has changed behaviour in response to green concerns.

(d) **Generally concerned** (90%) claim to be concerned about green issues.

Studies show that consumer behaviour varies in greenness according to the information which is available about the product, the regularity of purchase, the price-sensitivity of the purchase involved, their degree of brand loyalty to existing brands, the availability of substitutes and the credibility of green products.

Marketing at Work   Application

Green marketing

Being able to predict problems can produce great strategic advantages, but also some odd results. The problem of CFCs from aerosols, and their effects on the ozone layer, was known about from the early 1970s, and Johnson & Johnson abandoned the use of them in their products back in 1976. Consumer reactions to the product began in the late 1980s, and, of course, the firm was well prepared, but found itself in a very strange position, having to attach 'ozone friendly' labels to products which had, in fact, been modified more than ten years before.

This illustrates green marketing problems very well. Action is vital at the time when public perceptions threaten a product, rather than the manufacturer simply dealing with the environmental dangers which the product may pose. Green marketing practices will have to deal with more and more of these problems, and the old assumption that these worries are simply a moral panic which will run its course and disappear is surely now revealed as wishful thinking.

Nevertheless, resistance to green marketing within many companies is likely to remain strong. New products, new communications strategies and messages, new 'clean' plant and technology, new appointments of staff skilled in these areas, and very broad changes in organisational culture will all have to be 'sold' to powerful individuals and groups within organisations. Obviously, the internal politics of business organisations need to be taken into account by green practitioners.

Action Programme 4   Application

What are the implications of green issues for services marketing?

The **not-for-profit (NFP) sector**, would seem to be intrinsically greener since the profit motive has been blamed for generating wasteful and environmentally damaging over-consumption. Free market enthusiasts argue that not having to make a profit is more likely to promote waste and inefficiency, since the discipline of competition is absent. Even within the NFP sector, there are likely to be varying factors at work. For instance, government departments are more likely to feel a responsibility for the environment than smaller organisations.

Application/evaluation

You should, as part of your studies, read a quality daily newspaper so as to keep abreast of current marketing developments. Keep a special look out for articles about marketing and social responsibility. The examiner will be impressed if you are able to give up-to-date examples in your answers.

4.6.2 The legal environment

The legal system may be thought of as part of the political environment. It lays down the framework for business, with rules about business structure and ownership such as the Companies Act. It regulates business relationships with contract law and guarantees individual rights with employment law. There is a wide range of regulations dealing with general business activities such as health and safety regulations, rules about emissions into the environment and planning regulations.

5 Environmental analysis – the micro-environment

Pilot paper, 12/03, 6/04, 6/06, 12/06, 12/07

> **FAST FORWARD**
>
> An analysis of the **micro** environment concentres on **customers** and **competitors**.

The micro-environment is also known as the **task** environment. The nature of **competition** is a key element in the environment of commercial organisations. There are four main issues.

- Identifying the competitors
- The strength of the competition
- Characteristics of the market
- The likely strategies and responses of competitors to the organisation's strategies

> **FAST FORWARD**
>
> **Porter's five competitive forces** influence the state of competition in an industry and its profit potential.

In discussing competition, Porter (1996) distinguishes between factors characterising the nature of competition.

(a) **In one industry compared with another** (eg in the chemicals industry compared with the clothing retail industry). Which factors make one industry as a whole potentially more profitable than another?

(b) **Within a particular industry**. These relate to the competitive strategies that individual firms might select.

Key concept

> Five **competitive forces** influence the state of competition in an industry, which collectively determines the profit potential of the industry as a whole.
>
> (a)   The threat of **new entrants** to the industry
> (b)   The threat of **substitute** products or services
> (c)   The bargaining power of **customers**
> (d)   The bargaining power of **suppliers**
> (e)   The **rivalry** amongst current competitors in the industry

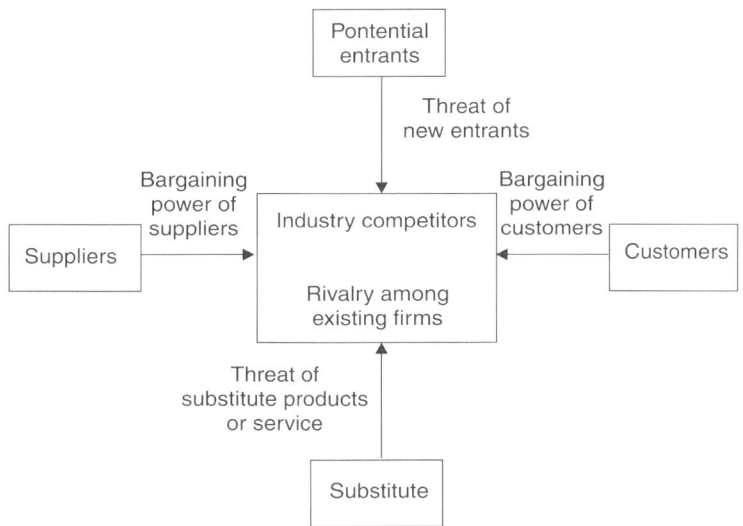

Source: adapted from Porter (1996)

5.1 The threat of new entrants (and barriers to entry to keep them out)

A new entrant into an industry will bring extra capacity and more competition. The strength of this threat is likely to vary from industry to industry, depending on:

- The strength of the **barriers to entry**. Barriers to entry discourage new entrants.
- The likely **response of existing competitors** to the new entrant.

5.2 The threat from substitute products

A **substitute product** is a good/service produced by **another industry** which satisfies the **same customer needs.** Substitutes put a lid on what firms in an industry can charge.

5.3 The bargaining power of customers

Customers want better quality products and services at a lower price. Satisfying this want might force down the profitability of suppliers in the industry. Customer strength depends upon such factors as how much the customer buys, or how price sensitive he or she happens to be.

5.4 The bargaining power of suppliers

Suppliers can exert pressure for higher prices, depending upon such factors as whether there are just **one or two dominant suppliers** to the industry, able to charge monopoly or oligopoly prices. It will also depend on whether the suppliers have **other customers** outside the industry, and do not rely on the industry for the majority of their sales.

Marketing at Work   Application

Food products in the UK are largely sold through supermarket chains, and it can be difficult for a new producer to get supermarket organisations to agree to stock its products. As retailers become more powerful, they are placing more and more demands on food producers: failure to comply can mean exclusion from the channel of distribution. Supplier bargaining power is low. Sophisticated marketing firms try to get round this by using advertising, for example, to stimulate customer demand by implementing 'pull strategies'. Such strategies can extend to point of sale advertising such as LCD screens in supermarket aisles, which may promote one or more products.

Other suppliers try to restrict distribution outlets to maintain high prices, particularly in the case of perfumes and cosmetics, by banning sales of these items in 'undesirable' outlets such as discount supermarkets.

5.5 Rivalry amongst current competitors in the industry

The **intensity of competitive rivalry** within an industry will affect the profitability of the industry as a whole. Competitive actions might take the form of price competition, advertising battles, sales promotion campaigns, introducing new products for the market, improving after sales service or providing guarantees or warranties. Intensity of competition is related to three main factors.

(a) **Whether there are many equally balanced competitors**. Markets involving a large number of firms are likely to be very competitive, but when the industry is dominated by a small number of larger firms, competition is likely to be less intense.

(b) **The rate of growth in the industry**. Fast growth is likely to benefit a larger number of firms, and so their rivalry will be less intense. Rivalry is intensified where growth is slow or stagnant.

(c) **Whether fixed costs are high**. If fixed costs are high, and variable costs are a relatively small proportion of the selling price, high volumes are necessary. It is tempting for firms to compete on price, even though this may mean a failure to cover fixed costs and make an adequate return in the longer run.

Competition may **help the industry to expand**, stimulating demand for new products. On the other hand, demand may be left unchanged, so that individual competitors will simply be spending more money, charging lower prices and making lower profits. The only benefits involve maintaining market share.

Marketing at Work

Application

The consequences of not monitoring the market can be illustrated with two examples. EverReady lost market leadership in the battery market by not keeping abreast of developments, and then reacting slowly to Duracell's alkaline product launch. An estimate of competitive retaliation was not undertaken by Cadbury's when they launched the Aztec bar against the might of Mars. Due to Mars' aggressive response, the launch failed.

5.6 Schemes for assessing competitors

Here are five key questions for the assessment of competitors.

- **Who** are we competing against?
- What are their **objectives**?
- What **strategies** are they pursuing, with what success?
- What **strengths and weaknesses** do they possess?
- How are they likely to react?

5.7 Customer analysis

Consumer behaviour can be defined as the behaviour that consumers display in searching for, purchasing, using, evaluating and disposing of products. It provides the foundation knowledge which guides subsequent marketing strategy.

5.7.1 Factors affecting customer behaviour

A number of factors influence the consumer buying process.

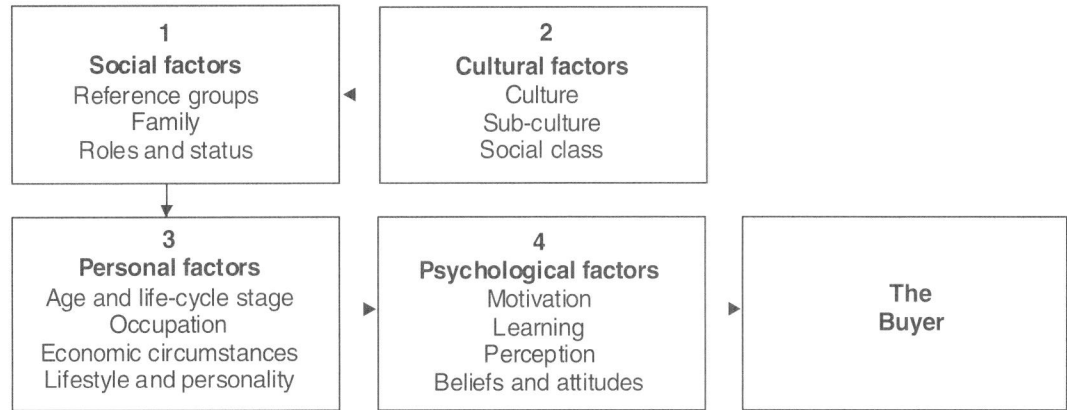

(a) **Cultural factors** exert the broadest and deepest influence on consumer behaviour. The culture in which we live determines our **values, beliefs and perceptions**. **Buying behaviour** is also affected by **subculture** and **social class**. Different social classes also display distinct brand preferences in areas such as clothing, decorative products and cars.

(b) A consumer's behaviour is also influenced by **social factors**. People are influenced in their buying by the groups they are members of, called **associate groups**, and by the groups whose behaviour they reject, called **disassociate groups**. Marketers, in planning their target market strategy, should try to identify the groups and the key individuals whose behaviours and lifestyles are followed. For example, football stars are used in advertising to appeal to the male youth market.

(c) A buyer's decisions are also influenced by **personal factors**.

   (i) The **family life cycle model** proposes that as we move through different phases of our lives, we buy different products and services and change our priorities.

   (ii) **Occupation** also influences consumption patterns.

   (iii) A person's **lifestyle** also influences what is deemed important to purchase, where they search for information on those goods and how they make the purchase decision.

(d) Finally **psychological factors** such as motivation, learning, perception, beliefs and attitudes influence the consumer buying process.

Exam tip

A consumer's buying process is the result of the complex interplay of cultural, social, personal and psychological influences. The marketing planner is unable to influence many of these factors. They are useful, however, in segmentation terms and they can suggest how you can develop a successful positioning concept and marketing mix to generate a strong and favourable consumer response and a good exam answer!

Action Programme 6

Application

Summarise the information needed for an appraisal of the task environment.

6 Internal appraisal

6/07

An **internal appraisal** assesses the company's **resources** and ability to **compete**.

Corporate resources are sometimes described as the **five Ms**.

- **Men:** its human resources and organisation
- **Money:** its financial health
- **Materials:** supply sources and products
- **Machines:** the production facilities, fixed assets, capacity
- **Markets:** its reputation, position and market prospects

In addition to this list it is also necessary to remember the less obvious **intangibles** like goodwill, brand names, patents, trademarks and development work in progress.

Action Programme 7

Application

For each of the five Ms identified above, give examples of the types of question which you would wish to ask in order to obtain information for use in an internal analysis.

Aspects of the internal appraisal

(a) **Past accounts and ratios.** By looking at **trends**, or by comparing ratios (if possible) with those of other firms in a similar industry, it might be possible to identify strengths and weaknesses in major areas of the business.

(b) **Product position and product-market mix.** Existing products and those in a late stage of development should be reviewed for market performance and potential. The overall balance of the product portfolio should be considered.

(c) **Cash and financial structure.** If a company intends to expand or diversify, it will need cash to acquire subsidiaries or for investing in new capacity.

(d) **Cost structure.** If a company operates **with high fixed costs and relatively low variable costs**, high volumes of production and sale might be required to break even. In contrast, a company with low fixed costs should be able to operate at a lower breakeven point.

(e) **Managerial ability.** Management may well overestimate their own ability or be unable to form a useful evaluation.

Typically, the analysis would use information from all areas of company activity. Here are some examples.

(a) **Marketing**

    (i)   Success rate of new product launches

    (ii)   Advertising: evaluating advertising strategies and individual campaigns

    (iii)   Market shares and sizes: is the organisation in a strong or weak position?

    (iv)   Portfolio of business units: new, growth, mature and declining markets

    (v)   Sales force organisation and performance

    (vi)   Service quality

    (vii)   Customer care strategies: nature of markets targeted

(b) **Products**

    (i)   Sales by market, area, product groups, outlets

    (ii)   Margins and contributions to profits from individual products

    (iii) Product quality

    (iv) Product portfolio: age and structure of markets

    (v)   Price elasticity of demand and price sensitivity of demand for products

(c) **Distribution**

    (i)   Delivery service standards – lead times for competitors and products

    (ii)   Warehouse delivery fleet capacity

    (iii) Geographical availability of products

(d) **Research and development (R & D)**

    (i)   R & D projects in relation to marketing plans

    (ii)   Expenditure on R & D relative to available assets

    (iii) Evaluation of R & D in new products/variations on existing products

    (iv) Appropriateness of R & D workload and schedules to competitor activity

(e) **Finance**

    (i)   Availability of short-term and long-term funds, cash flow

    (ii)   Contribution of each product to cash flow and return on investment

    (iii) Profitability of individual customers

    (iv) Accounting ratios to identify areas of strength or weakness in performance

    (v)   Availability of accurate cost data

(f) **Plant, equipment and other facilities**

    (i)   Age, value, production capacity and suitability of plant and equipment

    (ii)   Valuation of all assets

    (iii) Land and buildings: location, value, area, use, length of lease, book value

    (iv) Achievement of economies of scale

    (v)   Asset evaluation: age, condition, quality

(g) **Management and staff**

    (i)   Age profile

    (ii)   Skills and attitudes

    (iii) State of industrial relations, morale and labour turnover

    (iv) Training and recruitment facilities

    (v)   Manpower utilisation

    (vi) Management team strengths and weaknesses

(h) **Organisation**

    (i)   Organisation structure in relation to the organisation's needs

    (ii)   Appropriateness of management style and philosophy

    (iii) Communication and information systems

(i) **Raw material and finished goods stocks**

    (i)   The sources and security of supply

    (ii)   Number and description of items

    (iii) Turnover periods

    (iv) Storage capacity

    (v)   Obsolescence and deterioration

    (vi) Pilfering, wastage

7 SWOT analysis

> **FAST FORWARD**
>
> **SWOT analysis** is a commonly used technique to assess the current situation of the business. **Strengths** and **weaknesses** are features of the **organisation**; **opportunities** and **treats** are features of the **environment**.

Exam tip

> SWOT could come up in the compulsory case study question but perhaps less often as an essay question. It is a useful checklist – but you do not need SWOT for every answer. Place it within context: analysis tools for use in the marketing audit were examined in December 2005 and June 2007.
>
> To quote the syllabus notes, 'the SWOT should form the conclusion of the marketing audit and assist with the setting of marketing objectives'. We looked at marketing objectives in Section 3.

The features of the current situation can usually be summarised into **strengths, weaknesses, opportunities and threats**. This process is called **SWOT analysis**. Effective SWOT analysis does not simply require a categorisation of information, but also requires some assessment of the relative importance of the various factors.

Strengths and weaknesses are features of the organisation itself and its product/service range.

    (a)   **Strengths** are features from which the company may be able to derive competitive advantage. They are also known as core competences.

    (b)   **Weaknesses** are disadvantages that may have to be remedied. For example a company's growth is being hampered because its people have weak customer handling skills. A training programme could be introduced to help its people develop strong skills.

Opportunities and threats are features of the environment, particularly the immediate competitive or task environment.

A successful strategy is one that **exploits strengths** and **seizes opportunities**, while **remedying weaknesses** and **dealing effectively with threats**. Unfortunately, it is unusual for a company to possess all the strengths it needs to exploit its chosen opportunities and overcome the immediate threats. It is very common, therefore, for companies to undertake programmes of corporate development in which they attempt to overcome crucial weaknesses and build new strengths. There may also be attempts to convert threats into opportunities by the same process eg buying out a rival group of companies.

SWOT analysis is sometimes presented using a grid, popular with management gurus, as in the diagram in the following Action Programme.

Application

Give examples of political, economic, social and technological factors which might offer opportunities or be a source of threats.

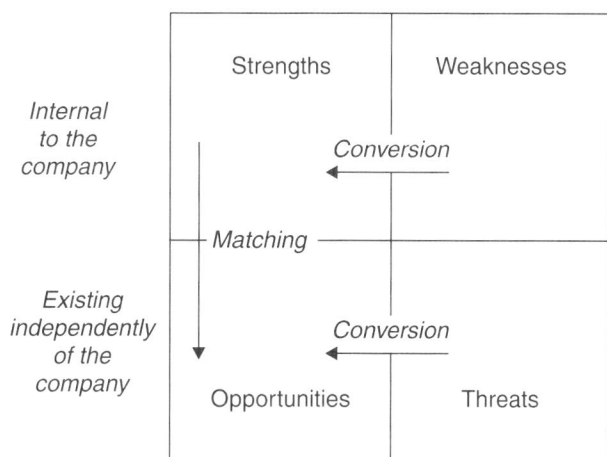

SWOT Analysis

Chapter Roundup

- **Strategic planning** begins with the definition of the corporate **mission**. Strategic objectives are then set which support the mission.

- **Marketing objectives** will support and flow from the overall corporate strategic objectives.

- A **marketing audit** must be comprehensive and objective and should be carried out regularly. It is a comprehensive review of a firm's marketing activities, covering:

  - The marketing environment
  - Marketing strategies
  - Marketing systems
  - Marketing organisation
  - Marketing function
  - Marketing productivity

- The setting of **objectives** is a key part of marketing planning.

- The wider **macro** environment may be analysed using the **PESTEL** mnemonic.

- An analysis of the **micro** environment concentres on **customers** and **competitors**.

- **Porter's five competitive forces** influence the state of competition in an industry and its profit potential.

- An **internal appraisal** assesses the company's **resources** and ability to **compete**.

- **SWOT analysis** is a commonly used technique to assess the current situation of the business. **Strengths** and **weaknesses** are features of the **organisation**; **opportunities** and **threats** are features of the **environment.**

- SWOT analysis is used to **sort information**; it does not provide ready made answers to strategic problems.

Quick Quiz

1   Define a mission statement.

2   How are typical corporate objectives expressed?

3   What is a marketing audit?

4   Give two examples of marketing objectives.

5   What is the business environment?

6   State four economic influences on business.

7   Summarise the effect of technological change on business.

8   What main factors determine the intensity of competition?

9   What are the five competitive forces?

10   What are the 5 Ms?

11   State six areas of marketing activity that would be examined during an internal appraisal.

12   What is a SWOT analysis?

Answers to Quick Quiz

1   A statement of what the organisation is aiming to achieve through the conduct of its business.

2   In concrete terms such as profitability and return on investment

3   A detailed analysis of marketing capacity and practice, which enables plans to be made with the aim of improving company performance.

4   Market share; sales levels.

5   All the factors that act on the company's markets, including its suppliers, competitors and customers.

6   Examples include:

- Inflation rate
- Interest rates
- Tax regime
- Unemployment rate
- Exchange rates
- Availability of credit

You may think of others.

7
- New products and services
- New methods and processes
- New means of delivering services
- New ways to identify markets

8
- A market with a large number of rivals is likely to be more competitive than one with a few.
- A fast rate of industry growth reduces competition; stagnation increases it.
- High fixed costs require high volumes and promote competition on price.

9   The threat of new entrants
The threat of substitutes
Bargaining power of customers
Bargaining power of suppliers
Rivalry amongst current competition

10   Men (ie staff resources)
Money
Materials
Machines
Markets

11   Six from:

- Market specifics eg advertising and customer care
- Products
- Distribution
- R&D
- Finance
- Plant and equipment
- Management and staff
- Organisation
- Stocks

12   The analysis of the current situation into strengths, weaknesses, opportunities and threats.

Action Programme Review

1 Each person's mission statement will be individual to him or her. Here are just some aspects that could be considered.

- Levels of educational attainment
- Career or occupational aspirations
- Treatment of colleagues and other people
- Attitudes to material possessions and wealth accumulation
- Type of lifestyle
- Approach to health and recreational activities
- Activities on environmental issues
- Travel, leisure and entertainment
- Attitude to progress and stability
- Political outlook and participation
- International and local identity
- Approaches to modernity, progress and conservatism
- Works of charity
- Attitudes to law and order
- Honesty and ethical behaviour
- Family and friends
- Involvement in the community
- Fulfilment of emotional needs
- Pursuit of happiness

This exercise may have benefits other than the personal. By enhancing your own self-awareness, you might well strengthen your market consciousness, helping you to be a more effective marketing professional.

2 Typical examples of decisions which sacrifice longer-term objectives.

- Postponing or abandoning capital expenditure, which would eventually contribute to (longer-term) growth and profits, in order to protect short-term cash flow and profits

- Cutting R&D expenditure to save operating costs, and so reducing the prospects for future product development

- Reducing quality control, to save operating costs

- Reducing the level of customer service, to save operating costs

3 • Comparative growth rates, inflation rates, interest rates and wage rates in other countries

- The extent of protectionist measures against imports

- The nature and extent of exchange controls

- The development of international economic communities such as the European Union and the prospects of international trade agreements between countries

- The levels of corporate and personal taxation in different countries

4 Here are some ideas.

(a) Even services industries use tangible assets such as buildings, stationery, vehicles and computers. It could be established policy that such assets should be, as far as possible, non-polluting; obtained from sustainable service; and recycled at the end of their lives.

(b) Service industries, like other organisations, can enhance their 'green' credentials by supporting worthy causes with donations and the use of facilities.

(c) Some services relate directly to the environment; examples are consultancy in the various energy sectors and agricultural management. Providers of such services can make it policy that their work will not be to the detriment of the environment, to the extent that it is possible.

5   Your own research.

6   (a) **Markets**. What changes are occurring in market trends – sales, profits, geographic distribution? What changes are occurring in market segments and niches?

(b) **Customers**. How do customers/potential customers rate us on aspects such as reputation, product quality, service, salesforce, advertising/price etc, relative to our competitors? What sorts of customers do we have? Are they changing? What is our customers' buying behaviour? Is it changing? How well do we understand our customers and their buying motives?

(c) **Competitors**. Who are our major competitors? What are their market shares? What are their strengths and weaknesses? Competitors' marketing strategies and likely responses to our marketing actions. Future changes in competition.

(d) **Distributors**. What are the major distributive channels in our markets? What are the channels' efficiency levels and growth trends?

(e) **Suppliers**. Outlooks for future supplies. Trends in patterns of buying/selling. Changes in power bases. Evaluations of suppliers against buying/ marketing criteria

(f) **Agencies**. What are the costs/availability outlooks for transportation services, for warehousing facilities, for financial resources etc? Just how effective are our advertising, PR and marketing research agencies?

(g) **Publics**. What publics offer particular opportunities or problems for us? What steps have we taken to deal effectively with each public?

7   Gathering this information involves obtaining answers to the following sort of questions.

(a) **Men and women**

(i) **Labour**. What is the size of the labour force? What are their skills? How much are they paid? What are total labour costs? What proportion of the organisation's added value or sales revenue is accounted for by labour costs? How efficient is the workforce? What is the rate of labour turnover? How good or bad are industrial relations?

(ii) **Management**. What is the size of the management team? What are its specialist skills? What management development and career progression exists? How well has management performed in achieving targets in the past? How hierarchical is the management structure?

(b) **Money**

(i) **Finance**. What are the company's financial resources? What are its debt and gearing ratios?

(ii) **Working capital**. How much working capital does the organisation use? What are the average turnover periods for stocks and debtors? What is the credit policy of the organisation? What credit is taken from suppliers? What is the level of bad debts? How is spare cash utilised by the treasury department? How are foreign exchange transactions dealt with? How profitable is our product portfolio?

(c) **Materials**

Where do they come from? Who supplies them? What percentage of the total cost of sales is accounted for by materials? What are wastage levels? Are new materials being developed for the market by suppliers?

    (d)   **Machines**

         Fixed assets. What fixed assets does the organisation use? What is their current value (on a going concern value and on a break-up value basis)? What is the amount of revenue and profit per £1 invested in fixed assets? How old are the assets? Are they technologically advanced or out of date? What are the organisation's repair and replacement policies? What is the **percentage fill** in the organisation's capacity? This is particularly important for service industries, such as cinemas, football grounds and trains, where fixed costs are high and resources need to be utilised as much as possible to earn good profits. R & D experience and level of technological expertise should also be assessed.

    (e)   **Markets**

         Market share, reputation, level of competition, deals with distributors and the level of goodwill. Is the company customer oriented and how is the customer contact/service perceived?

8   Opportunities and threats may arise in the following areas.

    (a)   **Political**: legislation involving, for example, pollution control or a ban on certain products would be a **threat** to various industries, but also an **opportunity** for selling lead-free petrol and suitable cars. Taxation incentives, rent-free factory buildings, or investment grants might be available for exploitation. Government policy may be to increase expenditure on housing, defence, schools and hospitals or roads and transport and this gives **opportunities** to private companies and the relevant government organisations alike. Political upheaval might damage market and investment prospects, especially overseas.

    (b)   **Economic**: unemployment, the level of wages and salaries, the expected total market behaviour for products, total customer demand, the growth and decline of industries and suppliers, general investment levels etc. At an international level, world production and the volume of international trade, demand, recessions, import controls, exchange rates.

    (c)   **Social**: Social attitudes will have a significant effect on customer demand and employee attitudes. Social issues such as environmental pollution, women's roles, and the need to solve social problems offer **opportunities** for new products and services. Demographic change and population structure will provide continuing product **opportunities**. There are recognised opportunities for growth in the personal pensions market. Unemployment will strongly affect the total spending power of consumers. This has been a chronic and long term **threat** in certain parts of the UK.

    (d)   **Technology**: new products appearing, or cheaper means of production or distribution will clearly have profound implications in these types of analysis.

Now try Question 3 at the end of the Study Text

Developing marketing strategies

Syllabus content – knowledge and skills requirements

- 2.6: Relationship between corporate objectives, business objectives and marketing objectives at an operational level
- 2.7: Concept of the planning gap and its impact on operational decisions
- 2.8: Segmentation, targeting and positioning within the marketing plan
- 2.9: Marketing budgets for mix decisions included in the marketing plan
- 2.10: Methods for evaluating and controlling the marketing mix
- 3.1: Role of strategy development in relation to developing market share and growth
- 3.2: How strategy formulation and decisions relating to the selection of markets impact at an operational level on the planning and implementation of an integrated marketing mix

Introduction

Having dealt with the marketing audit against the background of wider corporate planning, we now look more closely at marketing strategies. Section 1 discusses some important aspects of marketing strategy, including gap analysis. Once again, be aware that some of these ideas may be relevant at both the corporate and marketing department levels.

Market segmentation is a vital aspect of marketing strategy and is discussed in Section 2. Techniques for segmentation are covered in Sections 3 and 4 and the complementary ideas of targeting and product positioning in Sections 5 and 6. Section 7 covers the important topic of strategy evaluation and control.

1 Marketing strategies   6/04, 6/05, 12/05, 12/06

1.1 Gap analysis

> **FAST FORWARD**
>
> **Gap analysis** quantifies the size of the gap between the objective/targets for the planning period, and the forecast based on the extrapolation of the current situation. The organisation must then identify different strategies to fill the gap.

Key concept

> **Gap analysis** is a planning technique which identifies likely shortfalls in future performance and considers how best they can be filled.

Gap analysis starts with a comparison of what the organisation **wishes to achieve** and what it is **likely to achieve if nothing changes**.

The F_0 **forecast** is a forecast of future results assuming that the company continues to operate as at present. It is prepared in stages:

(a)   The analysis of revenues by units of sale and price, and the analysis of costs into variable, fixed, and semi-variable.

(b)   Projections into the future, based on past trends, to the end of the planning period.

(c)   Consideration of other factors affecting profits and return, such as the likelihood of deterioration in labour relations or machine servicability and the possibility of scarcity of raw materials.

(d)   Combination of these items into a single forecast.

When complete, the F_0 forecast may be compared with the organisation's objectives. Differences constitute the gap which has to be filled. The gap may have several elements such as a **profits gap** or a **sales gap**.

The **profit gap** is the difference between the target profits and the profits on the F_0 forecast. The options for bridging the gap need to be identified.

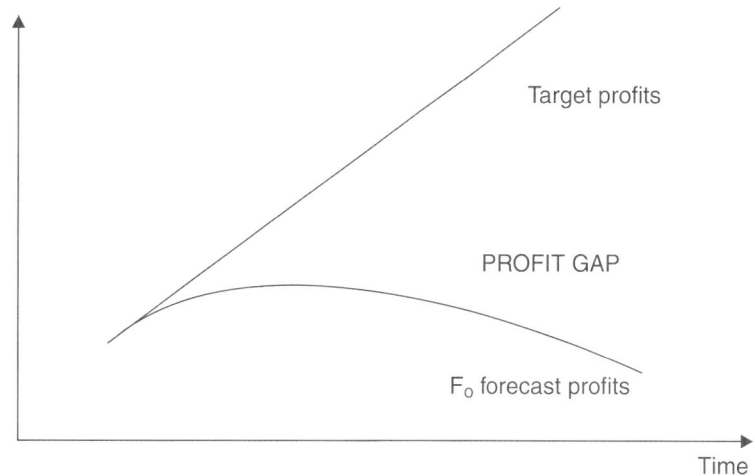

A **sales gap** can be filled by new product-market growth strategies as follows.

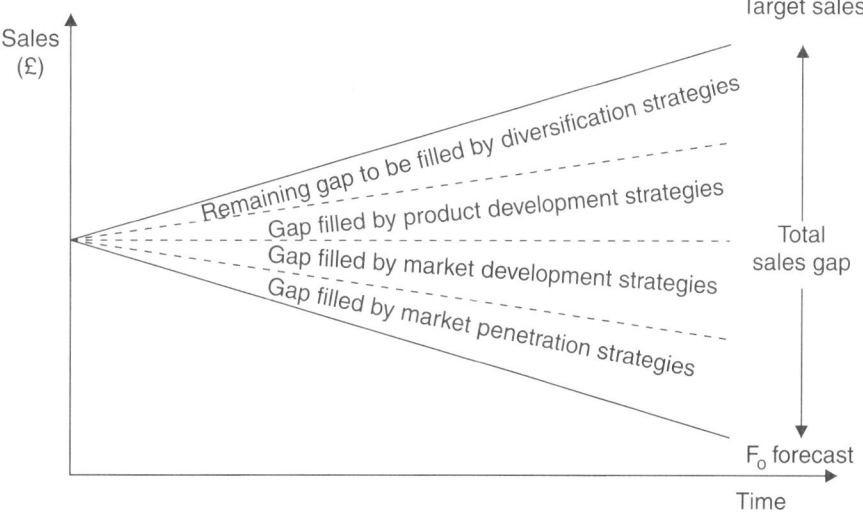

Exam tip

> The Pilot paper offers five marks for explaining the concept of gap analysis and a further five marks for using it in context. Gap analysis was also examined in June 2005.

The same basic technique can serve as the basis for formulating any particular strategy. In planning for human resources, gap analysis would be used to assess the difference over time between two quantities.

    (a)   What the organisation **needs to have** in terms of staff of differing skills and seniority
    (b)   What the organisation is **likely to have**, allowing for natural wastage of staff

A strategy would then be needed to fill the gap between target and current forecasts.

1.2 Competitive strategies

FAST FORWARD

> The purpose of **competitive strategy** is to provide the organisation with a competitive advantage.

1.2.1 Competitive advantage

Firms constantly strive for competitive advantage. Porter (1996) argues that strategy is essentially a method for creating and sustaining a profitable position in a particular market environment. The profit made by the firm depends first on the nature of its strategy and second on the inherent profitability of the industry in which it operates. An organisation in a basically profitable industry can still perform badly with an unsuitable strategy, while an organisation in an unprofitable industry may perform well with a more suitable strategy.

1.3 Growth strategies   Pilot paper, 12/03, 12/04, 6/05, 12/05, 6/06

FAST FORWARD ⟩⟩ **Ansoff's product/market matrix** is used for the analysis and determination of growth strategies. It suggests four possible options.

Ansoff's competitive strategies

Products

		Existing	New
Markets	Existing	Market Penetration 1	Product Development 4
	New	Market Development 2	Diversification 16

The numbers in the quadrants are an approximate indication of the risk attached to each strategy.

(a)   **Market penetration** involves increasing sales of the **existing products in existing markets**. This may include persuading existing users to use more (a credit card issuer might try to increase credit card use by offering higher credit limits or gifts based on expenditure); persuading non-users to use (for example, by, offering free gifts with new credit card accounts); or attracting consumers from competitors. Market penetration will, in general, only be viable in circumstances where the market is not already saturated. This is a low risk strategy.

(b)   **Market development** entails **expansion into new markets using existing products**. New markets may be different geographically, new market segments or new uses for existing products. This strategy requires swift, effective and imaginative promotion, but can be very profitable if markets are changing rapidly.

(c)   **Product development** involves the redesign or repositioning of existing products or the introduction of completely new ones in order to appeal to existing markets. Developments in the **mortgage market**, for example, illustrate product development as the traditional standardised mortgage account is rapidly being supplemented by variants which offer lower starting rates, special terms for particular types of customer and particular mixes of fixed and flexible repayment rates. This strategy relies on good service design, packaging and promotion and on company reputation to attract consumers.

(d)   **Diversification** is much more risky than the other three because the organisation is moving into areas in which it has little or no experience. Instances of pure diversification are consequently rare and as a strategic option it tends to be used in cases when there are no other possible routes for growth available.

Exam tip

> Ansoff's matrix features on the Pilot paper. New product development was examined in June 2005, and a product development strategy to expand a FMCG company's sales was the subject of a question on the December 2005 paper. Business growth strategies for a cruise company seeking to open up new business avenues and use its spare capacity formed part of the 50-mark question in the June 2006 sitting.

Most companies adopt, at least initially, a strategy of **market penetration** which carries the lowest risk. However, when market saturation is reached, a company needs to consider entering into new markets with existing products to maintain growth. Technological advance and competitive pressures will normally force companies into some degree of product development, ranging from cosmetic alterations through

tangible product improvements to revolutionary new products. Diversification may involve merger or takeover, but not necessarily.

Ansoff's matrix leads naturally into other marketing operations, such as research to identify new markets and new products, and the deployment of the marketing mix in exploiting product/market opportunities.

FAST FORWARD

PIMS is a diagnostic tool based on a database. It allows organisations to compare their strategic performance with that of other organisations.

PIMS, or Profit Impact of Marketing Strategy, is a large database covering more than 3,000 SBUs, developed largely in America but now adding a considerable number of European businesses to the portfolio. It is owned by the Strategic Planning Institute which has a London office. Clients input detailed confidential data on their expenditure and returns which are then computer-analysed to determine norms for groups of like businesses. This diagnostic tool thus enables a business to compare its own strategic performance (outputs relative to inputs) with the norm. The data claims to show in what respects the business is under-performing and how its performance might be improved.

1.3.1 The most influential determinants of profitability

(a)   The business' **competitive position** including market share and relative product quality

(b)   The **attractiveness of its served market** as indicated by growth rate and customer characteristics.

(c)   Its **production structure** including operational productivity and investment intensity.

Developing marketing objectives is a fundamental part of the marketing planning process.

One way to answer such a question is to draw the Ansoff Matrix, and explore each option in turn. For example, how do you increase market penetration? Sell more to current customers? Gain customers from competitors? For each of the four strategies you could have identified the supposed level of risk. Diversification as a means of increasing sales revenue is generally the most risky. (Don't assume that this guide is a formula which is always true. Market penetration is most risky if, for example, market structure and characteristics are changing rapidly.)

1.4 Strategy evaluation

Strategies are evaluated to decide whether they will help to achieve the organisation's objectives. The final list of desirable strategic opportunities will be a list for ranking in order of priority. Individual strategies could be tested against a list of criteria for acceptance as follows.

(a)   To what extent will the strategy contribute towards the company's **financial objectives** in both the short and long term?

(b)   Is the strategy consistent with the **social responsibilities** of the company?

(c)   Does the strategy **conform** to other strategies pursued by the company, or is it a completely new direction? (for example, conglomerate diversification, or investment in pure research might be proposed strategies which are currently not pursued by the company).

(d)   The element of **risk** attached to a proposed strategy should not be too high compared with the potential rewards. If the strategy can only be successful under the most favourable conditions, then the risk is probably too great.

(e)   Is the strategy capable of succeeding in spite of the likely reaction by **competitors**?

(f)   Will there be adequate **control**? A new strategy needs a careful check on performance to put any necessary remedial steps into effect, particularly in the early stages. The lack of an adequate control system may be a serious hindrance to effective decision making.

(g)   Is the strategy **preferable** to other, mutually exclusive strategies? Is there an option to combine two separate strategies into one action?

Here are six rather different criteria for testing strategy.

(a)   Can it be shown that the strategy gives the company an **expected return** with a given business risk attached, similar to the one expected by its shareholders?

(b)   Does the company have the necessary **competence** to carry out the strategy?

(c)   Does the strategy eliminate all the significant **weaknesses** of the company, as identified by the internal appraisal?

(d)   Does the strategy exploit any **opportunities** which have been identified as possibly arising in the future?

(e)   Does the strategy reduce the impact of any significant **external threats**?

(f)   Does the strategy call for action by the company which is objectionable on **social or moral** grounds?

The selection of strategies is formulated in a **policy statement**, which describes the planned long-term strategy of the company, identifying the objectives, constraints and strategies to be pursued over the corporate planning period. This statement should be short, and restricted to identifying a few key strategies. However, to sell the plan to junior managers and employees, the ideas in the statement might need to be internally marketed.

2 Market segmentation   Pilot paper, 6/04, 12/06

FAST FORWARD

It is extremely difficult for a business to be 'all things to all people'. **Market segmentation** is based on the recognition that every market consists of potential buyers with different needs, and different buying behaviour. These different customer attitudes may be grouped into segments' and a different marketing approach will be taken for each segment.

Marketing activity is more effective if groups can be identified and targeted. This is done by **market segmentation** which groups potential customers according to identifiable characteristics relevant to their purchasing behaviour.

Exam tip

A question on the Pilot paper asks about the benefits of segmentation.

Key concept

Market segmentation is the subdividing of a market into distinct subsets of customers, where any subset may conceivably be selected as a target market to be reached with a distinct marketing mix.

Kotler (1991)

The important elements of market segmentation are as follows.

(a)   While the total market consists of varied groups of consumers, each group has **common needs and preferences**, and may well react to market stimuli in the same way. For example, the market for umbrellas might be segmented according to sex. Women might seem to prefer umbrellas of a particular size and weight. The men's market might further be

subdivided by age or activity, for example, professionals, commuters, golfers. Each subdivision of the market will show increasingly common traits.

(b) **Each market segment can become a target market for a firm, requiring a unique marketing mix. Segmentation should enable a company to formulate an effective strategy for selling to a given group.** Objectives can then be set with reference to target segments.

> Effective market segmentation depends upon the **measurability**, **accessibility** and **sustainability** of the chosen segments.

There are many possible characteristics of buyers which could be chosen as segmentation variables and a variety of criteria which can be used to identify the most effective characteristics for use in market segmentation.

(a) **Measurability** is the degree to which information exists or is cost effectively obtainable on the characteristics of interest. Whilst a car manufacturer may have access to information about **location** of customers, **personality traits** are more difficult to obtain information about, because the required tests may be impractical to administer.

(b) **Accessibility** refers to the degree to which the company can identify and communicate with the chosen segments. Thus whilst a car dealer may be able to access potential corporate customers, by direct mail or tele-sales, identifying individual customers with family incomes in excess of £30,000 pa would not be so easy.

(c) **Substantiality** is the degree to which the segments are large enough to offer profitable returns. Thus, whilst a large number of people in social group DE aged over 65 could be identified, their potential profitability to a retailer is likely to be less in the long term than a smaller number of 17-18 year olds. This latter group might be worth cultivating, using a specially devised marketing approach, whereas the former might not be.

Action Programme 1   Evaluation

What do you think are the advantages of segmentation?

2.1 Key aspects of segmentation

Segmentation only makes sense if it brings appropriate benefits.

(a) Segmentation should increase benefits to consumers by providing **product features** more closely matching their needs.

(b) Segmentation enables the firm to identify those groups of customers who are most likely to buy. This ensures that **resources will not be wasted**, and marketing and sales activity can be **highly focused**. The result should be lower costs, greater sales and higher profitability (all key performance measures).

(c) Across the industry, segmentation will provide **greater customer choice** by generating a variety of products within a particular class from which consumers can choose.

Exam tip

Ten marks are on offer on the Pilot paper for a discussion of segmentation and targeting.

3 Segmenting consumer markets   **Pilot paper**

Consumer markets can be segmented, for example by location, by demography, by social class or by lifestyle.

3.1 Geographic segmentation

Segmentation based on location may be important for retailers, who need to get to know about the different groups of customers within their catchment area. Segmentation by location can also be a feature of international marketing strategy. Needs will be influenced by a range of factors including climate, religion, culture and infrastructure.

A national chain of supermarkets will use geographic segmentation because it interacts closely with the chain's outlet strategy. Each branch or group of retail outlets could be given mutually exclusive areas to service and so make more effective use of target marketing. The obvious advantage to customers is convenience of access, which is one of the major reasons why customers choose particular stores.

3.2 Demographic segmentation

Demography is the study of population and population trends. The following demographic factors have an impact on market segmentation.

(a)   Changes in national population and in regional distribution

(b)   Changes in the age distribution of the population. All over the developed world populations are ageing, as a result of improved health care and falling birth rates

(c)   The concentration of population into certain geographical areas

The total size of the population defines the total possible level of demand for a product. With the formation of the Single European Market in 1992, the market for UK companies became comparable in size to the US market.

The population is usually broken down into groups defined by demographic characteristics such as sex or age. The total size of each segment will suggest possible levels of demand for corresponding products.

3.2.1 Social class (socio-economics)

The social class of a person is also likely to influence buying habits and preferences. Although there are a number of factors involved in social class position, such as income, education and background the most commonly used classification, in the marketing world, is the **JICNARs scale**, based on the occupation of the main wage earner in the household. This involves the following classification scheme.

Social grade	Social status	Occupation
A	Upper middle class	Higher managerial, professional or administrative jobs.
B	Middle class	Middle managerial, professional or administrative jobs.
C1	Lower middle class	Supervisory or clerical jobs, junior management.
C2	Skilled working class	Skilled manual workers.
D	Working class	Unskilled and semi-skilled manual workers.
E	Those at the lowest level of subsistence	Pensioners, the unemployed, casual or low grade workers.

This scheme lacks precision as it divides the total population into just six large groups. It is very difficult to make significant distinctions between a B and a C1 class person. Also, because it is based on the occupation of the 'chief income earner' only, it does not reflect the income of the whole family unit, or the background and aspirations of members.

Computer databases using census details, market research and commercial data have over recent years made possible the use of segmentation systems based on a number of different household characteristics, from the names of occupants to the types of houses they occupy. By linking this to postcode data it is possible to identify very precisely the characteristics of consumers in a particular location, or to build up a profile of the types of people sending for goods by mail order, or completing hire purchase forms.

We will look at two more sophisticated approaches to geo-demographic segmentation, ACORN and MOSAIC, in the next section of this chapter.

3.2.2 Family life cycle

Family circumstances may be used to segment consumer markets. The segments are based on eight categories of **family decision making units**.

- Young and single
- Young, married, no children
- Young, married, youngest child under six years old
- Young, married youngest child over six years old
- Older, married, with children
- Older, married, no children under eighteen
- Older and single
- Other

The **family life cycle** (FLC) is a summary demographic variable. It brings together factors of age, marital status, career status (income) and the presence or absence of children. As a consequence, it is able to characterise the various stages through which households progress, with each stage involving **different needs and resources**.

3.2.3 Summary

Demographic segmentation methods are powerful tools especially when each of the bases is combined with other methods. The bases for demographic segmentation are clearly interdependent. Age and family life cycle stage are patently linked, as are housing and socio-economic group. Using a combination of these bases it is possible to define targets for marketing campaigns and sales activities.

3.3 Psychographic segmentation

Psychographic or **life style** segmentation seeks to classify groups according to their values, opinions, personality characteristics and interests. The ability to introduce new dimensions to existing customer information, for example customers' disposition towards savings, investment and the use of credit makes it extremely flexible.

Lifestyle refers to distinctive ways of living adopted by particular communities or sub-sections of society. It involves factors such as motivation, personality and culture, and depends on accurate description. When a group has been identified and characterised, products can be tailored and promoted for this particular group. It is possible for the same person to belong to several different psychographic groups at the same time.

3.4 Benefit segmentation

This form of segmentation is based on the different **benefits sought** by customer groups. In this form of segmentation, it is usual for varying customer groups to share the same benefits from the product or service. Benefit segmentation may be based on benefits sought or usage rates (see below).

In segmenting the market in terms of benefits sought, there is a need to identify common characteristics which the customer requires from the product or service.

| Marketing at Work | Application |

Banks and building societies have typically focused upon geographic, demographic, socio-economic and psychological characteristics to segment the market for financial services. These are not efficient predictors of future buying behaviour, so benefit segmentation by factor analysis is now being used to group building society customers in relation to their particular attitudes and behaviour. Certain benefits have been identified as being important to customers: personal service, investment, banking facilities, accessible cash, cash card, advice and money management. It seems that building societies and banks could use benefit segmentation to improve the effectiveness and efficiency of their marketing strategies.

3.4.1 Benefit segmentation of the toothpaste market

Segment name	Principal benefit sought	Demo-graphic strengths	Special behavioural character-istics	Brands disproport-ionately favoured	Personality character-istics	Lifestyle character-istics
The sensory segment	Flavour, product appearance	Children	Users of spearmint flavoured toothpaste	Colgate, Stripe	High, self–involvement	Hedonistic
The sociables	Brightness of teeth	Teens, young people	Smokers	Macleans, Ultra Brite	High sociability	Active
The worriers	Decay prevention	Large families	Heavy users	Crest	High hypo-chondriasis	Conservative
The independent segment	Price	Men	Heavy users	Brands on sale	High autonomy	Value-oriented

Individuals can be categorised by **usage patterns** – whether they are light, medium or heavy users of a product or service. The Target Group Index helps to identify usage groups for a wide range of products and services. This assists the marketer in developing distinct strategies aimed at specific users, based upon their existing consumption of a product or service. For example, banks and other financial institutions have introduced incentive schemes for customers when using their credit cards. This allows heavy users of the service to amass points and convert them into gifts.

Exam tip

> Both lifestyle and benefit segmentation are included in the Pilot paper. The question asked for recommendations as to how they could be used in the soft drink industry.

3.5 Segmentation in practice

When dealing with an individual customer, care needs to be taken **to avoid stereotypes** and not jump to conclusions. Sales staff may use segmentation as a benchmark, but should act cautiously on their assumptions.

Application

Make suggestions as to factors which might be used to segment each of the following markets.

- The market for adult education courses provided by a local authority
- The market for national magazines and periodicals
- The market for sports clubs and facilities across the UK

3.6 Fragmented industries and market segmentation

Industries begin to fragment and market segments proliferate when certain conditions prevail.

(a) Entry barriers are low and new firms can enter the market relatively easily.

(b) Economies of scale or learning curve effects are few, and so it is difficult for big firms to establish a significant overall cost leadership.

(c) Transport and distribution costs are high, and so the industry fragments on a geographical basis.

(d) Customer needs are extremely diverse.

(e) There are rapid product changes or style changes, to which small firms might react more quickly.

(f) There is a highly diverse product line, so that some firms are able to specialise in one part of the industry.

(g) There is scope for product differentiation, based on product design/quality differences or even brand images.

3.6.1 ACORN

ACORN is an acronym for A Classification of Residential Neighbourhoods. It is a geo-demographic segmentation approach which divides up the entire UK population in terms of the type of housing in which they live. For each of these areas, a wide range of demographic information is generated and the system affords the opportunity to assess product usage patterns, dependent upon the research conducted within national surveys.

Although the census is only conducted once every ten years, the ACORN database is updated annually to take account of latest population projections.

Application

Applications of the ACORN classifications.

(a) **Site Location Analysis**. Using ACORN profiles of the purchasing behaviour and socio-economic status of people living in the catchments of successful trading outlets, it is possible to identify sites with similar profiles for new stores or branches.

(b) **Market Research Sample Frames**. ACORN can help generate the most representative sample frames for market research, identifying areas with the right consumer mix.

(c) **Database Analysis. ACORN** can be used to profile both in-house customer files or bought-in lists by ACORN type, providing information which can be used to target people with similar characteristics.

(d) **Direct Mail. Selecting** from CACI's Electoral Roll database of 40 million names and addresses (according to the ACORN types relevant to particular products), can identify new prospect lists for direct mailings.

(e) **Door-to-Door Leaflet Campaigns**. ACORN can segment and define target markets by postal sector for effective and customised distribution planning in door-to-door promotions.

Marketing at Work
Application

Here are typical examples of ACORN categories in the UK produced by CACI Limited.

WEALTHY ACHIEVERS

A   Wealthy executives

1   Wealthy mature professionals, large houses
2   Wealthy working families with mortgages
3   Villages with wealthy commuters
4   Well-off managers with large houses

B   Affluent greys

5   Old affluent professionals
6   Farming communities
7   Old people, detached homes
8   Mature couples, smaller detached homes

C   Flourishing families

9   Older families, prosperous suburbs
10   Well-off working families with mortgages
11   Well-off managers, detached houses
12   Large families and houses in rural areas
13   Well-off older professionals, larger houses and converted flats
14   Older professionals in suburban houses and apartments
15   Affluent urban professionals, flats
16   Prosperous young professionals, flats
17   Young educated workers, flats
18   Multi-ethnic young, converted flats
19   Suburban privately renting professionals
20   Student flats and cosmopolitan shares
21   Singles and sharers, multi-ethnic areas
22   Low income singles
23   Student terraces

COMFORTABLY OFF

G   Starting out

24   Young couples, flats and terraces
25   White collar, singles/shares, terraces

H   Secure families

26   Younger white collar couples with mortgages
27   Middle-income, home owning areas
28   Working families with mortgages
29   Mature families in suburban semis
30   Established home-owning workers
31   Home-owning Asian family areas

I   Settled suburbia

32   Retired home owners
33   Middle-income older couples
34   Lower incomes, older people, semis

J   Prudent pensioners

35   Elderly singles, purpose built flats
36   Older people, flats

MODEST MEANS

L   Post industrial families

39   Skilled older families, terrace
40   Young working families

M   Blue collar roots

41   Skilled workers, semis and terraces
42   Home-owning families, terraces
43   Older people, rented terraces

Note: Altogether there are a total of 54 neighbourhood types. The above is an illustrative sample drawn from the full list.

3.6.2 MOSAIC

This system analyses information from a variety of sources.

(a)   **The census**, used to give housing, socio-economic, household and age data

(b)   **The electoral roll**, to give household composition and population movement data

(c)   **Post code address files** to give information on post 1981 housing, and special address types such as farms and flats

(d)   **CCN files/Lord Chancellor's office** to give credit search information and bad debt risk respectively

MOSAIC can provide information down to postcode level. The current classification includes 52 separate neighbourhood types.

4 Segmenting industrial markets

There are a variety of approaches to segmenting industrial markets.

Industrial markets are usually smaller and more easily identified than consumer markets. Segmentation may still be worthwhile, however, to identify and target specified groups within the total market.

Various segmentation schemes for industrial markets exist and may be used in combination. Databases have been developed to provide additional intelligence information which allows much tighter targeting of industrial customers. Industrial markets may be segmented using a variety of bases.

(a)   **By location**. Many business sectors are concentrated in particular locations (engineering in the West Midlands, computer companies along the M4 corridor).

(b)   **Company size** either by turnover or employees. This can give a good indication of their need for certain products or services.

(c)   **Usage rates**: Heavy, medium or light. This is most relevant in raw material and parts markets, and the market for some industrial services such as telecommunications and travel.

(d)   **Industry classification** indicates the nature of the business and may provide a useful method to classify sales leads. The UK Standard Industrial Classification is based on the European classification. It classifies businesses by their main type of economic activity. It is a hierarchical system using five levels of detail which start with 17 broad categories and work down to individual products such as soft furnishings.

(e)   **Product use**. An industrial organisation may buy a fleet of cars for use by its salesforce, or to hire out to the public as the basis for its service. Different uses are likely to be associated with different needs.

In industrial markets, just as in consumer markets, segmentation enables companies to devise strategies which more closely match the identified needs of customers. These smaller subgroups allow the marketing and sales team to get to know customers much better, and resources and efforts to be channelled towards the most profitable segments.

Remember that to be effective, segments must display three qualities.

- **Measurability**
- **Accessibility**
- **Substantiality**

5 Targeting   Pilot paper, 6/04, 12/06

Having carried out a segmentation exercise, the next step is to select **target markets**.

Limited resources, competition and large markets make it ineffective and inappropriate for companies to sell to the entire market; that is, every market segment. For the sake of efficiency they must select target markets. Marketing managers may choose one of the following policy options.

Key concepts

Undifferentiated marketing aims to produce a single product and get as many customers as possible to buy it. Segmentation is ignored.

Concentrated marketing attempts to produce the ideal product for a single segment of the market (eg Rolls Royce cars, Mothercare mother and baby shops).

Differentiated marketing attempts to introduce several versions of a product, each aimed at a different market segment (for example, the manufacture of several different brands of washing powder).

Identify one disadvantage of adopting a concentrated marketing approach and one disadvantage of adopting differentiated marketing.

The choice between these three approaches will depend on three factors.

(a)   The degree to which the product and/or the market can be considered homogeneous.

(b)   How far the company's resources are overextended as a consequence of differentiated marketing. Small firms, for example, may perform better by concentrating on only one segment.

(c)   How far the product is advanced in its life cycle. If it is in the early stages, segmentation and target marketing is unlikely to be profitable, because each segment would be too small.

The potential benefit of segmentation and target marketing is that the seller will have increased **awareness** of how product design and development stimulates demand in a particular section of the market. Also, the **resources** of the business will be more effectively employed, since the organisation should be more able to make products which the customer demands.

6 Positioning   6/04, 12/06

Key concept

Brand positioning. Brands can be positioned in relation to competitive brands on product maps in which space is defined in terms of how buyers perceive key characteristics.

Products may be positioned in the market by emphasising a variety of factors.

(a)   **Positioning by specific product features**. The most common approach to positioning, especially for industrial products. Most car advertisements, for example, stress the combination of product features available and usually also stress good value for money as well.

(b)   **Positioning by benefits, problems, solutions, or needs**. Benefits are emphasised. This is generally **more effective than positioning on product features**. Pharmaceutical companies position their products to doctors by stressing effectiveness and side effects.

(c)   **Positioning for specific usage occasions**. Similar to benefit positioning but this uses the occasion of usage as the main basis for the positioning. Johnson's Baby Shampoo is positioned as a product to use if you shampoo your hair every day.

(d)   **Positioning for user category**. Many breakfast cereal producers position by age.

(e)   **Positioning against another product**. Although Avis never mentions Hertz explicitly in its advertising, its positioning as Number 2 in the rent-a-car market is an example of positioning against a leader. 'Me too' products can always be related to leaders in this way.

(f)   **Product class disassociation**. This is a less common basis for positioning, but effective when introducing a new product clearly distinct from standard products in an established product category.

(g)   **Hybrid basis**. On occasion, a positioning strategy may be founded on several of these alternatives, incorporating elements from more than one positioning base. Porsche, for example, use a combination of the product benefits and user characteristics.

A basic **perceptual map** positions brands in **perceived price** and **perceived quality** terms.

Price and quality are clearly important elements in every marketing mix, but, in the customer's opinion, **they cannot be considered independent variables. A 'high' price will almost always be associated with high quality and low price with low quality**. Everybody would like to buy a bargain brand, but the problem to overcome is one of belief: will customers accept that a high quality product can be offered at a low price?

 Marketing at Work   Application

MFI would claim to be in the bargain quadrant. Many consumers perceive them to be at the lower end of the economy segment. Frequent sales and discounts in the store have the effect of overcoming at least some of the difficulties resulting from individuals using price as an assessment of quality. Thus, the price label shows the higher pre-discounted price and the low sale price. Customers appear to use the pre-sale price in order to confirm promotional claims about quality.

Public concern about such promotional pricing has resulted in the introduction of restrictions on the use of these techniques. Promotions have to be part of a genuine 'sale', and stores must provide evidence of this fact.

6.1 Gaps in the market

Market research into consumer perceptions can determine how customers locate competitive brands on a matrix.

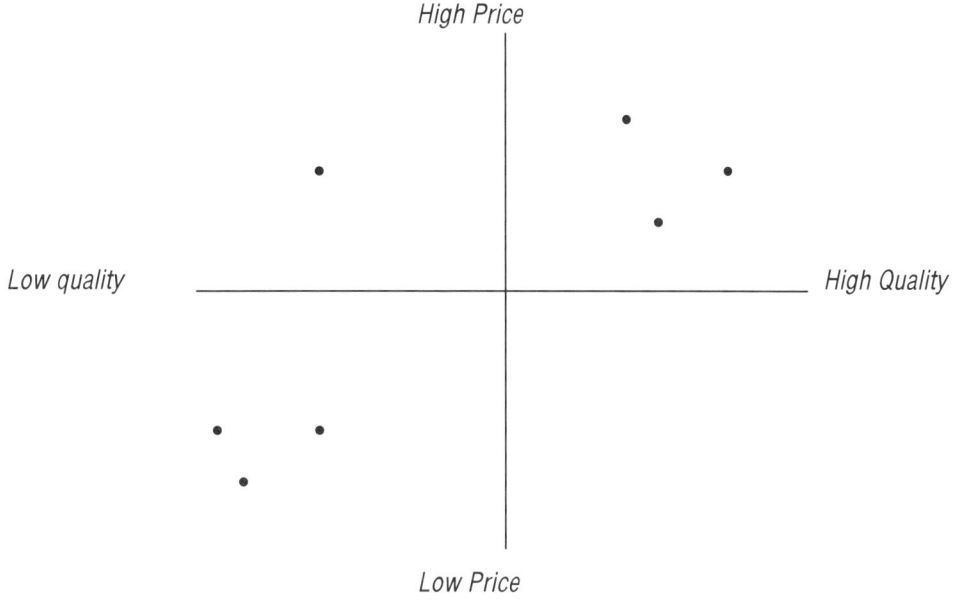

Restaurants in Anytown

The hypothetical model above shows a gap in the market for a moderately priced reasonable quality eating place. This is evident between clusters in the high price/high quality and the low price/low quality segments.

It would be wise to think before acting on this assumption. Why does the gap exist? Is it that no entrepreneurial restaurateur has noticed the opportunity? Or is it that, while there is sufficient demand for gourmet eating and cheap cafes, there are insufficient customers to justify a restaurant in the middle range segment? More research would be needed to determine which of these conditions apply.

6.2 Competitive positioning   6/04

Competitive positioning is concerned with 'a general idea of what kind of offer to make to the target market in relation to competitors' offers' (Kotler (1991)). Product quality and price are obviously important for competitive positioning, but Kotler identified a 3 × 3 matrix of nine different competitive positioning strategies.

Price	High	Medium	Low
Product quality			
High	Premium strategy	Penetration strategy	Superbargain strategy
Medium	Overpricing strategy	Average quality strategy	Bargain strategy
Low	Hit and run strategy	Shoddy goods strategy	Cheap goods strategy

7 Evaluation and control

6/05, 12/05, 6/06, 12/06

FAST FORWARD

The marketing control process can be broken down into four stages.

- Development of objectives and strategies
- Establishment of standards (critical success factors)
- Evaluation of performance
- Corrective action

Marketing at Work

Application

Motorola

The relationship between the corporate strategy and its implications for the marketing mix are shown by the example of Motorola, the US hi-tech manufacturer of mobile phones, television set-top boxes, microchips, emergency radios and flat-screen TVs.

Motorola competes against a large number of firms in many markets. It is too thinly spread. Each division has its own strategy. The chief executive officer, Ed Zander, intends to reduce the number of products and markets that the firm competes in, in order to focus on core areas.

For example, Motorola once dominated the mobile handset market, but its share is now around 15% compared to Nokia's share of 35%. Nokia won this position by its focus on the design of the handsets – the product element of the marketing mix.

Motorola's technology is respected but the firm, according to the *Economist* (10 January 2004) 'seems to lack a good grasp of what consumers want'.

Exam tip

Evaluation and control of the marketing plan is likely to a regular topic. Remember that the marketing audit is a control device which can be used as an input to the planning process – so any question about the marketing audit can mention the fact that it is a control over the marketing activity. The **marketing control process is vital** to the achievement of marketing objectives and the successful completion of marketing plans. Control is as important a feature of the role of the marketing manager as new product development or promotional creativity.

Key concept

To **control** is to measure results against targets and take any action necessary to adjust performance.

Marketing at Work

Examples of marketing measures

Feedback information	Standards	Control actions
Sales figures	Against budget	Simulate or dampen down demand
Complaints	Number, frequency, seriousness	Correct action
Competitors	Relative to us	Attack/defence strategies
Costs/profitability	Ratios	Cost cutting exercises
Corporate image	Attitude measures	Internal/external communications

BPP
LEARNING MEDIA

Because marketing is essentially concerned with people, **controlling marketing activities is particularly problematic**. Difficulties arise with information, timing and the cost aspects of marketing plans.

The marketing control process can be broken down into four stages.

- Development of objectives and strategies
- Establishment of standards (critical success factors)
- Evaluation of performance
- Corrective action

Note the importance of **critical success factors (CSFs)**, which are also relevant to controlling the marketing mix.

CSFs which relate to specific elements of the marketing mix

Activity	CSF
New product development	Trial rate
	Repurchase rate
Sales programmes	Contribution by region, salesperson
	Controllable margin as percentage of sales
	Number of new accounts
	Travel costs
Advertising programmes	Awareness levels
	Attitude ratings
	Cost levels
Pricing programmes	Price relative to industry average
	Price elasticity of demand
Distribution programmes	Number of distributors carrying the product

Part of the corrective action stage may well be to **adjust objectives and strategies** in the light of experience.

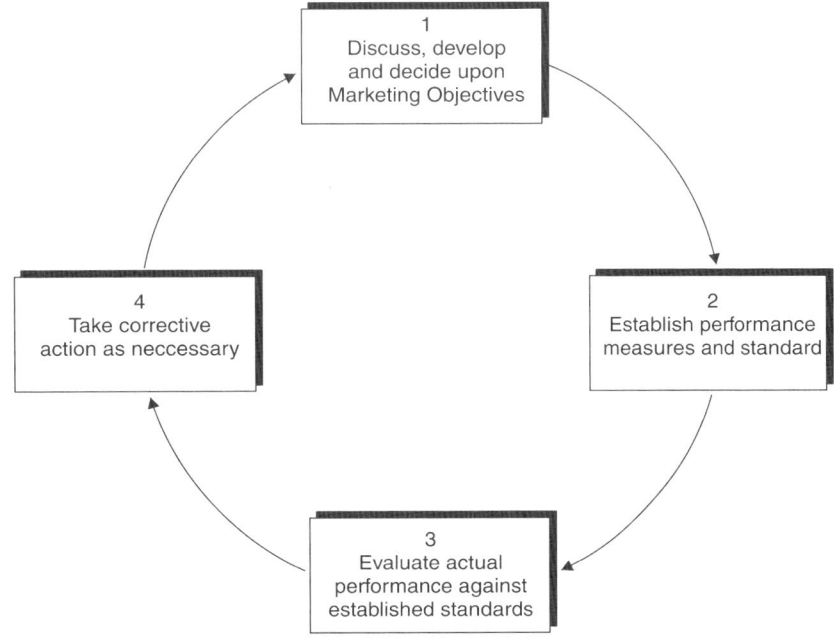

The marketing control process

7.1 Benchmarking and the market environment

Benchmarks may be established (using marketing research and competitor intelligence) to provide external targets of achievable performance.

Key concept

Benchmark: an external target of performance against which a firm measures its activities.

Benchmarks can be set against, say, the leading competitor on a variety of key performance indicators, as an objective form of control. In this case, marketing research and competitor intelligence would be needed to establish benchmarks and to monitor progress.

7.2 Monitoring competitor performance

When an organisation operates in a competitive environment, it should try to obtain information about the financial performance of competitors, to make a comparison with the organisation's own results. It might not be possible to obtain reliable competitor information, but if the competitor is a public company it will publish an annual report and accounts.

7.2.1 Financial information which might be obtainable about a competitor

(a)   Total profits, sales and capital employed

(b)   ROCE, profit/sales ratio, cost/sales ratios and asset turnover ratios

(c)   The increase in profits and sales over the course of the past twelve months (and prospects for the future, which will probably be mentioned in the chairman's statement in the report and accounts)

(d)   Sales and profits in each major business segment that the company operates in

(e)   Dividend per share

(f)   Gearing and interest rates on debt

(g)   Share price, and P/E ratio (stock exchange information)

Benchmarking **focuses on improvement in key areas** and sets targets which are challenging but achievable. What is really achievable can be discovered by examining what others have achieved: managers are thus able to accept that they are not being asked to perform miracles.

Benchmarking is, however, **reactive**; rather than imitating a competitor, another competitive strategy may be preferable. Furthermore, it is **not focused on the customer**. The firm should set itself targets that customers value.

7.3 Market share performance

Another useful measure of performance is the **market share** obtained by the organisation's product. A market share performance report should draw attention to the following.

(a)   The link between **cost and profit** and market performance in both the short term and the long term.

(b)   The performance of the **product or market segment** in the context of the product life cycle.

(c)   Whether or not the product is gaining or losing ground.

Changes in market share have to be considered against the change in the **market as a whole**, since the product might be increasing its share simply because the market is declining, with the competition losing

sales even more quickly. The reverse may also be true. The market could be expanding, and a declining market share might not represent a decline in absolute sales volume, but indicates a failure to grab more of the growing market.

7.4 Monitoring customers

Key customer analysis may be employed in industrial markets.

In some industrial markets or reseller markets, a producer might sell to a small number of key customers. The performance of these customers would therefore be of some importance to the producer: if the customer prospers, he will probably buy more and if he does badly, he will probably buy less. It may also be worthwhile monitoring the level of profitability of selling to the customer. **Key customer analysis** calls for seven main areas of investigation.

(a) **Key customer identity**

(i)   Name of each customer
(ii)   Location
(iii)   Status in market
(iv)   Products they make and sell
(v)   Size of firm (capital employed, turnover, number of employees)

(b) **Customer history**

(i)   First purchase date
(ii)   Who makes the buying decision in the customer's organisation?
(iii)   What is the average order size, by product?
(iv)   What is the regularity/periodicity of the order, by product?
(v)   What is the trend in size of orders?
(vi)   What is the motive in purchasing?
(vii) What does the customer know about the firm's and competitors' products?
(viii) On what basis does the customer reorder?
(ix)   Were there any lost or cancelled orders? For what reasons?

(c) **Relationship of customer to product**

(i)   Are the products purchased to be resold? If not, why are they bought?
(ii)   Do the products form part of the customer's service/product?

(d) **Relationship of customer to potential market**

(i)   What is the size of the customer in relation to the total end-market?
(ii)   Is the customer likely to expand, or not? Diversify? Integrate?

(e) **Customer attitudes and behaviour**

(i)   What interpersonal factors exist which could be affecting selling processes?
(ii)   Does the customer also buy competitors' products?
(iii)   To what extent may purchases be postponed?
(iv)   What emotional factors exist in buying decisions?

(f) **The financial performance of the customer**

How successful is the customer in his own markets? Similar analysis can be carried out as with competitors.

(g) **The profitability of selling to the customer**

7.5 Targets, budgets and ratios

In terms of strategic marketing management, **planned** results often comprise:

(a)   Targets for the overall **financial objective**, for each year over the planning period, and other financial strategy objectives such as productivity targets.

(b)   Subsidiary **financial targets**

(c)   Financial targets in the annual budget (including the sales budget and marketing expenditure budget)

(d)   Product-market strategy targets

(e)   Targets for each element of the **marketing mix**

7.6 Setting targets

The organisation's objectives provide the basis for setting performance targets and standards. Performance standards are set for two reasons.

(a)   Tell managers what they are **required to accomplish**, given the authority to make appropriate decisions

(b)   Indicate to managers how **well their actual results** measure up against their targets, so that control action can be taken where it is needed

It follows that in setting standards for performance, **it is important to distinguish between controllable or manageable variables and uncontrollable ones**. Any matter which cannot be controlled by an individual manager should be excluded from their standards for performance.

7.7 Budgets as a control device   6/05, 12/05, 6/06, 6/07, 12/07

FAST FORWARD

A **budget** is a plan representing the **resources** required to achieve objectives. There are various methods of setting the marketing budget, including the **objective and task** measures.

Key concepts

A **budget** is a consolidated statement of the resources required to achieve desired objectives, or to implement planned activities. It is a planning and control tool relevant to all aspects of management activities.

A **forecast** is an estimate of what might happen in the future.

7.7.1 Purposes of a budget

(a)   **Co-ordinates** the activities of all the different departments of an organisation; in addition, through participation by employees in preparing a budget, it may be possible to motivate them to raise their targets and standards and to archive better results.

(b)   **Communicates** the policies and targets to every manager in the organisation responsible for carrying out a part of that plan.

(c)   **Control** by having a plan against which actual results can be progressively compared.

Budgets perform a dual role.

(a) They **incorporate forecasting** and planning information.

(b) They **incorporate control measures**, in that they plan how resources are to be used to achieve the targets, and they can be flexed for corrective action.

7.7.2 Problems in constructing budgets

(a) **Unpredictability** in economic conditions or prices of inputs.

(b) Because of **inflation**, it might be difficult to estimate future price levels for materials, expenses, wages and salaries.

(c) **Managers might be reluctant to budget accurately**.

    (i) **Slack**. They may overstate their expected expenditure so that by having a budget which is larger than necessary, they will be unlikely to overspend the budget allowance. (They will then not be held accountable in control reports for excess spending.)

    (ii) They may **compete** with other departments for the available resources, by trying to expand their budgeted expenditure. Budget planning might well intensify inter-departmental rivalry and the problems of 'empire building'.

(d) **Inter-departmental rivalries** might ruin efforts towards co-ordination in a budget.

(e) Employees might resist budget plans either because the plans are not properly communicated to them, or because they feel that the budget puts them under pressure from senior management to achieve better results.

7.7.3 Setting the sales budget

(a) A **preliminary sales estimate** uses the following data.

    (i) A study of normal business growth
    (ii) A forecast of general business conditions
    (iii) A knowledge of potential markets for each product
    (iv) The practical judgement of sales and management staff
    (v) A realisation of the effect on sales of basic changes in company policy

(b) An **adjustment of the above preliminary sales estimate** may be required

    (i) Seasonal nature of the business
    (ii) Overall production or purchasing capacity
    (iii) Overall selling expenses and net profits
    (iv) The financial capacity of the business

(c) The adjusted anticipated sales by value and quantity contained in the sales budget should then be classified by commodities, departments, customers, salesmen, countries, terms of sale, methods of sale, methods of delivery and urgency of delivery.

7.7.4 The expense budgets related to marketing

(a)   *Selling expenses budget*

    (i)   Salaries and commission
    (ii)   Materials, literature, samples
    (iii)   Travelling (car cost, petrol, insurance) and entertaining
    (iv)   Staff recruitment and selection and training
    (v)   Telephones and telegrams, postage
    (vi)   After sales service
    (vii)   Royalties/patents
    (viii)   Office rent and rates, lighting, heating
    (ix)   Office equipment
    (x)   Credit costs, bad debts

(b)   *Advertising budget*

    (i)   Trade journal – space
    (ii)   Prestige media – space
    (iii)   PR space (costs of releases, entertainment
    (iv)   Blocks and artwork
    (v)   Advertising agents commission
    (vi)   Staff salaries, office costs
    (vii)   Posters
    (viii)   Cinema
    (ix)   TV
    (x)   Signs

(c)   *Sales promotion budget*

    (i)   Exhibitions: space, equipment, staff, transport, hotels, bar
    (ii)   Literature: leaflets, catalogues
    (iii)   Samples/working models
    (iv)   Point of sale display, window or showroom displays
    (v)   Special offers
    (vi)   Direct mail shots – enclose, postage, design costs

(d)   *Research and development budget*

    (i)   Market research – design and development and analysis costs
    (ii)   Packaging and product research – departmental costs, material, equipment
    (iii)   Pure research – departmental costs materials, equipment
    (iv)   Sales analysis and research
    (v)   Economic surveys
    (vi)   Product planning
    (vii)   Patents

(e)   *Distribution budget*

    (i)   Warehouse/deposits – rent, rates, lighting, heating
    (ii)   Transport – capital costs
    (iii)   Fuel – running costs
    (iv)   Warehouse/depot and transport staff wages
    (v)   Packing (as opposed to packaging)

7.7.5 Methods of setting the marketing budget

Method	Comment
Competitive parity	Fixing promotional expenditure in relation to the expenditure incurred by competitors (This is unsatisfactory because it presupposes that the competitor's decision must be a good one.)
The task method (or objective and task method)	The marketing task for the organisation is set and a promotional budget is prepared which will help to ensure that this objective is achieved. A problem occurs if the objective is achieved only by paying out more on promotion than the extra profits obtained would justify.
Communication stage models	These are based on the idea that the link between promotion and sales cannot be measured directly, but can be measured by means of intermediate stages (for example increase in awareness, comprehension, and then intention to buy).
All you can afford	Crude and unscientific, but commonly used. The firm simply takes a view on what it thinks it can afford to spend on promotion given that it would like to spend as much as it can.
Investment	The advertising and promotions budget can be designed around the amount felt necessary to maintain a certain brand value.
Rule-of-thumb, non-scientific methods	There include setting expenditure at a certain percentage of sales or profits.

Exam tip

> Methods of setting the marketing budget was worth 10 marks in the December 2007 exam.

7.8 Ratio analysis

Marketing relevant ratios are a **mix of financial ratios and non-financial ratios**. For example:

(a) **Financial ratio only**

    (i) Sales revenue or marketing expenditure can be compared: **over time**, against **budget** or against **competition**

	2004	2005
Revenue	£10m	£15m

    2004/2005 gives an increase of 1.5:1.

    (ii) There may be relationships between different variables. For example:

	2004	2005
Revenue	£10m	£15m
Bad debts	0.5m	1.2m
Bad debts/revenue	1:20 or 5%	2:25 or 8%

Comparing these over time suggests that while **income has increased**, the **quality of sales** (in terms of **creditworthiness**) has fallen, as bad debts are 8% of revenue rather than 5%. Perhaps the sales force has been too generous.

(b) **A mixture of financial ratios and non-financial data**

	2004	2005
Revenue	£10m	£15m
Sales personnel	50	60

Revenue has increased by 50% whereas the sales force has increased by 20%.

	2004	2005
Revenue per sales employee	£0.2m	£0.25m

The sales force was more productive in 2005 than in 2004.

(c)   **Non-financial data only**

This can of course refer to almost any aspect of a company's operations.

	2004	2005
Sales orders	250	300
Sales leads	1,000	1,025
Sales personnel	50	60

In 2004, 25% of leads turned into orders, whereas in 2005 this has increased to 29%, so the sales force is more effective. The number of orders by sales person has stayed the same.

7.9 Economy, efficiency and effectiveness

Economy, efficiency and effectiveness are all generally desirable features of organisational performance.

Key concepts

> **Economy** lies in operating at minimum cost. However, an over-parsimonious approach will reduce **effectiveness**.
>
> **Efficiency** consists of attaining desired results at minimum cost. It therefore combines **effectiveness** with **economy**.
>
> **Effectiveness** is achieving established objectives. There are usually several ways to achieve objectives, some more costly than others.

Some people use the word efficiency in a more restricted sense than that explained above, to mean the same thing as **productivity**; that is, the ratio of output to input. It is possible to be very productive in doing the wrong thing: no amount of efficiency will make a company profitable if it brings the wrong products to market.

7.10 Quantitative and qualitative targets

Performance can be measured in quantitative or qualitative terms.

(a)   **Quantitative measurements are expressed in figures**, such as cost levels, units produced per week, delay in delivery time and market penetration per product.

(b)   **Qualitative targets**, although not directly measurable in quantitative terms, may still be **verified by judgement and observation**.

Where possible, performance should be measured in quantitative terms because these are less subjective and liable to bias. Qualitative factors such as employee welfare and motivation, protection of the environment against pollution, and product quality might all be gauged by quantitative measures (such as employee pay levels, labour turnover rates, the level of toxicity in industrial waste, reject and scrap rates).

Action Programme 4   Evaluation

What are the disadvantages of using money as a measure when collecting management control information?

7.11 Marketing performance standards

Performance should be measured by obtaining data about actual results: **sales**, **costs** and **market share** are common measures.

The most common measures by which marketing performance is judged are **sales levels**, **costs** and **market shares**. However, responsible companies will also have ethical and social responsibility standards. The most marketing-orientated organisations will be likely to pursue **relationship marketing** which entails a high degree of customer care. Thus, in addition to sales measures, many companies will seek to measure **customer satisfaction**.

Performance standards could thus be set at sales of £X for the period, Y% market share and Z% profit, all set against a maximum number of customer complaints.

7.12 Evaluation of performance

The organisation monitors performance at given time intervals **by comparing actual results with the standards set** to determine whether it is on, above or below these targets.

7.13 Corrective action

Where performance against standard is below a tolerable level then remedial action needs to be taken. This may mean invoking **contingency plans** previously drawn up for this purpose or taking *ad hoc* actions such as initiating sales promotions. On reflection, it may be decided that the original target was, in fact, unattainable.

Action Programme 5   Application

Give examples of measures by which performance could be judged.

Chapter Roundup

- **Gap analysis** quantifies the size of the gap between the objective/targets for the planning period, and the forecast based on the extrapolation of the current situation. The organisation must then identify different strategies to fill the gap.

- The purpose of **competitive strategy** is to provide the organisation with a competitive advantage.

- **Ansoff's product/market matrix** is used for the analysis and determination of growth strategies. It suggests four possible options.

- **PIMS** is a diagnostic tool based on a database. It allows organisations to compare their strategic performance with that of other organisations.

- It is extremely difficult for a business to be 'all things to all people'. **Market segmentation** is based on the recognition that every market consists of potential buyers with different needs, and different buying behaviour. These different customer attitudes may be grouped into segments and a different marketing approach will be taken for each segment.

- Effective market segmentation depends upon the **measurability**, **accessibility** and **sustainability** of the chosen segments.

- **Consumer markets** can be segmented, for example by location, by demography, by social class or by lifestyle.

- There are a variety of approaches to segmenting industrial markets.

- Having carried out a segmentation exercise, the next step is to select **target markets**.

- The marketing control process can be broken down into four stages:

    – Development of objectives and strategies
    – Establishment of standards (critical success factors)
    – Evaluation of performance
    – Corrective action

- **Benchmarks** may be established (using marketing research and competitor intelligence) to provide external targets of achievable performance.

- **Key customer analysis** may be employed in industrial markets.

- A **budget** is a plan representing the **resources** required to achieve objectives. There are various methods of setting the marketing budget, including the **objective and task** measures.

- Performance should be measured by obtaining data about actual results: **sales**, **costs** and **market share** are common measures.

Quick Quiz

1   What does gap analysis involve?

2   What four options are suggested by Ansoff's product/market matrix?

3   What service does the PIMS database provide to participating companies?

4   What is Kotler's definition of market segmentation?

5   What are the three requirements for effective market segmentation?

6   What is the most commonly used classification in segmentation by social class?

7   What is psychographic segmentation?

8   What is ACORN?

9   Give four examples of how industrial markets might be segmented.

10 What is concentrated marketing?

11 Give five examples of characteristics which may be used to position products.

12 Name some critical success factors in relation to advertising

13 What is benchmarking?

14 What are some of the main areas of investigation in a key customer analysis?

15 Why might managers be reluctant to budget accurately?

16 Distinguish between efficiency and effectiveness.

Answers to Quick Quiz

1   A comparison of what the organisation wishes to achieve and what it is likely to achieve if nothing changes, followed by the development of plans for action that will lead to the gap's being filled.

2   Market penetration, market development, product development and diversification.

3   Norms of performance for groups of similar businesses.

4   The subdividing of a market into distinct subsets of customers, where any subset may conceivably be selected as a target market to be reached with a distinct marketing mix.

5   Segments should be measurable, accessible and substantial.

6   JICNARS

7   Lifestyle segmentation; that is, segmentation according to variables such as values, opinions, interests and activities.

8   ACORN divides up the entire UK population in terms of the type of housing in which they live.

9   By location; company size; usage rates; product use.

10 Concentrated marketing attempts to produce the ideal product for a single segment of the market.

11 Five from:

  • Positioning by specific product features
  • Positioning by benefits, problems, solutions or needs
  • Positioning by specific usage occasions
  • Positioning for user category

- Positioning against another product
- Product class dis-association
- Hybrid basis

12 Awareness levels; attitude rates; cost levels.

13 Benchmarking is the setting external targets of performance against which a firm measures its activities.

14
- Key customer identity
- Customer history
- Relationship to product
- Relationship to potential market

- Customer attitudes and behaviour
- Financial performance of customer
- Profitability of selling to the customer

15 There may be competition for resources, so they try to expand their budget, or inflate it to minimise the risk of overspending.

16 Effectiveness is getting things done. Efficiency is getting things done with the optimum use of resources

Action Programme Review

1 The following benefits can be identified.

- The identification of new marketing opportunities as a result of better understanding of consumer needs in each of the segments.

- Specialists can be developed and appointed to each of the company's major segments. Operating practices then benefit from the expertise of staff with specialist knowledge of the segment's business.

- The total marketing budget can be allocated more effectively, according to needs and the likely return from each segment.

- Precision marketing approaches can be used. The company can make finer adjustments to the product and service offerings and to the marketing appeals used for each segment.

- Specialist knowledge and extra effort may enable the company to dominate particular segments and gain competitive advantage.

- The product assortment can be more precisely defined to reflect differences between customer needs.

- Improved segmentation allows more highly targeted marketing activity. For instance, the sales team develops an in-depth knowledge of the needs of a particular group of consumers and can get to know a network of potential buyers within the business and there is an increased likelihood of referrals and recommendations.

- Feedback and customer problems are more effectively communicated. Producers develop an understanding in the needs of a target segment and expertise in helping to solve its problems.

2 (a) The market for adult education classes may be segmented by several criteria.

(i) Age (younger people might prefer classes in, say, yoga)

(ii) Sex (women might prefer self defence courses)

(iii) Occupation (apprentices may choose technical classes)

(iv) Social class (middle class people might prefer art or music subjects)

(v) Education (poorly educated people might prefer to avoid all forms of evening class)

(vi) Family life cycle (the interests of young single people are likely to differ from those of young married people with children)

(b)   In the magazines and periodicals market the segmentation may be by different criteria.

    (i)   Sex (Woman's Own)
    (ii)   Social class (Country Life)
    (iii)   Income (Ideal Home)
    (iv)   Occupation (Accountancy Age, Computer Weekly)
    (v)   Leisure interests (Practical Boat Owner)
    (vi)   Political ideology (New Statesman)
    (vii)   Age (Shout)
    (viii) Lifestyle (FHM)

(c)   The market for sporting facilities could be segmented in yet another way.

    (i)   Geographical area (rugby in Wales, ski-ing in parts of Scotland, sailing in coastal towns)

    (ii)   Population density (squash clubs in cities, riding in country areas)

    (iii)   Occupation (gymnasia for office workers)

    (iv)   Education (there may be a demand for facilities for sports taught at certain schools, such as rowing)

    (v)   Family life cycle or age (parents may want facilities for their children; young single or married people may want facilities for themselves)

3   Concentrated marketing runs the risk of relying on a single segment of a single market. This can lead to problems. Specialisation, nonetheless, can enable a firm to capitalise on a profitable, although perhaps temporary, competitive edge over rivals (such as Kickers specialising in leisure footwear).

The main disadvantage of differentiated marketing is the additional cost of marketing and production (extra product design and development costs, the loss of economies of scale in production and storage, extra promotion and administrative costs. When the costs of further differentiation of the market exceed the benefits from further segmentation and target marketing, a firm is said to have over-differentiated. Some firms have tried to overcome this by aiming the same product at two market segments, Johnson's baby powder, for example, is sold to adults for their own use.

4   (a)   The common assumption that all costs charged to a product or department are controllable by the manager is incorrect. A manager of a production department, for example, cannot control the prices of raw materials, nor the amount of production overhead charged to the department.

(b)   Costs and profits may not be the best way of comparing the results of different parts of a business.

(c)   Some managers may prefer to quantify information in non-monetary terms.

    (i)   The sales manager may look at sales volume in units, size of market share, speed of delivery, volume of sales per sales representative or per call.

    (ii)   A stores manager might look at stock turnover periods for each item, volume of demand, the speed of materials handling, breakages, obsolescence.

(d)   Where qualitative factors (notably human behaviour and attitudes) are important, monetary information is less relevant. This is one reason why strategic planning information, which relies more heavily on both external and qualitative factors, is generally more imprecise and not necessarily expressed in money terms.

5   Possible performance measures

- Sales levels
- Market share
- Marketing costs
- Profitability
- Customer satisfaction

Now try Questions 4,5 and 6 at the end of the Study Text

Part C
The extended marketing mix

The marketing communications mix

Syllabus content – knowledge and skills requirement

- 3.10:   The marketing communications mix and how it is co-ordinated with the marketing mix as part of a marketing plan

Introduction

Marketing communications are an important component of operational marketing. It is important that marketing communications are carefully planned and controlled so that the marketing communications mix supports the selected marketing mix.

Ultimately marketing communications might be characterised by two key questions:

- What is the message?
- What is the most appropriate media to deliver that message?

In this chapter we discuss the important background topics of consumer buying behaviour and the process of communication. Promotion is the means by which the marketer attempts to communicate with consumers in order to influence them in general terms and, in particular, to influence their buying decisions. It is therefore important to understand both how such decisions are made and the nature of the processes involved in communication.

Sections 1 and 2 look at consumer behaviour, starting with the wide range of factors that influence that behaviour, and then considering the way purchase decisions are made. Section 3 discusses communication, starting with a simple model of wide applicability and then considering the main stages of consumer response. Sections 4 and 5 draw the threads together by illustrating the way in which marketing communications fit into the overall marketing effort and support the marketing mix.

1 Factors influencing consumer buying behaviour

FAST FORWARD

Consumer buying behaviour is influenced by cultural, social, personal and psychological factors. Social class is a cultural factor; social factors include reference groups, opinion leaders and the family. Age, occupation, economic circumstances and lifestyle are all examples of personal factors. Psychological factors include motivation, perception, learning, beliefs and attitudes.

Marketing at Work

Application

The market for 'downloadable mobile content' is very much the domain of the young. Research suggests that people in their late teens and early-20s are most reliant on mobiles, and it is this age group that much of the download industry targets. However, the UK's aging population means there are twice as many over-65s as 15-to 24-year olds, so an untapped market exists for innovative download providers.

The market is dominated by ringtones, which account for about a third of traffic. Games, music downloads and gambling, meanwhile, are all emerging areas, likely to grow in the coming years.

www.brandrepublic.com – accessed 9 April 2008

Action Programme 1

Application

Apply the purchase of a mobile phone ring tone to the models that follow.

Key concept

Consumer buying behaviour can be defined as 'the decision processes and acts of individuals involved in buying and using products or services.' (Dibb *et al* (2001))

The core process of consumer buying behaviour will be influenced by a number of outside variables.

- Cultural
- Social
- Personal
- Psychological

1.1 Cultural factors

These are the most fundamental of the influencing factors, and include culture, subculture and social class.

Key concept

> **Culture** comprises the values, attitudes, beliefs, ideas and other symbols in the pattern of life adopted by people that help them to interpret and communicate as members of society.

Culture is largely the result of a learning process.

This broad set of values is then influenced by the **subcultures** in which we develop. Subcultural groups can be defined in terms of religion, ethnic characteristics, racial characteristics and geographical areas, all of which further influence attitudes, tastes, taboos and lifestyle.

1.2 Social factors

1.2.1 Opinion leaders

Opinion leaders are those individuals who reinforce marketing messages and to whom others look for information and advice. In addition, opinion leaders may communicate a marketing message to those members of the group who may have missed the original message. A person may be an opinion leader in certain circumstances but an opinion follower in others.

1.2.2 The family

Another major social influence is the family, particularly with regard to the roles and relative influence exerted by different family members. Research has indicated three patterns of decision making within the family and identified the sorts of product categories with which each is typically associated.

(a) **Husband dominated:** life insurance, cars and television.
(b) **Wife dominated:** washing machines, carpets, kitchenware and non living-room furniture.
(c) **Equal:** living-room furniture, holidays, housing, furnishings and entertainment.

1.3 Personal factors

Influencing factors that can be classified as personal include such things as **age and life cycle, occupation, economic circumstances and lifestyle**.

Age is particularly relevant to such products as clothes, furniture and recreation. However, consumption may also be shaped by the stage of the **family life cycle** within which an individual falls.

Occupation will influence consumption and the task for marketers is to identify the occupational groups that have an above average interest in their products and services.

There are four main facets to an individual's **economic circumstances**.

- Spendable income, its level, stability and time pattern
- Savings and assets, including the percentage that is liquid
- Borrowing power
- Attitude toward spending versus saving

People from the same subculture, social class and occupation may have completely different **lifestyles**. Marketers will search for relationships between their products and lifestyle groups.

1.4 Psychological factors

The process of buyer behaviour is also influenced by four major psychological factors: **motivation, perception, learning and beliefs** and **attitudes**.

1.4.1 Motivation

Key concept

> **Motivation** has been defined as an inner state that energises and channels behaviour towards goals.

Motivation arises from perceived needs. These needs can be of two main types – biogenic and psychogenic. **Biogenic needs** arise from physiological states of tension such as hunger, thirst and discomfort, whereas **psychogenic needs** arise from psychological states of tension such as the need for recognition, esteem or belonging.

1.4.2 Perception

Perception is defined as 'the process by which people select, organise and interpret sensory stimuli into a meaningful and coherent picture. The way consumers view an object (for example their mental picture of a brand or the traits they attribute to a brand)'.

1.4.3 Learning

Theories about learning state that learning is the result of the interplay of five factors

- Drives
- Stimuli
- Cues
- Responses
- Reinforcement

A **drive** is a strong internal force impelling action, which will become a motive when it is directed to a particular drive-reducing **stimulus** object (the product). **Cues** are minor stimuli (such as seeing the product in action) that determine when, where and how the person responds. Once the product is bought, if the experience is rewarding then the **response** to the product will be reinforced, making a repeat purchase more likely. Marketers must, therefore, build up demand for a product by associating it with strong drives, using motivating cues, and by providing positive **reinforcement**.

1.4.4 Beliefs and attitudes

A **belief** is 'a descriptive thought that a person holds about something' (Kotler 1991). Beliefs are important to marketers as the beliefs that people have about products make up the brand images of those products.

An **attitude** describes a person's 'enduring favourable or unfavourable cognitive evaluations, emotional feelings, and action tendencies toward some object or idea' (Kotler 1991). Attitudes lead people to behave in a fairly consistent way towards similar objects, by ensuring that they do not have to interpret and react to every object in a fresh way. Attitudes settle into a consistent pattern and to change one attitude may entail major changes to other attitudes. Marketers should ensure that their product fits into people's existing attitudes rather than try to change attitudes.

Exam tip

> You may have to integrate a number of areas. You might also have to justify plans by reference to theory, covered in Section 4 of this chapter. You should always be able to think about what you know about promotion generally, and then relate it to the market in question.

2 The purchase decision

Purchase decisions are of several types. Complex decision making may occur in high involvement purchases, which are the ones that are very important to the consumer. Simpler decision making occurs when the purchase is not seen as particularly important or if it is repetitive. In these cases limited decision making or brand loyalty take over.

Not all consumers behave in the same way. The decision processes involved in a major purchase, such as a car, are very different from the decision processes involved in the purchase of chocolate confectionery. There are two main dimensions.

- The extent of decision making
- The degree of involvement in the purchase.

	High involvement	Low involvement
Decision making (information search, consideration of brand alternatives	Complex decision making	Limited decision making
Habit (little or no information search, consideration of only one brand)	Brand loyalty	Inertia

High involvement purchases are those that are important to the customer in some way; for example, they may be closely tied to the customer's ego and self image. Such purchases involve risk. **Low involvement purchases are not as important to the customer** and therefore the level of risk is lessened. With such purchases it may not be worth the customer's while to engage in information search and evaluation and therefore a limited process of decision making usually occurs.

(a) **Complex decision making occurs when involvement is high and the consumer searches and considers alternatives**, such as in the purchase of major items like cars, brown goods and white goods.

(b) However, complex decision making will not occur every time and if the brand choice is repetitive the consumer learns from experience and **brand loyalty** is built up.

(c) **Low involvement decision making**.

    (i) Customers sometimes go through a decision making process even if not highly involved in the purchase, because they have little experience of the product area. This is called **limited decision making**.

    (ii) Limited decision making may also occur when the customer seeks variety. The brand switch is unlikely to be preplanned and may occur at the place of purchase.

(d) **Inertia**, comprises **low involvement** with the product and **no decision making**.

2.1 Complex decision making

The process of **decision making** begins with information search, which leads to the evaluation of alternatives. The marketer can aim to influence both of these processes. After making the purchase, the consumer experiences satisfaction or dissatisfaction, either of which influence the possibility of repeat purchases.

Complex decision making in purchasing behaviour corresponds neatly with the general stages in the buying process as identified by Kotler. This model is relevant to the topic of marketing communication.

- Need recognition
- Information search
- Evaluation of alternatives
- Purchase decision
- Post purchase evaluation

2.2 Need recognition

The process begins when the buyer recognises a need or problem. This can be triggered by internal stimuli, such as hunger or thirst, or external stimuli, such as lack of social esteem. If the need rises to a threshold level it will become a drive. The task for the marketer is to identify the circumstances and stimuli that trigger a particular need and use this knowledge to trigger consumer interest.

2.2.1 Information search

Once aroused, the customer will search for more information about the products that will satisfy the need. The information search stage can be divided into two levels. The first is **heightened attention**, where the customer simply becomes more receptive to information about the particular product category. The second stage is **active information search**.

In order to ensure that the brand has the best chance of being chosen by the consumer, the marketer has a range of options for action including the following.

(a) **Modifying the brand**. Redesigning the product so that it offers more of the attributes that the buyer desires. Kotler (1991) calls this 'real repositioning'.

(b) **Altering beliefs about the brand**. Kotler recommends that this course of action be pursued if the consumer **underestimates** the qualities of the brand, and calls it **psychological repositioning**.

(c) **Altering beliefs about competitors' brands**. This course of action would be appropriate if the consumer mistakenly believes that a competitor's brand has more quality than it actually has, and can be referred to as **competitive repositioning**.

2.2.2 Purchase decision

Having evaluated the range of brand choices the consumer may have formed a purchase intention to buy the most preferred brand. However, some factors could intervene between the purchase intention and the purchase decision. The first factor is the attitude of others. A strong negative opinion regarding the brand choice may influence the consumer to change his or her mind. Other factors could include a change in financial circumstances such as redundancy, or circumstances in which some other purchase becomes more urgent.

2.2.3 Post purchase evaluation

Having purchased the brand the consumer will experience some level of satisfaction or dissatisfaction, depending on the closeness between the consumer's product expectations and the product's perceived performance. These feelings will influence whether the consumer buys the brand again and also whether the consumer talks favourably or unfavourably about the brand to others.

3 The process of communication

The prime aim of marketing communications is to influence consumer's buying behaviour. To do this most effectively, marketers need to know how communication works. The simplest model starts with a **sender** who creates a **message** and sends it to a **receiver**. The next step in analysis is to recognise that most communication is a two-way process and involves an element of **feedback**. If you think about this you will realise that you rarely speak without expecting a reply and even writing a letter would usually elicit some kind of response. Feedback might not be in the same form as the message, though; it might take the form of some other kind of behaviour such as paying an overdue account, but whatever it is, it will indicate that the original message was at least received.

FAST FORWARD

Kotler's model of the communication process underscores many of the factors in effective communication. In particular, it discusses the importance of selectivity; selective attention, selective distortion and selective recall all tend to limit the success which is attainable in commercial communications.

3.1 Kotler's model

Kotler (1991) has put forward a more complex model of the communication process.

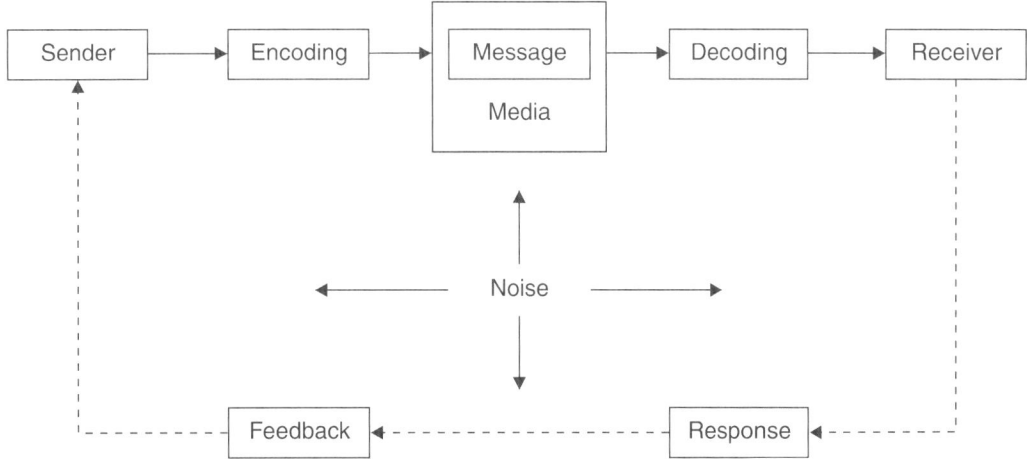

Noise can be defined as all those factors which prevent the decoding of a message by the receiver in the way intended by the sender.

The **sender** is the party sending the message, and may also be referred to as the communicator or the source. The **receiver** is the party who receives the message, and who may also be known as the audience or the destination.

The **encoding** process encompasses the means by which a meaning is placed into symbolic form such as words, signs, images and sound.

The **medium** is the communication channel or channels through which the message moves from sender to receiver.

The **decoding** process is carried out by the receiver who converts the symbolic forms transmitted by the sender into a form that makes sense to him. It is how the receiver interprets the message sent.

When the message has been decoded the receiver will react to it; this is the **response**.

Feedback is the part of the receiver's response that the receiver communicates back to the sender.

This model illustrates many of the factors in effective communication. Senders need to understand the **motivation of their audiences** in order to **structure messages** that the audience will **interpret** correctly through the decoding process. The sender also has to ascertain the most **effective communication media**

through which to reach the audience and also establish **effective feedback channels** in order to find out the receiver's **response** to the message.

Find some adverts – watch TV for half an hour or flick through a newspaper or a magazine. Analyse each ad in the above terms. Consider who are the parties involved (you may not be the intended receiver), what communication tools are used, what sort of codes are used, how they will be decoded (for example, by people in different income brackets or with different tastes), and what form feedback will take.

3.2 Noise and selectivity

This communication process is not carried out in isolation. There are many senders competing with their messages for the attention of the receiver. As a result there is considerable noise in the environment and an individual may be bombarded by several hundred commercial messages each day. The task of the sender is to get his message to the receiver but, as Kotler (1991) states, there are a number of reasons why the target audience may not receive the message.

3.2.1 Selective attention

Receivers will not notice all the commercial messages that they come into contact with, so the sender must design the message in such a way so as to win attention in spite of the surrounding noise.

3.2.2 Selective distortion

In many cases receivers may distort or change the information received if that information does not fit in with their existing attitudes, beliefs and opinions. In other words, people hear what they want to hear.

3.2.3 Selective recall

Receivers will retain in permanent memory only a small fraction of the messages that reach them.

3.3 Models of marketing communication

Response hierarchy models of marketing communication describe the sequence of mental stages that the consumer passes through on the way to a purchase. It is therefore possible to **prioritise the communication objectives** at various stages of the buying process. These objectives can be classified into three consecutive groups: **cognitive**, **affective** and **behavioural**.

(a) **Cognitive objectives** are concerned with creating knowledge or awareness in the mind of the consumer.

(b) **Affective objectives** are concerned with changing the consumer's attitude to the product as a whole, or a specific aspect of the product.

(c) **Behavioural objectives** are concerned with getting the consumer to act in some way (buy the product).

Some major response hierarchy models are regularly used in marketing.

- The AIDA model
- The adoption model
- DAGMAR (Defining Advertising Goals for Measured Advertising Response)
- Lavidge and Steiner's model

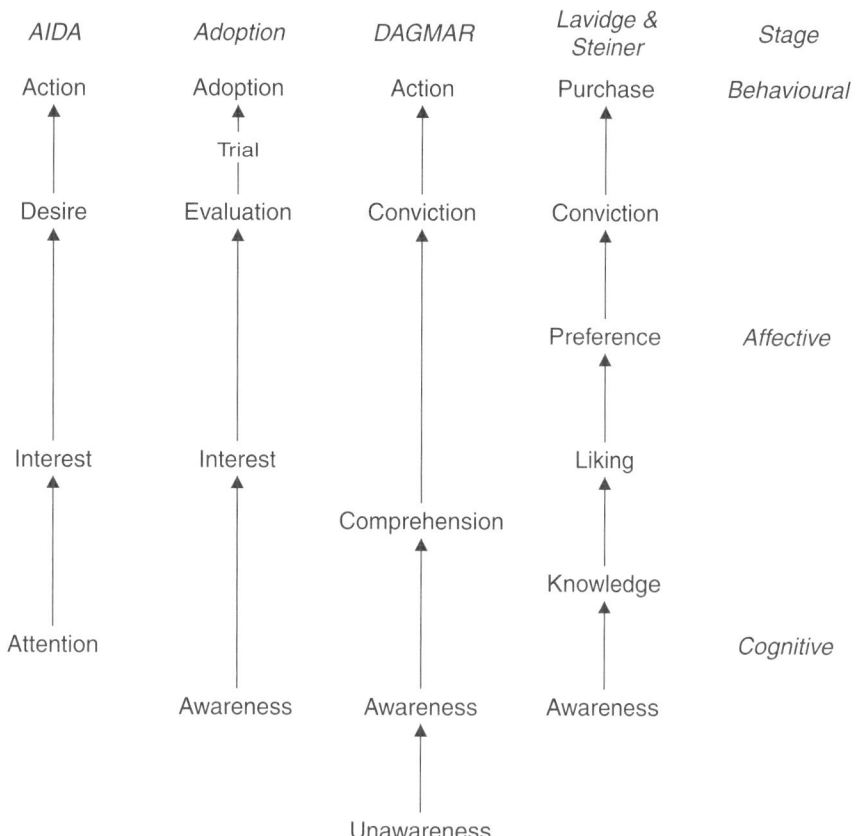

Adapted from PR Smith (2001)

It is clear that these models of communication are most applicable to **complex buying behaviour**. As described earlier, the consumer may not go through the stages of information search and evaluation of objectives before the purchase decision, as in the case of an impulse purchase. Buyers may also bypass the hierarchy of stages. For example, during the evaluation stage a buyer may go back to the information search stage in order to obtain more information before making the decision to buy.

4 The marketing communications mix

12/03, 12/04, 12/05, 12/06

FAST FORWARD

Models of consumer behaviour help to prioritise the communication objectives at various stages of the buying process, and thus assist with the selection of promotional tools. The process of promotion and the tools used should be integrated within the marketing communications process which, in turn, should support overall marketing objectives.

 Marketing at Work

Application

A threat to TV advertising?

TV advertising is core to the communications mix of many consumer products companies, as TV advertisements reach a large number of consumers effectively.

New digital technology such as the PVR (personal video recorder) threatens to undermine the TV mass advertising model. The PVR makes it far easier for consumers to skip advertisements in the programmes they record. (It is far easier to do this with a PVR than with a video cassette recorder.)

As those people edit out the ads, advertisers will refuse to pay for top TV spots. If PVRs do make a big impact:

(a)   TV companies will not be able to rely so much on advertising for revenue

(b)   Advertisers will have to find different ways of using TV, such as product placement and sponsorship slots at the start of a programme.

(c)   Consumers will watch TV programmes when it suits them

The diagram below shows a complete range of tools that can be used to influence a customer or potential customer.

Promotional influences on the customer

These tools represent the deployment of deliberate and intentional methods calculated to bring about a favourable response in the customer's behaviour. The diagram represents the most obvious promotion methods, though other parts of the marketing mix, including the product itself, pricing, policy and distribution channels, will also have decisive effects.

Choosing the correct tools for a particular promotions task is not easy. The process is still very much an art, though it is becoming more scientific because of the access to consumer and media databases. Matching consumer characteristics with media databases can be carried out very rapidly by computer and promotional budgets can be evaluated for a variety of different mixes.

At its most basic the choice of promotional tools should be exercised within the following top-down hierarchy of objectives.

At a more detailed level the choice of the correct promotion tools can be tackled like any other management problem. The following is a useful sequence of events.

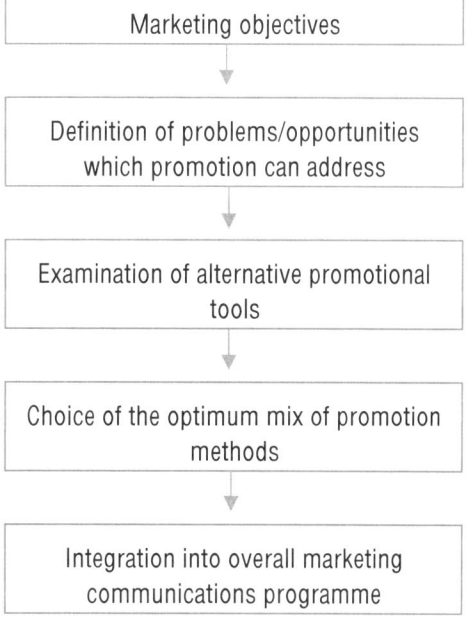

In reality, an experienced marketing manager is able to reach sensible conclusions almost intuitively, based on what has been successful in the past and on his intimate knowledge of both customers and competitors.

Exam tip

Keep this framework in mind. You may have to select promotional tools or techniques to satisfy particular media and other objectives.

4.1 Consumer and business-to-business markets

Consumer markets are categorised as consisting of mass audiences which are cost-effectively accessible by television or national newspaper advertising. The business-to-business markets involve a great deal of personal selling at different levels in the organisation. The needs of individual companies are different and therefore mass advertising would be inappropriate and wasteful. Building on these general comments it is possible to present the mix of appropriate tools in the following diagram.

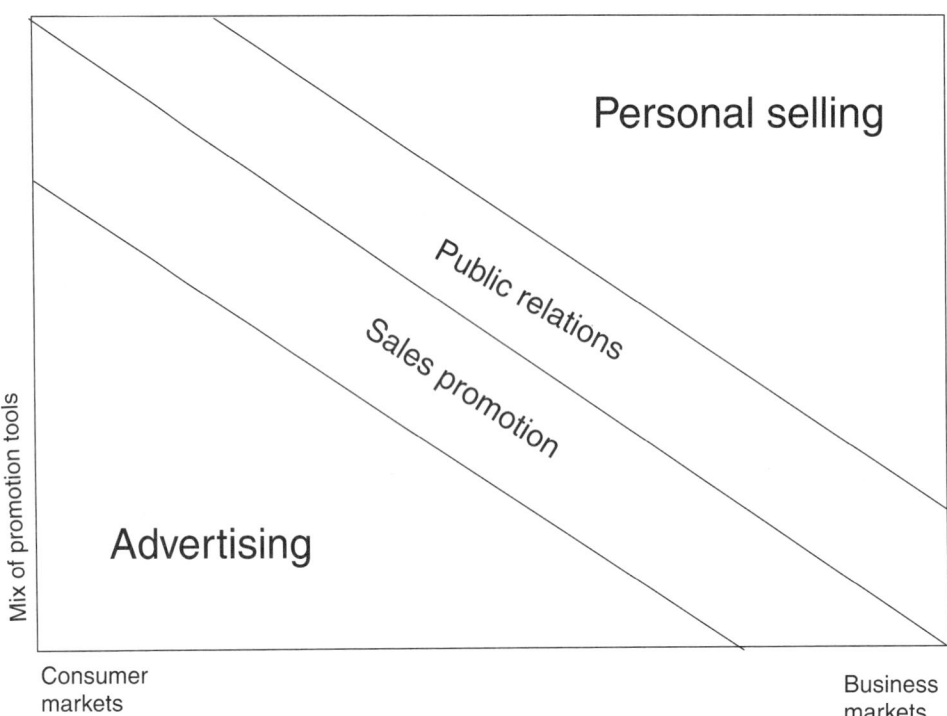

Variation of promotion tools with type of market

4.2 Integrated marketing communications

It is necessary to integrate all the promotional elements to achieve the maximum influence on the customer. **Integrated marketing communications** represent all the elements of an organisation's marketing mix that favourably influence its customers or clients. It goes beyond the right choice of promotion tools to the correct choice of the marketing mix. This is illustrated in the diagram below.

The integrated marketing communication process

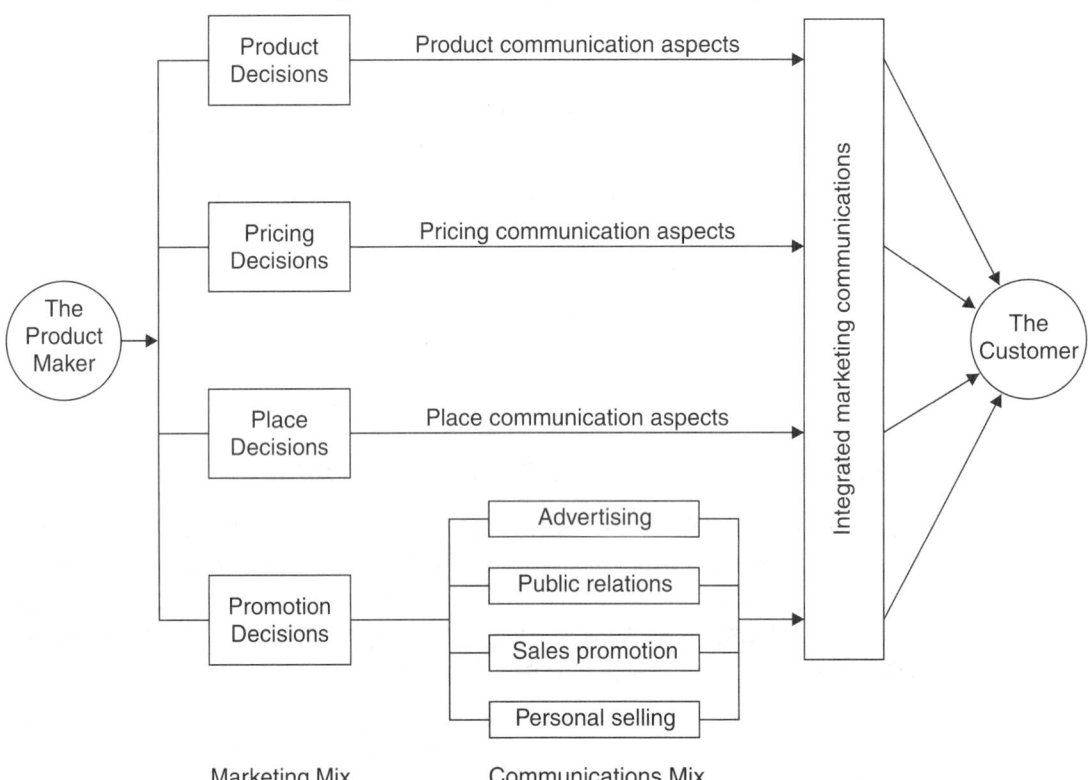

BPP
PROFESSIONAL EDUCATION

The background of theory can be used to explain, illustrate and justify chosen promotional techniques.

FAST FORWARD

In practice, marketing communication involves two key questions.

- What is the **message**?
- What is the most appropriate **medium**?

5 Delivering messages

Earlier we established the point that it is important to identify the company's marketing message, and to ensure that the most effective media are selected to deliver that message.

In practice, this entails making sure that the message is clear and that everyone in the organisation is totally professional and consistent, so that the target market does not receive mixed messages.

From a marketing management perspective, these external marketing messages must also be communicated internally, so that they are understood. This may entail internal briefings and training.

Marketing at Work

Application

These are values set out by the British Labour Party:

'The Labour Party is a democratic socialist party. It believes that by the strength of our common endeavour we achieve more than we achieve alone, so as to create for each of us the means to realise our true potential and for all of us a community in which power, wealth and opportunity are in the hands of the many, not the few.'

Policy in the Labour Party is made through a process called Partnership in Power, which is designed to involve all party stakeholders as well as the wider community in shaping party policy and support the relationship between the party in the country and the party in government.

Here are some key policy areas:

- Asylum and immigration
- Britain in the global economy
- Britain in the world
- Climate change and energy
- Crime and justice

- Education
- Families and pensioners
- Health
- Renewing our democracy
- Stronger communities

www.labour.org.uk – accessed 9 April 2008

Chapter Roundup

- **Consumer buying behaviour** is influenced by cultural, social, personal and psychological factors. Social class is a cultural factor; social factors include reference groups, opinion leaders and the family. Age, occupation, economic circumstances and lifestyle are all examples of personal factors. Psychological factors include motivation, perception, learning, beliefs and attitudes.

- **Purchase decisions** are of several types. Complex decision making may occur in high involvement purchases, which are the ones that are very important to the consumer. Simpler decision making occurs when the purchase is not seen as particularly important or if it is repetitive. In these cases limited decision making or brand loyalty take over.

- The process of **decision making** begins with information search which leads to the evaluation of alternatives. The marketer can aim to influence both of these processes. After making the purchase, the consumer experiences satisfaction or dissatisfaction, either of which influence the possibility of repeat purchases.

- **Kotler's** model of the communication process underscores many of the factors in effective communication. In particular, it discusses the importance of selectivity: selective attention, selective distortion and selective recall all tend to limit the success which is attainable in commercial communications.

- **Models of consumer behaviour** help to prioritise the communication objectives at various stages of the buying process and thus assist with the selection of promotional tools. The process of promotion and the tools used should be integrated within the marketing communications process which, in turn, should support overall marketing objectives.

- In practice, marketing communication involves two key questions.
  - What is the **message**?
  - What is the most appropriate **medium**?

Quick Quiz

1   What are four types of variable influencing consumer buying behaviour?

2   What are opinion leaders?

3   What determines a person's economic circumstances?

4   What five factors influence learning?

5   When does complex decision making take place?

6   What are the two stages of information search?

7   What can the marketer do to influence the consumer's evaluation of brands?

8   Sketch Kotler's model of the communication process.

9   Why may a target audience not receive the message sent?

10   What is the classification of communication objectives during the buying process?

11   What are the stages of the AIDA model of consumer buying behaviour?

Answers to Quick Quiz

1   Cultural, social, personal and psychological variables.

2   Those individuals who reinforce the marketing messages sent and to whom other receivers look for information, advice and opinion.

3   • Spendable income   • Savings and assets
     • Borrowing power   • Attitude to spending and saving

4   Drivers, stimuli, cues, responses and reinforcement.

5   When customer involvement is high.

6   Heightened attention and active information search.

7   Modify the brand itself; alter beliefs about the brand; alter beliefs about competitors' brands.

8

9   Noise; selective attention; selective distortion; selective recall.

10   • Cognitive objectives are concerned with creating knowledge or awareness.
     • Affective objectives are concerned with changing the customer's attitudes.
     • Behavioural objectives are concerned with stimulating action.

11   Attention; interest; desire; action.

Action Programme Review

1   The mobile phone ring tone decision can be modelled in several ways. It is likely to be a complex, high involvement decision, in that the buyer may want to shop around. Rather than buying out of habit, the buyer many actively choose to change his or her ring tone. As far as the level of involvement this will depend. Some may know exactly what they want.

Using the AIDA model, we have:

–   Awareness of the availability of ring tones and suppliers of ring tones
–   Interest in buying them – could be a result of social pressure
–   Desire
–   Action, the actual purchase decision, made easier by the phone company

2   This requires your own research.

Now try Question 7 at the end of the Study Text

6

Product

Syllabus content – knowledge and skills requirements

- 3.3: Branding and its impact on marketing mix decisions
- 3.4: Methods for maintaining and managing the brand
- 3.5: How a product or service portfolio is developed to achieve marketing objectives
- 3.6: The new product development process (including innovative, replacement, relaunched and imitative products) and the role of innovation

Introduction

This chapter deals with the product element of the marketing mix. The product life cycle is an important concept and can offer guidance on marketing activity. Portfolio analysis addresses how an organisation's products interrelate and affect one another. Both of these concepts are discussed in Section 1.

Section 2 deals with a related topic, new product development, which is essential for any market oriented company. The final elements of product input are dealt with in Section 3: brands and packaging.

Exam tip

The product life cycle and portfolio analysis occur regularly throughout the CIM syllabus, as they are models that can be used in almost any context.

1 The product life cycle and portfolio analysis   12/06, 6/07

FAST FORWARD

The **product life cycle** model describes the progress of a product from introduction to discontinuation in terms of sales and profitability. It can offer some guidance in the management of marketing and production.

1.1 The product

A product may be said to satisfy needs by possessing the following attributes.

(a) **Tangible attributes**

    (i)   Availability and delivery
    (ii) Performance
    (iii) Price

(b) **Intangible attributes**

    (i)   Image
    (ii) Perceived value
    (iii) Design

These features are interlinked. A product has a tangible **price**, for example, but for your money you obtain the **value** that you perceive the product to have. You may get satisfaction from paying a very high price for your wine glasses, because this says something about your status in life: the glasses become part of your self-image.

1.2 Product classification

The term **consumer goods** is used to distinguish goods that are sold directly to the person who will ultimately use them from goods that are sold to people who want them to make other products. The latter are known as **industrial goods**.

1.2.1 Classification of consumer goods

(a) **Convenience goods**. The weekly groceries are a typical example. There is a further distinction between **staple goods** like bread and potatoes, and **impulse buys**, like the bar of chocolate that you pick up at the supermarket checkout. Brand awareness is extremely important in this sector.

(b) **Shopping goods**. These are more durable items, like furniture or washing machines. This sort of purchase is usually only made after a good deal of **advance planning and shopping around**.

(c) **Speciality goods**. These are items like jewellery or more expensive items of clothing.

(d) **Unsought goods**. These are goods that you did not realise you needed! Typical examples would be the sort of items that are found in catalogues that arrive in the post.

Application

Think of three products that you have bought recently, one low-priced, one medium-priced, and one expensive item. Identify the product attributes that made you buy each of these items and categorise them according to the classifications shown above.

1.2.2 Classification of industrial goods

- **Installations**, eg major items of plant and machinery like a factory assembly line
- **Accessories**, such as printers for PCs
- **Raw materials:** plastic, metal, wood, foodstuffs chemicals
- **Components:** the Intel microchip in most PCs
- **Supplies:** office stationery, cleaning materials

There are very few **pure products** or **pure services**. Most products have some service attributes and many services are in some way attached to products. However, we shall consider some of the features that particularly characterise service marketing later on in this chapter.

1.3 The product life cycle

Key concept

The **product life cycle** asserts that products are born (or introduced), grow to reach maturity and then enter old age and decline.

Despite criticisms, the product life cycle (PLC) has proved to be a useful control device for monitoring the progress of new products after introduction.

The profitability and sales position of a product can be expected to change over time. The product life cycle is an attempt to recognise distinct stages in a product's sales history. Here is the classic representation of the PLC.

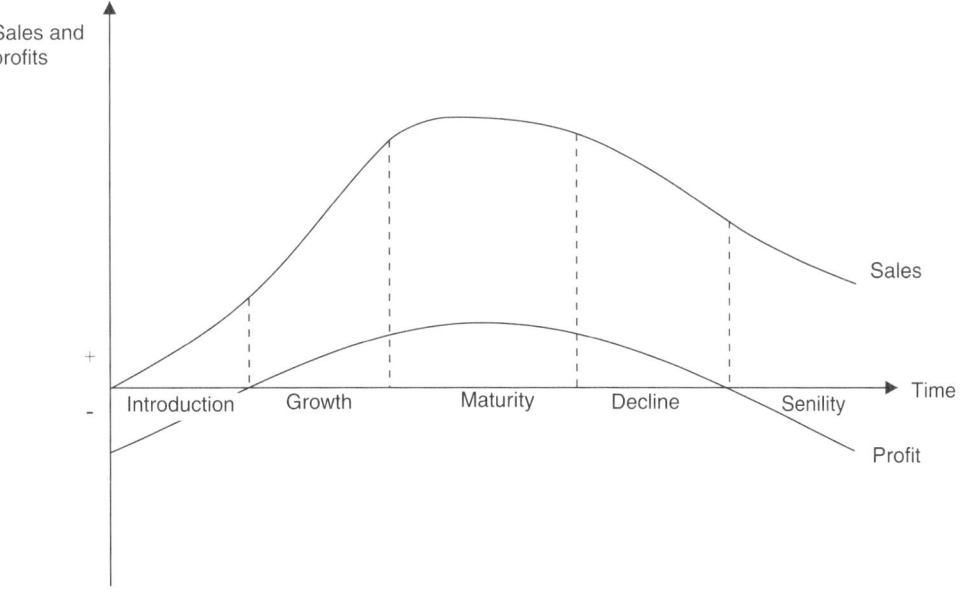

(a) **Introduction**. A new product takes time to find acceptance and there is a slow growth in sales. Unit costs are high because of low output; there may be early teething troubles with production technology and prices may be high to cover production and sales promotion costs. Pocket calculators, video cassette recorders and mobile telephones were all very expensive when launched. The product, for the time being, is a **loss maker**.

(b) **Growth**. Sales will eventually rise more sharply and the product starts to make profits. As production rises, unit costs fall. Since demand is strong, prices tend to remain fairly static for a time. However, the prospect of cheap mass production and a strong market will attract competitors so that the number of producers is increasing. With the increase of competition, manufacturers must spend a lot of money on product improvement, sales promotion and distribution to obtain a dominant or strong position in the market.

(c) **Maturity**. The rate of sales growth slows down and the product reaches a period of maturity which is probably the longest period of a successful product's life. Most products on the market will be at the mature stage of their life. Eventually sales will begin to decline so that there is **overcapacity of production in the industry**. Severe competition occurs, profits fall and some producers leave the market. The remaining producers seek means of prolonging the product life by modifying it and searching for new market segments.

(d) **Decline**. Many producers are reluctant to leave the market, although some inevitably do because of falling profits. If a product remains on the market too long, it will become unprofitable and the decline stage in its life cycle then gives way to a 'senility' stage.

Action Programme 2

Application

Can you think of any products that have disappeared in your lifetime or are currently in decline?

Marketing at Work

Application

The technology underpinning the music industry has changed. With easy Internet downloads, you might assume that the market for CD-singles would disappear, and many music industry people are worried about this. It is possible that people *are* willing to pay for CDs, but not at current prices.

Mobile phone ring tones outsell CD singles and earn more revenue for music companies.

1.4 Buying participants through PLC stages

The introductory stage represents the highest risk in terms of purchasing a new and, as yet, untested product. Buyers at this stage reflect this: they typically consist of the relatively wealthy, to whom the risk of a loss is relatively small, and the young, who are more likely to make risky purchases.

In the growth and mature stages the mass market needs to be attracted. By the time decline sets in the product is well tested with all its faults ironed out. At this stage enter the most risk-averse buyers, termed **laggards**. These are the mirror image of those who participated in the introductory stage, being the poorer and older sections of the community.

1.5 How are life cycles assessed?

It is plausible to suggest that products have a life cycle, but it is not so easy to sort out how far through its life a product is, and what its expected future life might be. To identify these stages, the following should be carried out.

(a) There ought to be a **regular review** of existing products.

(b) The future of each product should be estimated in terms of both **sales revenue and profits**.

(c) **Estimates of future life and profitability should be discussed with any experts available** to give advice, for example, R & D staff about product life, management accountants about costs, and marketing staff about prices and demand.

Once the assessments have been made, decisions must be taken about what to do with each product. There are three possibilities.

(a) **To continue selling** the product, with no foreseeable intention of stopping production.

(b) To initiate action **to prolong a product's life**, perhaps by advertising more, by trying to cut costs or raise prices, by improving distribution, or packaging or sales promotion methods, or by putting in more direct selling effort.

(c) To plan **to stop producing the product** and either replace it with new ones in the same line, or diversify into new product-market areas.

Costs might be cut by improving the productivity of the workforce, or by redesigning the product slightly.

Action Programme 3	Application

Where do you consider the following products or services to be in their product life cycle?

- Mobile telephones
- Baked beans
- Satellite television
- Cigarettes
- Carbon paper

- Mortgages
- Writing implements
- Car alarms
- Organically grown fruit and vegetables

1.6 Criticisms of the product life cycle

(a) Stages cannot easily be defined.

(b) Some products have no maturity phase, and go straight from growth to decline. Others have a second growth period after an initial decline. Some have virtually no introductory period and go straight into a rapid growth phase.

(c) **Strategic decisions can change a product's life cycle**: for example, by repositioning a product in the market, its life can be extended. If strategic planners decide what a product's life is going to be, opportunities to extend the life cycle might be ignored.

(d) Competition varies in different industries, and the strategic implications of the product life cycle will vary according to the nature of the competition. The traditional life cycle presupposes increasing competition and falling prices during the growth phase of the market and also the gradual elimination of competitors in the decline phase. This pattern of events is not always found in financial markets, where there is a tendency for competitors to follow-my-leader very quickly. Competition may build up well ahead of demand. The rapid development of various banking services is an example of this.

There must be many products that have been around for as long as you can remember. Companies like Cadbury's have argued that they spend so much on brand maintenance that they should be able to show a value for their brands as an asset in their accounts.

Think of some examples of products that go on and on from your own experience, and try to identify what it is about them that makes them so enduring.

1.7 The strategic implications of the product life cycle

The strategic implications of the product life cycle might be as follows.

	Phase			
	Introduction	**Growth**	**Maturity**	**Decline**
Product	Initially, poor quality Product design and development are a key to success No standard product and frequent design changes (eg microcomputers in the early 1980s)	Competitor's products have marked quality differences and technical differences Quality improves Product reliability may be important	Products become more standardised and differences between competing products less distinct	Products even less differentiated. Quality becomes more variable
Customers	Initial customers willing to pay high prices Customers need to be convinced about buying	Customers increase in number	Mass market Market saturation Repeat-buying Markets become segmented	Customers are sophisticated buyers of a product they understand well
Marketing issues	High advertising and sales promotion costs High prices possible Distribution problematic	High advertising costs still, but as a % of sales, costs are falling Prices falling More distributors	Segment specific Choose best distribution Brand image	Less money spent on advertising and sales promotion
Competition	Few or no competitors	More competitors enter the market Barriers to entry can be important	Competition at its keenest: on prices, branding, servicing customers, packaging etc	Competitors gradually exit from the market Exit barriers can be important

	Phase			
	Introduction	**Growth**	**Maturity**	**Decline**
Profit margins	High prices but losses due to high fixed costs	High prices. High contribution margins, and increasing profit margins High P/E ratios for quoted companies in the growth market	Falling prices but good profit margins due to high sales volume High prices in some market segments	Still low prices but falling profits as sales volume falls, since total contribution falls towards the level of fixed costs. Some increases in prices may occur in the late decline stage
Manufacturing and distribution	Overcapacity High production costs Few distribution channels High labour skill content in manufacture	Undercapacity Move towards mass production and less reliance on skilled labour Distribution channels flourish and getting adequate distribution is a key to marketing success	Optimum capacity Low labour skills Distribution channels fully developed, but less successful channels might be cut	Overcapacity because mass production techniques still used Distribution channels dwindling

1.8 Product portfolio planning

> Product portfolio planning aims to achieve a portfolio of products which fit well together in financial, marketing and production terms. New product development is another aspect of product portfolio management and is about bringing innovation successfully to market.

A company's product mix (or product assortment or portfolio) is all the product lines and items that the company offers for sale.

	Characteristics of company's product line
Width	Number of product lines
Depth	Average number of items per product line
Consistency	Closeness of items in product range in terms of marketing or production characteristics

The product mix can be extended in a number of ways.

- Introducing **variations** in models or style
- Changing the **quality** of products offered at different price levels
- Developing **associated items**, such as a paint manufacturer introducing paint brushes
- Developing **new products** that have little technical or marketing relationship to the existing range

Managing the product portfolio involves broad issues such as what role should a product play in the portfolio, how should resources be allocated between products and what should be expected from each product. Maintaining balance between well-established and new products, cash-generative and cash-using products and growing and declining products is very important. If products are not suitable for the market

or not profitable, then corporate objectives will be jeopardised. Equally, if potentially profitable products are ignored or not given sufficient support then crucial marketing opportunities will be lost.

It follows that **there are benefits to be gained from using a systematic approach to the management of the product range**. Marketing is not an exact science and there is no definitive approach or technique which can determine which products should remain, which should be pruned and how resources should be shared across the current product range. There are, however, techniques which can aid decision making.

1.9 Product-market matrices

The product-market matrix is used to classify a product or even a business **according to the features of the market and the features of the product**. It is often used at the level of corporate strategy to determine the relative positions of businesses and select strategies for resource allocation between them. The same techniques are **equally valuable when considering products and the management of the product portfolio**. The two most widely used approaches are the **Boston Consulting Group (BCG) growth-share matrix and the General Electric (GE) Business Screen**.

1.9.1 The BCG matrix

The matrix, illustrated below, classifies products (or businesses) on the basis of their market share relative to that of their competitors and according to the rate of growth in the market as a whole. The split on the horizontal axis is based on a market share identical to that of the firm's **nearest competitor**, while the precise location of the split on the vertical axis will depend on the rate of growth in the market. Products are positioned in the matrix as circles with a diameter proportional to their sales revenue. The underlying assumption in the growth-share matrix is that a larger market share will enable the business to benefit from economies of scale, lower per unit costs and thus higher margins.

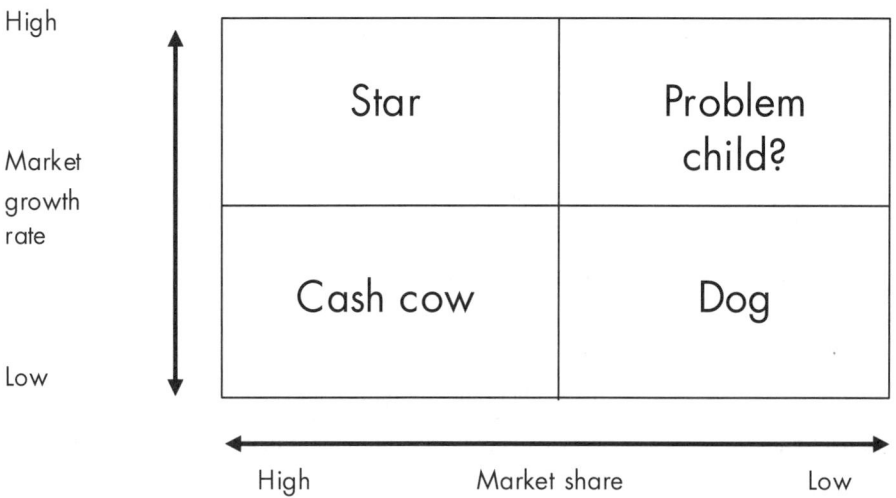

On the basis of this classification, each product or 'strategic business unit' will then fall into one of four broad categories.

(a)   **Problem child?**: a small market share but in a high growth industry. The generic product is clearly popular, but customer support for the company brand is limited. A small market share implies that competitors are in a strong position and that if the product is to be successful it will **require substantial funds**, and a new marketing mix. If the market looks good and the product is viable, then the company should consider a **build** strategy to increase market share. This would require the commitment of funds to permit more active marketing. If the future looks less promising then the company should consider the possibility of withdrawing the product. The problem child is sometimes referred to as the **question mark**.

(b)   **Star**: this is a product with a high market share in a high growth industry. By implication, **the star has potential for generating significant earnings** currently and in the future. However, at this stage it may still require substantial marketing expenditure to maintain its position, but would probably be regarded as **a good investment for the future**.

(c)   **Cash cow**: a high market share but in a mature slow growth market. Typically, a well established product with a high degree of consumer loyalty. Product development costs are typically low and the marketing campaign is well established. **The cash cow will normally make a substantial contribution to overall profitability**. The appropriate strategy will vary according to the precise position of the cash cow. If market growth is reasonably strong then a **holding** strategy will be appropriate, but if growth and/or share are weakening, then a **harvesting** strategy may be more sensible: cut back on marketing expenditure and maximise short-term cash flow.

(d)   **Dog**: a product characterised by low market share and low growth. Again, typically a well established product, but one which is apparently losing consumer support and may have cost disadvantages. The usual strategy would be to consider **divestment** unless cash flow position is strong, in which case the product would be **harvested** in the short term prior to deletion from the product range.

Implicit in the matrix is the notion that markets are dynamic. The typical new product is likely to appear in the problem child? category to begin with; with effective marketing it might be expected to become a star, then, as markets mature, a cash cow and finally a dog. The suggestion that most products will move through these stages does not weaken the role played by marketing. On the contrary, it strengthens it, since poor marketing may mean that a product moves from being a problem child? to a dog without making any substantial contribution to profitability. Equally, of course, good marketing may enable the firm to prolong the star and cash cow phases, thus maximising cash flow from the product.

The framework provided by the matrix can offer guidance in terms of developing **appropriate strategies** for products and in maintaining a **balanced product portfolio**, ensuring that there are enough cash-generating products to match the cash-using products.

However, there are a number of **criticisms**.

(a)   The BCG matrix **oversimplifies product analysis**. It concentrates only on two dimensions of product markets, size and market share, and therefore may encourage marketing management to pay too little attention to other market features.

(b)   It is not always clear what is meant by the terms 'relative market share' and 'rate of market growth'. **Not all companies or products will be designed for market leadership**, in which case describing performance in terms of relative market share may be of limited relevance. Many firms undertaking this approach have found that all their products were technically dogs and yet were still very profitable, so they saw no need to divest. Firms following a 'niche' strategy will commonly find their markets are (intentionally) small.

(c)   The matrix **assumes a relationship between profitability and market share**. There is empirical evidence for this in many but not all industries, particularly where there is demand for more customised products.

(d)   The basic approach **may oversimplify the nature of products** in large diversified firms with many divisions. In these cases, each division may contain products which fit into several of the categories.

Despite these criticisms, the BCG matrix can offer guidance in achieving a balanced portfolio. However, given the difficulty of generalising to deal with all product and market situations, its recommendations should be interpreted with care.

1.10 The General Electric Business Screen

The basic approach of the GE Business Screen is similar to that of the BCG matrix but it tries to avoid the criticism levelled against that technique by including a broader range of company and market factors in assessing the position of a particular product or product group. A typical example of the GE matrix is provided below. This matrix classifies products (or businesses) according to **industry attractiveness** and **company strengths**. Typical examples of the factors which determine industry attractiveness and company strength are the following.

(a) **Industry attractiveness:** market size, market growth, competitive climate, stability of demand, ease of market entry, industry capacity, levels of investment, nature of regulation, profitability.

(b) **Company strengths:** relative market share, company image, production capacity, production costs, financial strengths, product quality, distribution systems, control over prices/margins, benefits of patent protection.

Although a broader range of factors are used in the classification of products, this is a highly subjective assessment. Products are positioned on the grid with circles representing market size and segments representing market shares. The strategy for an individual product is then suggested on the basis of that position. It is interesting to note the apparent similarity in recommendations between the BCG matrix and the GE matrix; the basic difference arises from the method of classification.

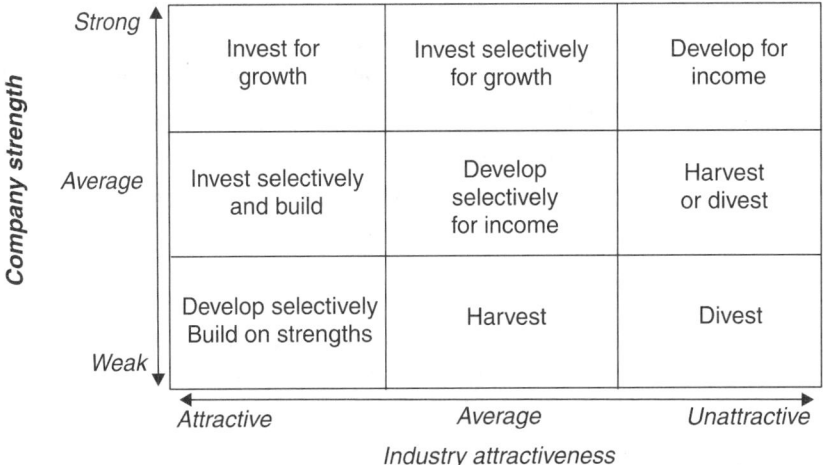

The broader approach of the GE matrix emphasises the attempt to match distinctive competences within the company to conditions within the market place. Difficulties associated with measurement and classification mean that again the results of such an exercise must be interpreted with great care and not seen as a prescription for strategic decisions.

1.11 New and old products

The energy and effort placed into adding new products and brands to the portfolio is seldom mirrored by a similar effort to identify and weed out the weak or declining. One of the benefits of effective marketing strategy is to ensure the organisation's resources are directed to the most suitable market segments; this can easily be thrown away by a **proliferation of products**.

Fashions in dieting come and go.

(a)   Diet clubs such as Weight Watchers and Slimming World, which originally were based on calorie counting, now design their diets to make it easier for people to undertake dieting without having to weigh food and count calories.

(b)   The Atkins diet, with a dedicated product range to support it, does not require dieters to turn up to meetings. The clientele of Weight Watchers and Slimming World are primarily women.

(c)   Weight Watchers endorses some foods. Heinz has a Weight Watchers range in its product portfolio. Supermarkets have 'healthy eating' or 'low fat' options to cater for the weight conscious segments.

2 New product development

Pilot paper, 12/03, 6/04, 6/05, 12/05, 6/07

Innovation is the life blood of a successful organisation and the management of innovation is central to this success.

(a)   **New products** may be developed as a result of a technical breakthrough, or as a consequence of changes in society, or simply to copy and capitalise on the success of existing products. They may therefore be a **reactive response** to competitive innovation

(b)   Management, however, can adopt a **proactive approach to product development** by establishing research and development departments to look into ideas for new products, although they do not have to come through this formal departmentalised system. Management, sales people, customers and competitors can all generate new product ideas.

Exam tip

> 'Reactive' and 'proactive' strategy features in the Pilot paper.

2.1 What is a new product?

- One that opens up an entirely new market
- One that replaces an existing product
- One that broadens significantly the market for an existing product

An old product can be new:

- If it is introduced to a new market
- If it is packaged in a different way
- If a different marketing approach is used
- If a mix variable is changed

Action Programme 5

Can you think of examples of new products and 'new' old products to fit into each of the above categories?

There are several degrees of newness.

(a)   **The unquestionably new product**. Marks which distinguish such a new product include technical innovation, high price, performance problems and patchy distribution. An example is the MP3 music player.

(b)   **The partially new product**. The mark distinguishing such a product is that it performs better than the old ones did. An example would be the Pentium microchip.

(c)   **Major product change**, such as the transistor radio. The mark distinguishing this product is the radical technological change which alters the accepted concept of the order of things.

(d)   **Minor product change**, such as styling changes. It is these extras which give a boost to a product.

Marketing at Work	Application

Many retailers are switching to organic foods and adding organic food to their portfolios.

Firms such as Seeds of Change and Green & Black make branded organic products. Other firms produce organic versions of their existing brands (such as organic Weetabix).

There is evidence that the market for organic food is a **growth market**. New entrants, such as Seeds of Change, have an opportunity.

It is useful to think of new products under the following headings

(a)   **Replacement product** – a product intended to take over market position of an established product reaching the decline stage of its life cycle eg in a cosmetics product revitalised by a new name, packaging or promotion.

(b)   **Relaunched product** – a newish product that has not achieved its planned market success – relaunch will be largely based on new promotion, but may include other features of the marketing mix such as improved distribution, changed price and possibly changes to the core product itself.

(c)   **Imitative product** – a 'me too' or 'copy cat' product introduced to exploit the market created by a competitor's unprotected product – probably with a small price advantage – similar to an 'own brand' product.

Exam tip

> The syllabus refers specifically to replacement, relaunched and imitative products. These feature on the Pilot paper as well.

2.2 Sources for new products

- Licensing (eg Formica, Monopoly)
- Acquisition (buy the organisation making it)
- Internal product development
- Customers (listen to and observe them, analyse and research – this is how the Walkman developed)
- External inventors (Kodak and IBM rejected Xerox)
- Competition (Kodak instant cameras, following the Polaroid concept)

- Patent agents
- Academic institutions (for example, the pharmaceutical industry funds higher education department research)

Exam tip

The Pilot paper contains a 25-mark question on various aspects of innovation and new product development. The July 2005 and December 2005 papers both contained questions on product development. It is likely to be a regularly examined topic.

2.3 Screening new product ideas

The mortality rate of new products is very high.

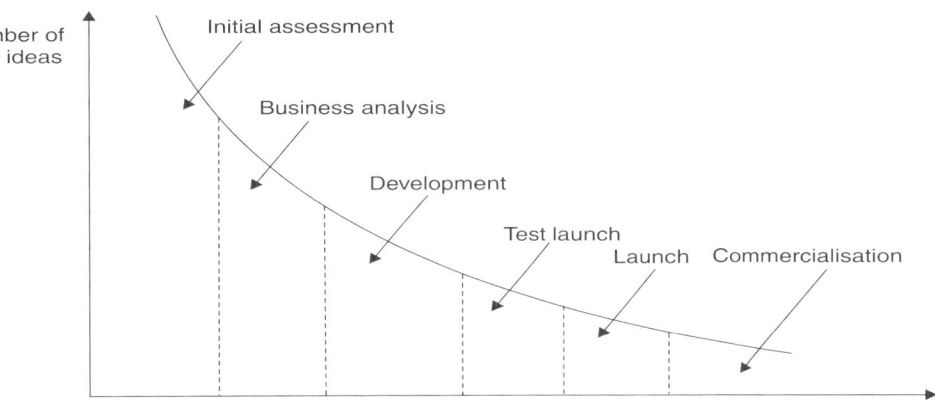

To reduce the risk of failure new product ideas should always be **screened**. There is some evidence that the product screening process is becoming more effective.

2.4 New product development plan

New products should only be taken to advanced development if they satisfy three conditions.

- Adequate **demand**
- Compatibility with existing **marketing** ability
- Compatibility with existing **production** ability

2.5 Initial concept testing

At a preliminary stage the concept for the new product should be tested on potential customers to obtain their reactions. It is common to use the company staff as guinea pigs for a new product idea although their reaction is unlikely to be typical. But it is difficult to get sensible reactions from customers. Consider the following examples.

(a) **New designs for wallpaper**. When innovative new designs are tested on potential customers it is often found that they are conditioned by traditional designs and are dismissive of new design ideas.

(b) **New ideas for chocolate confectionery** have the opposite problem. Potential customers typically say they like the new concept (because just about everyone likes chocolate bars) but when the new product is launched it is not successful because people continue to buy old favourites.

2.6 Product testing

A working prototype of the product, which can be tried by customers, is constructed. This stage is also very useful for making preliminary explorations of whether the product could be produced in sufficient quantities at the right price were it to be launched. The form the product test takes will depend on the type of product concerned. To get realistic responses the **test should replicate reality as clearly as possible**.

(a) If the product is used in the home, a sample of respondents should be given the product to use **at home**.

(b) If the product is chosen from amongst competitors in a retail outlet (as with chocolate bars) then the product test needs to rate response against **competing products**.

(c) If inherent **product quality** is an important attribute of the product, then a 'blind' test could be used in which customers are not told who is producing the new product.

(d) An industrial product could be used for a **trial period** by a customer in a realistic setting.

2.7 Quality policy

Different market segments will require products of different price and quality. When a market is dominated by established brand names, one entry strategy is to tap potential demand for a cheaper, lower quality 'me-too' item.

Customers often judge the quality of an article by its price. Quality policy may well involve fixing a price and then manufacturing a product to the best quality standard that can be achieved within these constraints, rather than making a product of a certain quality and then deciding what its price should be.

Quality should also be related to the expected physical, technological and social life of the product.

(a) There is no value in making one part of a product good enough to have a physical life of five years, when the rest of the product will wear out within two years (unless the part with the longer life has an emotional or symbolic appeal to customers; for example, a leather covering may be preferred to plastic).

(b) If technological advances are likely to make a product obsolescent within a certain number of years, it is wasteful and uneconomic to produce an article which will last for a longer time.

(c) If fashion determines the life of a product, the quality required need only be sufficient to cover the period of demand; the quality of fashion clothes, for example, is usually governed by their fashion life. Fashion items are only intended to be worn a relatively small number of times, while non-fashion items are more durable.

Quality policy must be carefully integrated with sales promotion. If a product is branded and advertised as having a certain quality, and customers then find this is not true, the product will fail. The quality of a product must be established and maintained before a promotion campaign can use it as a selling feature.

2.8 Test marketing

The purpose of test marketing is to obtain information about **how consumers react to the product** in selected areas thought to be representative of the total market. This avoids a blind commitment to the costs of a full scale launch, while permitting the collection of market data. The firm will use the sales outlets it plans to use in the full market launch, and the same advertising and promotion plans it will use in the full market. Test marketing helps to forecast sales, and can also be used to identify flaws in the product or promotional plans which can be dealt with before a full-scale launch.

2.9 The diffusion of innovation

The **diffusion** of the new product refers to the **spread of information about the product** in the market place. **Adoption** is the process by which consumers incorporate the product into their buying patterns. The diffusion process is assumed to follow a similar shape to the PLC curve. Adoption is thought to follow a normal bell shaped distribution curve. The classification of adopters is shown below.

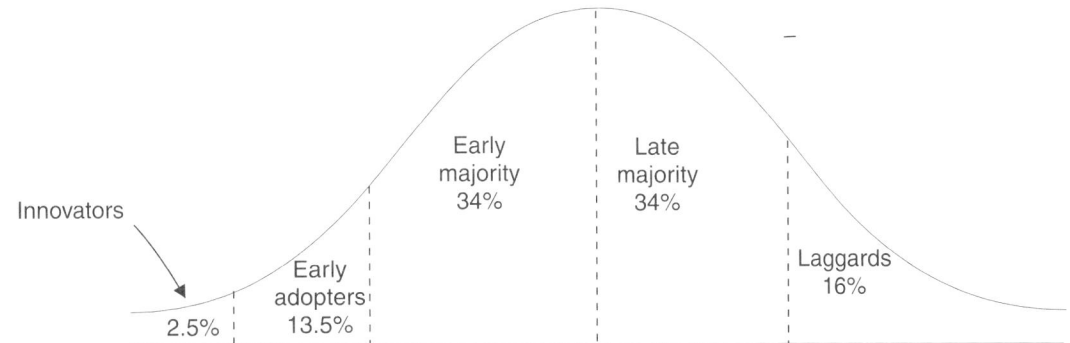

Early adopters and innovators are thought to operate as 'opinion leaders' and are therefore targeted by companies in order to influence the adoption of a product by their friends.

Marketing at Work   Application

The i-pod is a portable device which permits music downloads. It combines the convenience of the Sony Walkman or Discman with the digital download of music.

3 Brands   12/03, 6/04, 12/04, 6/05, 12/05, 6/06, 6/07

FAST FORWARD

> **Branding** is a form of product differentiation and can help to create customer loyalty. Brand strategies include brand extension, multi-branding and family branding.

Key concept

> A **brand** is a name, term, sign, symbol or design intended to identify the product of a seller and to differentiate it from those of competitors. It amounts to a promise of consistent quality and value.

Not long ago most products were sold unbranded from barrels and bins. Today in developed countries hardly anything goes unbranded. Even salt, oranges, nuts and screws are branded. There has however been a recent return to generics. These are cheap, unbranded products, packaged plainly and not heavily advertised.

Branding is a very general term covering brand names, designs, trademarks, symbols, jingles and the like. A **brand name** refers strictly to letters, words or groups of words which can be spoken. A **brand image** is created using the **values** the company would like to be associated with the brand, and distinguishes a company's product from competing products in the eyes of the user.

Branding and a **firm's reputation** are linked. the important thing to remember is that a brand is something that **customers** value. A brand is the link between a company's marketing activities and the customer's perception.

Application

In suburban Philadelphia is a retail establishment called Ed's Beer Store. Customers know what they can buy there, and if they have a complaint they know whom to talk to.

But what about companies with names like Agere, Agilent or Altria? Or Diageo, Monday and Verizon? Or Accenture, Cingular and Protiviti?

Except for Monday, which may be a strange thing to call a company but is nonetheless a real word, all these names are made up, solely for the companies to use as their names. What's more, none of them, even Monday, tells potential customers anything about the businesses they are in. Plus, they sound so contrived that you might conclude they will do nothing but elicit snickering and confusion in the market place.

According to marketing professors at Wharton, however, that is not necessarily the case. They say peculiar names, by themselves, may mean nothing to begin with. But if backed by a successful branding campaign, they will come to signify whatever the companies want them to mean.

Action Programme 7   Application

What characteristics do the following brand names suggest to you?

- Brillo (scouring pads)
- Pampers (baby nappies)
- Cussons Imperial Leather (soap)
- Kerrygold (butter)

- Hush Puppies (shoes)
- Bombay Sapphire (Gin)
- Seeds of Change (organic food)
- Smile (Internet bank)

Branding is a form of **product differentiation**.

(a)   **Brand identity** conveys a lot of information very quickly and concisely. This helps customers to identify and select goods or services, and so helps to create a **customer loyalty** to the brand which is a means of increasing or maintaining sales.

(b)   Advertising needs a brand name to sell to customers, and advertising and branding are very closely related aspects of promotion; the more similar a product (whether an industrial good or consumer good) is to competing goods, the more branding is necessary to **create a separate product identity**.

(c)   Branding leads to a readier acceptance of a manufacturer's goods by **wholesalers and retailers**.

(d)   It **facilitates self-selection** of goods in self-service stores and also makes it easier for a manufacturer to obtain display space in shops and stores.

(e)   It reduces the importance of **price differentials** between goods.

(f)   Brand loyalty in customers gives a manufacturer more **control over marketing strategy** and his choice of channels of distribution.

(g)   Other products can be introduced into a brand range to 'piggy back' on the articles already known to the customer (but ill-will as well as goodwill for one product in a branded range could be transferred to all other products in the range). Adding products to an existing brand range is known as **brand extension strategy**.

(h)   It eases the task of **personal selling**.

(i) **Branding makes market segmentation easier**. A range of products under one brand may be developed to meet specific needs of categories of users.

The relevance of branding does not apply equally to all products. The cost of intensive brand advertising to project a brand image nationally may be prohibitively high. Goods which are sold in large numbers, on the other hand, promote a brand name by their existence and circulation.

Where a brand image promotes an idea of quality, customers will be disappointed if their experience of a product fails to live up to their expectations. **Quality control is therefore an important element in branding policy. It is especially a problem for service industries** such as hotels, airlines and retail stores, where there is less possibility than in a manufacturing industry of detecting and rejecting the work of an operator before it reaches the customer. Bad behaviour by an employee in a face-to-face encounter with a customer will reflect on the entire company and possibly deter the customer from using any of the company's services again.

The decision as to whether a brand name should be given to a range of products or whether products should be branded individually depends on quality factors.

(a) If the brand name is associated with **quality**, all goods in the range **must** be of that standard. An example of a successful promotion of a brand name to a wide product range is Virgin.

(b) If a company produces different quality (and price) goods for different market segments, it would be unwise to give the same brand name to the higher and the lower quality goods because this would deter buyers in the high quality/price market segment.

3.1 Branding strategies

Branding strategy	Description	Implies
Family branding	The power of the family name to help products	Image of family brand applicable across a range of goods
Brand extension (or stretching)	Adding new products to the brand range	High consumer loyalty to existing brand
Multi-branding	Different names for similar goods serving similar consumer tastes	Consumers make random purchases across brands

Family branding: the power of the family name to assist all products is being used more and more by large companies, such as Heinz. In part, this is a response to retailers own-label goods. It is also an attempt to consolidate highly expensive television advertising behind just one message rather than fragmenting it across the promotion of numerous individual items. Individual lines can be promoted more cheaply and effectively by other means such as direct marketing and sales promotions.

Brand extension: new additions to the product range are beneficial for two main reasons.

(a) They require a **lower level of marketing investment** (part of the image already being created).

(b) The extension of the brand presents **less risk to consumers** who might be worried about trying something new. Recent examples of brand extension include Easy Jet transferring into car rental and Internet cafes.

Multi-branding: the introduction of a number of brands that all satisfy very similar product characteristics.

(a)   This can be used where little or no brand loyalty is noted, the rationale being to run a large number of brands and so pick up buyers who are constantly changing brands.

(b)   The best example is washing detergents. The two majors, Lever Brothers and Procter & Gamble, have created a barrier to fresh competition as a new company would have to launch several brands at once in order to compete.

A manufacturer might supply large retailers with goods under their own brand names, (own label or dealer brands). The major examples are the own brands of supermarkets and major chain stores. This industrial structure has developed for several reasons.

(a)   A high level of sales may be necessary to cover **fixed costs of production**; supplying dealer branded goods may be a way of achieving a profitable sales level. New market segments can be covered profitably at less risk and outlay to the producer.

(b)   Large retailers with a high sales turnover and considerable control over the retail trade may **insist on having their own brand**, and supplying dealer branded goods may be essential to retain their business.

(c)   A manufacturer may wish **to concentrate on production only**, leaving the problem of design, quality and distribution to a multiple retailer.

3.1.1 Advantages of dealer brands to dealers

(a)   The use of a brand helps to create **customer loyalty** to the store.

(b)   The buying-in price is lower and cost of sales promotion negligible, therefore the price of dealer branded goods to customers can be lower.

(c)   'Me-too' products may benefit from the **generic promotion effect** of the market leader's success, but enjoy a price advantage.

3.2 Brand management

It is usual to appoint a marketing professional to manage a brand, or group of brands. This **brand manager** is responsible for the long-term integration of the corporate effort that goes into making the brand a success. A matrix style of management is indicated here, since the brand manager is unlikely to have direct authority over the resources needed by the brand. Inputs will be needed from all departments and top management is likely to take a close interest. The primary role of the brand manager is therefore co-ordination. The job may require a small team of marketing people for each major brand.

The most important aspect of this co-ordination is the **promotion of a customer orientation**. The brand manager must be the focus for all communication to and from the customer. In particular, complaints should be dealt with by the brand management team.

A secondary role for the brand manager is to act as the **brand's advocate** in the internal contest for organisational resources.

3.3 Brand values

In the Key Concept box at the start of this section we remark that a brand amounts to a promise of consistent quality and value. The overall object of branding is that the customer should perceive greater value in the branded good than in the unbranded equivalent. There may be some objective basis for this perception, but much brand value in fact exists exclusively in the mind of the purchaser. The customer places a subjective valuation on such brand messages as style, quality, masculinity, sophistication and reliability. These are known as **brand values**.

Clearly, such customer perceptions are extremely valuable and can lead to higher than average returns. They must also be protected from erosion or dilution of brand values by neglect, or the hostile action of competitors. Manufacturers of exclusive brands will go to great lengths to ensure that they are distributed only through up-market outlets, for instance.

3.4 Brand valuation

Brands can be valued in money terms; when mergers and acquisitions take place, some part of the purchase price may represent **brand value**. However, current accounting practice does not allow brands to be shown as assets on the balance sheet. This is because a brand's value can be extremely volatile, depending on both good management and market conditions.

3.5 Threats to the brand

There are three main threats to a brand.

(a) **Competition**. Brands must be protected against competition. The principal way of doing this is by promotion aimed at establishing the brand's unique identity and values.

(b) **Infringement of intellectual property rights**. Trademarks, designs and text are all forms of intellectual property and can be granted legal protection against unlicensed use.

(c) **Generic names**. A brand can be too successful. If a brand name comes into common, everyday use as the generic name of a particular type of product, its owners may forfeit their rights over it. It is for this reason that Rolls-Royce take action against claims that such-and-such a product is the 'Rolls-Royce' of its market. It is important that 'Rolls-Royce' does not become established in everyday speech as a synonym for best. **Nylon** and **aspirin** were once brand names.

4 Packaging

FAST FORWARD

Packaging has a number of practical functions such as protecting the product and assisting the shopper, as well as contributing to promotional objectives.

Packaging has several functions.

(a) **Protection of contents** during distribution.

(b) **Selling**, as the design and labelling serve promotional objectives of providing information and conveying an image.

(c) **User convenience**, as an aid to storage and carrying, such as aerosol cans and handy packs.

(d) **Security**, for example small valuable items are packaged in large containers to deter shoplifting.

(e) **Choice of offering** for example Coca Cola comes in various sizes and packages. There is a range of plastic bottles pitched at different users, and also cans. In bars and pubs there are traditional glass bottles.

(f) Compliance with **government regulations** for example, by providing a list of ingredients and contents by weight, as in food packaging.

Remember that goods are usually packaged in more than one layer. Consumer goods might be packaged for sale to individual customers, but delivered to resellers in cartons or some similar bulk package.

Upmarket retailers also utilise packaging for promotional purposes.

Smarties were introduce in 1937 and are now one of Nestlé's major confectionery brands. Now manufactured in Hamburg, Smarties are brightly coloured, sugar coated sweets with a milk chocolate centre. The mix comprises eight colours – red, yellow, orange, green, purple, pink, brown and blue.

In 2005, Nestlé's Rowntree division announced that is was changing the traditional cylindrical tube packaging for a hexagonal tube design as part of a new 'fresh and funky' approach.

According to Nestlé', nearly 17,000 Smarties are eaten every minute in the UK.

www.just-food.com – accessed 9 April 2008

4.1 The qualities required of a pack

(a)   The **range of sizes and varieties should be minimised** in order to keep down purchasing, production and distribution costs, but it should succeed in making the product attractive and distinctive to the target consumer.

(b)   In industries where **distribution** is a large part of total costs, packaging is an important issue. Packs should do four things.

    (i)   Protect, preserve and convey the product to its destination in the desired condition

    (ii)   Fit into the practices of mechanised handling and storage systems and use vehicle space cost effectively

    (iii)   Be space efficient, but also be attractive as display items

    (iv)   Convey product information to shoppers effectively

(c)   Packaging is an **important aid to selling**. Where a product cannot be differentiated by design techniques, the pack takes over the design selling function. This is crucial where there are no real product differences between rival brands, or in the case of commodities such as flour.

    (i)   A pack should help to **promote the advertising/brand image**. In addition, a **logo** should be clearly identifiable on the package, to apply customer brand loyalty to a range of products.

    (ii)   Shape, colour and size should relate to **customer motivation** for value or quantity.

    (iii)   It should be the **appropriate size** for the expected user of the product (for example, family size packets of food).

    (iv)   Some may be designed to **promote impulse buying,** such as snack foods.

    (v)   A **convenience pack** (tubes, aerosols) should be provided where this is an important attribute.

    (vi)   Packaging should maintain product **quality standards**.

    (vii)   It should **attract attention** of potential customers, where appropriate.

Packaging must appeal not only to consumers, **but also to resellers**. A reseller wants a package design that will help to sell the product, but also one which minimises the likelihood of breakage, or which extends the product's shelf life, or makes more economic use of shelf space.

The **packaging of industrial goods** is primarily a matter of maintaining good condition to the point of use. This is a selling aid in itself in future dealings with the customer. Large, expensive and/or fragile pieces of equipment must be well packaged.

Application

Packaging innovations

No one could accuse the packaging industry of running short of ideas. The past few years have brought such user-friendly designs as baby bottle-style closures on water bottles; recloseable, plastic pour devices on milk cartons and large-opening ends of beer and soft drinks cans. Even petfood is available in single-serve squeezable pouches.

Packaging is no longer designed just to protect the contents, but has become a sophisticated marketing tool that consumers expect to meet certain performance standards.

Consumers' attitudes have changed too. Packaging was seen as a 'necessary evil' in the late 1980s and early 1990s and was heavily criticised for creating excessive waste.

Environmental concerns have not gone away, but many consumers have tired of – or at least got used to – the waste issues.

Convenient, easy to use containers and a wide choice of options now seem to be the top priorities for consumers. Changing lifestyles, virtually world-wide, are causing a sharp rise in snacking, de-skilling of cookery practices in the home and a breakdown of the structured family meal time.

Much innovation has focused on the plastics industry. One important trend is the move away from glass to PET (polyethylene terephthalate) jars for foods such as premium soup, pasta sauce, jams and jellies. These jars are safe and non-breakable and incorporate moulded side grips for easy handling.

Also big news in plastic at present are oxygen-scavenging materials inside the walls and closures of containers. These remove excess oxygen inside a container, thereby lengthening the product's shelf-life.

Hilary Schrafft, Financial Times

Chapter Roundup

- The **product life cycle** model describes the progress of a product from introduction to discontinuation in terms of sales and profitability. It can offer some guidance in the management of marketing and production.

- **Product portfolio planning** aims to achieve a portfolio of products which fit well together in financial, marketing and production terms. New product development is another aspect of product portfolio management and is about bringing innovation successfully to market.

- **Branding** is a form of product differentiation and can help to create customer loyalty. Brand strategies include brand extension, multi-branding and family branding.

- **Packaging** has a number of practical functions such as protecting the product and assisting the shopper, as well as contributing to promotional objectives.

Quick Quiz

1   What are the stages of the product life cycle (PLC) and how do they affect profitability?

2   What are the criticisms of the PLC concept?

3   What are the marketing implications of the introductory phase of the PLC?

4   What are the axes of the BCG matrix?

5   What degree of marketing expenditure does a star need?

6   What are the axes of the GE Business Screen?

7   What degrees of 'newness' can you discern in products?

8   What are 'early adopters'?

9   What is the advantage of branding in distribution?

10   How can packaging help selling?

Answers to Quick Quiz

1   Introduction; growth; maturity; decline; senility.

2   •   Where technology remains unimproved, products can be perennial
     •   Some products appear to go directly from growth to decline
     •   A product's life cycle can be managed and its progress affected by marketing decisions
     •   The model presupposes a particular pattern of competition that does not exist in all industries

3   High promotion costs; high prices possible; distribution problematic

4   Market share and market growth rate

5   Substantial, probably

6   Company strength and industry attractiveness

7   Unquestionably new; potentially new; major change; minor change

8   A kind of opinion leader; they adopt new products early

9   It helps acceptance of goods by both wholesalers and retailers

10   Pack design and labelling provide information, so they are a form of promotion

Action Programme Review

1   Your own research.

2   Some ideas to start you off are manual typewriters, unleaded petrol and vinyl records. Also, almost anything subject to fads or fashions.

3   You could perhaps pin down some of these items, but most are open to discussion, especially if you take an international perspective. For many you may consider that the PLC is not valid, and you will not be alone.

4   Here are some examples: Mars bar; Oxo cube; Burberry trench coat; Hunter gum boots.

5   You should try to think of your own examples, but these suggestions may help.

New product
Entirely new market   Web browsers, National Lottery
Replacing an existing product   Faster PCs
Broadening the market   Cable for satellite TV and telephones

'New' old product
In a new market   German confectionery (in the UK)
New packaging   Anything
New marketing   French wine competing with Australian wine

Now try Question 8 at the end of the Study Text

7

Price and place

Syllabus content – knowledge and skills requirements

- 3.7: Pricing frameworks available to, and used by, organisations for decision marketing
- 3.8: How pricing is developed as an integrated part of the marketing mix
- 3.9: The channels of distribution and logistics to be used by an organisation and developing a plan for channel support

Introduction

The main material dealt with in this chapter relates to **pricing**. This is one of the most important and difficult parts of business decision making, and is normally controlled at a high level. There are many factors to be considered when setting prices, from the existence or otherwise of a prevailing market price, through the reality of breakeven analysis to various rules of thumb.

All of these factors are considered in Sections 1, 2, and 3.

The second important topic of this chapter is **place** and, in particular, the vital areas of distribution and logistics. These matters are covered in Section 4.

1 Price
12/03, 6/04, 12/05

Price is the only element of the mix which generates revenue rather than creating cost. It must be consistent with the other elements of the marketing mix and is particularly associated with **perceptions of quality**. Economic theory deals with price in terms of market forces; its most useful aspect for the marketer is the idea of **price elasticity of demand**, which measures the extent to which a change in **price** is reflected by a proportionate change in **demand**.

Key concept

Price can be defined as a measure of the value exchanged by the buyer for the value offered by the seller. It might be expected, therefore, that the price would reflect the costs to the seller of producing the product and the benefit to the buyer of consuming it.

Pricing is the only element of the mix which generates revenue rather than creating costs. It also has an important role as a competitive tool to **differentiate** a product and an organisation and thereby exploit market opportunities. Pricing must also be **consistent** with other elements of the marketing mix since it contributes to the overall image created for the product. No organisation can hope to offer an exclusive high quality product to the market with a low price – the price must be consistent with the overall **product offer**.

Action Programme 1
Application

In what circumstances would you expect price to be the main factor influencing a consumer's choice?

Although pricing can be thought of as fulfilling a number of roles, in overall terms a price aims to produce the desired level of sales in order to meet the objectives of the business strategy. Pricing must be systematic and at the same time take into account the internal needs and the external constraints of the organisation.

The ultimate objective of pricing, as with other elements of the marketing mix, is to produce the required level of sales so that the organisation can achieve its specified objectives. **Two broad categories of objectives may be specified for pricing decisions**.

   (a)   **Maximising profits** is concerned with maximising the returns on assets or investments. This may be realised even with a comparatively small market share, depending on the patterns of cost and demand.

(b) **Maintaining or increasing market share** involves increasing or maintaining the customer base which may require a different, more competitive approach to pricing. The company with the largest market share may not necessarily earn the best profits.

Either approach may be used in specifying pricing objectives, and they may appear in some combination, based on a specified rate of return and a specified market share. As always, it is important that stated objectives are consistent with overall corporate objectives and corporate strategies.

1.1 Price setting in theory

> Economic theory suggests that price for any good is set by market forces. Under conditions of perfect competition, an **equilibrium price** will exist such that demand and supply are perfectly matched and there is neither surplus or shortage of the good in question.

Market pricing is illustrated in the diagram below. The upward sloping supply curve shows the natural tendency of manufacturers to enter a market if prices are high and to leave it if they are low. The downward sloping demand curve reflects the unwillingness of consumers to buy at a high price and their willingness to buy at a low one. The vertical co-ordinate of the point where the two curves cross is the prevailing equilibrium price; the horizontal co-ordinate shows the amount of the good in question bought and sold in the market. The equilibrium price is also called the **clearing price**, because it clears the market; there is neither unsatisfied demand nor unsold goods.

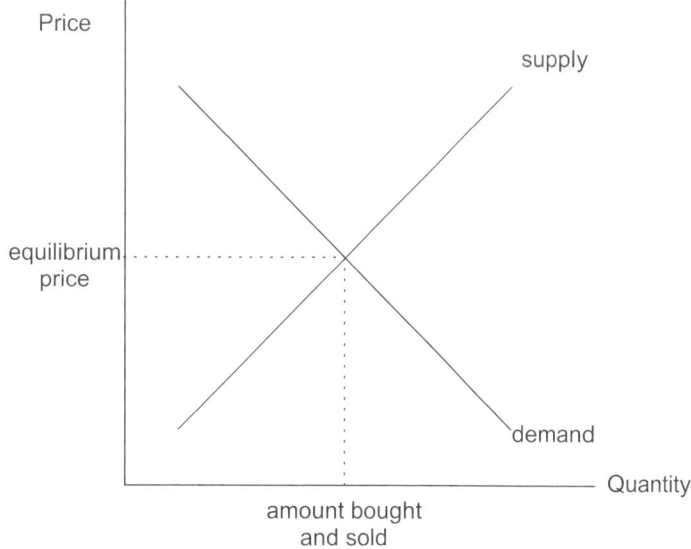

This simple mechanism gives a reasonable picture of **commodity markets**, in which there are many buyers and sellers and none has significant **market power**. More complex models are used to describe markets in which a supplier or group of suppliers has market power.

(a) A **monopolist** is the sole supplier in a market and is able to prevent other suppliers from entering. Monopolists are in a strong position to exploit the consumer.

(b) **Oligopolists** are members of a small group who between them control supply in a market. Oligopoly is characterised by price 'stickiness'. That is to say, oligopolists typically compete with one another but only in matters **other than price**.

(c) Suppliers under **monopolistic competition** attempt to obtain some of the monopolist's market power by supplying a **differentiated** product. The success of this depends on the willingness of the consumer to accept that the product is, in fact, different. Clearly, this is a very important area for the marketer.

Exam tip

The Pilot paper for this subject includes a 10 mark part-question on two aspects of pricing theory: **'marginal analysis'**, which is a term sometimes used to refer to the type of economic analysis dealt with above, and **'breakeven analysis'**, which is dealt with in Section 4. The December 2005 paper had a question on pricing in international markets.

Price elasticity of demand

Key concept

Price elasticity of demand is a measure of the degree of change in demand for a good when its price changes. If the change in demand is large in proportion to the change in price, demand is said to be **elastic**. If the change in demand is small in proportion to the change in price, demand is said to be **inelastic**.

Price elasticity of demand is measured as:

$$\frac{\text{The change in quantity demanded, as a \% of demand}}{\text{The change in price, as a \% of the price}}$$

Since the demand goes up when the price falls, and goes down when the price rises, the elasticity has a negative value, but it is usual to ignore the minus sign. Values greater than 1 indicate elastic demand, while values less than 1 indicate inelastic demand.

1.2 Example

The price of a product is £1.20 per unit and annual demand is 800,000 units. Market research indicates that an increase in price of 10 pence per unit will result in a fall in annual demand of 75,000 units. What is the price elasticity of demand?

Solution

Annual demand at £1.20 per unit is 800,000 units.

Annual demand at £1.30 per unit is 725,000 units.

% change in demand $\qquad \dfrac{75,000}{800,000} \times 100\% = 9.375\%$

% change in price $\qquad \dfrac{10p}{120p} \times 100\% = 8.333\%$

Price elasticity of demand = $\dfrac{-9.375}{8.333} = -1.125$

Ignoring the minus sign, price elasticity is 1.125.

The demand for this product, at a price of £1.20 per unit, would be referred to as *elastic* because the price elasticity of demand is greater than 1. Now try the following exercise yourself.

Action Programme 2

Application

If the price per unit of X rises from £1.40 to £1.60, it is expected that monthly demand will fall from 220,000 units to 200,000 units.

What is the price elasticity of demand?

1.3 Elastic and inelastic demand

The value of demand elasticity may be anything from zero to infinity. Where demand is **inelastic, the quantity demanded falls by a smaller percentage than the percentage rise in price,** and where demand is **elastic, demand falls by a larger percentage than the percentage rise in price**.

There are three special values of price elasticity of demand; 0, 1 and infinity.

(a) **Demand is perfectly inelastic**. There is no change in quantity demanded, regardless of the change in price. The demand curve is a vertical straight line. Demand for tobacco is almost perfectly inelastic in the short term, for any reasonable increase in duty, as Chancellors of the Exchequer know.

(b) **Perfectly elastic demand** (infinitely elastic). Consumers will want to buy an infinite amount, but only up to a particular price level. Any price increase above this level will reduce demand to zero. The demand curve is a horizontal straight line. This is illustrated by a market price in a commodity market.

(c) **Unit elasticity of demand. Total revenue for supplies** (which is the same as total spending on the product by households) **is the same whatever the price**.

1.4 The significance of price elasticity of demand

The price elasticity of demand is relevant to **total spending** on a good or service. When demand is **elastic**, an increase in price will result in a fall in the quantity demanded, and the supplier's **total revenue will fall**. When demand is **inelastic**, an increase in price will still result in a fall in quantity demanded, but **total revenue will rise**.

Information on price elasticity of demand indicates how consumers can be expected to respond to different prices. Business people can make use of information on how consumers will react to pricing decisions as it is possible to trace the effect of different prices on total revenue and profits. Information on price elasticities of demand will be useful to a business which needs to know the price decrease necessary to clear a surplus (excess supply) or the price increase necessary to eliminate a shortage (excess demand).

1.5 Factors influencing price elasticity of demand for a good

The main factors affecting price elasticity of demand are as follows.

(a) **The availability of close substitutes.** The more substitute goods there are, especially close substitutes, the more elastic will be the price elasticity of demand for a good. The elasticity of demand for a particular brand of breakfast cereal is much greater than the elasticity of demand for breakfast cereals as a whole, because the former have much closer substitutes. **This factor is probably the most important influence on price elasticity of demand**.

(b) **The time period**. Over time, consumers' demand patterns are likely to change, and so, if the price of a good is increased, the initial response might be very little change in demand (inelastic demand). As consumers adjust their buying habits in response to the price increase, demand might fall substantially. The time horizon influences elasticity largely because the longer the period of time which we consider, the greater the knowledge of **substitution possibilities** by consumers and the provision of substitutes by producers.

(c) **Competitors' pricing**. A market dominated by a small number of large suppliers is called an **oligopoly**. In an oligopoly, firms are very sensitive to price changes by their competitors. If the response of competitors to a price increase by one firm is to keep their prices unchanged, the firm raising its prices is likely to face elastic demand for its goods and lose business. If the response of competitors to a reduction in price by one firm is to match the price reduction themselves, the firm is likely to face inelastic demand but at lower prices. That is, all the firms in the market are likely to retain their market share, but at a lower price. As a result, oligopolists tend to compete in ways other than by price reductions. The diagram below illustrates the **kinked demand curve** perceived by the individual oligopolist.

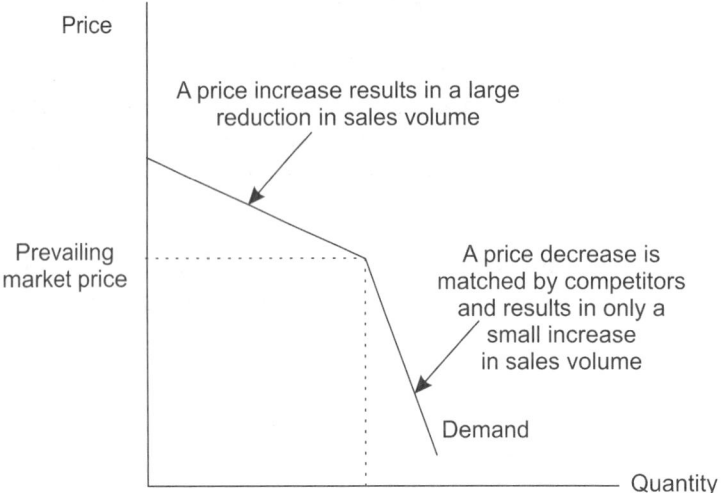

Action Programme 3

Application

What are the limitations of price elasticity as a factor in determining prices?

1.6 Price setting in practice

There are three main influences on price setting in practice: **costs, competition and demand**.

1.6.1 Costs

Cost is the most important influence on price. Many firms base price on simple **cost-plus** rules: in other words, costs are estimated and then a profit margin is added in order to set the price. This method is fairly easy to apply and ensures that costs are covered. Costs are available from accounting records, sometimes in great detail.

The price may be based on **direct costs** or **full costs**, the difference being that full cost includes overheads whereas direct cost does not. In either case, a suitable **margin** is added to cost; under the direct cost method this has to cover overheads as well as profit. Under the full cost method, the margin represents profit only. While appearing to ignore demand, this method can take account of market conditions by adjusting the margin applied.

A common example occurs with the use of **mark-up** pricing. This is used by retailers and involves a fixed margin being added to the buying-in price of goods for resale. This fixed margin tends to be conventional within product classes. In the UK, for example: fast moving items, such as cigarettes, carry a low 5-8% margin (also because of tax factors); fast moving but perishable items, such as newspapers, carry a 25% margin; while slow moving items which involve retailers in high stockholding costs, such as furniture or books, carry 33%, 50% or even higher mark up margins.

The problems with cost-plus pricing arise out of difficulties in defining direct costs and allocating overheads. Because the cost-plus approach leads to price stability, with price changing only being used to reflect cost changes, it can lead to a marketing strategy which is **reactive** rather then **proactive**. In addition, there is very limited consideration of **demand** in cost-based pricing strategies. From a marketing

perspective, cost-based pricing may lead to **missed opportunities** as little or no account is taken, particularly in the short run, of the price consumers are **willing** to pay for the brand, which may actually be higher than the cost-based price.

Particular problems may be caused by the use of cost-based pricing for a **new brand**, as **initial low production levels** in the introduction stage may lead to a **very high average unit cost and consequently a high price**. A longer term perspective may thus be necessary, accepting short-term losses until full production levels are attained.

1.6.2 Competition

We have already looked at price behaviour under oligopoly. In reality, the kinked demand curve theory would produce **going rate pricing** in which some form of average level of price becomes the norm.

In some market structures **price competition may be avoided by tacit agreement**, leading to concentration on non-price competition; the markets for cigarettes and petrol are examples of this. Price-setting here is influenced by the need to **avoid retaliatory responses by competitors** which would result in a breakdown of the tacit agreement, and so lead to price competition. Price changes based on real cost changes are led in many instances by a representative firm in the industry and followed by other firms. This may then be followed by a resumption of the tacit agreement. Often such actions are the result of external factors at work on the industry.

Industry level agreements do not necessarily preclude short-term price competition for specific brands, especially where sales promotion devices, such as special offers, are used.

Action Programme 4   Application

There is at least one service industry in which this practice is the norm and which is regularly reported in the headlines. Can you think of it?

Competitive bidding is a special case of competition-based pricing. Many supply contracts, especially concerning local and national government purchases, involve suppliers submitting a **sealed bid tender**. In this case, the firm's submitted price needs to take account of expected competitor bid prices. Often the firms involved will not even know the identity of their rivals but successful past bids are published by purchasers and, if this is so, it is possible to use this data to formulate a current bid price.

If the firm has the particular problem of bidding for a number of contracts before the result of any one bid is known, the **production (or supply) capacity may be important**. The firm may need only to win some contracts.

If past bid data is not published, then there is very little data on which to base bid price setting. The firm may have to rely on trade gossip, on conjecture or on an estimate of likely competitors' cost and profit requirements.

If the contract is not awarded purely on price (that is, if the lowest bid is not automatically accepted) **the problem is more acute**. In the case of the supply of branded goods, the relative value of each brand must be considered on a **'value for money'** basis by the purchaser. The bidder may have to rely on subjective 'feel of the market' analysis in arriving at bid prices. There are, of course, numerous instances where cases of actual and attempted bribery of officials have been uncovered as firms employ underhand means in the attempt to win contracts.

1.6.3 Demand

Rather than cost or competition as the prime determinants of price, **a firm may base pricing strategy on the intensity of demand**. Cost and competition factors, of course, remain influences or constraints on its freedom to set price. **A strong demand may lead to a high price, and a weak demand to a low price**.

Whenever there is a single price for a good, some consumers enjoy a **consumer surplus**. This is because of the downward slope of the demand curve. **If prices were to rise, there would be some purchasers who would pay the higher price**. The difference between the market price and the higher price a purchaser is prepared to pay is the consumer surplus. In elasticity terms, the demand of that purchaser is price inelastic. If such consumers can be identified and a higher price charged to them, the supplier obviously benefits. This is called **price discrimination** or **differential pricing**.

In practice, measurement of price elasticity and implementing differential pricing can be very difficult. There are a number of bases on which discriminating prices can be set.

(a)   **By market segment.** A cross-channel ferry company would market its services at different prices in England, Belgium and France, for example. Services such as cinemas and hairdressers are often available at lower prices to old age pensioners and juveniles.

(b)   **By product version.** Many car models have 'add on' extras which enable one brand to appeal to a wider cross-section of customers. Final price need not reflect the cost price of the add on extras directly: usually the top of the range model would carry a price much in excess of the cost of provision of the extras, as a prestige appeal.

(c)   **By place.** Theatre seats are usually sold according to their location so that patrons pay different prices for the same performance according to the seat type they occupy.

(d)   **By time.** This is perhaps **the most popular type of price discrimination**.

  Marketing at Work   Application

Off-peak travel bargains, hotel prices, telephone and electricity charges are all attempts to increase sales revenue by covering variable cost of provision. UK rail operators are successful price discriminators, charging more to rush hour rail commuters whose demand is inelastic at certain times of the day.

Price discrimination can only be effective if a number of conditions hold.

(a)   The market must be **segmentable in price terms**, and different sectors must show different intensities of demand. Each of the sectors must be identifiable, distinct and separate from the others, and be accessible to the firm's marketing communications.

(b)   There must be little or no chance of a **black market** developing so that those in the lower priced segment can resell to those in the higher priced segment.

(c)   There must be little chance that competitors will **undercut** the firm's prices in the higher priced market segments.

(d)   The cost of segmenting and administering the strategy should not exceed the extra revenue derived from it.

The firm could use a **market test** to estimate the effect on demand of a price change. This would involve a change of price in one region, and a comparison of demand with past sales in that region and with sales in similar regions at the old prices. **This is a high risk strategy**: special circumstances may affect the test area (such as a competitor's advertising campaign) which could affect the results. Customers may switch from the test brand if a price rise is being considered and become loyal to a competitive brand; they may not switch back even if the price is subsequently lowered.

Alternately, a **direct attitude survey** may be used with respondents. **Pricing research is notoriously difficult**, especially if respondents try to appear rational to the interviewer or do not wish to offend him or her. **Usually there is a lack of realism in such research**; the respondent is not actually faced with having to pay out hard earned income and therefore may give a hypothetical answer that is not going to be translated into actual purchasing behaviour. Nevertheless, pricing research is increasingly common as firms struggle to assess the perceived value customers attribute to a brand to provide an input to their pricing decisions.

2 Pricing policy Pilot paper, 6/06, 6/07

FAST FORWARD

> **Cost-plus pricing** is widely used because it is fairly easy to do and should lead to profitable prices. It can take account of demand by adjusting the margin added for profit. Competitor action, whether actual or expected, influences real-world price setting, especially under conditions of oligopoly and competitive bidding. Some customers enjoy a **consumer surplus** because they are prepared to pay a higher price. **Differential pricing** enables the supplier to exploit this willingness.

Price sensitivity will vary amongst purchasers. **Those who can pass on the cost of purchases will be least sensitive** and will respond more to other elements of the marketing mix.

(a) Provided that it fits the corporate budget, **the business traveller** will be more concerned about the level of service and quality of food when looking for hotel accommodation than price. In contrast, a family on holiday are likely to be very price sensitive.

(b) In industrial marketing, the **purchasing manager is likely to be more price sensitive than the engineer** who might be the actual user of new equipment that is being sourced. The engineer and purchasing manager are using different criteria in making the choice. The engineer places product characteristics as first priority, the purchasing manager is more price oriented.

2.1 Finding out about price sensitivity

FAST FORWARD

> **Pricing policy** is determined in the light of the customers' sensitivity to price, the objectives and actions of suppliers, competitors and intermediaries and the interplay of forces like inflation and income levels. Price strategies include penetration, skimming, cash recovery and product line promotion.

Research on price sensitivity has had some interesting results.

(a) Customers have a good concept of a 'just price' – **a feel for what is about the right price** to pay for a commodity.

(b) Unless a regular purchase is involved, **customers search for price information before buying**, becoming price aware when wanting to buy but forgetting soon afterwards.

(c) Customers will buy at what they consider to be a bargain price without full regard for need and actual price.

(d) For consumer durables it is the **down payment** and **instalment price** rather than total price which is important to the buyer.

(e) In times of rising prices the **price image tends to lag** behind the current price, which indicates a resentment of the price increase.

2.2 Factors affecting price decisions

2.2.1 Intermediaries' objectives

If an organisation distributes products or services to the market through independent intermediaries, **the objectives of these intermediaries have an effect on the pricing decision**. Such intermediaries are likely to deal with a range of suppliers and **their aims concern their own profits rather than those of suppliers**. Also, the intermediary will take into account the needs of its customers. Thus conflict over price can arise between suppliers and intermediaries which may be difficult to resolve.

Many industries have traditional margins for intermediaries; to deviate from these might cause problems for suppliers. In some industries, notably grocery retailing, the power of intermediaries (the large supermarkets) allows them to dictate terms to suppliers. The relationship between intermediaries and suppliers is therefore complex, and price and the price discount structure is an important element.

2.2.2 Competitors' actions and reactions

An organisation, in setting prices, **sends out signals to rivals. These rivals are likely to react** in some way. In some industries (such as petrol retailing) pricing moves in unison; in others, price changes by one supplier may initiate a price war, with each supplier undercutting the others.

2.2.3 Suppliers

If an organisation's suppliers notice that the prices for an organisation's products are rising, they may seek a rise in the price for their supplies to the organisation, arguing that it is now more able to pay a higher price. This argument is especially likely to be used by the trade unions in the organisation when negotiating the 'price' for the supply for labour.

2.2.4 Inflation

In periods of inflation the organisation's prices may need to change in order to **reflect increases in the prices of supplies**, labour and rent. Such changes may be needed to keep relative (real) prices unchanged (this is the process of prices being adjusted for the rate of inflation).

2.2.5 Quality connotations

In the absence of other information, customers tend to judge quality by price. A price rise may be taken to indicate quality improvements and a reduction may signal reduced quality, perhaps through the use of inferior components. Thus any change in price needs to take such factors into account.

2.2.6 New product pricing

Most pricing decisions for existing products relate to price changes. Such changes have a **reference point** from which to move (the existing price). But **when a new product is introduced for the first time there may be no such reference point**; pricing decisions are most difficult to make in such circumstances. It may be possible to seek alternative reference points, such as the price in another market where the new product has already been launched, or the price set by a competitor.

2.2.7 Income effects

In times of rising incomes, price may become a less important marketing variable than, for instance, product quality or convenience of access. When income levels are falling and/or unemployment levels rising, price will become a much more important marketing variable.

2.2.8 Multiple products

Most organisations market not just one product but a range of products. These products are commonly interrelated, perhaps being complements or substitutes. The management of the pricing function is likely to focus on the profit from the whole range, rather than that on each product. Take, for example, the use of **loss leaders**: a very low price for one product is intended to make consumers buy other products in the range which carry higher profit margins. Another example is selling razors at very low prices whilst selling the blades for them at a higher profit margin. People will buy many of the high profit items but only one of the low profit items – yet they are 'locked in' to the former by the latter. Loss leaders also attract customers into retail stores where they will usually buy normally priced products as well as the loss leaders.

2.2.9 Sensitivity

Price decisions are often seen as highly sensitive and as such may involve top management more clearly than other marketing decisions. As already noted, price has a very obvious and direct relationship with profit.

2.3 Price setting strategies

(a) **Market penetration objective**: here the organisation sets a **relatively low price** for the product or service in order to **stimulate growth of the market and/or to obtain a large share** of it. This strategy was used by Japanese motor cycle manufacturers to enter the UK market. It worked famously: UK productive capacity was virtually eliminated and the imported Japanese machines could then be sold at a much higher price and still dominate the market.

Such sales maximisation is appropriate under three conditions.

(i)   Unit costs will fall with increased output (economies of scale).
(ii)   The market is price sensitive and relatively low prices will attract additional sales.
(iii) Low prices will discourage new competitors.

(b) **Market skimming objective**: Skimming involves **setting a high initial price for a new product in order to take advantage of those buyers who are ready to pay a high price**. A typical strategy would be initially to set a premium price and then gradually to reduce the price to attract more price sensitive segments of the market. This strategy is really an example of price discrimination over time. It may encourage competition, and growth will initially be slow.

This strategy is appropriate under three conditions.

(i)   There is insufficient production capacity and competitors cannot increase capacity.
(ii)   Some buyers are relatively insensitive to high prices.
(iii) High price is perceived as high quality.

(c) **Early cash recovery objective**: an alternative pricing objective is to recover the investment in a new product or service as quickly as possible, to achieve a minimum payback period. The price is set to facilitate this objective. This objective would tend to be used in three circumstances.

(i)   The business is high risk.
(ii)   Rapid changes in fashion or technology are expected.
(iii) The innovator is short of cash.

(d) **Product line promotion objective**: here, management of the pricing function is likely to focus on **profit from the range of products** which the organisation produces **rather than to**

treat each product as a separate entity. The product line promotion objective will look at the whole range from two points of view.

    (i)   The interaction of the marketing mix.

    (ii)   Monitoring returns to ensure that net contribution is worthwhile.

(e)   **Intermediate customers**. Some companies set a price to distributors and allow them to set whatever final price they wish. A variant involves publishing an inflated **recommended retail price** so that retailers can offer large promotional discounts.

(f)   **Cost-plus pricing**. A firm may set its initial price by marking up its unit costs by a certain percentage or fixed amount, as already discussed.

(g)   **Target pricing**. A variant on cost-plus where the company tries to determine the price that gives a specified rate of return for a given output.

(h)   **Price discrimination (or differential pricing)**. The danger is that price cuts to one buyer may be used as a **negotiating lever** by another buyer. This can be countered in three ways.

    (i)   Buyers can be split into clearly defined segments, such as overseas and home.

    (ii)   Own branding, where packaging is changed to that of a supermarket, is a variation on this.

    (iii)   Bulk buying discounts and aggregated rebate schemes can favour large buyers.

(i)   **Going rate pricing**. Try to keep in line with industry norm for prices, as discussed earlier.

(j)   **Quantum price**: in retail selling the concept of a **quantum point** is often referred to. When the price of an item is increased from, say, £9.65 to £9.95, sales may not be affected because the consumers do not notice the price change. However, if the price is increased from £9.95 to £10.05 a major fall in sales may occur, £10 acting as a quantum point which can be approached but not passed if the price is not to deter would be purchasers.

(k)   **Odd number pricing**: sometimes referred to as psychological pricing, the odd number pricing syndrome (pricing at £1.95, say, rather than £2) is said to have originated not as a marketing concept but in department stores in order to ensure the honesty of sales assistants. The customer has to wait for change from £1.95 when, as is usual, they offer £2 in payment, so the assistant has to use the till.

(l)   **One coin purchase**: confectionery firms have used another **psychologically based concept** of a one coin purchase. Rather than change price to reflect cost changes, such firms often alter the quantity in the unit of the product and keep the same price. This is a case of 'price-minus' pricing. The firm determines what the market will bear and works backwards, planning to produce and market a brand which will be profitable to them, selling at the nominated retail price.

(m)   **Gift purchases**: gift purchasing is often founded on the idea of price which is taken to reflect quality. Thus if a gift is to be purchased in an unfamiliar product category, a price level is often fixed by the buyer and a choice made from the brands available at that price. Cosmetics are often priced at £4.99 and £9.99 to appeal to gift purchasers at the £5 and £10 price level. Importantly, **packaging is a major part of the appeal** and must reflect a quality brand image, an important part of the psychology of gift choice.

2.3.1 Product line pricing

When a firm sells a range of related products, or a product line, its theoretical pricing policy should be to set prices for each product in order to maximise the profitability of the line as a whole. A firm may therefore have a **pricing policy for an entire product line**.

(a) There may be a **brand name** which the manufacturer wishes to associate with high quality and high price, or reasonable quality and low price and so forth. All items in the line will be priced accordingly. For example, all major supermarket chains have an own brand label which is used to sell goods at a lower price than the major named brands.

(b) If two or more products in the line are **complementary**, one may be priced as a **loss leader** in order to attract more demand for all of the related products.

(c) If two or more products in the line share joint production costs (**joint products**), prices of the products will be considered as a single decision. For example, if a common production process makes one unit of joint product A for one unit of joint product B, a price for A which achieves a demand of, say, 17,000 units, will be inappropriate if associated with a price for product B which would only sell, say, 10,000 units. 7,000 units of B would be unsold and wasted.

2.3.2 Price changes caused by cost changes in the firm

During the prolonged period of inflation dating back to the 1970s, price increases generated by **increased costs to the manufacturer** were a common experience. The effect of inflation on price decisions was very noticeable and different organisations reacted in different ways.

(a) Some firms raised their prices regularly.

(b) Other firms gave advance warning of price rises, especially in an industrial market. Customers might then be persuaded to buy early in order to avoid paying the higher price at a later date.

(c) A firm which did not raise its prices was reducing its prices in real terms.

2.4 Pricing under oligopoly

As discussed earlier under **oligopoly**, in established industries dominated by a few major firms it is generally accepted that a **price initiative by one firm** will be countered by a **price reaction** by competitors. Here, prices tend to be fairly stable, unless pushed upwards by inflation or strong growth in demand. Consequently, in industries such as breakfast cereals (dominated in Britain by Kellogg's, Nabisco and Quaker) or canned soups (Heinz, Crosse & Blackwell and Campbells) a certain **price stability might be expected** without too many competitive price initiatives, except when cost inflation pushes up the price of one firm's products with other firms soon following.

In the event that a **rival cuts prices** expecting to increase market share, a firm has several options.

(a) It will **maintain its existing prices** if the expectation is that only a small market share will be lost, so that it is more profitable to keep prices at their existing level. Eventually, the rival firm may drop out of the market or be forced to raise its prices.

(b) It may **maintain its prices** but respond with a **non-price counter-attack**. This is a more positive response, because the firm will be securing or justifying its current prices.

(c) It may **reduce its prices**. This should protect the firm's market share at the expense of profitability. The main beneficiary from the price reduction will be the consumer.

(d) It may **raise its prices** and respond with a **non-price counter-attack**. The extra revenue from the higher prices might be used to finance promotion on product changes. A price increase would be based on a campaign to emphasise the quality difference between the firm's own product and the rival's product.

2.4.1 Price leadership

Given that price competition can have disastrous consequences for all suppliers in conditions of oligopoly, it is not unusual to find that large corporations emerge as **price leaders**. A price leader will dominate price levels for a class of products; **increases or decreases by the price leader provide a direction to market price patterns**. The price dominant firm may lead without moving at all. This would be the case if other firms sought to raise prices and the leader did not follow. The price leader generally has a large, if not necessarily the largest, market share. The company will usually be an efficient low-cost producer with a reputation for technical competence.

The role of price leader is based on a track record of having initiated price moves that have been accepted by both competitors and customers. Often, this is associated with a mature well established management group. Any dramatic changes in industry competition, (a new entrant, or changes in the board room) may endanger the price leadership role.

Marketing at Work

Application

The price of a credit card may include an annual fee and an interest rate. The interest rate may be influenced by the actual rate and any period of free credit.

Interest rates vary, and price discrimination is used for different groups of customers.

- Some customers who are low risk can get low rates
- Others are charged high rates

To capture business, card companies offer:

- Interest free or low interest periods
- Free balance transfers
- Reward points

In other words, price is consciously used to attract new customers.

The only major innovation in the 'packaging' of credit cards has been changes in the shape of the card.

---

3 Cost accounting and breakeven analysis   Pilot paper

FAST FORWARD

Pricing decisions should be based on detailed information including knowledge of costs. Cost accountants use two main approaches: **absorption costing** and **direct costing**. Direct costs and **contribution** should always be used for making decisions about prices and assessing profitability. Contribution is also used in **breakeven analysis**. The extent by which budgeted sales exceed the breakeven point is called the **margin of safety**.

We looked briefly at the two main approaches to accounting for costs when we considered cost-plus pricing methods. The approaches are usually known as **absorption costing** and **direct costing**.

3.1 Classification of costs

Key concepts

We may regard costs of production as being divided into two main categories. These are **direct costs** and **overheads**.

Direct costs are also called **variable costs** or, very frequently, **marginal costs**. They are the **costs which can be identified as directly associated with the process of producing an item of a good or service**.

Overheads are incurred whether production takes place or not.

Direct costs include the material which goes into the product, the labour used to produce it and any expenses traceable to it, such as power for the machine which was used to make it. The point about these costs is that **they do not arise until a unit of product is made**. They are called variable costs because they **vary with the volume of production**. Overheads include such items as rent, heat and insurance and will probably be far larger than the direct costs. Cost accounting schemes in large organisations usually only concern themselves with **manufacturing overheads**, marketing and administrative overheads being dealt with separately – though some organisations will absorb them into product cost as well.

Absorption costing calculates a cost for a product **including overheads**. This method is widely used.

(a)   It is **required by law** for valuation of stock in the published accounts of limited companies and plcs.

(b)   It allows a very **simple cost-plus approach to price**. This is frequently used for one-off, special orders. Cost plus pricing should ensure that the company makes a profit.

(c)   It draws management attention to the **control of overheads**.

However, absorption costing has several disadvantages. We need to consider two in the context of pricing.

(a)   The process of **allocating overheads to products is extremely arbitrary**; two cost accountants working separately might arrive at quite different results.

(b)   Since overheads are fixed in the short term, they are **irrelevant for decision making in the short term**; Pricing is a short-term decision.

As a result, the direct cost of a product should be used when making decisions about prices or comparing the financial performance of different products. This requires the use of **contribution**.

Key concept

Contribution is defined as sales value less all variable costs of sale. These will include direct manufacturing costs and any direct selling costs such as a sales promotion or distribution cost per item. 'Contribution' is an abbreviation for **contribution to fixed costs and profit** and is widely used in product management. The **contribution/sales (c/s) ratio** is calculated as contribution divided by selling price. Contribution can be calculated per item or in total.

3.2 Breakeven analysis

Breakeven analysis is a useful application of marginal costing. Before a company starts to make a profit during a trading period, it must first earn **enough contribution to cover its fixed costs**. The volume of sales at which this occurs is known as the **breakeven point** and may be expressed in units or value. At this volume of sales, revenue just covers fixed costs plus variable costs and this implies that **contribution at this point equals fixed costs**. As total contribution equals contribution per unit times number of units sold, **the number of units of sales required to breakeven** is equal to:

$$\frac{\text{Total fixed costs}}{\text{Contribution per unit}}$$

3.3 Example

Expected sales   10,000 units at £8 = £80,000
Variable cost   £5 per unit
Fixed costs   £21,000

Required

Compute the breakeven point.

Solution

The contribution per unit is £(8 – 5)	=	£3
Contribution required to break even	=	fixed costs = £21,000
Breakeven point (BEP)	=	£21,000 ÷ £3 = 7,000 units
In revenue, BEP	=	(7,000 × £8) = £56,000

Sales above £56,000 will result in profit of £3 per unit of additional sales, and sales below £56,000 will mean a loss of £3 per unit for each unit by which sales fall short of 7,000 units. In other words, profit will improve or worsen by the amount of contribution per unit.

	7,000 units	7,001 units
	£	£
Revenue	56,000	56,008
Less variable costs	35,000	35,005
Contribution	21,000	21,003
Less fixed costs	21,000	21,000
Profit	0 (= breakeven)	3

The sales revenue required to break even can be calculated by dividing fixed costs by the c/s ratio.

3.4 Example

In the example in Paragraph 3.3 the C/S ratio is $\dfrac{£3}{£8}$ = 37.5%

Breakeven is where sales revenue = $\dfrac{£21,000}{37.5\%}$ = £56,000

At a price of £8 per unit, this represents 7,000 units of sales.

The contribution/sales ratio is a measure of how much contribution is earned from each £1 of sales. The C/S ratio of 37.5% in the above example means that for every £1 of sales, a contribution of 37.5p is earned. Thus, in order to earn a total contribution of £21,000, and if contribution increases by 37.5p per £1 of sales, sales must be:

$$\frac{£1}{37.5p} \times £21,000 = £56,000$$

An important application of breakeven analysis is the determination of **margin of safety**. This is simply the extent to which budgeted sales exceed break even. Knowledge of the magnitude of the margin of safety enables a reasoned response when sales do not reach budget. A small incursion into the margin of safety can probably be dealt with by a policy of 'wait and see', but if sales fall, more drastic action may be needed. Any adjustment of price will, of course, require a re-computation of the breakeven point and must be made in the light of what is known about price elasticity of demand.

Application

Pricing is often a real headache for marketing managers, and an area where they are least certain that they are doing well. The rewards of a better pricing strategy are an increase in profit without heavy upfront costs. For example, announcing a fall in sales the UK retailer Marks & Spencer indicated that its new product range was well received, but that consumers preferred lower prices.

Some consumers are prepared to pay more if value is added: this is how US retailers have competed effectively against Wal-Mart.

4 Place   6/05, 12/05

FAST FORWARD

Distribution channels provide transport, stockholding and storage, local knowledge, promotion and display. **Direct distribution** occurs when the product goes direct from producer to consumer.

4.1 Distribution channels

Independently owned and operated distributors may well have their own objectives, strategies and plans. In their decision-making processes, these are likely to take precedence over those of the manufacturer or supplier with whom they are dealing. This can lead to conflict. Suppliers may solve the problem by buying their own distribution route or by distributing direct to their customers.

In order for a product to be distributed a number of basic functions usually need to be fulfilled.

Transport	This function may be provided by the supplier, the distributor or may be sub-contracted to a specialist. For some products, such as perishable goods, transport planning is vital.
Stock holding and storage	For production planning purposes, an uninterrupted flow of production is often essential, so stocks of finished goods accumulate and need to be stored, incurring significant costs and risks.
	For consumer goods, holding stock at the point of sale is very costly; the overheads for city centre retail locations are prohibitive. A good stock control system is essential, designed to avoid stockouts whilst keeping stockholding costs low.
Local knowledge	As production has tended to become centralised in pursuit of economies of scale, the need to understand local markets has grown, particularly when international marketing takes place. The intricacies and idiosyncrasies of local markets are key marketing information.
Promotion	Whilst major promotional campaigns for national products are likely to be carried out by the supplier, the translation of the campaign to local level is usually the responsibility of the local distributor, often as a joint venture.
Display	Specialist help from merchandisers can be bought in but presentation decisions on layout and display need to be taken by local distributors, often following patterns produced centrally.

Action Programme 5

Evaluation

For many goods, producers use retailers as middlemen in getting the product to the customer. Try to think of some of the disadvantages of doing this, from the producer's point of view.

4.1.1 Points in the chain of distribution

(a) **Retailers**. These are traders operating outlets which sell directly to households. They may be classified in a number of ways.

    (i) Type of goods sold (eg hardware, furniture)

    (ii) Type of service (self-service, counter service)

    (iii) Size

    (iv) Location (rural, city-centre, suburban shopping mall, out-of-town shopping centre)

    (v) **Independent retailers** (including the local corner shop, although independents are not always as small as this)

    (vi) **Multiple chains**, some of which are associated with one class of product while others are 'variety' chains, holding a wide range of different stocks

    (vii) Still others are **voluntary groups** of independents, usually grocers

(b) **Wholesalers**. These are intermediaries who stock a range of products from competing manufacturers to sell on to other organisations such as retailers. Many wholesalers specialise in particular products. Most deal in consumer goods, but some specialise in industrial goods, such as steel stockholders and builders' merchants.

(c) **Distributors and dealers**. These are organisations which contract to buy a manufacturer's goods and sell them to customers. Their function is similar to that of wholesalers, but they usually offer a narrower product range, sometimes (as in the case of most car dealers) the products of a single manufacturer. In addition to selling on the manufacturer's product, distributors often promote the products and provide after-sales service.

(d) **Agents**. Agents differ from distributors

    (i) Distributors **buy** the manufacturer's goods and **re-sell** them at a profit.

    (ii) Agents do not purchase the manufacturer's goods, but earn a commission on whatever sales they make.

(e) **Franchisees**. These are independent organisations which, in exchange for an initial fee and (usually) a share of sales revenue, are allowed to trade under the name of a parent organisation. Most fast food outlets are franchises. Franchising has become a popular means of growth both for suppliers and for franchisees. The supplier gains additional outlets quickly and exerts more control than is usual in distribution.

(f) **Multiple stores** (eg **supermarkets**) buy goods for retailing direct from the producer, many of them under their 'own label' brand name.

4.2 Types of distribution channel

Choosing distribution channels is important for any organisation, because once a set of channels has been established, subsequent changes are likely to be costly and slow to implement. Distribution channels fall into one of two categories: **direct** and **indirect channels**.

Direct distribution means the product going directly from producer to consumer without the use of a specific intermediary. These methods are often described as **active** since they typically involve the **supplier** making the first approach to a potential customer. Direct distribution methods generally fall into two categories: those using **media** such as the press, leaflets and telephones to invite response and purchase by the consumer and those using a **sales force** to contact consumers face to face.

Indirect distribution is a system of distribution, common among manufactured goods, which makes use of intermediaries; wholesalers, retailers or perhaps both. In contrast to direct distribution, these methods are often thought of as being **passive** in the sense that they rely on consumers to make the first approach by entering the relevant retail outlet.

In building up efficient channels of distribution, a manufacturer must consider several factors.

(a) How many **intermediate stages** should be used and how many dealers at each stage?

(b) What **support** should the manufacturer give to the dealers? It may be necessary to provide an after-sales and repair service, and regular visits to retailers' stores. The manufacturer might need to consider advertising or sales promotion support, including merchandising.

(c) To what extent does the manufacturer wish to **dominate a channel of distribution**? A market leader might wish to ensure that its market share is maintained, so that it could, for example, offer **exclusive distribution contracts** to major retailers.

(d) To what extent does the manufacturer wish to **integrate its marketing effort** up to the point of sale with the consumer? Combined promotions with retailers, for example, would only be possible if the manufacturer dealt directly with the retailer (rather than through a wholesaler).

4.3 Channel design decisions

FAST FORWARD

Channels are designed bearing in mind the characteristics of customers, the product, the available distributors and the methods used by competitors. There are factors encouraging both direct distribution and the use of intermediaries.

In setting up a channel of distribution, the supplier must consider five things.

- Customers
- Product characteristics
- Distributor characteristics
- The channel chosen by competitors
- The supplier's own characteristics

4.3.1 Customers

The number of potential customers, their buying habits and their geographical locations are key influences. The use of mail order for those with limited mobility (rural location, illness) is an example of the influence of customers on channel design. Marketing industrial components to the car industry needs to take account of the geographic distribution of the car industry in the UK. The growth of Internet trading, both in consumer and business to business markets, has been built on the rapid spread of fast Internet access.

4.3.2 Product characteristics

Some product characteristics have an important effect on the design of the channel of distribution.

(a) **Perishability**

Fresh fruit and newspapers must be distributed very quickly or they become worthless. Speed of delivery is therefore a key factor.

(b) **Customisation**

Customised products tend to be distributed direct. When a wide range of options is available, sales may be made using demonstration units, with customised delivery to follow.

(c) **After-sales service/technical advice**

Extent and cost must be carefully considered, staff training given and quality control systems set up. Training programmes are often provided for distributors by suppliers.

4.3.3 Distributor characteristics

The capability of the distributor to take on the distributive functions already discussed above is obviously an important influence on the supplier's choice.

4.3.4 Competitors' channel choice

For many consumer goods, a supplier's brand will sit alongside its competitors' products and there is little the supplier can do about it. For other products, distributors may stock one name brand only (for example, in car distribution) and in return be given an exclusive area. In this case, new suppliers may face difficulties in breaking into a market if all the best distribution outlets have been taken up.

4.3.5 Supplier characteristics

A strong financial base gives the supplier the option of buying and operating their own distribution channel. Boots the Chemist is a prime example. The market position of the supplier is also important: distributors are keen to be associated with the market leader.

4.3.6 Factors favouring the use of direct selling

(a) An expert sales force will be needed to demonstrate products, explain product characteristics and provide after sales service.

(b) Intermediaries may be unwilling or unable to sell the product. For example, the ill-fated Sinclair C5 eventually had to be sold by direct mail.

(c) Existing channels may be linked to other producers, reluctant to carry new product lines.

(d) The intermediaries willing to sell the product may be too costly, or they may not be maximising potential sales.

(e) If specialised transport requirements are involved, intermediaries may not be able to deliver goods to the final customer.

(f) Where potential buyers are geographically concentrated the supplier's own sales force can easily reach them (typically an industrial market). One example is the financial services market centred on the City of London.

4.3.7 Factors favouring the use of intermediaries

(a) There may be insufficient resources to finance a large sales force.

(b) A policy decision to invest in increased productive capacity rather than extra marketing effort may be taken.

(c) The supplier may have insufficient in-house marketing 'know-how' in selling to retail stores.

(d) The assortment of products may be insufficient for a sales force to carry. A wholesaler can complement a limited range and make more efficient use of his sales force.

(e) Intermediaries can market small lots as part of a range of goods. The supplier would incur a heavy sales overhead if its own sales force took small individual orders.

(f) The existence of large numbers of potential buyers spread over a wide geographical area. This is typical of consumer markets.

4.4 Making the channel decision

Producers have a number of decisions to make.

(a)   What types of distributor are to be used (wholesalers, retailers, agents)?

(b)   How many of each type will be used? The answer to this depends on what degree of market exposure will be sought.

    (i)   **Intensive** – blanket coverage
    (ii)   **Exclusive** – appointed agents for exclusive areas
    (iii)   **Selective** – some but not all in each area

(c)   Who will carry out specific marketing tasks?

    (i)   Credit provision
    (ii)   Delivery
    (iii)   After sales service
    (iv)   Sales and product training
    (v)   Display

(d)   How will the performance of distributors be evaluated?

    (i)   In terms of cost?
    (ii)   In terms of sales levels?
    (iii)   According to the degree of control achieved?
    (iv)   By the amount of conflict that arises?

To develop an integrated system of distribution, the supplier must consider all the factors influencing distribution combined with a knowledge of the relative merits of the different types of channel available.

4.5 Multi-channel decisions

A producer serving both industrial and consumer markets may decide to use intermediaries for his consumer division and direct selling for his industrial division. For example, a detergent manufacturer might employ salesmen to sell to wholesalers and large retail groups in their consumer division. It would not be efficient for the sales force to approach small retailers directly. The distribution channels appropriate for industrial markets may not be suitable for consumer markets.

4.6 Industrial and consumer distribution channels

Industrial markets may be characterised as having fewer, larger customers purchasing expensive products which may be custom built. It is due to these characteristics that industrial distribution channels tend to be more direct and shorter than for consumer markets. It has to be remembered, however, that the most appropriate distribution channels will depend specifically on the objectives of the company regarding market exposure. There are specialist distributors in the industrial sector, which may be used as well as, or instead of, selling directly to the companies within this sector.

There are fewer direct distribution channels, from the manufacturer to the consumer in the **consumer market**. Examples may be found in small 'cottage' industries or mail order companies. It is more usual for companies in consumer markets to use wholesalers and retailers to move their product to the final consumer.

(a)   **Wholesalers** break down the bulk from manufacturers and pass products on to retailers. They take on some of the supplier's risks by funding stock. Recently in the UK there has been a reduction in importance of this type of intermediary.

(b)   **Retailers** sell to the final consumers. They may give consumers added benefits by providing services such as credit, delivery and a wide variety of goods. In the UK, retailers

have increased in power whilst wholesalers have declined. Retailing has also become more concentrated with increased dominance of large multiples.

4.7 Distribution strategy

There are three main strategies.

(a)   **Intensive distribution** involves concentrating on a segment of the total market, such as choosing limited geographical distribution rather than national distribution.

(b)   Using **selective distribution**, the producer selects a group of retail outlets from amongst all retail outlets on grounds of the brand image, or related to the retailers' capacity to provide after sales service.

(c)   **Exclusive distribution** is an extension of selective distribution. Particular outlets are granted exclusive handling rights within a prescribed geographical area. Sometimes exclusive distribution, or franchise rights, are coupled with making special financial arrangements for land, buildings or equipment, such as petrol station agreements.

4.8 Channel dynamics

FAST FORWARD

A key factor to consider when discussing distribution channels is the identity of the channel 'captain'. Does the power lie with the supplier, the manufacturer or retailer?

Channels are subject to conflicts between members. This need not be destructive as long as it remains manageable. Manufacturers may have little influence on how their product is presented to the public. Conflicts are usually resolved by arbitration rather than judicial means.

(a)   A distribution system with a central core organising marketing throughout the channel is termed a **vertical marketing system**. Vertical marketing systems provide channel role specification and co-ordination between members.

(b)   In **corporate marketing systems** the stages in production and distribution are owned by a single corporation. This common ownership permits close integration and therefore the corporation controls activities along the distribution chain. For example, Laura Ashley shops sell goods produced in Laura Ashley factories.

(c)   **Contractual marketing systems** involve agreement over aspects of distribution marketing. One example of a contractual marketing system that has become popular over the last decade is franchising.

(d)   If a plan is drawn up between channel members to help reduce conflict this is often termed an **administered marketing system**.

Channel leadership or channel captaincy gives power to the member of the channel with whom it lies. In industrial markets where channel lengths are generally short, power often lies with manufacturers of products rather than 'middlemen'. In consumer markets, power often lies with the retailer because they are fewer and relatively bigger than their suppliers and producers.

Nestlé is the world's biggest food company. According to a spokesperson 'Ten years ago we were in a cockfight with the retailers. But we must not forget that they invested in very, very expensive distribution systems that brought prices down and contributed to our volume growth. So now we want to be a partner, not a supplier.'

There is a widespread view in the markets that branded goods groups, such as Nestlé or its US rivals, will lose in confrontations with large retailers, whether Wal-Mart or European discounters such as Germany's Aldi.

Nestlé accept that concentration in retailing is a fact but argues that relationships with suppliers will not suffer as retailers become bigger. They believe that the growth of such groups such as Wal-Mart, Carrefour or Tesco has helped both sides – as well as consumers – by cutting the complexity of distribution, one of the biggest cost factors in the business.

Exam tip

Distribution is often not represented and easy to ignore, but is key to issues of speed and profitability. Each channel has different needs and requirements. It is likely to be regularly examined, and indeed it appeared on both of the 2005 papers.

Action Programme 6

One of the fastest growing forms of selling in the US over the past decade has been the factory outlet centres. Discount factory shops, often situated on factory premises, from which manufacturers sell off overmakes, slight seconds, or retailers' returns are already well-established in the UK, and in the US developers have grouped such outlets together in purpose-built malls.

What would you suggest are the advantages of this method of distribution for customers and manufacturers?

4.9 International channels   12/05

As markets open to international trade, channel decisions become more complex. A company can export using host country middlemen or domestic middlemen. These may or may not take title to the goods. Implications of channel management in the case of exporters include a loss of control over product policies like price, image, packaging and service. A producer may undertake a joint venture or licensing agreement or even manufacture abroad. All will have implications for the power structure and control over the product.

4.10 Logistics management and Just-in-Time

Key concept

Logistics management involves physical distribution and materials management encompassing the inflow of raw materials and goods and the outflow of finished products.

Logistics management has developed because of an increased awareness of:

(a) customer benefits that can be incorporated into the overall product offering because of efficient logistics management

(b) the cost savings that can be made when a logistics approach is undertaken

(c) trends in industrial purchasing that necessarily mean closer links between buyers and sellers, for example, Just-in-Time purchasing and computerised purchasing.

Logistics managers organise inventories, warehouses, purchasing and packaging. There are benefits to consumers of products that are produced by companies with good logistics management. There is less likelihood of goods being out of stock, delivery should be efficient and overall service quality should be higher.

Marketing at Work   Application

The Internet has greatly facilitated the rise of home shopping. Most grocery firms however use Internet shopping as a supplement to their traditional model.

Perhaps more interesting is the importance of Internet distribution to financial services companies such as banks. Many banks use the Internet as a means to escape the cost of a network of branches.

Research suggests that:

(a)   for transaction processing, Internet banking is an added convenience for customers

(b)   customers prefer face to face contact when they are discussing more complex issues such as mortgages. These are often sold in branches, which, effectively become retail environments.

Chapter Roundup

- **Price** is the only element of the mix which generates revenue rather than creating cost. It must be consistent with the other elements of the marketing mix and is particularly associated with **perceptions of quality**. Economic theory deals with price in terms of market forces; its most useful aspect for the marketer is the idea of **price elasticity of demand**, which measures the extent to which a change in **price** is reflected by a proportionate change in **demand**.

- **Cost-plus pricing** is widely used because it is fairly easy to do and should lead to profitable prices. It can take account of demand by adjusting the margin added for profit. Competitor action, whether actual or expected, influences real-world price setting, especially under conditions of oligopoly and competitive bidding. Some customers enjoy a **consumer surplus** because they are prepared to pay a higher price. **Differential pricing** enables the supplier to exploit this willingness.

- **Pricing policy** is determined in the light of the customers' sensitivity to price, the objectives and actions of suppliers, competitors and intermediaries and the interplay of forces like inflation and income levels. Price strategies include penetration, skimming, cash recovery and product line promotion.

- Pricing decisions should be based on detailed information including knowledge of costs. Cost accountants use two main approaches: **absorption costing** and **direct costing**. Direct costs and **contribution** should always be used for making decisions about prices and assessing profitability. Contribution is also used in **breakeven analysis**. The extent by which budgeted sales exceed the breakeven point is called the **margin of safety**.

- **Distribution channels** provide transport, stockholding and storage, local knowledge, promotion and display. **Direct distribution** occurs when the product goes direct from producer to consumer.

- **Channels are designed** bearing in mind the characteristics of customers, the product, the available distributors and the methods used by competitors. There are factors encouraging both direct distribution and the use of intermediaries.

- A key factor to consider when discussing distribution channels is the identity of the channel 'captain'. Does the power lie with the supplier, the manufacturer or retailer?

Quick Quiz

1   What is price elasticity of demand?

2   How does a seller exploit consumer surplus?

3   What is the difference between market penetration and market skimming?

4   What is price leadership?

5   What is the formula for breakeven point in units?

6   How is the C/S ratio used to calculate breakeven point?

7   Differentiate between wholesalers, distributors and agents.

8   How do product characteristics influence distribution?

Answers to Quick Quiz

1   A measure of the extent of change in demand for a good when its price changes.

2   By identifying the consumers who would be prepared to pay a higher price and charging them more: price discrimination.

3   Market penetration aims for high turnover in units early on in a product's life by charging a low price. Market skimming charges a high initial price to exploit the customers who are prepared to pay it, thus achieving maximum positive cash flow while volumes are still low.

4   Under oligopoly, a price leader (usually the largest producer) gives a lead in price movements.

5   $$\frac{\text{Total fixed costs}}{\text{contribution per unit}}$$

6   Sales revenue required to breakeven equals:

$$\frac{\text{Total fixed costs}}{\text{c/s ratio}}$$

7   Wholesalers stock a wide range of goods, often from competing manufacturers, while distributors deal in the goods of a small number of non-competing manufacturers. Agents, unlike both wholesalers and distributors, do not buy the manufacturers goods: they sell them for commission.

8   Perishables must be distributed rapidly; customised units are normally distributed direct; where extensive after-sales service is required, distributors must be properly trained.

Action Programme Review

1   You might have identified a number of different factors here. Perhaps the most important general point to make is that price is particularly important if the other elements in the marketing mix are relatively similar across a range of competing products. For example, there is a very wide variety of toothpastes on the market, most of them not much differentiated from the others. The price of a particular toothpaste may be a crucial factor in its sales success.

2   Monthly demand at £1.40 per unit = 220,000 units.

Monthly demand at £1.60 per unit = 200,000 units.

% change in demand $\dfrac{20,000}{220,000} \times 100\% = 9.09\%$

% change in price $\dfrac{20}{140} \times 100\% = 14.29\%$

Price elasticity of demand = $\dfrac{-9.09}{14.29} = -0.64$

Demand is inelastic at a price of £1.40 per unit, because the price elasticity of demand (ignoring the minus sign) is less than 1.

3   The main problem is that, unless very detailed research has been carried out, the price elasticity of a particular product or service is likely to be unknown. As a theoretical concept, it is useful in gaining an understanding of the effects of price changes; but it is of little use as a practical tool in determining prices.

4   The industry referred to is the financial services industry. When economic factors cause alterations in interest rates (one of the main 'costs' borne by building societies and banks, because of their interest payments to investors), the societies reduce or increase their lending rates (for example, the price of their mortgage products). It is usual to see one of the larger societies leading the way, after which the others fall into line.

5   Your answers might include some of the following points.

   (a)   The middleman's margin reduces the revenue available to the producer.

   (b)   The producer needs an infrastructure for looking after the retailers – keeping them informed, keeping them well stocked – which might not be necessary in, say, a mail order business.

   (c)   The producer loses some control over the marketing of the product. The power of some retailers (for example, W H Smith in the world of book publishing) is so great that they are able to dictate marketing policy to their suppliers.

6   Prices are up to 50% below conventional retail outlets and shoppers can choose from a wide range of branded goods that they otherwise might not be able to afford. They can also turn a shopping trip into a day out, as factory outlet centres are designed as 'destination' shopping venues, offering facilities such as playgrounds and restaurants.

Manufacturers enjoy the ability to sell surplus stock at a profit in a controlled way that does not damage the brand image. They have also turned the shops into a powerful marketing tool for test-marketing products before their high street launch, and selling avant-garde designs that have not caught on in the main retail market.

Now try Questions 9 and 10 at the end of the Study Text

Services marketing

Syllabus content – knowledge and skills requirements

- 3.11: The importance of customer relationships to the organisation and how they can be developed and supported by the marketing mix
- 3.12: How a plan is developed for the human element of the service encounter, including staff at different levels in the organisation
- 3.13: How the physical evidence element of the integrated marketing mix is developed
- 3.14: How a plan covering the process or systems of delivery for a service is developed
- 4.3: How marketing plans and activities vary in organisations that operate in a virtual marketplace and develop an appropriate marketing mix
- 4.4: An effective extended marketing mix in relation to design and delivery of service encounters (SERVQUAL)

Introduction

Element 3 of your syllabus (which constitutes 50% of it) is entitled 'The extended marketing mix and related tools'. This choice of phrase indicates the importance of services marketing.

We commence our consideration of services marketing with the basics: what services are, why they are important and what is special about services marketing. These topics are covered in Sections 1 and 2.

Section 3 explains services marketing in terms of the 7Ps of the extended marketing mix, the new elements being people, process and physical evidence. Of these, people are critical to the success of the services organisation and Section 4 emphasises this.

Measuring and controlling quality in service encounters is far more difficult than with a tangible product. Models of service quality are dealt with in Section 5.

Section 6 moves on from services marketing to the connected topic of the organisation's general relationship with the customer (and other stakeholders), and the concept of relationship marketing.

The virtual marketplace is a recent and important economic development. Of course, products are marketed through such marketplaces just as much as services, but the inherent nature of direct and Internet marketing means that if is appropriate to cover these topics in this chapter. They are dealt with in Sections 7 and 8.

1 Services marketing 6/04, 12/04

FAST FORWARD

The extension of the service sector, and the application of market principles across many public sector and ex-public sector organisations, has made a large number of service providers much more marketing-conscious. **Services marketing** differs from the marketing of other goods in a number of crucial ways, and five specific characteristics of services marketing have been proposed.

Exam tip

Services are an important area of the British economy and account for more employment than the manufacturing sector. They will feature regularly on exam papers.

There are a number of reasons why services marketing is more important today than in the past. These include the following.

(a) **The growth of service sectors in advanced industrial societies**. More people now work in the service sector than in all other sectors of the economy and the major contributors to national output are the public and private service sectors. Invisible earnings from abroad are of increasing significance for Britain's balance of trade. In fact about 80% of the UK's economy is made up of services of one kind or another.

(b) **An increasingly market-oriented trend within service-providing organisation**. This has been particularly apparent within the public sector with the advent of internal markets, market testing and the chartermark.

The public sector in Britain includes service provision in the legal, medical, educational, military, employment, transportation, leisure and information fields. Increasingly, there is a focus on profits in many of these areas. The private sector embraces not-for-profit areas such as the arts, charities and religious and educational organisations and includes business and professional services in travel, finance, insurance, management, the law, building, commerce and entertainment.

Key concepts

> **Services: some definitions**
>
> (a) ' ... those separately identifiable but intangible activities that provide want-satisfaction, and that are not, of necessity, tied to, or inextricable from, the sale of a product or another service.'
>
> *Cowell* (1995)
>
> (b) ' ... any activity of benefit that one party can offer to another that is essentially intangible and does not result in the ownership of anything. Its production may or may not be tied to a physical product.'
>
> *Kotler* (2002)

The marketing of services faces a number of distinct problems, and as a consequence, the approach adopted must be varied, and particular marketing practices developed.

2 Characteristics of services marketing

Characteristics of services which make them distinct from the approach to the marketing of goods have been proposed. These are five major differences.

- Intangibility
- Inseparability
- Heterogeneity
- Perishability
- Ownership

2.1 Intangibility

Intangibility is the lack of physical substance in service delivery. Clearly, this creates difficulties and can inhibit the propensity to consume a service, since customers are not sure what they have.

We can view insubstantiality as a continuum, as shown in the diagram below.

The Goods - Services Continuum

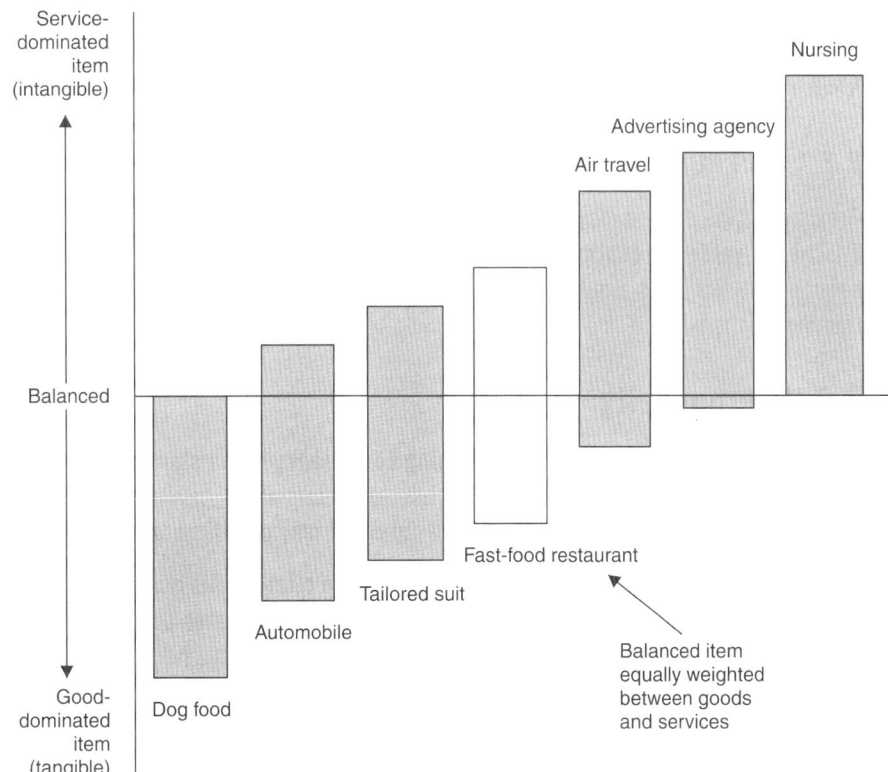

Clearly, for each service, the number, complexity and balance of the various elements involved will vary a great deal. What is experienced remains insubstantial, although many parts of the process (the machines, buildings and staff of an airline, for instance) are very substantial.

The consumer needs **information** to form some grounds for **judgement**, and to cut down **risk**. The marketer wishes to make the choice of the product safer and make consumers feel more comfortable about paying for something that has no physical form.

The intangibility may be countered in two ways.

- By the consumer **seeking opinions** from other consumers
- By the marketer offering the consumer **something tangible** to represent the purchase

2.1.1 Marketing implications

Dealing with the problems may involve strategies to **enhance tangibility**.

(a) **Increasing the level of tangibility**. When dealing with the customer, staff can use physical representations or illustrations to make the customer feel more confident as to what it is that the service is delivering.

(b) **Focusing the attention of the customer on the principal benefits of consumption.** This could take the form of communicating the benefits of purchasing the service so that the customer visualises its appropriateness. Promotion and sales material could provide images or records of previous customers' experience.

(c) **Differentiating the service and reputation-building**. This is achieved by enhancing perceptions of service and value through offering excellence in the delivery of the service and by promoting values of quality, service reliability and value for money. These must be attached as **values** to brands, which must then be managed to secure and enhance their market position.

2.2 Inseparability

A service often cannot be separated from the provider of the service. The **performance of a service often occurs at the same instant as its consumption**. Think of having dental treatment or going on a journey. Neither exists until actually consumed by the purchaser.

2.2.1 Marketing implications

Provision of the service may not be separable from the provider. Consequently, increasing importance is attached to **values of quality and reliability** and a customer service ethic which can be transferred to the service provision. This emphasises the need for customer orientation, high quality people and high quality training for them.

2.3 Heterogeneity

Many services face a problem of **maintaining consistency in the standard of output**. Variability of quality in delivery is inevitable, because of the number of factors which may influence it. This may create problems of operations management. For example, it may be difficult or impossible to attain:

(a) **Precise standardisation of the service offered**. The quality of the service may depend heavily on who delivers the service and when it takes place. Booking a holiday may well be quite different on a quiet winter afternoon than on a hectic spring weekend, and will vary according to the staff member dealing with the client.

(b) **Influence or control over perceptions of what is good or bad customer service**. From the customer's perspective, it is very difficult to obtain an idea of the quality of service in advance of purchase.

As a result, it is necessary to monitor customer reactions constantly and to maintain an attitude and organisational culture which emphasises three things.

- Consistency of quality control
- Consistency of customer service
- Effective staff selection, training and motivation

2.3.1 Other important matters

(a) Clear and objective quality measures

(b) Standardising as much as possible within the service

(c) The **Pareto principle** (80 percent of difficulties arise from 20 percent of events surrounding the provision of the service). Therefore, identify and respond most closely to these potential troublespots.

2.4 Perishability

Services cannot be stored. They are innately **perishable**. Performances at a theatre or the services of a chiropodist consist in their availability for periods of time, and if they are not occupied, the service they offer cannot be used later.

This presents specific marketing problems. **Meeting customer needs in these operations depends on staff being available when they are needed**. This must be balanced against the need to minimise unnecessary expenditure on staff wages. Anticipating and responding to levels of demand is, therefore, a key planning priority. There are two risks.

- Low level of demand will be accompanied by substantial fixed cost
- Excess demand may result in lost custom through inadequate service provision.

Policies must seek to match demand with supply by price variations and promotions to stimulate off-peak demand.

2.5 Ownership

Services do not result in the transfer of property. In the case of purchasing a product, there is permanent transfer of title and control over the use of an item. An item of service provision is often defined by the length of time it is available.

This may very well lessen the perceived customer value of a service, and consequently make for unfavourable comparisons with **tangible** alternatives. Attempts have been made to overcome this problem by providing **symbolic** tangible items which can be taken away and kept. Car brochures, theatre programmes and the plethora of corporate giftwares such as golf umbrellas, pens and keyrings, are all examples of this.

Action Programme 1   Application

What are the marketing implications of the lack of ownership of a service received?

3 The extended marketing mix for services

> An extended marketing mix has been suggested for services marketing. Booms and Bitner suggested an additional 3 Ps. Here, we have taken an approach which analyses an additional **4 Ps**.

The standard 4 P approach to the marketing of products should be extended for services by the addition of **three more Ps**.

- People
- Process
- Physical evidence or ambience

Services are provided by **people** for people. If the people providing the service are not up to standard, the service is spoiled. In the case of a bus service, a cheap fare, a clean vehicle and a frequent service can be spoiled by a surly driver.

Services are usually provided in a number of sequential steps. This is **process. The service can be spoiled or enhanced at any step in the sequence.**

Finally, there is the **physical evidence** or **ambience**. The latter can be a maker or spoiler of experience of the service, but note that an important aspect of physical evidence is the provision of a physical token of the service provided, such as a brochure or other documentation, to overcome in part the absence of tangibility.

An alternative approach identifies four extra Ps.

- Personal selling ⎫
- Place of availability ⎬ the 'process'
                     ⎭
- People and customer service
- Physical evidence

3.1 Personal selling

Personal selling is very important in the marketing of services, because of the **greater perceived risk** involved and greater uncertainty about quality and reliability. The reputation of the supplier may be of greater importance, and the customer places greater reliance on the honesty of the individual salesperson. When consumers seek reassurance, personal contact with a competent, effective representative may provide the necessary confidence. Conversely, inappropriate selling may generate increased anxiety.

3.2 Place of availability

Place of availability is really covered by the distribution system, but there are special problems for services in **operations management**. The place and frequency of availability are key service variables but service resources must be used economically.

The level and quality of service are sensitive to the **efficiency of the processes** by which services are delivered. There are three key factors.

(a) **Capacity utilisation**: matching demand sequences to staff utilisation to avoid both the costs of overstaffing and the lost revenue of underprovision

(b) **Managing customer contact** to avoid crowding and customer disruption, meet needs as they arise, and increase employee control over interactions

(c) **Establishing objectives within the not-for-profit sector**, for example, standards for teachers or medical staff

Interactions **between customers** are a key strategic issue. Customers often interact to gather information and form views about the service they are contemplating purchasing. Minimising exposure to negative feedback, and promoting the dissemination of positive messages about the service are important objectives.

3.3 People and customer service

For some services, the **physical presence of people performing the service is a vital aspect of customer satisfaction**. For example, staff in catering establishments are performing or producing a service, selling the service and liaising with the customer to promote the service, gathering information and responding to customer needs.

Customers will tend to use cues to establish a view about the organisation from the demeanour and behaviour of staff. The higher the level of customer contact involved in the delivery of a service, the more crucial is the staff role in adding value. In many cases, the delivery of the service and the physical presence of the personnel involved are completely inseparable. **Technical competence and skill in handling people are of equal importance** in effective delivery of the service.

Action Programme 2   Application

All levels of staff must be involved in customer service. To achieve this end, it is vital for senior management to promote the importance of customer service. How do you think that this might be achieved?

3.4 Physical evidence

Physical evidence is an important remedy for the intangibility of the product. This may be a physical item **associated with the service itself**, (for example, credit cards which represent the service available to customers); **built up by identification with a specific individual** (a 'listening' bank manager); or **incorporated into the design and specification of the service environment,** involving the building, location or atmosphere.

Action Programme 3   Application

What do you think that design can achieve in services marketing?

4 The importance of people

As a consequence of the importance of **people**, service marketing organisations have certain common areas of emphasis.

(a)   **Selection** and **training**: staff with an aptitude for delivering service to a high standard should be selected and all staff should receive thorough ongoing training. All training should emphasise the importance to the customer of satisfactory service and, by implication, its importance to the success of the service organisation.

(b)   Internal marketing to promote the **culture of service** within the firm

(c)   Ensuring conformance with **standards**

      (i)   Behaviour
      (ii)   Dress and appearance
      (iii)   Procedures
      (iv)   Modes of dealing with the public

(d)   **Automating** procedures where possible

(e)   Constantly **auditing** staff performance and behaviour

(f)   **Extending the promotion** of the service and its qualities into the design of service environments, and the engineering of interactions between staff and customers and among the customers themselves.

Action Programme 4

Application

The role of people in services marketing is especially important. What human characteristics improve the quality of client service?

5 Service quality   Pilot paper, 12/04, 6/05, 12/05, 6/07

FAST FORWARD

> **Service quality** can be defined as the difference between what customers expect and what they perceive themselves to be receiving. Improved service quality leads to higher profits and is a key task for service marketers.

Service quality is a significant basis which customers use for differentiating between competing services. Second only to market share in the PIMS research, relative quality is a key contributor to **bottom line profit performance**.

Quality can only be defined by customers. It occurs where a firm supplies products to a specification that satisfies their needs. Customer expectations serve as standards against which subsequent service experiences are compared. When service performance falls short of customer expectations, dissatisfaction occurs.

There are two ways firms can gain from improving their quality of service.

(a)   **Higher sales revenues** and improved marketing effectiveness brought about by improved customer retention, positive word-of-mouth recommendations and the ability to increase prices.

(b)   **Improved productivity and reduced costs** because there is less rework, higher employee morale and lower employee turnover.

Grönroos (1984) introduced the concept of 'perceived service quality' in 1982 and extended this in the development of his widely cited **model of service quality**.

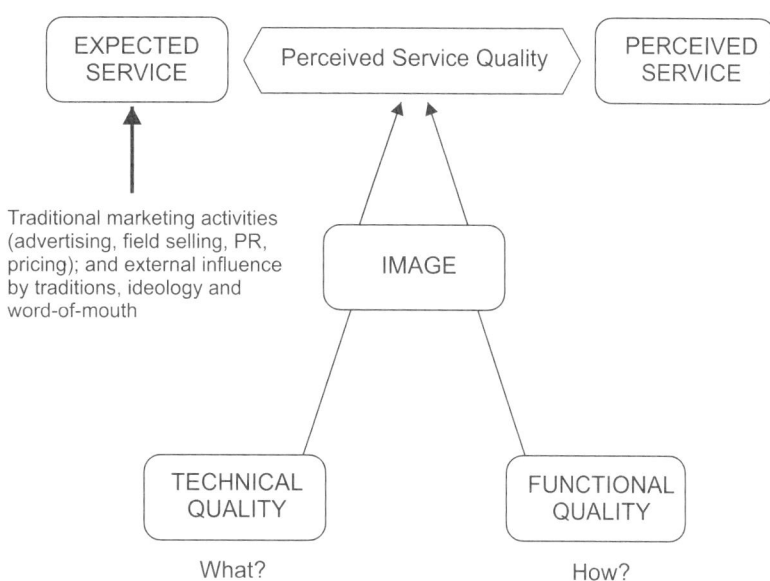

Grönroos Service Quality Model

The model suggests that the quality of a given service is the outcome of an evaluation process where **consumers compare what they expected to receive with what they perceive that they actually received**. Consumer expectations are influenced by marketing mix activities, external traditions, ideology and word-of-mouth communications. Grönroos also suggests previous experience with the service will influence expectations.

In terms of perceived service quality, Grönroos suggests there are two principal components of quality, **technical** and **functional**, with a third, **image**, acting as a mediating influence.

(a)   **Technical quality** is what the customer is left with, when the production process is finished. For example, in higher education this would be perceived as the level of attainment and understanding achieved at the end of the course. This can be much more easily measured by the consumer.

(b)   **Functional quality**, on the other hand, is more difficult to measure objectively because it involves an evaluation of **how the consumer receives the technical quality** in the interactions between customer and service provider and other customers. Grönroos' suggestion that **service quality is dependent both on what you receive and how you receive it** emphasises the importance of service interactions, contact employees and managing the service experience.

(c)   **Image**. Grönroos also suggests that both expectations and perceptions are affected by the consumer's view of the company and by its image. If a consumer has a **positive image** of a university or lecturer but has a negative experience, for example a rather confused lecture, the consumer may still **perceive** the service to be satisfactory because he or she will find excuses for the negative experience. Correspondingly, Grönroos suggests that a **negative image** may increase perceived problems with service quality.

5.1 Quality gaps

Zeithaml, Parasuraman and Berry (1990) developed the most widely applied model of service quality in 1985. The researchers developed their model via interviews with fourteen executives in four service businesses and twelve customer focus groups. The executive interviews resulted in the idea of **five gaps** which are potential hurdles for a firm in attempting to deliver high quality service.

```
                        ┌─────────────────────────┐
                        │      Expectations       │
                        └─────────────────────────┘
              Gap 5                   ↕
                        ┌─────────────────────────┐
                        │      Perceptions        │
   The Customer         └─────────────────────────┘

   ═══════════════════════════════════════════════════════════
   Gap 1

   The Firm       ┌──────────────────────┐      ┌──────────────────────────┐
                  │   Service delivery   │ ←──→ │  External communications │
                  └──────────────────────┘      └──────────────────────────┘
              Gap 3            ↕              Gap 4
                  ┌──────────────────────────┐
                  │ Service quality specifications │
                  └──────────────────────────┘
              Gap 2            ↕
                  ┌──────────────────────────┐
                  │  Management perceptions  │
                  └──────────────────────────┘
```

Gap 1   **Customer expectations and management perceptions gap**

Essentially managers may not know what features connote high quality, what features a service must have or what levels of performance are required by customers.

Gap 2   **Management perceptions and service quality specification gap**

Resource constraints, market conditions and/or management indifference may result in this gap.

Gap 3   **Service quality specifications and service delivery gap**

Guidelines may exist but contract employees may not be willing or able to perform to the specified standards.

Gap 4   **Service delivery and external communications gap**

Exaggerated promises or lack of information will affect both expectations and perceptions.

Gap 5   **Expected service and perceived service gap**

This gap was defined as service quality. The authors argue that Gap 5 five is influenced by the preceding four gaps, so if management want to close the gap between performance and expectations it becomes imperative to design procedures for measuring service performance against expectations.

In 1988, the researchers developed the **SERVQUAL** questionnaire which purports to be a global measure of Gap 5 across all service organisations. This measures the five generic criteria that consumers use in evaluating service quality.

---

1   **Tangibles**: physical facilities, equipment, appearance of personnel
2   **Reliability**: ability to perform the promised service dependably and accurately
3   **Responsiveness**: willingness to help customers and provide prompt service
4   **Assurance**: knowledge and courtesy of employees and their ability to convey trust and confidence
5   **Empathy**: caring, individualised attention

Respondents are asked first to give their expectations of the service on a seven point scale, then to give their evaluation of the actual service on the same scale. Service quality is then calculated as the difference between perception and expectations, weighted for the importance of each item.

Exam tip

'SERVQUAL' is specifically referred to in the syllabus.

Once a firm knows how it is performing on each of the dimensions of service quality it can use a number of methods to try to improve its quality.

(a) Development of a customer orientated **mission statement** and clear senior **management support** for quality improvement initiatives

(b) Regular **customer satisfaction research** including customer surveys and panels, mystery shoppers, analysis of complaints and similar industry studies for benchmarking purposes

(c) Setting and **monitoring standards** and communicating results

(d) Establishment of systems for customer **complaints and feedback**

(e) Encouragement of **employee participation**, ideas and initiative, often through the use of quality circles and project teams

(f) **Rewarding** excellent service

Action Programme 5

Application

What evidence do you see of firms implementing quality programmes and continually improving service quality? How does your company, or one you have worked for in the past, measure service quality?

Exam tip

There is a 10-mark question on the Pilot paper on perceptions of service quality. A question on the June 2007 paper linked service improvements to staff training and a recognition of the importance of customer relationships.

6 Customers and other stakeholders

FAST FORWARD

Customers are stakeholders. This means that they should be valued and not taken for granted. They differ in their characteristics and can be analysed or segmented to increase profitability.

6.1 Stakeholders

Key concept

Stakeholders: groups or individuals whose interests are directly affected by the activities of a firm or organisation. The stakeholder concept suggests a wider concern than the traditional marketing approach of supplying goods and services which satisfy immediate customer needs.

Here are the main stakeholder groups.

Stakeholder group	Members
Internal stakeholders	Employees, management
Connected	Shareholders, customers, suppliers, lenders
External	The government, local government, the public

Stakeholder groups can exert influence on strategy. The greater the power of a stakeholder group, the greater that influence will be. Each stakeholder group has different expectations about what it wants, and the expectations of the various groups will conflict. It is important to realise that satisfying customers cannot be achieved in isolation from other objectives.

6.2 Stakeholders' objectives

Here is a broad checklist of stakeholders' objectives.

(a) **Employees and managers**

    (i)   Job security (over and above legal protection
    (ii)   Good conditions of work (above minimum safety standards)
    (iii) Job satisfaction
    (iv) Career development and relevant training

(b) **Customers**

    (i)   Satisfaction of expectations
    (ii)   After sales service
    (iii) Consistent quality

(c) **Suppliers**: to be offered regular orders in return for reliable delivery and good service

(d) **Shareholders**: to provide an appropriate return

(e) **Society as a whole**

    (i)   Control pollution
    (ii)   Financial assistance to charities, sports and community activities
    (iii) Co-operate with the government in minimizing health risks in the product

The customer is central to the marketing orientation, but so far we have not considered this important concept in detail. Customers make up one of the groups of **stakeholders** whose interests management should address. The supplier-customer relationship extends beyond the basic transaction. The customer needs to **remain** satisfied with his purchase and positive about his supplier long after the transaction has taken place. If his satisfaction is muted or grudging, future purchases may be reluctant or non-existent and he may advise others of his discontent.

Not all customers are the same. Some appear for a single cash transaction and are never seen again. Others make frequent, regular purchases in large volumes, using credit facilities and building up a major relationship. Yet another type of customer purchases infrequently but in transactions of high value. This variation will exist to a greater or lesser extent in all industries, though each will have a smaller typical range of behaviour. However, even within a single business, customers will vary significantly in the frequency and volume of their purchases, their reasons for buying, their sensitivity to price changes, their reaction to promotion and their overall attitude to the supplier and the product. **Segmentation** of the customer base can have a major impact on profitability, perhaps by simply tailoring promotion to suit the most attractive group of customers.

Many businesses sell to intermediaries rather than to the end consumer. Some sell to both categories; they have to recognise that **the intermediary is just as much a customer as the eventual consumer**. Examples are manufacturers who maintain their own sales organisation but appoint agents in geographically remote areas and companies who combine autonomous operations with franchising. While it is reasonable to give the highest priority to the needs of the ultimate consumer and insist on some control over the activities of the intermediary, it must be recognised that he will only perform well if his own needs are addressed. For instance, a selling agent who has invested heavily in stock after being given exclusive rights in an area should be consulted before further demands are made on his cash flow by the launch of a new product.

6.3 Customer retention

Customer retention is an important contribution to profitability since each customer can represent a lifetime's cash flow and creating a new customer requires far more promotional and administrative effort than retaining an existing one. The vital factor in customer retention is the skill and approach of the front-line staff.

Variation in customer behaviour was mentioned above. The most important aspect of this variation is whether or not the customer comes back for more. Customers should be seen as potentially providing a lifetime of purchases so that **the turnover from a single individual over time might be very large indeed**. It is widely accepted that there is a non-linear relationship between customer retention and profitability in that **a fairly small amount of repeat purchasing generates significant profit**. This is because it is far more expensive in promotion and overhead costs to convert a non-buyer into an occasional buyer than to turn an occasional buyer into a frequent buyer. The repeat buyer does not have to be persuaded to give the product a try or be tempted by special deals; he needs less attention from sales staff and already has his credit account set up. New customers usually have to be won from competitors.

Today's highly competitive business environment means that customers are only retained if they are **very satisfied** with their purchasing experience. **Any lesser degree of satisfaction is likely to result in the loss of the customer**. Companies must be active in monitoring customer satisfaction **because very few will actually complain. They will simply depart.** Businesses which use intermediaries must be particularly active, since research shows that even when complaints are made, the principals hear about only a very small proportion of them.

The most satisfactory way to retain customers is to offer them products which they perceive as providing superior benefits at any given price point. However, there are specific techniques which can increase customer retention.

Marketing at Work   Application

Loyalty schemes such as frequent flyer programmes augment the product in the customer's eyes. The club concept, as used by Sainsbury and Tesco, offers small discounts on repeated purchases. The principal benefit of both these types of scheme, however, is the enhanced knowledge of the customer which they provide. Initial registration provides name, address and post code. Subsequent use of the loyalty card allows a detailed purchasing profile to be built up for individual customers. This enables highly targeted promotion and cross-selling later.

Research indicates that **the single largest reason why customers abandon a supplier is poor performance by front-line staff**. Any scheme for customer retention must address the need for careful selection and training of these staff. It is also a vital factor in **relationship marketing**.

6.4 Relationship marketing   12/03

Relationship marketing is more than customer retention. It is the fostering of a mutually beneficial relationship by precision in meeting the needs of individual customers. It uses powerful computer database systems.

Key concept

> **Relationship marketing** is defined very simply by Grönroos as the management of a firm's market relationships.

Application

Much has been written in recent years on relationship marketing.

Gummesson suggests it is a 'paradigm shift' requiring a dramatic change in marketing thinking and behaviour, not an add-on to traditional marketing.' In his book *Total Relationship Marketing*, he suggests that the core of marketing should no longer be the 4Ps, but 30Rs, which reflect the large number of complex relationships involved in business.

Kotler (1991) says 'marketing can make promises but only the whole organisation can deliver satisfaction'.

Adcock (2000) expands on this by remarking that relationship marketing can only exist when the marketing function fosters a customer-oriented service culture which supports the network of activities that deliver value to the customer. The metaphor of marriage has been used to describe relationship marketing, emphasising the nature of the necessary long term commitment and mutual respect.

Relationship marketing is thus as much about attitudes and assumptions as it is about techniques. The marketing function's task is to inculcate habits of behaviour at all levels and in all departments which will enhance and strengthen the alliance. It must be remembered, however, that the effort involved in long-term relationship building is more appropriate in some markets than in others. Where customers are purchasing intermittently and switching costs are low, there is always a chance of business. This tends to be the pattern in commodity markets. Here, it is reasonable to take a **transactions approach** to marketing and treat each sale as unique. A **relationship marketing approach** is more appropriate where switching costs are high and a lost customer is thus probably lost for a long time. Switching costs are raised by such factors as the need for training on systems and high capital cost.

The conceptual or philosophic nature of relationship marketing leads to a simple principle, that of **enhancing satisfaction by precision in meeting the needs of individual customers**. This depends on extensive two-way communication to establish and record the customer's characteristics and preferences and build a long-term relationship. There are three important practical methods which contribute to this end.

- Building a customer database
- Developing customer-oriented service systems
- Extra direct contacts with customers

Modern **computer database systems** have enabled the rapid acquisition and retrieval of the individual customer's details, needs and preferences. Using this technology, relationship marketing enables telephone sales staff to greet the customer by name, know what he purchased last time, avoid taking his full delivery address, know what his credit status is and what he is likely to want. It enables new products to be developed that are precisely tailored to the customer's needs and new procedures to be established which enhance his satisfaction. It is the successor to **mass marketing**, which attempted to be customer-led but which could only supply a one-size-fits-all product. The end result of a relationship marketing approach is a mutually satisfactory relationship which continues indefinitely.

Relationship marketing extends the principles of **customer care**. Customer care is about providing a product which is augmented by high quality of service, so that the customer is impressed during his transaction with the company. This can be done in ignorance of any details of the customer, other than those implicit in the immediate transaction. The customer is anonymous. **Relationship marketing is about having the customer come back for further transactions**. The culture must be right; the right people must be recruited and trained; the structure, technology and processes must all be in place.

It is inevitable that **problems** will arise. A positive way of dealing with errors must be designed into the customer relationship. Front line sales people cannot usually deal with the causes of mistakes as they **are built into the products, systems and organisation structure**. It is therefore necessary for management to promote vertical and horizontal interaction in order to spur changes to eliminate the **sources** of mistakes.

It is inevitable that there will be multiple contacts between customer and supplier organisations. Each contact is an opportunity to enhance or to prejudice the relationship, so staff throughout the supplier organisation must be aware of their marketing responsibilities. Two way communication should be encouraged so that the relationship can grow and deepen. There is a link here to the database mentioned above: extra contacts provide more information.

6.4.1 Differences between transactional and relationship marketing

Transactional	Relationship
Importance of single sale	Importance of customer relation
Importance of product features	Importance of customer benefits
Short time scale	Longer time scale
Less emphasis on service	High customer service
Quality is concern of production	Quality is concern of all
Competitive commitment	High customer commitment
Persuasive communication	Regular communication

6.4.2 The relationship marketing mix

By now you are familiar with the 4Ps of the basic marketing mix. Relationship marketing is highly dependent upon a fifth P: **people**. The features of the basic 4Ps must support the commitment to developing mutually beneficial customer relationships. The **behaviour of the people** involved in the customer relationship is even more important, because relationship marketing success depends on their motivation to achieve it. In turn, that motivation depends to a great extent upon the leadership exercised by marketing managers. It is not enough to expect self-motivation because all staff are involved, not just those with a sales role.

6.5 Key accounts

FAST FORWARD

Customers can be analysed for their value to the business. **Key account management** allows the most valuable customers to be given an enhanced service.

So far we have considered the retention of customers as an unquestionably desirable objective. **However, for many businesses a degree of discretion will be advisable**. 'Key' does not mean large. A customer's **potential** is very important. The definition of a key account depends on the circumstances.

Customers can be assessed for desirability according to the following criteria.

- The profitability of their accounts
- The prestige they confer
- The amount of non-value adding administrative work they generate
- The cost of the selling effort they absorb
- The rate of growth of their accounts
- The turnover of their own businesses
- Their willingness to adopt new products
- Their credit history.

Such analyses will almost certainly conform to a Pareto distribution and show, for instance that 80% of profit comes from 20% of the customers, while a different 20% generate most of the credit control or administrative problems. Some businesses will be very aggressive about getting rid of their problem customers, but a more positive technique would be to concentrate effort on the most desirable ones. These are the **key accounts** and the company's relationship with them can be built up by appointing **key account managers**.

Key account management is often seen as a high level selling task, but should in fact be a business wide team effort about relationships and customer retention. It can be seen as a form of co-operation with the customer's supply chain management function. The key account manager's role is to integrate the efforts of the various parts of the organisation in order to deliver an enhanced service. This idea has long been used by advertising agencies and was successfully introduced into aerospace manufacturing over 40 years ago. It will be the key account manager's role to maintain communication with the customer, note any developments in his circumstances, deal with any problems arising in the relationship and develop the long term business relationship.

The key account relationship may progress through several stages.

(a)   At first, there may be a typical **adversarial** sales-purchasing relationship with emphasis on price and delivery. Attempts to widen contact with the customer organisation will be seen as a threat by its purchasing staff.

(b)   Later, the sales staff may be able to foster a mutual desire to increase understanding by wider contacts. **Trust** may increase.

(c)   A **mature partnership** stage may be reached in which there are contacts at all levels and information is shared. The key account manager becomes responsible for integrating the partnership business processes and contributing to the customer's supply chain management. High 'vendor ratings', stable quality, continuous improvement and fair pricing are taken for granted.

7 Direct marketing

FAST FORWARD

Direct marketing involves both direct selling and the use of IT to develop customer databases. A wide variety of media are used to communicate with the target market; a well developed database allows individually targeted mail shots and telephone selling. Lists may be developed in-house or purchased. Fulfilment is the keeping of the promise to the customer and is a vital part of the direct marketing process.

Key concept

(a)   The Institute of Direct Marketing in the UK defines **direct marketing** as 'The planned recording, analysis and tracking of customer behaviour to develop relational marketing strategies'.

(b)   The Direct Marketing Association in the US defines direct marketing as 'An interactive system of marketing which uses one or more advertising media to effect a measurable response and/or transaction at any location'.

It is worth studying these definitions and noting some key words and phrases.

(a)   **Response**. Direct marketing is about getting people to respond by post or telephone to invitations and offers.

(b)   **Interactive**. The process is two-way involving the supplier and the customer.

(c)   **Relationship**. Direct marketing is in many instances an on-going process of selling again and again to the same customer.

(d)   **Recording and analysis**. Response data are collected and analysed so that the most cost-effective procedures may be arrived at.

(e)   **Strategy**. Direct marketing should be seen as a part of a comprehensive plan stemming from clearly formulated objectives.

Because direct marketing **removes all channel intermediaries** apart from the advertising medium and the delivery medium, there are no resellers, therefore avoiding loss of control and loss of revenue.

7.1 Components of direct marketing

Direct marketing encompasses a wide range of media and distribution opportunities.

- Television
- Radio
- Direct mail
- Telemarketing

- Inserts
- Take-ones
- Mail order
- Computerised home shopping

7.2 The growth of direct marketing

There has been a major increase in the amount spent on direct marketing activities. A number of factors have contributed to this growth.

The **nuclear family** is no longer the dominant group within the population. Single parent families and co-habitants now form over 35% of the households in the UK. This trend will lead to the **emergence of new customer groups** with a diverse range of needs, which will require a more **individualistic marketing strategy**.

Retailers have acquired much information about consumers through the use of loyalty cards and bar-coded goods. This gives them the ability to launch and target new goods and services more effectively.

The continued growth in use of **credit cards** has provided financial institutions, multiple retailers and mail order companies with a plethora of personal information which gives the ability to target tightly-defined customer groups.

Action Programme 6   Evaluation

In the light of these comments, how effective do you think your bank is at targeting you and your personal financial needs?

There has been a significant rise in the **real cost of television advertising**. The advent of satellite and cable television will fragment further the potential audience, and unless advertising rates adequately reflect the changing structure of the market, advertisers will seek more cost effective forms of advertising.

Consumers are becoming more **educated** in terms of what they are purchasing and, as a consequence, are much more likely to try out alternatives. The shift away from habitual **brand loyalty** coupled with a constant array of **new products** in the market place means that customers have to be more precisely segmented and targeted.

Over 90% of UK households now own a **telephone**, which has improved accessibility for the direct marketers.

Direct Line

Direct Line, the insurance company, turned the motor insurance industry on its head through its ability to by-pass the traditional brokers and offer the average consumer not only a cheaper form of insurance but a high degree of service.

Above all, the power of the **computer** has transformed the processes by which marketers relate to their customers. Improvements in database software and reductions in the cost of computer systems, now provide the opportunity for the smallest of operations to develop and benefit from the information era.

7.3 Direct mail and direct response media

Direct mail has been the fastest growing advertising medium during the past ten years. Direct mail tends to be the main medium of **direct response advertising**. The reason for this is that other major media such as newspapers and magazines are familiar to people in advertising in other contexts. Newspaper ads can include coupons to fill out and return, and radio and TV can give a phone number to ring. However, direct mail has a number of strengths as a direct response medium.

    (a)   **The advertiser can target down to individual level** and the communication can be personalised. Known data about the individual can be used, whilst modern printing techniques mean that parts of a letter can be altered to accommodate this.

    (b)   **Testing potential is sophisticated**: a limited number of items can be sent out to a 'test' cell and the results can be evaluated. As success is achieved, so the mailing campaign can be rolled out.

    (c)   What you do is **less visible to your competitors** than other forms of media.

There are, however, a **number of weaknesses** with direct mail.

    (a)   It **does not offer sound or movement**, although it is possible for advertisers to send out audio or video tapes, and even working models or samples.

    (b)   There is obvious concern over the **negative associations of junk mail** and the need for individuals to exercise their right to privacy.

    (c)   **Lead times may be considerable** when taking into consideration the creative organisation, finished artwork, printing, proofing, inserting material into envelopes where necessary and, finally, the mailing.

    (d)   The most important barrier to direct mail is that **it can be very expensive on a per capita basis**. A delivered insert can be around 30 times more expensive than a full page colour advert in a magazine. It therefore follows that the mailshot must be very powerful and, above all, well targeted to overcome such a cost penalty.

The cornerstone upon which direct mailing is based is the **mailing list**. It is far and away the most important element in the list of variables, which also include the offer, timing and creative content.

7.4 Building the database

A database is a collection of available information on past and current customers together with future prospects, structured to allow for the implementation of effective marketing strategies. Database marketing is a customer oriented approach; it is only possible if modern computer database systems are used. It enables the company to do three things.

- To **extend help** to a company's target audience
- To **stimulate** further demand
- To **stay close** to them

Recording and keeping a record of customers and prospects and of all communications and commercial contacts helps to improve all future contacts.

The database may be used to meet a variety of objectives with numerous advantages over traditional marketing methods.

- Focusing on prime prospects
- Evaluating new prospects
- Cross-selling related products
- Launching new products to potential prospects
- Identifying new distribution channels

An effective database can provide important management information.

- **Usage patterns**, for example, reasons for account closures
- **Evaluation** of marketing activities, for example response rates
- **Segmentation** analysis to ensure accurate targeting
- **Account analysis**, for example value, duration, product type
- Updated **market research** information

The database should not be seen as a tool simply to generate the one-off sale, requiring the marketing effort to be re-engaged time and time again.

7.4.1 Obtaining information

The type of information required for database marketing to operate can easily be obtained from both internal and external sources. This will typically include customer, market and competitor information. A large amount of this data is often already collected for invoicing or control purposes, but is frequently not in a format suitable for use by the marketing department.

Information on the firm's existing customers will form the core of the database, with the sales invoice being perhaps the most valuable input. Whilst the invoice is created for financial purposes, it contains a considerable amount of customer data which can be made immediately available to marketers. A typical selection of data recorded on a sales invoice is shown below.

Information	Marketing use
Customer title	Sex, job description identification
Customer first name	Sex coding, discriminates households
Customer surname	Ethnic coding
Customer address	Geodemographic profiling and census data
Date of sale	Tracking of purchase rates, repurchase identification
Items ordered	Benefit/need analysis, product clusters
Quantities ordered	Heavy/light/medium use
Price	Lifetime value of customer

7.4.2 Buying lists from elsewhere

The sources of data available to an organisation from its own database are finite and will ultimately diminish as customers cease to trade with the organisation. Therefore, it is necessary to go outside to other sources.

- **List owners and managers** may rent direct or through a broker
- **List brokers** are independent of both compiler and user

- **List compilers**, who manage and rent their lists directly
- **Directories** (telephone and commercial)
- **Exhibition organisers**
- **Publishers**
- **Associations and clubs**
- **Professional organisations**

Some of the best lists will be those which are noted as **mail responsive**. People who have responded by mail or telephone to anything in the past will be likely to do so again.

In the process of evaluating lists, the following are some of the questions to which answers will be needed.

- What is the source?
- Who is the owner?
- Are there names as well as addresses?
- Is it mail responsive or compiled from other sources?
- How active are the names?
- How up-to-date are the addresses?
- Are they buyers or enquirers?
- How frequently do they buy?
- How much do they spend?
- How did they pay?

Possibly the major problem with any list is the task of keeping it up to date. A list bought in from outside may have to be checked to ensure that it is up-to-date and accurate.

7.5 Budgeting

One of the methods in determining the direct marketing budget is to ask how much the business can afford to spend on recruiting an extra customer. One of the oldest methods available is to calculate the **allowable cost-per-order**. This is calculated by constructing a mini profit and loss statement for an average sale, including the desired profit level, but **excluding the promotional costs**.

	£	£
Selling price		60
Less returns		5
Net order value		55
Costs		
Cost of goods	18	
Fulfilment (see below)	6	
Bad debts	4	
		28
Contribution to break even		27
Desired profit		8
Allowable cost per order		19

By undertaking such a calculation, the amount which can be budgeted for the direct marketing effort is precisely determined.

The next step is to calculate the required response rate which is needed, by building in the costs of the promotion and the quantity to be mailed.

Using the data from the above example, suppose the promotional cost is £38,000. How many orders do we need to get if the allowable cost per order is £19?

$$\text{Number of orders} = \frac{£38,000}{£19} = 2,000 \text{ orders}$$

If we are to carry out a mailing of 60,000 potential customers, then the required response rate is as follows.

$$\text{Response rate} = \frac{2,000}{60,000} \times 100 = 3.33\%$$

In building up the costs of a direct marketing campaign, the following costs need to be considered.

- Press advertising
- Agency artwork
- List preparation
- Printing
- Mailing
- Response handling
- Fulfilment costs
- Bad debts/returns

Action Programme 7   Application

The selling price of an item is £75 with returns estimated at £5. The cost of goods sold is £20 and bad debts £3. The desired level of profit is £15 per unit. The total promotional costs are budgeted at £45,000 and the total number of customers to be mailed is 150,000.

Calculate:

(a)   The allowable cost-per-order
(b)   The number of orders required
(c)   The response per thousand

7.6 Fulfilment

Perhaps the most important element, and the vital link in the direct marketing plan, is the extent to which the promise to the customer is kept. Direct marketing by definition requires a response, and **fulfilment is the act of servicing the customer's response**. The act of fulfilment may take on a number of different activities including handling customer complaints, taking orders, offering advice, providing service and despatching goods. In all of these cases, it is safe to assume that the customer requires a prompt, courteous and effective response.

Typical activities carried out within the fulfilment stage

- Processing requests
- Picking, packaging and despatch
- Credit card validation and processing
- Analysing and reporting response data

Whether carried out within the company or handled by an external agency, **the area of fulfilment is a potential disaster area**, where even the most professional of organisations can come unstuck.

(a)   **Inaccurate forecasting** by the organisation in the take-up of a particular offer may lead to items being out-of-stock, resulting in unhappy customers.

(b)   Fulfilment operations can lead to extensive demands upon the organisation in terms of **human resources**, and **work space**. Organisations need to consider the trade-off between the costs of setting up the fulfilment service and the volume of business that will be generated by direct marketing activity. A decision has to be made whether to set up in-house or utilise an outside fulfilment house.

(c)   **Delays** in stock delivery and pilferage of stock can lead to frustrated customers.

(d)   **Human error** when inputting data can result in the wrong items being despatched to the wrong address. Errors of this type require careful handling when the complaints arise.

7.7 Telemarketing

Key concept

> **Telemarketing** is the planned and controlled use of the telephone for sales and marketing opportunities.

Unlike all other forms of direct marketing, telemarketing allows for **immediate two-way communication**.

Telemarketing is a quick, accurate and flexible tool for gathering, maintaining and helping to exploit relevant up-to-date information about customers and prospects. It can be utilised at all stages, from the point of building highly targeted mailing lists through to screening respondents to determine the best type to follow up, and supporting the salesforce.

7.7.1 Characteristics of telemarketing

(a)   **Targeted**. The message is appropriately tailored to the recipient.

(b)   **Personal**. Telemarketers can determine and respond immediately to the specific needs of individuals, building long-term personal and profitable relationships.

(c)   **Interactive**. Since the dialogue is live, the conversation can be guided to achieve the desired results; the representative is in control.

(d)   **Immediate**. Every outbound call achieves an immediate result, even if it is a wrong number or 'not interested'.

(e)   **High quality**. Minimum amounts of information can be gathered accurately, kept up-to-date and used to select and prioritise leads for follow up calls.

(f)   **Flexible**. Conversations can be tailored spontaneously as the representative responds to the contact's needs. There are no geographical constraints on calls and they can be timed to suit the contact.

(g)   **Accountable**. Results and effectiveness can be checked continuously.

(h)   **Experimental**. Campaign variables can be tested quickly, and changes made whilst the campaign is in progress.

7.7.2 Problems with telemarketing

Telemarketing can be costly. There are few economies of scale, and techniques such as direct mail and media advertising can work out to be cheaper. Labour overheads are potentially high, although this can be counterbalanced by operating the business from a central point.

A telemarketer can only contact around 30 to 40 customers in a day, whereas media advertising can reach a mass audience in a single strike. Media advertising married with a telephone contact number can be a very powerful combination.

If poorly handled, telemarketing may be interpreted as intrusive. This may alienate the customer and lead to lost sales opportunities.

Where telemarketing has been outsourced to a foreign call centre it is important that the operatives are properly trained and are aware of cultural differences.

7.7.3 Telemarketing as an integrated marketing activity

Telemarketing has several important ancillary functions.

(a) **Building, maintaining, cleaning and updating databases**

(b) **Market evaluation and test marketing**. Almost any feature of a market can be measured and tested by telephone. Feedback is immediate so response can be targeted quickly to exploit market knowledge.

(c) **Dealer support**. Leads can be passed on to the nearest dealer.

(d) **Traffic generation**. The telephone, combined with postal invitations, is the most cost effective way of screening leads and encouraging attendance at promotional events.

(e) **Direct sales and account servicing**. The telephone can be used at all stages of the relationship with prospects and customers. This includes lead generation, establishing buying potential and defining the decision-making process.

(f) **Customer care and loyalty building**. Every telephone contact opportunity can demonstrate to customers that they are valued.

(g) **Crisis management**. If, for example, there is a consumer scare, immediate action is essential to minimise commercial damage. A dedicated hotline number can be advertised to provide information and advice.

8 The Internet

FAST FORWARD

The **Internet** is already in use for commercial purposes. It is most productively used in the giving and receiving of information. Web-surfers need to know a site is there, so indexes and key words are important. Sites must be carefully designed if they are to be useful.

8.1 Web strategies

The Internet is widely seen as revolutionising many aspects of business. It certainly has huge potential wherever data and communication are important, and is currently used for business in several different ways.

It can enhance **customer service** and thus promote stronger marketing relationships. Two good examples of this are software fixes that can be downloaded from IT manufacturers' web sites and the publication of flight schedules.

Manufacturers' web sites can be used to provide information on new uses for old products; this very simple type of **market development** can mean increased sales. They are also very useful as an ancillary to advertisements in other media: 'See our website for full catalogue, for example.

Web sites can be used for **direct sales**. Sometimes this amounts to little more than a modern version of catalogue selling, but the 'Add to shopping cart' approach can help the customer by making it unnecessary to complete and add up an order form. There are a number of useful techniques.

(a) Give something away, charge for something else. For example, give away the abstract but charge for the book; give away a fuzzy picture, but charge for a clear one.

(b) Precede the free download with a commercial for something else.

(c) Use 'today only' offers; a website can be changed extremely quickly.

As always, where material goods are involved, **fulfilment** is crucial to the success of the venture. No problem exists where the goods can themselves be delivered over the Internet, as is the case with

software, music and images. However, where material goods must be physically delivered, a much more complex problem exists. The solution to this problem will require consideration of the factors discussed in Chapter 7, in Section 4 on **place**. In particular, Internet traders dealing in physical goods must accept that their ability to satisfy their customers depends largely on the effectiveness of their chosen distribution channel.

Media companies can use their web sites to provide a new dimension of information and entertainment, which leads to increased product involvement and hence enhanced perceived value. Examples are newspaper web editions and home pages for movies.

Information can be obtained from site visits since the Internet is interactive and visitors can be asked questions. One popular approach is to run competitions; filling in the entry form can glean significant information. Such information is invaluable for database marketing purposes.

8.2 Customer management

The Internet provides many opportunities.

(a) A website is available 24 hours a day, 365 days a year. It can provide a **continual dialogue** between customer and company. In the B2B sector this continual availability is essential. Technical data or new product information can be accessed and downloaded. Different customers can be given access to different types of information using access passwords.

(b) The **interactivity** of the Internet allows problems to be overcome quickly. Information can be exchanged. Thus customer relationships can be enhanced and developed.

(c) The **Intranet**, where public access is denied, can help to develop relationships between the customer and the business. Often in B2B markets customers know each other and meet regularly at, for example, trade fairs and conferences. The Intranet can provide a constant open channel of communication.

(d) The Internet can also be used to develop a **total relationship strategy** with other related groups. For example, the six-market model (*Christopher et al*) of relationship marketing identifies internal influence, referral, employee, supplier and customer markets. The Internet can be used to recruit employees, set up meetings between suppliers and customers and distribute press releases for the media.

(e) Face to face contact is largely not needed and the opportunity to develop **on-line relationships** instead is evident. The need for businesses to develop **databases** is therefore apparent. Such databases will need to hold considerable amounts of up to date information which can also be accessed by customers. Such availability and exchange of information will enable customers to be managed far more effectively.

8.3 Marketing strategy and the Internet

(a) **Products** – a large number of information based products/services can be developed to be easily accessed by both existing and potential customers. These could include product technical data, latest trends for the industry, product availability schedules and discussion forums for customers.

(b) **Markets** – physical nearness is no longer a problem. Worldwide markets can be developed and those nearer home can be serviced without costly sales teams making face to face contact.

(c) **Services** – the Internet will speed up the move from transaction based marketing to relationship marketing. All businesses will need to invest in the new technology to provide the services that will be demanded. The investment needed will include training for both management and employees as well as the purchase of 'state of the art' systems.

(d) **Communications** – the Internet is a mass communications medium which must be integrated into existing communication strategies. The constant availability of the medium along with its potential for interactivity means that new promotional strategies will have to be developed.

(e) **Brands** – the worldwide nature of the Internet means that businesses are not restricted to using local providers. This is particularly so in the services area eg consultancy, design, market information. New global service brands may start emerging.

(f) **Distribution channels** – an organisation can now supply a world market from a small centralised base. Expensive market entry strategies may not be needed as the Internet becomes sophisticated in terms of access and the use of technology.

8.4 Rules for Internet success

If a site is to succeed it **must seize attention immediately**.

(a) It is important to use a fast computer and connection.

(b) Attention grabbers should appear early in the text, based on the chosen web strategy. For instance, a media company might offer free browsing of back issues.

(c) Anything new about the site should be emphasised early.

(d) There should be early interactivity in the text.

Long download times may produce beautiful graphics and video, but few people will wait for them.

Selling must offer **price savings** over normal shopping; customers know that Internet selling costs are much reduced.

It is important to **cross-promote** a site. The Internet is unlike traditional direct mail methods in that it does not intrude into the potential customer's life: the customer must come looking for the website. It is therefore essential to register with major web indexes such as Yahoo! Using the right key words will help customers find a site.

8.5 Page design

Unfortunately, the website designer does not have total control over page layout or use of colour because of the nature of the system. Presentation and colour palette depend on the browser in use.

Action Programme 1   Evaluation

If you have Internet access, look critically at commercial websites and assess them against the ideas outlined above.

Chapter Roundup

- The extension of the service sector, and the application of market principles across many public sector and ex-public sector organisations, has made a large number of service providers much more marketing-conscious. **Services marketing** differs from the marketing of other goods in a number of crucial ways, and five specific characteristics of services marketing have been proposed.

- An extended marketing mix has been suggested for services marketing. Booms and Bitner suggested an additional 3 Ps. Here, we have taken an approach which analyses an additional **4 Ps**.

- **Service quality** can be defined as the difference between what customers expect and what they perceive themselves to be receiving. Improved service quality leads to higher profits and is a key task for service marketers.

- **Customers are stakeholders**. This means that they should be valued and not taken for granted. They differ in their characteristics and can be analysed or segmented to increase profitability.

- **Customer retention** is an important contribution to profitability since each customer can represent a lifetime's cash flow and creating a new customer requires far more promotional and administrative effort than retaining an existing one. The vital factor in customer retention is the skill and approach of the front-line staff.

- **Relationship marketing** is more than customer retention. It is the fostering of a mutually beneficial relationship by precision in meeting the needs of individual customers. It uses powerful computer database systems.

- Customers can be analysed for their value to the business. **Key account management** allows the most valuable customers to be given an enhanced service.

- **Direct marketing** involves both direct selling and the use of IT to develop customer databases. A wide variety of media are used to communicate with the target market; a well developed database allows individually targeted mail shots and telephone selling. Lists may be developed in-house or purchased. Fulfilment is the keeping of the promise to the customer and is a vital part of the direct marketing process.

- The **Internet** is already in use for commercial purposes. It is most productively used in the giving and receiving of information. Web-surfers need to know a site is there, so indexes and key words are important. Sites must be carefully designed if they are to be useful.

Quick Quiz

1. What are the five marketing characteristics of services?

2. What are the marketing implications of the intangibility of services?

3. What issues arise from the perishability of services being marketed?

4. What are the additional 'Ps' in the service marketing mix?

5. In what areas should rigorous procedures be applied to take account of the importance of people in services marketing?

6. In what two ways can firms gain by improving their quality of service to customers?

7. What is 'quality' in marketing terms?

8. What is the main medium of direct response advertising?

9. Give five types of information which could be obtained from an effective database.

10. Give four characteristics of telemarketing.

11. What are the rules for successful selling on the Internet?

Answers to Quick Quiz

1 Intangibility, inseparability, heterogeneity, perishability, ownership.

2 Strategies are required to do three things.

- Increase the degree of tangibility
- Focus attention on benefits
- Differentiate the service

3 Since services cannot be stored, customer needs can only be met if staff are available.

4
- People
- Process **OR**
- Physical evidence

- Personal selling
- Place availability
- People and customer service
- Physical evidence

5
- Selection and training
- Culture of service
- Standards
- Mechanisation
- Audit of performance
- Design of service environments and interactions

6 Higher revenue and improved productivity.

7 Quality is defined by the customer.

8 Direct mail

9 Usage patterns; evaluation of marketing activities; segmentation analysis; account analysis; market research information

10 Four from:

- Targeted
- Personal
- Interactive
- Immediate

- High quality
- Flexible
- Accountable
- Experimental

11 Seize attention quickly; keep down load times short; offer price savings; cross-promote the site by using the right indexes and key words

Action Programme Review

1   Possible marketing implications

(a)   Promote the advantages of non-ownership. This can be done by emphasising, in promotion, the benefits of paid-for maintenance, and periodic upgrading of the product. Radio Rentals have used this as a major selling proposition with great success.

(b)   Make available a tangible symbol or representation of ownership (certificate, membership of professional association). This can come to embody the benefits enjoyed.

(c)   Increasing the chances or opportunity of ownership (eg time-shares, shares in the organisation for regular customers)

2   There must be continuous development of service-enhancing practice.

- Policies on selection
- Programmes of training
- Standard, consistent operational practices ('MacDonaldisation')
- Standardised operational rules
- Effective motivational programmes
- Managerial appointments
- The attractiveness and appropriateness of the service offer
- Effective policies of staff reward and remuneration

3   Things design can do:

- Convey the nature of the service involved
- Transmit messages and information
- Imply aesthetic qualities, moral values, or other socio-cultural aspects of a corporate image
- Reinforce an existing image
- Reassure
- Engender an emotional reaction in the customer, through sensory and symbolic blends

4   The following are all dimensions of client service quality.

- **Problem solving creativity**: looking beyond the obvious and not being bound by accepted professional and technical approaches

- **Initiative**: anticipating problems and opportunities and not just reacting

- **Efficiency**: keeping client costs down through effective work planning and control

- **Fast response**: responding to enquiries, questions, problems as quickly as possible

- **Timeliness**: starting and finishing service work to agreed deadlines

- **Open-mindedness**: professionals not being 'blinkered' by their technical approach

- **Sound judgement**: professionals dealing with the wider aspects of their technical specialisations

- **Functional expertise**: need to bring together all the functional skills necessary from whatever sources to work on a client project

- **Industry expertise**: clients expect professionals to be thoroughly familiar with their industry and recent changes in it

- **Managerial effectiveness**: maintaining a focus upon the use of both the firm's and the client's resources

- **Orderly work approach**: clients expect salient issues to be identified early and do not want last minute surprises before deadlines

- **Commitment**: clients evaluate the calibre of the employee and the individual attention given

- **Long-range focus**: clients prefer long-term relationships rather than 'projects' or 'jobs'

- **Qualitative approach**: a whole business appreciation, not just the numbers

- **Continuity**: clients do not like firms who constantly change the staff that work with them – they will evaluate staff continuity as part of an ongoing relationship

- **Personality**: clients will also evaluate the friendliness, understanding and co-operation of the service provider

5   Your own research.

6   One way of measuring is to see how much of what your bank sends you ends up in the bin! Arguably, the UK High Street banks are better at collecting information than at using it intelligently, though this is gradually changing.

7   (a)   £32
      (b)   1407 (round up)
      (c)   10 in every thousand need to respond. (The precise answer is 9.375)

Now try Question 11 at the end of the Study Text

Part D
Marketing in different contexts

International marketing

Syllabus content – knowledge and skills requirement

- 4.1: How marketing plans and activities vary in organisations that operate in an international context, develop an appropriate marketing mix

Introduction

International marketing presents a new set of challenges for the marketer. First, the marketing information needs are great, and cannot be satisfied as easily as at home. The marketing environment is different, with each country having its own characteristic laws and culture. Regional trade alliances between countries present a new set of difficulties and opportunities which must be addressed if the organisation's strategy is to be successful. Key decisions relate to adapting the marketing mix (Sections 2-5) and the means by which a firm will enter the overseas market.

A key aspect to consider is the differences and similarities between markets. Good risk management requires differences to be identified and acknowledged. However, the seeds of marketing opportunities are likely to be found in identifying similarities between markets.

1 International marketing   12/04, 6/05, 12/05, 6/06

FAST FORWARD

International marketing is an increasingly important area. There is a range of specific problems to be addressed.

Exam tip

International marketing will feature regularly in the exam. You might be asked to identify a company and write a case history about it. You might need to consider other aspects of marketing operations in an international context. Alternatively you might have to consider specific international marketing issues, such as market entry strategies. The June 2005 paper contained a question on the marketing mix for attracting international customers, while the December 2005 paper asked about different pricing frameworks for international market segments. In June 2006, the question focused upon the complications and difficulties associated with international marketing, such as barriers to entry and the need to adapt the marketing mix.

Companies will enter into international marketing for a number of different reasons.

(a)   **Growth**. If the domestic market is static or growth is slow, or if competition is excessively fierce, a company may seek to explore new areas within which it can hope to compete or operate without competition.

(b)   **Economies of scale**. Since volume of output and unit cost are related, increased volume may lead to lower costs. Expanding into international markets may provide the level of sales necessary to benefit from economies of scale.

(c)   **International competition**. Markets of all kinds are becoming globalised. International trade becomes a necessity. In many industries, those who are unable to compete globally may find themselves reduced to subcontracting for the main players.

(d)   **National necessity**. Imports must be paid for with foreign currency, and exports provide the means of acquiring this currency. Governments typically encourage exports.

1.1 Marketing information needs

FAST FORWARD

In order to develop an effective marketing plan, information about the markets into which the company intends to go is essential. In the case of domestic markets, the normal step would be to undertake research which would provide that information. International marketing, however, requires a different approach to marketing research, and presents its own peculiar problems.

International marketing research faces a number of challenges which mark it out from home research.

- Lack of secondary data and the difficulty of establishing comparability and equivalence
- Cost of collecting primary data
- Complexity of research design
- Co-ordination of research and data collection across countries

1.2 Secondary data

There is little comparability between countries' available data. For example, it is by no means easy to compare census data. Different countries gather it in different ways and at different time intervals.

- Every 10 years in the USA
- Every 5 years in Japan and Canada
- Every 27 years in Germany

In addition, data may well imply quite different things, even when the same instruments are used in the data collection process. A cross-national comparison of consumer research measures showed that even with the same scales, measuring the same product attributes, different levels of reliability appear.

Marketing at Work   Application

A report titled "China replacing United States as world's biggest consumer" issued by the Washington-based Earth Policy Institute in February 2005 indicated that China has now surpassed the USA in consumption of goods such as fridges, television sets and mobile phones.

China watched one and a half times as many television sets as the USA and uses one and two thirds as many mobile phones. The report reveals that China now leads the world in the consumption of commodities such as meat, grain, coal and steel.

Currently China trails the USA only in car usage. However, currently car sales are doubling on an annual basis in China and at this rate, car ownership may well match that of the USA in the foreseeable future.

The report predicts that as Chinese incomes rise at a record rate, use of footstuffs, energy, raw material and sales of consumer goods will continue to escalate.

"China is no longer just a developing country. It is an emerging economic superpower, one that is writing economic history."

Various sources

1.3 Primary data collection

In the case of primary research, participation is often difficult to obtain. In many cultures, men will not discuss shaving habits with anyone, particularly women interviewers, while respondents in the Netherlands and Germany are unwilling to discuss personal finances. The Dutch are more willing to discuss sexual behaviour.

1.4 Research design

Methods of data collection may also vary between countries. For example, face-to-face interviews at home or work are very popular in the UK and Switzerland, while interviews in shopping areas are favoured in the Netherlands and France. The Japanese consumer prefers personal, face to face discussions to telephone or mail.

Overseas data is frequently aggregated, and consequently does not satisfy the needs of a firm which is focusing on one product. In this case, **market assessment by inference** becomes a useful tool. This approach uses **available facts about related products or other foreign markets** as a basis for deriving appropriate information.

Three inference bases are commonly used.

(a) Inference based on a **related product**, for example replacement tyre market based on car ownership.

(b) Inference based on **related market size,** for example, a known need in one country may be used as a basis for countries with similar economic development levels, and consumption patterns.

(c) Inference based on **related environmental factors** such as similar shifts in socio-economic variables.

1.5 Marketing environment differences

The marketing environment is different in international marketing. Most aspects of **cultural systems** vary between countries, sometimes quite significantly.

Even between neighbouring countries such as France and Spain, or China and Vietnam cultural differences can be very great. Marketing planning must consider the main aspects of cultural systems.

- Material culture
- Social institutions
- Belief systems
- Aesthetics
- Language

(a) **Material culture** affects the following.

(i) The **level of demand**. For instance, the lack of electricity will restrict the demand for electronic items.

(ii) **Quality and types of products demanded**. Difference in disposable income influences the kinds of goods demanded. Note also the **symbolic** importance of particular goods which may be used primarily as status symbols. For instance, the ownership of a European brand car confers a level of status in Australia, where they are more expensive than Japanese cars.

(iii) **Social characteristics**. Demand for snack food and the habit of 'grazing' has been stimulated in the UK by changes in the social roles of women, and in the activities which take place within the home.

(iv) The **nature of products demanded**. 'Menu meals' are a product intended to help in the preparation of quality food when people cannot spare time for shopping and cooking, because many households are now characterised by full-time employment.

(b) **Social institutions** give a society its distinctive form, and develop around particular aspects of the life experience such as the care and raising of children, or coping with conflict or suffering. The form of social institutions has profound implications for the ways in which goods are regarded, since they provide the foundations for value systems, and through them, attitudes and behaviour.

(i) **Social organisation**. Tightly knit family units, in which social roles are bound up with responsibility to the family, influence both the kinds of products demanded, and the ways in which purchase decisions are made.

(ii) **Political structures**. The political system sets the agenda for consumption through policy and example.

(iii) **Educational system**. Literacy is a key factor in promotional and advertising activity.

(iv) **Family or household roles**. Roles played by family members in decision making are one area in which culture shapes consumption. Also, the way in which the household is actually used and regarded are very important for consumption. For instance, the modern household actually forms the focus for leisure activity far more than it did in the past.

(c) **Belief systems** include **religious, philosophical, and political ideologies**. Generalised belief systems are all-pervasive, even in societies which consider themselves secularised. Our holidays and gift giving occasions are formed around the religious calendar; the foods we eat reflect moral and aesthetic judgements as much as nutritional good sense. Many religions proscribe particular forms of consumption, such as coffee, alcoholic drinks, 'provocative' clothes and certain music.

(d) **Aesthetics** and what counts as beauty or ugliness is tied into quite specific values which a marketer must be aware of in a foreign culture.

(e) Marketing literature is full of examples of linguistic *faux pas*, such as the Vauxhall Nova, which means 'doesn't go' in Spanish. Advertising slogans need to beware of the pitfalls of the local **language**; successful slogans may not work in another language, or may be unintentionally funny or offensive.

Marketing at Work   Application

Cars in the West are designed with most of the facilities such as the heating/air conditioning, radio and lighting controlled by the driver. In China, where society is structured on a more communal and consensual basis, consumers prefer to have controls accessible to the passengers sitting in the back.

This culture of sharing is mirrored in the catering industry. In the West, the chef controls the portions placed on the plate. The waiter then makes the allocation decision. In Chinese restaurants (and households) all the food is placed in the middle of the table and everybody helps themselves according to their own needs, but mindful of the needs of the other participants.

1.6 Regional trade alliances and markets

FAST FORWARD

International marketing operations are affected by **regional trade alliances** and markets. Free trade areas have low or no internal tariff barriers. Customs unions add a common external tariff. An economic union creates a single internal market.

Trade between nations is of such significance that rules governing it have been established. Economic theory predicts mutual benefits for nations trading internationally, but there are two opposing pressures.

- The desire to **expand the domestic economy** by selling to other nations
- The desire to **protect indigenous sources** of employment by restricting imports

1.7 Regional trading groups

While the World Trade Organisation encourages free trade, the opposite force of protectionism has led to the creation of regional trading organisations, which seek to encourage trade between members but introduce hurdles to non-members. An example is the European Union (EU). These regional trading groups can take progressively more integrated forms.

- Free trade areas
- Customs unions
- Economic unions

(a)   **Free trade areas** have members who agree to lower barriers to trade amongst themselves. There is little other form of economic co-operation. Examples include Mercosur and the Andean Community in South America, and the North American Free Trade Agreement, comprising Canada, the USA and Mexico. In underdeveloped countries, attempts to form such associations have led to problems as members seek to protect their embryo economies, and fear the effects of free trade with member states.

(b)   **Customs unions** not only provide the advantages of free trade areas, but also agree a common policy on barriers to external countries. Currently the EU is the leading example of this type of union, and is seen as the prototype for other unions elsewhere.

(c)   Economic unions represent the ultimate step - the submission of all decisions relating to trade, both internal and external, from member states to the union itself. **In effect the members become one for economic purposes**.

2 Product

FAST FORWARD

> Within the marketing mix, standardisation or customisation of the product must be considered. **Extension** requires no significant change to the product. **Adaptation** can be undertaken in terms of the product, the way it is promoted, or both. The great advantage of extension is increased scale economies.

2.1 To standardise or to customise?

Products successfully marketed within one country cannot necessarily be moved into an alien market without problems. Products have symbolic and psychological aspects as well as physical attributes. As a result, entry into a market with a different set of cultural, religious, economic, social and political assumptions may cause extreme reactions to a product concept or marketing mix.

The problem derives from an inherent tension between two important ideas in marketing. Target marketing and segmentation suggest that the way to maximise sales is to identify specific consumer needs and hence to **adapt** a product for a new foreign market. At the same time, it is impractical to create separate products for every conceivable segment, and it is more profitable to produce a **standardised** product for a larger market. This is resolved by considering the costs and benefits of alternative marketing strategies.

There are five approaches to the problem of adaptation, which are defined by decisions about the product and about promotion. They are summarised in the diagram below. **Extension** of product or promotion means that no significant change is made.

| | | **PRODUCT** | | |
		Extension	Adaptation	New
PROMOTION	Extension	Straight Extension	Product Adaptation	Product invention
	Adaptation	Communication Adaptation	Dual Adaptation	

(a) **Straight extension** has the advantages discussed in Paragraph 2.1.1.

(b) **Product adaptation** is normally undertaken so that the product can either fulfil the same function under different conditions, as when an electrical device is adapted to conform to a different voltage, or to overcome cultural problems such as taste.

(c) **Communications adaptation** is a way of marketing an unchanged product to fulfil a different need, as when garden implements are promoted as agricultural equipment in less-developed countries where plot sizes tend to be small. This can be very cost effective. Similarly, food consumed in one way in one country may be eaten in a different way in another country eg cakes are eaten with afternoon tea in Britain, but may be marketed as a component of a continental breakfast in Europe.

(d) **Dual adaptation** is expensive, but applies to most products since there tend to be at least small differences in the ways they are used in new markets.

(e) **Product invention** is commonly used to enter less sophisticated markets where products must be simple and cheap.

 **Marketing at Work**   Application

Guinness

Nigeria is one of Guinness's largest markets, after the UK and the Republic of Ireland. However, the products sold in the UK (and Ireland) and Nigeria are different. Guinness Nigeria uses local ingredients, and this gives the beer a sweeter flavour. In fact, Nigerian (and Ghanaian) Guinness is imported to the UK, in part for West African people living in London and other centres.

The promotion and branding is subtly different in Nigeria than in the UK or Ireland, as this is governed by local laws. Parts of Nigeria operate under Sharia (Islamic) law.

2.1.1 Arguments in favour of product standardisation

(a) **Economies of scale**

(i) **Production**

    – Plant confined to one country and used to maximum capacity
    – Exporting rather than difficult licensing deals

(ii) **Research and development**. Product modification is costly and time consuming

(iii) **Marketing**. Promotion which can use the same images and themes is in advertising is clearly more cost effective when only the soundtrack, or the printed slogan, has to be changed. Similarly, standardisation of distribution systems, salesforce training, aftersales provisions and other aspects of the marketing mix can save a great deal of money.

(b) **Consumer mobility**. Finding a familiar brand name is important for the growing numbers of travellers moving across national boundaries.

(c) **Technological complexity**. The microelectronics market illustrates the inherent danger of diversity in technically complex products. Even the endorsement of powerful Japanese companies could not sustain the Betamax VCR system or non-standard PC systems. The international market selected VHS and IBM respectively.

What are the arguments in favour of product adaptation?

2.2 New products in international markets

Product ideas, both internally and externally generated, must be screened in order to identify potentially marketable and profitable products. Product screening may be carried out at a centralised location, although this poses the threat of alienating management at remote subsidiary plants where many ideas may originate. If this does cause problems, some measure of decentralisation in the screening process may be necessary.

2.2.1 Criteria for product screening

Products are screened against the firm's capabilities and characteristics.

(a) **Producing the product**. This may involve existing resources, diversification.

(b) **Marketing the product**. If existing marketing resources suffice, then so much the better. A new system could involve substantial outlay and disruption.

(c) **Researching the new market**. This might involve the deployment of existing resources, particularly if the firm is already established and operating in a related area. If there is no related market involvement, there is greater uncertainty and risk.

(d) **Marketing internationally**. Orientation to a specific market will reduce the economies of scale involved in multinational marketing. Products are likely to be rejected if they cannot be produced for international markets.

(e) **Motivation to introduce and market the new product effectively**. Why is the new product being introduced?

(f) **Organisational suitability to marketing the new product**. Are suitable support and maintenance systems available?

2.2.2 Product screening in practice

International firms exist partly because operations spread across several countries reduce overall risk. The more diverse the operations of the firm, however, the more difficult they are to co-ordinate.

2.2.3 A checklist for new products

Some factors can be assigned a variable weighting, since they are likely to be of varying importance in differing circumstances. Some are **critical**, and failure in these areas will **disqualify** a product from international marketing.

2.2.4 Requirements for a new product

It must:

- Fall within a company's terms of incorporation (critical)
- Be profitable in the short term
- Be profitable in the long term (critical)
- Have a realistic payback period
- Be distinct from previously patented products (critical)
- Be protected by patent or trademark in all overseas markets

- Comply with national safety standards
- Be compliant with regulations, and profitable when taking account of import duties
- Be capable of being produced in a number of countries
- Be able to be introduced in either a standardised or suitably adapted form

3 Place

FAST FORWARD

Distribution is a complex issue in international marketing, and a wide range of channels can be identified.

A range of factors affect the selection, establishment, and running of international distribution systems. A wide range of channels can be developed.

Using an **Export Management Company** (EMC) which handles all aspects of exporting, can be an attractive option. It requires minimal investment and no company personnel are involved. The EMC already has an established network of sales offices, and extensive international marketing and distribution knowledge. From the company's point of view, however, there is a loss of control.

Another alternative is **export agents**. These provide more limited services than EMCs, are focused on one country and do not perform EMC marketing tasks, but concentrate on the physical movement of products. The main problem here is that a company requires several agents to cover a range of markets.

Direct exporting can be attractive. In-house personnel are used, but they must be well trained and experienced. Also, the volume of sales must be sufficient to justify employing them.

Import middlemen, or distributors who are experts in their local market needs, can play a key part, being able to source goods from the world market. They operate to purchase goods in their own name, and act independently of the manufacturer. They are able to exploit good access to wholesale and retail networks.

3.1 Developing an international distribution strategy

As in domestic marketing, there must be **consistency of purpose** in the way in which elements within the marketing mix operate. **Three key strategic areas** are involved.

- **Distribution density** – exposure or coverage desired
- **Channel length, alignment and leadership** – number, structure and hierarchy relationships of the channel members
- **Distribution logistics** – physical flow of product

3.1.1 Distribution density

Distribution density depends on a knowledge of how customers select dealers and retail outlets, by segment. If less shopping effort is involved, as in the case of convenience goods, an extensive system would be appropriate. If more shopping effort is used, as in the case of premium priced goods, then a selective or exclusive system would be required.

3.1.2 Channel members

After strategy has been formulated, marketers must select **channel partners** capable of implementing the overall strategy. Since it can be difficult to change partners once contracted, this choice is very sensitive indeed. There are several important criteria for selection.

- Cost
- Capital requirement
- Product nature
- Control achievable
- Synergy

Cost falls into three categories. The **initial cost** of locating and setting up the channel, **maintenance costs** such as employing sales people, paying travel expenses, auditing and controlling, the profit margin paid to middlemen, and **logistics costs** such as transportation, storage, breaking bulk and customs administration.

The **least profitable approach to distribution is that of direct exporting** to retailers in the host country. The **most profitable involves selling to a distributor** in a country with its own marketing channels. **Capital requirements** here are offset by cash flow patterns. In order to arrive at the right decision, costs must be evaluated between channels. For example, an import distributor will often pay for goods received before they are sold on to the retailer or industrial customer. An agent, however, may not pay anything until payment by the end customer is received.

Product nature is also relevant. Perishable or short shelf-life products need shorter channels, and this bears on costs and hence profits. High tech products require either direct sales effort or skilled and knowledgeable channel partners.

Synergy arises when the components of a channel complement one another to the extent that they produce more than the sum of their individual parts. Such synergy may arise if, for example, the chosen partner has some key skill which allows quicker access to the market.

3.1.3 Logistics

Logistics systems are expensive and can be very damaging to corporate profitability if badly handled. There are several areas which are crucial to international logistics.

- Traffic and transportation management
- Inventory control
- Order processing
- Materials handling and warehousing
- Fixed facilities location management

Traffic and transportation management deals primarily with the main mode of transport involved in moving goods. Three main criteria are employed in this choice – lead times, transit time and costs.

Inventory control relates cost with service levels. Inventory reduces potential profit by using up working capital; the management aim here is to reduce inventories to an absolute minimum.

3.2 Retailing

There are certain key global trends in international distribution. **Larger scale retailers** are partly a consequence of economic development and growing affluence. Increasing car ownership, increasing fridge/freezer ownership and the changing role of women all encourage one-stop shopping. At one stage, Tesco had shut down two-thirds of its small in-town stores (less than 10,000 square feet) in favour of larger stores. This is a global trend deriving from a reduction in distribution costs and increased sophistication of retailers.

International retailers like Marks & Spencer have developed for the same reasons. Companies might see limited growth opportunities at home, and move to overseas markets. This allows manufacturers to build relationships with retailers active in a number of different markets. This internationalisation process is prompted by improved data communications, new forms of international financing, more open international markets and lower barriers to entry. In the EU for instance, the Single European Market motivates retailers to expand overseas, as they see international retailers entering their domestic markets.

In 1996 two US academics by the names of Boze and Patton posed a simple question: how many global brands are there? Their answer was surprising. Defining a brand as 'global' if it was sold in 33 countries or more, only a few brands (apart from the usual suspects such as Coca-Cola) made the grade. Over half the brands sold by major players such as Colgate, Kraft, Procter & Gamble and Unilever were sold in less than three countries, whilst most of the rest were sold in under 30.

Since then, it has become all the rage to cut brand 'tails' and focus investment on big global brands. Yet things haven't changed much. A recent study of 200 'billion-dollar brands' by A C Nielsen found that only 43 brands passed the global test – and a pretty weak test it was too. Nielsen's definition of 'global' was: selling in each of the world's four main economic regions, and with at least five per cent of its sales outside its home region. In other words, despite years of global brand building, 78 per cent of the biggest brands are still only regional or generate more than 95 per cent of their sales in their 'home' territories.

What are we to make of this huge gap between rhetoric and reality? It's created by a combination of three key factors. First, for the most part, consumers do not want global brands. Yes, there are some brands, such as Visa, for whom 'being global' is important. But a housewife in Bolton probably does not really care whether her peers in Buenos Aires and Boston use the same brand.

Yet, if consumers don't want global brands, companies certainly do – globalising brands presents huge opportunities to cut costs and achieve new economies of scale. It's all about producer push, not consumer pull.

Direct marketing is growing rapidly all over the world using IT systems to bypass the wholesale – retail network, and go direct to customers.

Information technology has had an enormous impact. Computerised retail systems allow better monitoring of consumer purchases, lower inventory costs and quicker stock turns alongside a better assessment of product profitability. Internet selling is widely expected to revolutionise business (though it depends on traditional fulfilment).

3.3 Communications

Market communications face additional barriers internationally. In developing an effective promotional mix, experience plays a key role. Costs and the overall effectiveness of measures are also important considerations. The elements to be considered are as follows.

(a) **Push-oriented strategy**. In a domestic setting, this emphasises personal selling. This may be more expensive if employed abroad since minor equipment or supplies in large UK firms may be 'major equipment' overseas and require more involved personal selling effort. A long non-domestic channel, involving many non-domestic intermediaries, increases costs, reduces the effect of personal selling, and poses severe control problems.

(b) **Pull-oriented strategy** is characterised by a greater dependence upon advertising and is typically employed for FMCG marketing to very large market segments. It is generally more appropriate for long channels, where relatively simple products are being sold. However, not all countries have the same access to advertising media and the quality of media varies greatly.

4 Price   12/05

FAST FORWARD Prices in foreign markets are likely to be determined by local conditions, with each market separate.

4.1 Getting the price right

Prices in foreign markets are likely to be determined by local conditions, with each market separate. The organisation's degree of control over pricing is likely to be higher if it has wholly owned subsidiaries in each of the markets, and lower if it conducts business through licensees, franchisees or distributors.

Action Programme 2   Application

Market conditions are the most important influence on pricing. What other factors do you think influence pricing?

The diversity of markets within a region is important. If markets are unrelated, the seller can successfully charge different prices. Pressures for price uniformity often come from large groupings such as free trade areas or the EU, and from increases in international business activity. Companies can control price in several ways.

- Direct distribution to customers
- Resale price maintenance
- Recommended prices
- Agreed margins between parent and subsidiary companies
- Centralised control over prices within several subsidiary companies

5 Promotion

FAST FORWARD Elements of the promotional mix must also be considered. The Internet is of increasing importance.

Sales promotions may be affected by different retailing norms and government regulations. For example, coupons, much used in the UK and the USA, are prohibited in Germany and Greece. Reduction in price promotions are often restricted to a percentage of full price. As a consequence, standardising sales promotion tools is extremely difficult. Sales promotions are usually handed over to local experts.

Sports promotions and sponsorships are widely used. The key methods involved are advertising during sports programming on TV, positioning of stadium or arena signs and sponsorship of individuals, teams or events. What type is used depends on the country involved and the circumstances and regulations which they apply. In Germany, for example, TV advertising cannot be used within sports shows so alternative approaches are needed.

5.1 Advertising

Sources of **media problems**

(a)   **Availability**. Media may be more important and effective in some countries than in others (for instance, cinema in India, radio in the USA), while there may be a lack of specific media in others.

(i)   **Newspapers** may not be widely available because of low levels of literacy, or even specific policies on the part of the government.

      (ii)   **Magazines**, which are important for specialist products such as industrial machinery, may be very restricted.

      (iii)   **TV commercials** are restricted, or even banned in many countries. For instance, advertising specifically directed at children is banned in some Scandinavian countries. It is also sometimes very difficult to gauge effectiveness because of missing or incomplete data.

      (iv)   **Billboards, direct mail** and other forms of promotion may be unfamiliar or ineffective (there is very limited usage of billboards in some formerly communist countries).

(b)   **Financial aspects**. Costs may be very difficult to estimate in some countries, since negotiation and the influence of intermediaries might be greater. There may also be expectations of gift-giving in the negotiation process.

(c)   **Coverage of media (or reach of advertising message)**. This relates to the forms of media employed as well as the physical characteristics of the country. Inaccessible areas may rule out the use of direct mail, or posters; scarcity of telephones may rule out this form of advertising promotion. It may also be difficult to monitor advertising effectiveness.

The Internet. Selling over the Internet is discussed elsewhere in this text. However, it is worth revisiting the topic in the context of international marketing.

(a)   **Web searches**. A well presented website, known to portals such as Yahoo! and easily found via keywords by search engines such as Google, is a powerful tool for contacting new customers. Contacts made in this way are particularly valuable since they are initiated by potential customers.

(b)   **International business**. Because the web transcends national boundaries, international orders become matters of routine. Customers can place orders wherever they are and, assuming payment by credit card, the orders can be fulfilled with a minimum of administration. However, there is a growing realisation on the part of national authorities that Internet trade can circumvent customs and excise duty, and shipping administration is likely to increase.

6 Structure choices

There are five basic alternatives for structure when entering a foreign market.

- Exporting
- Licensing
- Franchising
- Trading companies
- Manufacturing abroad

When considering exporting for the first time a company has to decide upon the degree of involvement which is appropriate, and the level of commitment. There are five basic alternatives when entering a foreign market.

(a)   **Simple exporting**, often based on the need to dispose of excess production for a domestic market, is the commonest form of export activity.

(b)   The second main form is **licensing**, based on patents, designs and trade marks.

(c) **Franchising** is the third main option. It is very similar to licensing, in terms of advantages and disadvantages. There is minimal risk, but also modest returns. **Joint ventures** are more likely to produce good returns, but they are much riskier.

(d) **Trading companies** may be established in the target countries.

(e) **Manufacturing abroad** may be undertaken. This will require major investment.

6.1 Exporting

Exporting can involve minimum effort, cost and risk and is relatively flexible. Exporting can be direct to buyers or more normally through export organisations of various kinds. An export agent acts as an intermediary between buyers and sellers, taking a commission from the transactions. Export merchants/export houses buy products from different companies and sell them to other countries.

In most cases these export organisations have long-established contacts in foreign countries and a purchasing headquarters in, say, London. The exporter thus deals in English, under the English legal system, gets paid by a resident bank, is not involved in shipping and may not have to alter products in any way. It is simple and risk free, but naturally the rewards are not as potentially great as other options.

6.2 Licensing

Licensing usually involves only a small capital outlay and this approach is favoured by small and medium sized companies. It is the least profitable method of entry, and has the least associated risks.

The licensee pays a royalty on every product item produced or sold in addition to a lump sum paid for the license. Licensing is used particularly when local manufacture, technical assistance and market knowledge offer advantages. It is an alternative to investing directly and is particularly advantageous if an overseas country should be politically unstable.

Licensing is also attractive for medium-sized companies wishing to launch a successful home market brand internationally. Fashion houses such as Yves St Laurent and Pierre Cardin have issued hundreds of licences and Löwenbrau has expanded sales worldwide without having to expend capital building its own breweries overseas.

6.3 Joint ventures

Joint ventures in Europe have become particularly prevalent. They involve collaboration with one or more foreign firms. They offer reduced economic and political risks and a ready made distribution system. Where there are barriers to trade, they may be the only way to gain entry to foreign markets.

Quite a number of vehicle manufacturers have initiated joint ventures or strategic alliances, including Chrysler with Mitsubishi and Alfa Romeo with both Nissan and Fiat.

6.4 Trading companies

This structure avoids involvement in manufacturing. A trading company simply buys in one country and sells to buyers in another country. It will sometimes also act as a consultant advising buyers and sellers on market conditions, quality/price issues etc. For example, long-established trading companies control much of the world's food market for commodities such as cereals, or indeed any items that are able to be stored in bulk and moved rapidly in response to shortages.

6.5 Direct ownership

Setting up a company in a foreign country may be appropriate if growth prospects and political stability make a long-term commitment attractive.

Manufacturing abroad requires major investment and is only justified by very heavy demand. However, it may offer advantages such as those below.

Advantages may include:

- Lower labour costs
- Avoidance of import taxes
- Lower transport costs

These may be offset by the degree of management effort required, and higher levels of risk.

Multinationals will have directly owned subsidiaries in many countries. These can offer considerable operating and tax advantages. Some car manufacturers such as General Motors and Ford in the US actually import cars built by foreign subsidiaries.

Chapter Roundup

- **International marketing** is an increasingly important area. There is a range of specific problems to be addressed.

- In order to develop an effective marketing plan, information about the markets into which the company intends to go is essential. In the case of domestic markets, the normal step would be to undertake research which would provide that information. International marketing, however, requires a different approach to marketing research, and presents its own peculiar problems.

- The marketing environment is different in international marketing. Most aspects of **cultural systems** vary between countries, sometimes quite significantly.

- International marketing operations are affected by **regional trade alliances** and markets. Free trade areas have low or no internal tariff barriers. Customs unions add a common external tariff. An economic union creates a single internal market.

- Within the marketing mix, standardisation or customisation of the product must be considered. **Extension** requires no significant change to the product. **Adaptation** can be undertaken in terms of the product, the way it is promoted, or both. The great advantage of extension is increased scale economies.

- **Distribution** is a complex issue in international marketing, and a wide range of channels can be identified.

- **Prices** in foreign markets are likely to be determined by local conditions, with each market separate.

- Elements of the promotional mix must also be considered. The Internet is of increasing importance.

- There are five basic alternatives for structure when entering a foreign market.

  - Exporting
  - Licensing
  - Franchising
  - Trading companies
  - Manufacturing abroad

Quick Quiz

1   Why do companies enter into international marketing?

2   What is the main problem with using secondary data in international market research?

3   What is the significance of material culture in international marketing?

4   What are the two main opposing pressures on international trade?

5   What are the arguments in favour of product standardisation?

6   What is product screening?

7   What factors influence the choice of channel members?

8   Distinguish between a push-oriented strategy and a pull-oriented strategy.

9   What media problems may arise in international marketing?

10   What is licensing?

Answers to Quick Quiz

1   To achieve growth and economies of scale; to respond to global competition and in response to government encouragement.

2   Lack of basic comparability; varying implications of the data collected.

3   It affects the following.

- Level of demand
- Social characteristics
- Quality and type of goods produced
- Nature of products demanded

4   The desire to expand domestic production by selling overseas and the desire to protect domestic production by restricting imports.

5   Achievement of economies of scale in production, R&D and marketing; presentation of known brands to mobile consumers.

6   Assessment of potential new products against the company's capabilities and characteristics.

7   Overall cost; capital required; nature of the product(s); degree of control achievable; degree of synergy achievable.

8   'Push' emphasises personal selling; 'pull' emphasises other forms of promotion.

9   Availability of media may vary between countries; costs maybe difficult to estimate and control and standards of financial probity may vary; media coverage may be limited by geography or stage of economic development.

10 Licensing is an alternative to setting up production: the licensee pays a sum for a license to produce and a royalty on sales. Risk is low, as is the potential for high profits.

Action Programme Review

1 (a) **Greater sales potential**, where this also means greater profitability, which it may not!

(b) **Varied conditions of product** *use* may force a company to modify its product.

(i) Climatic variations, for instance cars produced for dry climates may suffer corrosion in wet ones

(ii) Literacy or skill levels of users such as languages which can be used on a computer

(iii) Cultural, social, or religious factors such as religious or cultural requirements for food products like Halal slaughtering of New Zealand lamb for Middle Eastern Markets or dolphin-friendly tuna catching methods for Europe and the USA)

(c) **Variation in market factors**. Consumer needs are by nature idiosyncratic, and there are likely to be distinctive requirements for each group not met by a standard product.

(d) **Governmental or political influence**. Taxation, legislation or pressure of public opinion may force a company to produce a local product.

2 Other factors

(a) **Cost**: full cost of supplying goods to consumers. Relevant costs could include administrative costs, a proportion of group overheads, manufacturing costs, distribution and retailing costs.

(b) **Inflation**, particularly in the target market and in raw material suppliers.

(c) **Official regulations**. Governments may well intervene in pricing policies. This may involve *acceptable* measures such as import duties and tariffs, and generally *unacceptable* measures such as non-tariff barriers, import quotas and price freezes. Price controls may also be used.

(d) **Competition**. 'Price leaders' may well be undercut by competitors. The effectiveness of this policy will vary according to the significance of other marketing activities, and the capacity of competitors to match these.

Now try Question 12 at the end of the Study Text

10

Business-to-business marketing

Syllabus content – knowledge and skills requirement

- 4.2: Marketing plan and marketing mix for an organisation operating in any context such as FMGG, business-to-business, (supply chain), large or capital project-based, services, voluntary and not-for-profit sales support (eg SMEs)

Introduction

Business-to-business, or industrial marketing, is a very important marketing context that differs significantly from the usual retail environment. The general nature of this type of marketing is covered in Section 1, and target marketing in Section 2. Target marketing is likely to be easier in industrial marketing than consumer marketing because of the easy availability of large amounts of analysed data.

The business-to-business marketing mix is likely to be very different from any retail mix, as shown in Section 3, with a heavy emphasis on personal contact and product features. Industrial marketers must be prepared to seek competitive advantage where they can, because product differentiation may not be possible. The nature of organisational buying can be a source of competitive advantage, if it is understood. This is covered in Section 4.

1 Business-to-business marketing

FAST FORWARD

Industrial marketing, or marketing **business-to-business**, is different in nature from consumer marketing. Buying motivations (the criteria which consumers apply) and the nature of the buying process itself are quite different. There are four basic categories of industrial market.

- Capital goods
- Components and materials
- Supplies
- Business services

Although many of the products involved in industrial markets are the same as those bought within the ordinary consumer markets, (for example motor vehicles), **the reasons they are bought will be quite different**. Buying motivations, the criteria which consumers apply, and the nature of the buying process itself will be quite different.

Organisational buyers are buying for their organisations, and what they buy is part and parcel of the business activity of the organisation involved – it is part of the process of earning a profit.

Industrial marketing involves widely varying products and services. It is not just about raw materials, or about the selling of specialised, heavy duty machinery or equipment.

1.1 Products

Industrial goods and services are bought by manufacturers, distributors and other private and publicly owned institutions, such as schools and hospitals, to be used as part of their own activities, rather than for resale.

1.1.1 Categories of industrial market

(a) **Capital goods** include such items as buildings, machinery and motor vehicles. Accounting procedures involve recognition of depreciation in their value over time.

(b) **Components and materials** include raw, partly and wholly processed materials or goods which are incorporated into the products sold by the company.

(c) **Supplies** are goods which **assist** production and distribution. They are not regarded as a capital investment, however. This category would include small but important items such as machine oil, computer disks and stationery, janitorial wares and other 'consumables'.

(d) **Business services** are services used by businesses.

Industrial products are **distinctive** in several ways.

(a) **Conformity with standards**. Industrial products are often bound by **legal or quality standards**, and as a consequence, products within a particular group are often similar. Differentiation, which is such a key dimension of consumer goods, is more difficult here. At the same time, buyers lay down their own specifications to which manufacturers must adhere.

(b) **Technical sophistication**. Many products in this area require levels of complexity and sophistication which are unheard of in consumer products. Often the industry standard gradually influences the consumer equivalent as, for instance, in the case of power tools in the DIY market. After-sales and maintenance contracts have become essential in certain areas.

(c) **High unit values**. As a consequence of (a) and (b), many industrial goods, particularly capital equipment, are very often extremely costly items. Even in the case of supplies, although the unit value of components and materials may be comparatively low, the quantity required frequently means that individual orders and total sales to individual customers usually have a very high value.

(d) **Irregularity of purchase**. Machinery used to produce consumer goods is not bought regularly. Materials used to produce the goods certainly are, but components and materials are often bought on a contract basis, so that the opportunity to get new business may not arise very often.

1.2 Characteristics of industrial markets

Three kinds of economic activity have been defined.

(a) **Primary or extractive industries** cover activities like agriculture, fishing, mining and forestry.

(b) **Secondary or manufacturing industries** include manufacturing and construction.

(c) **The tertiary sector includes the service industries**. Services are becoming extremely important within our modern economy and services marketing is exerting a big influence on the way in which marketing is developing.

1.3 The importance of marketing for the industrial sector

A marketing orientation is just as valid within the industrial sector as it is in the consumer goods sector. Customers seek answers to their problems. Industrial products must be full of customer benefits, providing answers to customers' problems rather than simply being 'good products'.

1.3.1 The marketing manager within the organisation

This implies a need for well co-ordinated activity, around a common, market-oriented, mission. Marketing management has several functions.

- It acts as catalysts within the firms
- It informs technical management about market trends
- It monitors competitive activity
- It informs corporate planning decisions
- It directs R & D

They are not simply concerned with customers, but in linking and co-ordinating various activities within the firm.

1.4 Special practices

(a) **Reciprocal trading** is evident in some markets. This closes markets off for newcomers and restricts trading.

(b) **Joint ventures** often involve large industrial and commercial organisations which pool their resources in order to accomplish particular contracts. This may be necessary because of the scale of the project, or because of cultural, legal or technical advantages which the co-operation confers on both parties.

(c) **Consortiums** are more permanent partnerships.

(d) **Project management** involves special techniques to bring a single unique development to completion. Projects may involve research, design, manufacturing and logistic activities.

(e) **Turnkey operations** may be similar to project management or may involve continuing responsibility to the customer for services and maintenance.

(f) More and more **machinery is being leased rather than bought**. In the construction industry, leasing deals also involve lessors tying the machinery to exclusive purchasing of other items such as raw materials.

(g) **Licensing** enables new products to be introduced to customers without the risks and high costs associated with the development and launch of a new product. It also significantly reduces the time to launch.

2 Target marketing in industrial markets

FAST FORWARD

Target markets for industrial marketing tend to be easier to identify than consumer market segments. Data is generally more easily available on businesses than on consumers. Sources include government and privately-published statistics.

Business-to-business target markets tend to be easier to identify than consumer market segments, mainly because more data is readily available on businesses than on groups of people within the general public. Much information about industrial markets is published in government statistics. Production statistics, available monthly and quarterly for manufacturing companies, are broken down into ten major Standard Industrial Classifications (SICs). Each major heading is broken down into smaller groups. Under each heading is given such detail as number of employees, number of establishments, value of shipments, exports and imports and annual growth rates.

Action Programme 1   Application

Find some examples of government publications which might provide a useful source of statistics.

Official statistics are also published by bodies such as the United Nations and local authorities.

2.1 Privately published statistics

(a) Companies and other organisations specialising in the provision of economic and financial data (eg the *Financial Times* Business Information Service, the Data Research Institute, Reuters and the Extel Group)

(b) Directories and yearbooks, such as Kompass or Kelly's Directory

(c)   Professional institutions (eg Chartered Institute of Marketing, Industrial Marketing Research Association, Institute of Practitioners in Advertising)

(d)   Specialist libraries, such as the City Business Library in London, collect published information from a wide variety of sources

(e)   Trade associations, trade unions and Chambers of Commerce

(f)   Commercial organisations such as banks and TV networks

(g)   Market research agencies

2.2 Buying in data

The sources of secondary data identified above are generally free because they are in the public domain. However, the information is non-specific and needs considerable analysis before being useable.

A middle step between adapting secondary data and commissioning primary research is the purchase of data collected by market research companies or business publishing houses. The data tend to be expensive but less costly than primary research.

There are a great many commercial sources of secondary data, and a number of guides to these sources are available. Commonly used sources of data on particular industries and markets are:

- Key Note Publications
- Economist Intelligence Unit
- Mintel publications
- *Market Research GB*, Euromonitor

3 Marketing mix differences in industrial marketing

FAST FORWARD

There are differences in the marketing mix for industrial marketing when compared to the characteristic mix adopted for consumer markets.

The industrial marketing mix differs from the marketing mix for consumer products. Often industrial products are not packaged for resale, prices tend to be negotiated with the buyer and distribution tends to be more direct. The promotional mix is also generally different in that consumer goods are often advertised heavily on TV and in mass media, whereas industrial marketing companies tend to restrict advertising to trade magazines.

Much more reliance is placed on personal selling. An industrial buyer purchases off the page, especially where capital goods are concerned. Whereas most FMCG are purchased on a self-service basis, industrial goods involve a great deal more personal contact. Industrial marketers also use **exhibitions and demonstrations** to quite a high degree when promoting their products.

3.1 Product

Most business-to-business marketing mixes will include **elements of service** as well as product. Pre-sales services may involve technical advice, quotations, opportunities to see products in action and free trials. After-sales service will include Just-in-Time delivery, service and maintenance and guarantees. Products will also be custom-built to a much greater degree than for consumer marketing mixes. Frequently, products will have to be tested to laid down conditions. Packing will be for protection rather than for self-service. Some of these elements can comprise a powerful differential competitive advantage. For example, ICI offers laboratory testing of various metals so that industrial customers can be assured of the one most suitable for given corrosive conditions.

When buying machine tools, **efficiency features** can be the most powerful buying motive. Other product-unique features may be the ease of or safety of operation. If an operator can manage two machines rather than one, his potential output is doubled. Training of operators is another service often provided by manufacturers of industrial equipment.

3.2 Price

Price is not normally fixed to the same degree as in consumer markets. Particularly where products or services are customised, price is a function of buyer specification. Price is negotiable to a much greater extent and may depend upon the quantity, add-on services and features and sometimes the total business placed per year. Retrospective annual discounts act as loyalty incentives. Mark downs and special offers as used in consumer markets have spread to industrial market pricing.

Trade discounts can apply in those cases where industrial and commercial goods are marketed through middlemen (see below on distribution). In some industrial markets, especially construction, prices are set under a **tendering system**.

3.3 Promotion

Within the promotional mix, personal selling is very important in business-to-business marketing. Some industrial products are quite complex and need explaining in a flexible way to non-technical people involved in the buying process.

Buying in business-to-business marketing is often a group activity and, equally, selling can be a team effort. Salespeople are expected to follow-up to ensure that the products are working properly and that the business buyer is perfectly satisfied. Where an industrial equipment manufacturer markets through an industrial dealer, the manufacturer's salesforce may be required to train the dealer salesforce in product knowledge.

The partnership approach is present to a much greater degree in industrial selling, where the buyer needs information and services and the seller is seeking repeat business in the long term.

The types of **media** used for advertising differ greatly from those in consumer markets. Mass media are rarely used. Advertising is usually confined to **trade magazines**, which reach more precise targets. Direct mail is used to supplement personal selling.

Industrial exhibitions are popular as a means of personal contact with particular target markets, and factory visits are used as a means of engendering confidence in the manufacturer's abilities and standards. More industrial marketers are using PR, through agencies, as a means of gaining favourable publicity in the trade media and to build up their corporate images.

3.4 Place

Industrial marketers tend to deliver direct where agents are used, as in international markets. UK manufacturers will usually deliver direct to overseas business clients.

Sometimes, however, business to business distributors are employed, particularly for consumable and lower-value goods. **Business to business channels** are

- Manufacturer   → Business buyer
- Manufacturer   → Agents → Business buyer
- Manufacturer   → Business distributor → Business buyer
- Manufacturer   → Agents → Business distributor → Business buyer

On-time delivery can be an extremely important requirement in industrial markets, especially where valuable contracts can be held up for want of a relatively small piece of equipment. In such circumstances, the premium on delivery is so great that penalty clauses for lateness are invoked.

3.5 Services

Business organisations are also significant buyers of services, for example insurance, banking, management consultancy and information technology, payroll services and office cleaning. The growth of outsourcing means that suppliers and customers need to establish good relationships and each need to know exactly what is expected of the relationship. The quality of the people and process elements of the service marketing mix are probably more important than physical evidence.

Marketing at Work   Application

The UK's National Health Service

In the UK, medical provision is offered free at the point of use and is funded by the taxpayer. This is unlike healthcare systems elsewhere in the world, where medical care is funded by employers, individual patients or insurance schemes. (British citizens can pay for treatment by private sector providers if they wish.) The organisation that provides such services is the National Health Service (NHS).

The NHS is a large employer, in overall charge of local doctors' surgeries (General Practitioners – GPs) and hospitals throughout the UK. The NHS has many stakeholders: the government has placed the effectiveness of the NHS at the top if its priorities. Although the NHS is government run, some NHS hospitals will operate more like businesses. The NHS , like any other customer, is concerned about cost and value for money.

A large organisation has problems with management. The NHS has undergone a number of restructuring exercises in the last decade. Some aspects of healthcare provision are managed on a regional basis. Some hospitals are independent trusts. The National Institute for Clinical Excellence (NICE) exists to spread best practice in treatment and to review the costs and benefits of drugs and medical techniques. The NHS is a major customer of the global pharmaceutical industry. Other steps have involved giving patients (or their GPs) the right to choose where they are treated. Moreover it is a major user and buyer of information systems.

Applications for information systems

At time of writing, the UK government has instituted a fundamental overhaul in the NHS's use of information technology. According to the *Financial Times* from 2004 to 2012, '800,000 staff in England will be electronically linked to the medical records of more than 50m patents'.

- Hospital appointments and eventually appointments with GPs will be booked online.
- Patient records and prescriptions will be held digitally – as will images of x-ray scans.
- Doctors will have access to online diagnostic tests.

Cost and management

The UK Government is seeking to improve the workings of the NHS by improving its **information systems**. The cost is staggering – about £4bn. Key issues are:

- Doctors must be persuaded that this is the right thing to do – many regional health authorities have developed their own information systems.

- Patients must be reassured that the data is secure and accurate.

- The Government must be reassured that the IT industry will deliver on its premises.

The programme is so large that the procurement process has been intensely competitive. Most major suppliers are working in consortia with others. Each consortia has had to show how the systems produced by its members will work together. The NHS is a key component of the UK's taxpayer-funded welfare state. The continuation of this model depends on the success of projects such as this. However, there is a tension between centrally-imposed and local solutions. For example, the most difficult users to convert to a new system often fall into two groups: enthusiasts for their own systems and the technologically illiterate. The NHS is already a heavy user of IT, but different regions and hospitals are in charge of their own procurement. The NHS's failure to provide IT in the past' means there is a big credibility problem.

4 Competitive edge

FAST FORWARD   **Competitive advantage** may be obtained from an understanding of the industrial buying process.

When competing for business, the industrial product manufacturer is likely to have to conform to laid down standards or quote to tight specifications. **This means it is more difficult to gain a differential advantage in the product itself.** However, a variety of add-on services, such as technical advice pre-sale and rapid spares availability after-sales, can provide competitive advantage.

4.1 Buyers

The relationship with the industrial buyer may also provide competitive advantage and it is important to understand and exploit the customer's buying process.

Organisational buying is a transaction between a number of individuals rather than an action by one person. Buying decisions are likely to be made by a group called a **decision making unit** (DMU). The **purchasing officer** (PO) will usually be part of the DMU but may play one of a variety of roles. Small and routine purchases will normally be the PO's territory and other members of staff may make only small input. For larger or less frequent purchases the PO may lead the team or may be relegated to an **administrative** or **gatekeeper** role. Other members of the DMU will also vary in their influence and involvement.

(a)   The **specifier** is very important and lays the ground rules for the buying decision, though this person may not have the final say. The specification process is often complete before sales negotiations commence and it may not be easy to influence the specifier.

(b)   The **user** may be the same person as the specifier, but not necessarily. The user and the specifier may have different ideas about the good or service to be purchased and the sales person may be able to exploit such differences.

(c)   The **finance** person decides what can be spent. Again, this person may play another role, since purchasing is often a matter of applying budgets and the budget holder may well be the specifier or the user. It is the role of the financier to ensure that value for money is obtained and to approve things like credit arrangements.

Differences between consumer behaviour and organisational buying can be summarised as follows from the viewpoint of the **buying centre**.

(a)   At an organisational level, the decision process is a group buying process, in which the people involved make up the DMU or buying centre.

(b)   The complexity of the products is usually greater.

(c)   The needs of users are more varied and difficult to satisfy.

(d)   The impact of an unsuccessful purchase decision poses much greater personal and organisational risks than the average consumer decision process, for both groups and individuals involved in the purchase.

(e)   There is more interdependence between buyer and vendor in industrial markets because there are smaller numbers of goods and customers. Therefore, not only are sellers dependent on buyers for an assured outlet for their goods, but buyers are dependent on sellers for the continued source of inputs for their processes.

(f)   Post-purchase processes are much more important.

Action Programme 2

What external factors do you think influence organisational buying behaviour?

There are also, of course, **organisational** forces affecting buying.

Centralisation	The physical and managerial location of the decision-making authority.
Formalisation	The degree to which rules and procedures are stated and adhered to by the employees of the organisation.
Specialisation	The degree to which the organisation is divided up into specialised departments according to job function and organisational activities.
Organisational culture	Informal but influential habits, practices and attitudes.

4.2 Models of organisational buying

A number of models have attempted to deal with the complex relations between the factors involved in organisational buying.

4.2.1 The American Marketing Association model

The American Marketing Association model proposes that there are four main influences on organisational buying decisions.

- The inherent priorities of the buyer and the buying department
- Pressures applied to the buyer by the organisation
- Environmental influences on the buyer, including increased professionalism
- Environmental influences on the wider organisation and the way it does business

Departmental influences

	Within purchasing department	Between departments
Intra-firm influence	**Cell 1** **The Purchasing Agent** Social factors Price/cost factors Supply continuity Risk avoidance	**Cell 2** **The Buying Centre** Organisational structure Power/conflict processes Gatekeeper role (1)
Inter-firm influence	**Cell 3** **Professionalism** Word-of-mouth communication Trade shows, journals Advertising, PR, promotion Supplier purchase reciprocity	**Cell 4** **Organisational Environment** (2) Technological change Nature of suppliers Co-operative buying

Organisational influences

Notes

(1)   The gatekeeper role is the buyer's reaction to pressure from other departments; the buyer tends to defend his territory.

(2)   Research suggests that as technological change accelerates, the purchasing agent is less likely to be an important influence in the process. The nature of the supplier is also likely to influence the buying process, with larger firms presenting less risk to their customers, while smaller firms may be preferable to ensure continuity of supply.

4.2.2 The Sheth model

The Sheth model is based on the Howard-Sheth (1969) model of Consumer Behaviour (CB) which gives a central place to **learning** following behaviourist principles. This model illustrates the intricacy of the organisational processes involved, and suggests that the relationships between the individuals concerned in cell 2 of the American Marketing Association model may hold the key to understanding the process.

Three aspects of organisational buyer **behaviour** are identified.

- **Psychological environments** of the individuals in the buying decision
- Conditions which precipitate joint decision making
- Joint decision-making process and conflict resolution amongst decision makers

Joint decision making. The model recognises that a number of individuals, and often a number of different departments, are involved in the decision to buy. Purchasing agents, quality control engineers and production management, for instance, may be involved, and all have different backgrounds, expertise, and exposure to information. Individuals have very different requirements of the products involved, because of these differences.

Five main factors influence the psychological environments of individuals involved in organisational buying decisions.

- **Backgrounds** of individuals such as education and lifestyles

- **Information sources** available to them

- **The degree of active search** in which they are involved

- **Perceptual distortion** affecting the way they see the problem

- **Satisfaction with past purchases** – again, backgrounds will influence how satisfactory the performance of the product was judged to be

Factors precipitating **joint** rather than **autonomous** decision making can be divided into **product specific** and **company specific**.

(a)   **Product specific** factors include perceived risk, type of purchase and time pressure. Each of these has implications for the degree of risk and joint expectations which the product is expected to satisfy.

(b)   **Company specific** factors include company size, degree of centralisation, and company orientation. Clearly, the nature of the company, and the relationships between the individuals and departments involved will all bear on the way in which purchases are approached.

This model does not examine autonomous buying decisions in any detail, but **concentrates on joint decision making**. Conflict is seen almost as a natural and inevitable aspect of such decision processes. Resolution is an essential aspect of organisational structure.

There are four main ways in which this takes place.

- Problem solving
- Persuasion
- Bargaining
- Politicking

The first two of these are rational, and although time consuming, lead to good decisions, according to this model. The others tend to be used when there are irremediable conflicts between interested parties, and they lead to resolution of conflicts, but poor decisions are often made, since they imply that the requirements of some parties remain unsatisfied or frustrated.

4.3 Other ways of creating differential advantage

Other ways of creating differential advantage arise directly from the close relationship involved in industrial marketing. Here are some examples.

(a) **Product**

    (i)   Offer to finish product in any colour to match factory/warehouse decor

    (ii)   Offer to add customer's logo to casings

    (iii)   Emphasise the benefits of any unique product features

(b) **Pre-sales services**

    (i)   Technical advice

    (ii)   Free demonstrations, perhaps at other customers' premises

(c) **After-sales service**

    (i)   Spares immediately available from stock

    (ii)   Rapid maintenance and repair service

    (iii)   Guarantees for longer periods than competitors

(d) **Price**

    (i)   Leasing arrangements made upon request

    (ii)   Discounts for quantity

    (iii)   Package prices for supply, installation and maintenance

(e) **Promotion**

    (i)   Sales engineers who take a partnership approach

    (ii)   Video presentations

    (iii)   Models and samples

(f) **Distribution**

    (i)   Direct delivery

    (ii)   Just-in-Time service

Chapter Roundup

- Industrial marketing, or marketing **business-to-business**, is different in nature from consumer marketing. Buying motivations (the criteria which consumers apply) and the nature of the buying process itself are quite different. There are four basic categories of industrial market.

  - Capital goods
  - Components and materials
  - Supplies
  - Business services

- **Target markets** for industrial marketing tend to be easier to identify than consumer market segments. Data is generally more easily available on businesses than on consumers. Sources include government and privately-published statistics.

- There are differences in the marketing mix for industrial marketing when compared to the characteristic mix adopted for consumer markets.

- **Competitive advantage** may be obtained from an understanding of the industrial buying process.

Quick Quiz

1   What are the four categories of industrial market?

2   Give four examples of non-government sources which could be used in targeting industrial markets.

3   How does 'product' differ in industrial marketing when compared to consumer marketing?

4   How does distribution differ in industrial marketing when compared to consumer marketing?

5   What are the four influences on organisation buying as identified by the AMA?

6   What are the five factors which influence the individuals involved in organisational buying?

Answers to Quick Quiz

1   •   Capital goods   •   Supplies
       •   Materials and components   •   Business services

2   Directories and yearbooks
      Professional indexes
      Specialist libraries
      Trade associations
      Commercial organisations

3   There will usually be a high degree of service built into the product offering.

4   The distribution channel will usually be short, with many supplier delivering direct.

5   •   The buyer's priorities

      •   Organisational pressure on the buyer

      •   Environmental influences on the buyer, especially pressure to analyse professional conduct and competence

      •   Environmental influences on the organisation

6   •   Personal background
      •   Information available
      •   Degree of active search
      •   Perceptual distortion
      •   Satisfaction with past purposes

Action Programme Review

1   Examples of government publications include:

- The **Annual Abstract of Statistics** and its monthly equivalent, the **Monthly Digest of Statistics**. These contain a wide variety of data about manufacturing output, housing, population and so on

- The **Digest of UK Energy Statistics** (published annually)

- **Housing and Construction Statistics** (published quarterly)

- **Financial Statistics** (monthly)

- **Economic Trends** (monthly)

- **Census of Population**. The Office for National Statistics publish continuous datasets including the **National Food Survey**, the **Household Survey** and the **Family Expenditure Survey**

- **Census of Production** (annual). This has been described as 'one of the most important sources of desk research for industrial marketers'. It provides data about production by firms in each industry in the UK

- **Employment Gazette** (monthly) giving details of employment in the UK

- **British Business**, published weekly by the Department of Trade and Industry, giving data on industrial and commercial trends at home and overseas

- **Business Monitor** (published by the Business Statistics Office), giving detailed information about various industries

- **Social Trends** (annually)

2   These include the following.

- **Political/legal**. Government attitude toward business; international tariffs; trade agreements and government assistance to selected industries; legal and regulatory forces at the local and national levels which affect the industrial decision-making process

- **Economic**. Interest rates; level of unemployment; consumer and wholesale price index; growth in GNP. Changes in different economic conditions will impact different sections of the market in differing degrees

- **Physical influences**. Climate, geography, locations, labour supply, choice of raw materials

Now try Question 13 at the end of the Study Text

11

Charity and not-for-profit marketing

Syllabus content – knowledge and skills requirement

- 4.2: Marketing planning and marketing mix for an organisation operating in any context such as FMCG, business-to-business (supply chain), large or capital project-based, services, voluntary and not-for-profit, sales support (eg. SMEs)

Introduction

The objectives of charities and not-for-profit organisations are different from those of most other commercial organisations. While they may carry on economic activities their main purpose is not profit maximisation (Section 1). Although the marketing concept does involve profit, marketing techniques such as segmentation and targeting, can be applied by non-profit sectors to further their objectives (Sections 2 and 3).

1 Charity and not-for-profit marketing   12/03

FAST FORWARD

NFP and **charitable organisations** are usually viewed as a single type, even though this is a varied sector containing both public and private operations.

In the United Kingdom, charitable status is governed by statute law. For a body to qualify as a **charity** its purposes must fall within certain fairly widely defined categories such as the promotion of education or religion. The rather wider category of **not-for-profit (NFP) organisations** might be defined as organisations which do not have increasing the wealth of the owners as a primary objective, though the larger co-operative and mutual societies probably do not count as NFP bodies. Also, many NFP bodies undertake clearly commercial ventures, such as shops and concerts, in order to generate revenue.

Key concept

We could define **not-for-profit** enterprises by recognising that their first objective is to be 'non-loss' operations in order to cover their costs and that profits are only made as a means to an end such as providing a service, or accomplishing some socially or morally worthy objective.

Dibb *et al* suggest that non-business marketing can conveniently be split into two sub-categories.

(a)   **Non-profit organisation marketing,** for example, for hospitals and colleges.

(b)   **Social marketing** seeks to shape perceived beneficial social attitudes such as protecting the environment, saving scarce resources or contributing towards good causes.

1.1 Is marketing relevant to this sector?

FAST FORWARD

Marketing has a lot to offer this sector in terms of marketing auditing and research and the development of strategies to include a clear understanding of segmentation, targeting and positioning.

 Marketing at Work   Application

The **public sector** has recently needed marketing skills to cope with changes in funding and increased competition as a result of compulsory competitive tendering for council services. The Army struggles to recruit able employees often attracted by higher salaries in the commercial sector. Many NFP organisations have introduced initiatives to raise money, such as hospitals selling paramedical services to local industry, and universities developing commercial centres to sell research and consultancy skills.

Marketing management is now recognised as equally valuable to both profit orientated and NFP organisations. The tasks of marketing audit, setting objectives, developing strategies and marketing mixes and controls for their implementation can all help in improving the performance of charities and NFP organisations.

2 Distinctive characteristics

Each element of the marketing mix can be used to achieve the organisation's objectives and marketing control can help to ensure these are achieved.

Whilst the basic principles are appropriate for this sector, Dibb *et al* suggest that **four key differences** exist, related to **objectives**, **target markets**, **marketing mixes** and controlling **marketing activities**.

(a) **Objectives** will not be based on profit achievement but rather on **achieving a particular response from target markets**. This has implications for reporting of results. The organisation will need to be open and honest in showing how it has managed its budget and allocated funds raised. Efficiency and effectiveness are particularly important in the use of donated funds.

Action Programme 1   Application

List possible objectives for NFP and charitable organisations.

(b) **The concept of target marketing** is different in the not-for-profit sector. There are no buyers but rather **a number of different audiences**. A target public is a group of individuals who have an interest or concern about the charity. Those benefiting from the organisation's activities are known as the client public. Relationships are vital with donors and volunteers from the general public. In addition, there may also be a need to lobby local and national government and businesses for support.

There are four types of customers for charities.

(i) **Beneficiaries** include not only those who receive tangible support, but also those who benefit from lobbying and publicity.

(ii) **Supporters** provide money, time and skill. Voluntary workers form an important group of supporters. Those who choose to buy from charities are supporters, as are those who advocate their causes.

(iii) **Regulators** include both formal bodies, such as the Charities Commission and local authorities, and less formal groups such as residents' associations.

(iv) **Stakeholders** have rights and responsibilities in connection with charities and include trustees, managers, staff and representatives of beneficiaries.

(c) Charities and NFP organisations often deal more with services than products. In this sense the **extended marketing mix of people, process and physical evidence** is important.

(i) **Appearance** should be business-like rather than appearing extravagant.

(ii) **Process** is increasingly important; for example, the use of direct debit to pay council tax, reduces administration costs, thus leaving more budget for community services.

(iii) **People**, whether employed or volunteers, must offer good service and be caring in their dealings with their clients.

(iv) **Distribution channels** are often shorter with fewer intermediaries than in the profit making sector. Wholesalers and distributors available to business organisations do not exist in most non-business contexts.

(v) **Promotion is often dominated by personal selling** with street corner and door-to-door collections. Advertising is often limited to public service announcements due to limited budgets. Direct marketing is growing due to the ease of developing databases. Sponsorship, competitions and special events are also widely used.

(vi) **Pricing** is probably the most different element in this sector. Financial price is often not a relevant concept. Rather, **opportunity cost**, where an individual is persuaded of the value of donating time or funds, is more relevant.

(d) **Controlling activities** is complicated by the difficulty of judging whether the **non-quantitative objectives** have been met. For example, assessing whether a charity has improved the situation of client publics is difficult to research. To control NFP marketing activities, managers must specify what factors need to be monitored and permissible variance levels. Statistics related to product mix, financial resources, size of budgets, number of employees, number of volunteers, number of customers serviced and number and location of facilities, may be useful.

3 The charity marketing mix

Charity marketing is akin to service marketing and the extended service marketing mix is appropriate. The guiding philosophy of the charity says what it is for and how it goes about its business. Clearly, just as the components of the normal marketing mix must be in harmony with one another, so too must they be in harmony with the charity's philosophy.

A charity's **products** include **ideas** as well as goods and services. Ideas are very important in fund-raising, pressure-group activity and communicating with the public.

(a) When a supporter provides money to a charity, the idea of what the money will be used for is a kind of product, providing satisfaction to the supporter.

(b) Pressure groups work, in part, by promoting new ideas into the public consciousness, so that bodies with power can be persuaded to take a desired course of action.

(c) Ideas can also be promoted to the public with the aim of changing their behaviour. Governments often take this approach, as, for instance, with energy conservation and road safety campaigns.

Price is very important to larger charities since sales of goods and services provide their largest single source of income. Proper cost accounting techniques must be applied where appropriate.

Since supporters are crucial to a charity's income and beneficiaries are the reason why it exists, **processes** must be as customer-friendly as possible. This is certainly an area where philosophy is important.

Place. It is common for charities to have significant problems with the distribution of physical goods when they rely on volunteer labour. This is especially true of charities that operate internationally, unless they are well established. In particular, the type of charity fund that is set up to relieve a disaster overseas is likely to have great difficulty moving the necessary supplies to where they are needed.

On the other hand, charities that merely disburse funds within one country, to the poor, for instance, or to pay for medical research, may have very short and easily managed distribution chains.

Action Programme 2   Application

You have just joined a small charity which is currently without a formal marketing function. You have been asked to prepare a report which outlines the relevance of marketing in this sector.

Chapter Roundup

- **NFP** and **charitable organisations** are usually viewed as a single type, even though this is a varied sector containing both public and private operations.

- Marketing has a lot to offer this sector in terms of marketing auditing and research, the development of strategies to include a clear understanding of segmentation, targeting and positioning.

- Each element of the marketing mix can be used to achieve the organisation's objectives and marketing control can help to ensure these are achieved.

Quick Quiz

1   Define NFP marketing.

2   How do Dibb *et al* split NFP marketing?

3   What are the four distinctive characteristics in this sector?

4   How might a charity use the tools of the promotional mix?

Answers to Quick Quiz

1   Marketing is a means to an end other than profit such as a socially or morally worthy objective.

2   Marketing in not-for-profit organisations such as charities and marketing directed at shaping perceived beneficial social attitudes.

3   Non-profit objectives; target marketing aimed at groups in addition to consumers; a particular profile applied to the extended services marketing mix; and complexity of measuring success across a range of objectives and publics.

4   Emphasis on value for money; caring; short or non-existent distribution channels; emphasis on personal selling.

Action Programme Review

1   Possible objectives include the following.

- Surplus maximisation (equivalent to profit maximisation)
- Revenue maximisation (as for a commercial business)
- Usage maximisation (as in leisure centre swimming pool usage)
- Usage targeting (matching the capacity available as in the NHS)
- Cost recovery (minimising subsidy)
- Budget maximisation (maximising what is offered)
- Producer satisfaction maximisation (satisfying the wants of staff and volunteers)
- Client satisfaction maximisation (the police generating the support of the public)

2   The charity has objectives which it wants to attain.

Plans will be developed and implemented to achieve these non-profit objectives. The various publics to whom the charity will be communicating will need to be identified. This is in keeping with profit orientated organisations' application of marketing, namely, 'to identify, anticipate and satisfy customer requirements profitably' (CIM). Whilst the profit element is not included in our activities, we are still seeking to make the best use of our resources.

The anticipation of our target markets' needs is vitally important. Our 'customers' in this sense are the people that the charity supports. Other 'customers' include the volunteers working for the charity. In return for their time, support and enthusiasm we must satisfy their needs for team-spirit, and social activities, for example. The donors to the charity will need to feel that their funds are being used wisely and for the purposes they intended. By satisfying the needs of our various stakeholders, we can satisfy our own goals.

Charities are in the business of attracting volunteers and donors and developing a long term relationship with them. To achieve this, the development of trust is vital, and can be fostered through effective communications as in commercial markets.

Part of our work is about education of the public, and choosing the correct communication channels and message is just as important as it is in advertising a bar of chocolate. The issues involved are more serious but the process is the same. The difference really lies in the results desired – one is to increase awareness, the other is to prompt action to purchase. Much commercial advertising is intended to increase awareness, change attitudes and increase knowledge. We will be using our communications in relation to the charity aims rather than profit objectives.

Marketing has a valuable contribution to make in achieving the charity's goals. It emphasises the needs of the various customer groups and directs our attention towards satisfying their needs. We can do this by using the tools of marketing which include marketing planning, implementation and control and in particular the techniques offered by marketing communications, including advertising, direct marketing, sponsorship and public relations. A marketing orientation also emphasises the need for a quality service to achieve customer satisfaction and for relationship management to ensure loyalty and support.

Now try Question 14 at the end of the Study Text

BPP
LEARNING MEDIA

Question and Answer bank

1 Ethics and responsibility   40 mins

As a journalist for a business publication, you have been asked to prepare an article which explains the importance of marketing ethics and social responsibility in business today. Put together a draft document using appropriate examples to illustrate your arguments.   **(25 marks)**

2 Control and evaluation   40 mins

Your magazine recently published a reader questionnaire to help it to focus more closely on areas of interest to marketing executives. You have been asked to analyse the responses and choose a number of topics which could form the basis for future articles. In the first batch of replies, a recurrent theme is that, although companies are spending significant amounts on marketing activities, they seem to obtain very little in the way of feedback on those activities.

Prepare an article for the magazine which explains different approaches to marketing control and evaluation. Provide details of possible approaches to implementation in a retail environment and suggest who should be involved.   **(25 marks)**

3 Environment   40 mins

Your company produces computer software for small businesses. In your role as marketing manager, you have been asked to prepare a report for your board of directors which explains how aspects of the marketing environment could affect the company's activities. Your report should cover aspects of the wider (macro) marketing environment.   **(25 marks)**

4 Ansoff   40 mins

Lewis Upholstery manufactures and sells craftsman produced seating furniture for the home user. There is one showroom which features three-piece suites. The company attracts price-conscious customers by placing advertisements in the local newspaper which emphasise buying direct from the manufacturer. The Managing Director wants to increase sales and has employed a marketing consultant to assist.

As the marketing consultant, use Ansoff's growth matrix as the basis of your report. This should outline a number of specific marketing strategy alternatives, and go on to recommend and justify the best strategies to implement in the short and medium term.   **(25 marks)**

5 IKEA   80 mins

Swedish furniture manufacturer and retailer IKEA was formed in 1943 by Ingvar Kamprad. Between 1954, when the first store opened, and 1990 the company underwent massive expansion from a single Swedish outlet to more than 80 spread through 21 different countries, with over 70% of revenue generated outside Scandinavia. The IKEA concept comprises large retail outlets (around 80,000 square metres) situated on the edge of sizeable towns and cities, selling a full range of furniture and furnishings. The outlets sell everything from beds to lounge suites, kitchen utensils to carpets, curtains, pictures and lighting: everything the customer needs to set up and update the home. The stores also offer instore restaurant and child care facilities to make the shopping experience a pleasant one. To help in the selling effort, the company produces an extensive catalogue, giving details of the items for sale, prices, colours, measurements and availability. In 1990 alone, around 35 million US dollars were spent producing 40 million copies in 12 different languages.

IKEA operates with an up market brand image, linked to stylish and sophisticated Swedish taste, but its products are aimed clearly at the mass market. The company is not a market nicher and to maintain its growth must attract large numbers of customers of low as well as high incomes. To keep its prices low, IKEA must keep costs down. This is achieved by a clever combination of buying in bulk, making buying centres compete for orders, having large stores with self-service facilities and products which are flat packed, for self assembly at home.

The IKEA company mission is clearly stated 'We shall offer a wide range of furnishing items of good design and function, at prices so low that the majority of people can afford to buy them'. This philosophy is backed up by the following aims.

- IKEA should keep costs low and assist customers

- products should combine good quality, durability and be functional

- profit should be used to build and expand

- a keen understanding of the company's cost base must be maintained and good results achieved with careful investment

- energy must be concentrated carefully and time used efficiently

- simple solutions should be found to product and company problems

- IKEA should take responsibility and put things right

- IKEA should find alternative solutions to problems by experimenting

Currently IKEA seems to appeal particularly to customers aged in their 20s and 30s who are furnishing a home for the first time. These customers want their homes to look stylish and smart, but with relatively low disposable incomes they must carefully consider price. The company is also keen to attract other customer types, from many different countries and of all ages and lifestyle stages. Although IKEA does not formally use demographics and psychographics to segment its market, it divides its markets into different geographical areas, each with a standard product range but having the flexibility to include products which match local, cultural requirements.

Answer the following questions with reference to the IKEA case.

(a)   Briefly define marketing planning and say why it is important for IKEA to use it.   (10 marks)

(b)   How should the marketing planning process relate to IKEA's corporate planning?   (10 marks)

(c)   Describe the elements of a detailed marketing plan and show within this framework what types of information might be included in a marketing plan for IKEA.   (30 marks)

(50 marks)

6 Segmentation   40 mins

Many organisations recognise the benefits offered by the careful application of market segmentation. However, exactly how the process works is less widely understood. For example, some managers regard the identification of target markets as the key stage in the segmentation process. Others are more interested in identifying appropriate segmentation variables with which to group customers.

You have been asked to make a presentation to your organisation which explains the segmentation, targeting and positioning elements of the market segmentation process. Using examples from business to business markets to illustrate your explanation, draft a document which details the areas you intend to cover.

(25 marks)

7 Models
40 mins

Prepare a short paper on the value of behavioural models in seeking to understand the promotional process. Illustrate your answer with three different models. Specifically illustrate applications and limitations of each model.
(25 marks)

8 New products for growth
40 mins

Your company is seeking to develop a strategy which will enable the business to expand rapidly, growing turnover fourfold in four years. Prepare a statement for the board of directors that indicates the most appropriate methods of examining new and existing products in order to identify those most likely to enable the business to reach the growth goals outlined above.
(25 marks)

9 Pricing policy
40 mins

Construct a report to marketing management that explains the factors that should be taken into consideration when pricing for a product line.
(25 marks)

10 Physical distribution and marketing
40 mins

The company for which you work is considering the idea that physical distribution should become a component part of marketing, rather than being the final delivery part of the production process. Your line manager has asked you to prepare a report for the board of directors outlining how such an arrangement might improve service to customers.
(25 marks)

11 Service marketing
40 mins

You have applied for a job with a small hotel company which is establishing a formal marketing function for the first time. As part of the interview process, you have been asked to make a short presentation which explains the characteristics of marketing in the service sector. Prepare some notes which detail the areas you intend to cover in your presentation.
(25 marks)

12 Modes of entry
40 mins

You are a freelance journalist who specialises in writing articles on international marketing for a variety of publications. Decide upon the publication you wish to target and write a short article which explains the difference between structure choices such as exporting, licensing, joint ventures, trading companies and direct ownership. The article should also outline the factors which organisations should take into account when selecting which structure to adopt.
(25 marks)

13 Industrial marketing
40 mins

You are employed as a marketing manager by an industrial organisation producing moulded plastics for the car industry. Your managing director has asked you to prepare a presentation for junior marketing recruits explaining the characteristics of industrial marketing and how they apply to your organisation. Draft a document which details the areas you will cover in your presentation.
(25 marks)

14 Charity

40 mins

You have recently taken up a new position with a well-known national charity. Your job is to oversee and organise marketing activities for the charity. Your previous work experience has been entirely in the commercial sector so not-for-profit marketing is new to you.

Your new boss, the charity's director, has asked you to make some notes on the similarities and differences you expect to find between your new and old positions. Prepare a document which does this and explains how these contrasts will affect the marketing activities which you carry out. **(25 marks)**

1 Ethics and responsibility

Title: Marketing Ethics and Social Responsibility: an opportunity for competitive advantage, or a constraint on marketing decisions?

Marketing professionals are increasingly being influenced by a demand for higher standards in terms of ethics and social responsibility. Recent examples of this trend include the positive publicity given to The Cooperative Bank when it severed ties with two fox-hunting associations, a peat extraction company and companies that test products on animals. In contrast, Ford experienced negative publicity for taking out black employees from photographs used in Eastern European advertising.

Ethics operate as a set of moral principles and values that act as a guide to an individual's conduct. Henderson has developed a matrix to illustrate the different positions a company can take towards this issue:

1. Ethical and Legal	**3. Ethical but Illegal**
Ideal option - decisions are both legal and ethical	Decisions require a trade-off of legality in favour of ethical choices
2. Unethical but Legal	**4. Unethical and Illegal**
Decisions require a trade-off of ethics for legality	Decisions both illegal and unethical should be avoided

Positions 2 and 3 pose problems for marketing managers, especially when operating internationally. For example, bribes in many African countries are often standard practice; managers have to decide whether to behave in line with local expectations or adhere to home country values. Many people consider it unethical to sell arms to oppressive nations but this practice is not illegal. This comes into sharp focus when marketing to children, and when marketing cigarettes and alcohol, illustrated by the debate surrounding the advertising of Hooch, the alcoholic lemonade.

Another issue which highlights the importance of marketing ethics in business today is the opportunity it presents for developing a competitive position. The Cooperative Bank in 1992 repositioned itself as 'the ethical bank', based on the bank's core values of responsible sourcing and distribution of funds. A loss of £6m in 1991 turned into a profit of nearly £18m in 1993 following this repositioning.

Social responsibility is different from ethics. It refers to a company's obligation to maximise its positive impact and minimise its negative impact on society. However it is similar in the sense that it is also poses problems for marketers, because society is made up of diverse groups and satisfying everybody is difficult. For example, airline companies tread a fine line between satisfying the needs of smokers and non-smokers.

Social responsibility can be usefully considered under three headings: consumer issues, community relations and green marketing. Many companies are now proactive in terms of responding to these issues. Linking community relations and green marketing together, IBM has an environmental policy and community programmes plan which includes environmental improvement projects, software and teaching packs and secondees to the Department of Environment. ICI have significantly reduced their hazardous waste since 1990, Bass Brewers use CFC free cellar coolers and The Body Shop regard all three areas as vitally important.

Marketing ethics and social responsibility are both constraints on marketing decisions and opportunities for competitive advantage.

Gas flares and oil pipelines above ground in Nigeria coupled with the Brent Spar controversy have earned Shell a tarnished reputation and provoked consumer protest, while the Cooperative Bank has turned around its fortunes on the basis of its sound ethical policies.

2 Control and evaluation

Introduction

In any control and evaluation process, a useful starting point would be a detailed breakdown of marketing expenditure for the last five years, together with a full review of current marketing control and evaluation procedures.

This would be followed by thorough audits of current marketing effectiveness (strategies, organisation, marketing operations) using the formats recommended by Kotler.

These documents will help readers with specific indicators for their own operations, but for general purposes, I am assuming that the organisation is involved in all the marketing activities normally associated with a medium-sized or large company.

The marketing control process in outline

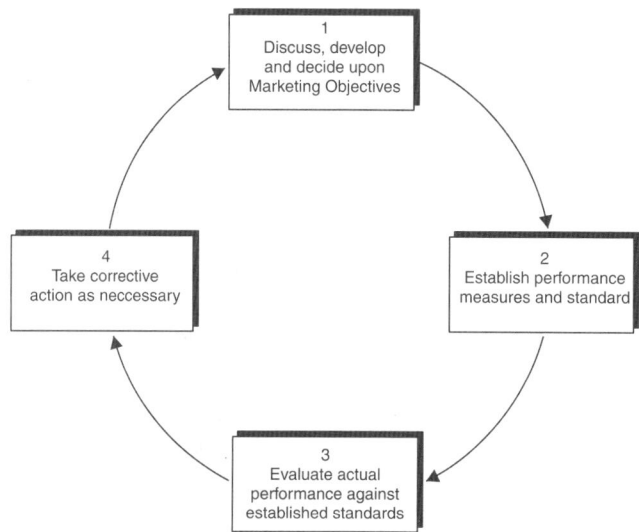

The following explanatory notes should be read in conjunction with the above diagram.

1. Marketing objectives

The starting point is the organisation's **marketing objectives** which should show clearly where it wants to be at particular points in time. Without knowing clearly where it wants to be, it cannot possibly establish the extent to which it is getting there, or indeed whether it has arrived. Objectives should be achievable given prevailing market conditions and resources.

Realistic objectives will be based upon past performance and internal and external audits, the latter supplemented by marketing research.

2. Performance measures

There are a number of **measures by which performance can be judged** and these should at least include:

- Sales levels
- Market share
- Marketing costs
- Profitability
- Customer satisfaction

Performance standards can now be set at £x for the period, Y% market share and £z marketing costs, all set against a maximum number of customer complaints.

3.   **Evaluation**

The organisation is now in a position to monitor and **evaluate actual performance** against these standards.

4.   **Corrective action**

Where performance is below a tolerable level, the organisation should **take corrective action**. This may mean invoking contingency plans previously drawn up for this purpose.

Information will be needed at all stages of the process, ie information of the right type, in the right place and at the right time. The types of information the organisation should be seeking include:

- Competitor market shares, strategies, products, prices etc
- Sales by product, by area, by retail outlet, by week
- Total market and forecasted trends. Market segments and brand positionings.

Different approaches to control and evaluation

Control methods can be formal or informal or a mixture of both. Some formal methods have been outlined above and are largely quantitative in nature. However, matters like brand image and customer satisfaction are more qualitative. Informal methods of evaluation and control include peer pressure, staff appraisal meetings and informal discussions.

More detailed evaluation and control techniques for a retail company could include:

- Mystery retail shoppers
- Formal store checks
- Retail audits
- Consumer surveys
- On pack offer responses
- Hall tests for presentation, packaging
- Taste tests and focus group discussion for new product introductions
- Test marketing

Implementation

In a fully marketing orientated company everyone is involved directly or indirectly in marketing and therefore in marketing evaluation and control. This can be achieved by encouraging discussion and comments at meetings and through suggestion boxes. All staff should be asked their opinions and those of relatives and friends outside the company.

More specifically however, formal marketing evaluation and control procedures should be the responsibility of the marketing director, implemented downwards through marketing, sales and retail management/personnel. Advertising, PR and marketing research agencies would also play a part in the evaluation process.

3 Environment

Tutorial note. The impact of the macro-environment on a computer software company forms the basis of this question. It is a relatively straightforward question requiring application of the generally well understood 'PEST' framework. The most important aspect of the question is the requirement to apply this framework to the context and provide interesting and relevant examples.

Report: Effect of Macro Environment on the Company
To: The Board of Directors
From: The Marketing Manger
Date: June 200X

Introduction

1.   The marketing environment defined

Every company is affected by both its internal and external environment. The external environment audit directs managers to consider the likely affects of political, economic, social and technological factors on the company's operations. In addition, customer, competitor, supplier and distributor activities should be monitored. Such activity is often referred to as MACRO and MICRO environmental analysis. This should highlight opportunities and threats for the organisation to consider in its planning activities.

The focus for this report is how aspects of the macro environment could affect our computer software company when selling to small businesses.

2.   The external marketing environment

2.1   Political/Legal factors

The change of government in 1997 has resulted in some significant changes. The National Minimum Wage Regulations and the Working Time Regulations both require the keeping of records to prove compliance; there are opportunities for us here.

The government claims to support small businesses and the many regional programmes can be used to assist purchase. Regional priorities may be adjusted in the wake of Welsh and Scottish devolution.

The 1998 Data Protection Act has replaced the 1984 legislation and has wider implications for us and for our clients. The new legislation considerably strengthens the position of the individual in relation to others who possess data about him. Processing such data will be forbidden except in certain tightly controlled circumstances. We can add value to our products by providing good advice on the implications of the legislation.

The political environment further afield is also of interest. A lasting peace in Ireland could increase the viability of a sales subsidiary in that country. Similar international opportunities should be evaluated with consideration for political stability.

At a more tactical level we should be aware of the legal standards imposed by statutory bodies such as the Advertising Standards Association and the legal requirements of legislative Acts such as Trade Descriptions and Health and Safety.

2.2   Economic factors

The local economy is very relevant to us and, more particularly, our customers. Whilst we are able to spread our risk through a national network, small businesses are much more dependent on the local economic climate. We should use local employment and economic indicators available through the HMSO and Monthly Digest of Statistics to anticipate changes.

On the national scale, the economy should be evaluated on a regular basis. There is currently significant debate over interest rates, with tension between the Bank of England's brief to contain inflation and the sluggish performance of small manufacturing businesses. The possibility of adopting the Euro makes the effect of future monetary policy difficult to forecast.

Social and cultural factors determine people's basic assumptions and habits. This is particularly important for us as we deal mostly with owner managed businesses. Larger organisations may display a greater tendency towards entirely logical decision making; the owner manager is more influenced by impressions and innate preferences. The crucial factor here is the imbalance in computer literacy between the generation which controls the budget and the generation which actually uses our product. We must offer the decision makers comfort and security while providing the operators with the facilities they need. References from satisfied customers will be invaluable.

3.   **Conclusion**

To conclude, effective environmental scanning systems and flexible, adaptive marketing planning processes are required by our company so we can avoid threats and exploit opportunities presented by the macro environment.

4 Ansoff

Tutorial note. The Ansoff matrix is a key tool for generating a number of alternative marketing strategy options. This question therefore tests candidates' ability to apply this matrix and make decisions regarding the most appropriate options to select, given the scenario presented. It is important to apply the theory to the specifics of the question. Note here that Lewis Upholstery is probably a small business (no senior marketing staff, advertises in a local newspaper) and therefore has limited resources. Also, furniture is a shopping good, which is probably purchased only after a good deal of planning and shopping around.

Report: Strategic options for increasing sales at Lewis Upholstery
To: Managing Director
From: Marketing Consultant
Date: December 200X

1.   **Consultancy brief**: to outline a number of marketing strategy alternatives which will increase sales for Lewis Upholstery. To go on to recommend and justify the best strategy to adopt in the short and medium term.

2.   **Ansoff matrix framework**: the matrix which will be used was developed by Ansoff and covers four different routes to increased sales for an organisation. These include:

- Market penetration
- Market development
- New product development
- Diversification

Market penetration involves thinking about options to enable the company to sell more of its current products and services to current customers. According to Ansoff, this is the least risky option as the firm has experience in both areas.

After this, market development is suggested. Here the company considers if there are any markets, distribution channels or customer segments who could be persuaded to buy the firm's current products.

New product development is the third option, usually considered more risky than market development because the failure rate for launching and growing new product sales is high, particularly in the consumer products sector.

Finally, diversification is a route to more sales but this is very risky because it entails getting involved with new markets and new products.

Having outlined the basic tool, I will now apply the strategies outlined for each option in the matrix above to Lewis Upholstery.

PRODUCTS

	EXISTING	NEW

	EXISTING	NEW
M A R K E T S **EXISTING**	**Market penetration** • More purchase and usage from existing customers • Gain customers from competitors • Convert non-users	**New product development** • Product modifications • Different quality levels • 'New' products
NEW	**Market development** • New market sectors • New distribution channels • New geographic areas eg international marketing	**Diversification** • Horizontal integration • Vertical integration • Concentric diversification • Conglomerate diversification

3. Application to Lewis Upholstery

The firm has limited financial and marketing resources. While considering all possibilities, therefore, it may be that some will seem impractical.

3.1 Market penetration

3.1.1 **More purchase and usage from existing customers**: encourage repeat sales with sale offers, discounts on multiple purchases and setting up a database and mailing customers with relevant offers and supplementary product ideas. Train showroom staff in 'selling up' and link sales techniques.

3.1.2 **Gain customers from competitors**: create differential advantage, emphasise 'custom made suites' and customers' ability to specify their requirements (style, fabric, finish) and see them being made. Review the design and layout of the showroom - consider a re-launch day with free food and drink and prize draw. Reduce prices.

3.1.3 **Convert non-users into users**: increase promotion spend, use direct mail, yellow pages, local radio, sales promotion and step up efforts to gain local publicity. Another option is to offer existing and previous customers an incentive for recommendations to family and friends that results in an order.

3.2 Market development

3.2.1 **New distribution channels**: consider additional showrooms in the region. Consider manufacturing for a local or national retail chain. Mail-order catalogue or mail-order advertising would be an additional route to market.

3.2.2 **New markets**: in terms of new market segments you could consider quality conscious rather than price conscious customers, emphasising 'craftsman manufactured' and 'tailor-made' thereby increasing profits perhaps rather than sales. Employ a sales person to target the business, hotel and leisure markets for reception suites and furniture.

3.2.3 **New geographic areas**: you could expand out of the local area and go regional, national or explore export markets. Marketing research would be advisable for these options.

3.3 **Product development**

3.3.1 **Product modification**: add 2 seater suites, arm chairs, stools, bedroom suites, garden chairs

3.3.2 **Different quality levels**: manufacture a value range, a standard range and a deluxe range

3.3.3 **'New' products**: add curtains, fabrics, tables, bookcases, lighting

3.4 **Diversification**

3.4.1 **Horizontal integration**: moving into high quality suites, kitchen units, TV cabinets and tables for a made to measure premium market. Manufacture new products for pubs, sports centres and office reception areas.

3.4.2 **Vertical integration** is probably impractical as the minimum efficient scale for fabric manufacturing and the timber trade is beyond your investment capacity.

3.4.3 **Concentric integration** seeks marketing and technical synergy. An example might be to acquire or develop a fabrics business with an emphasis on soft furnishings and replacement made to measure loose covers.

3.4.4 **Conglomerate**: you may decide to change your business area completely and go into an entirely new, unrelated business area - catering for example. This would be highly risky.

4. **Recommendation and justification**

On the basis of risk, core competence and resource criteria, market penetration followed by product and market development seems sensible.

In the short term there exist a number of market penetration options which could be easily resourced and quickly implemented. You have a basic replacement demand, then you have new housing developments and friends and family of current customers. This will require more sophisticated marketing communications which I would be happy to help you with.

In the medium term, I would recommend you add products to your range which can be sold to current and new customers. It would be sensible to combine this with market development to begin to target more affluent, less price sensitive customers. The most successful position for small, niche companies is one of differentiation focus where you concentrate on high quality at a high price. It seems very possible that your company has the skills to do this.

Perhaps longer term the business market has potential, but as this requires both new products and developing an understanding of new customers I feel this is too risky at present. I look forward to discussing this report with you in due course.

5 IKEA

(a) Marketing planning is the regular, systematic, customer-centred and controlled series of activities a company will undertake to meet business objectives, secure long-term profitability and realise its product/market strategy effectively and competitively. Planning activity exists over the short term (1 year), the medium term (2 - 3 years), and the long term (3 - 6 years). Marketing planning is an essential management tool for IKEA to use for the following reasons.

(i) Planning pre-supposes an organised and structured approach to business - essential for IKEA to stay competitive.

(ii) Marketing plans, effectively implemented, can be a spur to action for all concerned with their execution.

(iii) Marketing planning provides a market orientation to customers, and a control mechanism to keep corporate activity on track.

(iv) Marketing planning helps stimulate the creation of an open, action-centred culture.

(v) Marketing planning focuses the organisation on the customer, and helps the organisation become more pro-active.

(b) The marketing planning process should be fully integrated with the IKEA corporate planning process.

(i) Marketing is an 'organisation-wide' function. Successful organisations realise that there are internal as well as external customers, and that successful marketing depends on the quality of relationships people have with each other and with customers.

(ii) Marketing strategy is developed from corporate objectives and informs the corporate planning process.

The following approaches will facilitate the integration of marketing planning with IKEA corporate objectives.

(i) Ensure marketing is represented at senior executive level.

(ii) Create a culture where participation, motivation and self-development are encouraged, and where there is dedication to customer service.

(iii) Ensure the management information systems within IKEA are linked to a market intelligence system, to facilitate speedy and reliable information flow back to the organisation.

(iv) Develop marketing tactics from marketing strategy and test them against the requirements of corporate objectives.

(v) The control mechanisms used to test the effectiveness of marketing planning should also be able to be used as tools to indicate to what extent corporate objectives are being achieved.

(c) The marketing plan will begin with a marketing audit which will examine in full the business environment of the firm, the internal marketing system of the firm, and the specific marketing activities which are currently being carried out. IKEA management will use the information gathered from this exercise to gain an overall picture of the firm's current trading and improve marketing effectiveness. Two specific marketing tools are used.

(i) SWOT analysis - which will indicate to IKEA the company's current strengths, weaknesses, business opportunities and competitive threats.

(ii) PEST analysis - which will indicate to IKEA the influences of political, economic, social and technical factors on the firm's business activities.

A number of key strategic questions emerge.

- Who and where are our potential customers?
- When and where will they buy our products?
- Can we reach all of them with our existing or planned resources?
- Why do our customers buy from us?
- Who are our main competitors and what inducements to buy are they offering?
- What key external factors currently constrain our business activities?
- What key internal factors currently constrain our business activities?

The next components of the planning process are the assumptions and actions that IKEA management make and take in order to drive the planning process forward.

(i)   Timescales are placed on identified and agreed required actions.

(ii)   Marketing objectives are then set for IKEA over the short, medium and long terms. These should be quantifiable where possible. The objectives state what the company seeks to achieve with the products, and in the markets in which it trades.

(iii)   Marketing strategy is clearly set out. This enables IKEA management to set down the methods it will use to meet the marketing objectives.

(iv)   Marketing tactics will then be established; these will illustrate how the staff (who must deliver the plan) will carry out marketing activities.

(v)   A selling and sales management organisation will then need to be determined. This will consist of all the supporting activities and office structures needed to enable the marketing tactics to happen.

Levels of planning

Time Horizon

Strategic Planning

Which businesses should the organisation be in?

How should they be financed?

How should the organisation be structured?

How should resources be allocated?

5 years +

Tactical Planning

What products should be added or deleted?

What capital investment or divestment is necessary to meet strategic plans?

What is the best pricing pattern?

What new facilities, systems or methods are needed to meet strategic plans?

1-5 years

Operational planning

What is the best production/marketing etc plan to meet objectives?

What materials, facilities are needed for operations?

What is the best method of organising operations?

1-12 months

Operations and Transactions

What operations should be performed with existing facilities to meet the specified output requirements in the next operational period?

Now

Increasing Scope

Increasing Detail

(vi)   IKEA will need to staff the plan effectively. They must have the right people with the right knowledge and skills in the right place at the right time to carry out the plan successfully.

(vii) Contingency measures will need to be drawn up. These are used to address failures in expected outcomes, and are used as insurances against the product/market strategy not delivering the forecasted results.

(viii)   IKEA will need to have drawn up effective mechanisms for feedback and review. These are controls such as targets (individual objectives), budgets (used to finance the plan) and audits (used to test its effectiveness). Feedback information will feed both the marketing planning and corporate planning activities and will be used to initiate the next planning cycle.

6 Segmentation

Tutorial note. This question asks students to demonstrate a sound understanding of the underlying principles and process of market segmentation. The application to the business to business context provides an opportunity for candidates to illustrate the concept's practical value.

Presentation: the market segmentation process

Structure of the presentation

1.   Introduction

2.   The three elements
2.1   Segmentation
2.2   Targeting
2.3   Positioning

3.   Conclusions & Discussion

Materials for presentation

OHT, Flip chart, Pens, Handouts

1.   **Introduction**

Good morning ladies and gentlemen. This presentation will last for approximately 45 minutes during which time I will outline the principles and benefits of the market segmentation process and provide a number of business to business applications of the concept. We should have time for questions and discussion at the end.

Market segmentation has been defined by Dibb et al (1994) as the process by which customers in markets with some heterogeneity can be grouped into smaller, more homogenous segments. Market segmentation is a process made up of three distinct activities: segmentation, targeting and positioning. Market segmentation allows a company to decide which groups of customers it can service most effectively and to design marketing mix programmes so that the needs of these targeted groups are then more closely met. Specific benefits include a better understanding of customers, a clearer view of the competitive situation and effective resource allocation.

2.   **The three elements of the process**

2.1   **Segmentation**

Segmenting a total market involves the identification of variables which divide the market into sub-segments with similar characteristics.

Business to business markets, such as packaging, photocopier and computer markets, can be segmented with many of the bases used in consumer markets such as geography, usage rate and benefits sought. Traditional industrial market bases include customer type, use of product, customer size and purchasing procedures. So for example, a company selling protective packaging may segment its market by the customer types of consumer goods manufacturers, publishing companies and consumer durable manufacturers. It may further segment these by customer size and product application. So for instance

packaging may be required for presenting the product, protecting each product or over-wrapping a group of products. The handling of books may require different packaging from tinned food and video recorders.

The base used to segment the total market should result in a group of customers who are:

(a) **Measurable** - information on customer characteristics should be obtainable so that the marketer knows who is in the segment and therefore the size of the segment.

(b) **Accessible** - it should be possible to communicate effectively with the chosen segment

(c) **Substantial** - large enough to consider for separate marketing activity

(d) **Meaningful** - customers who have different preferences and vary in market behaviour/ response to marketing efforts

Once the market has been segmented, a more detailed profile of typical customers in each segment should be developed.

2.2 Targeting

Following on from the segmentation process is the targeting process which involves evaluation of the attractiveness of each segment and the decision concerning which segments to target. A number of factors should be taken into consideration in evaluating segment attractiveness; the structure and size of the market, the company's brand and market share, the intensity of competition, production/marketing scale economies and the capabilities of the company in matching with the target markets' needs relative to competition. Following this, two targeting strategies are possible - the concentration strategy or the multi-segment strategy. So for example if the photocopying market was segmented on the basis of photocopying volume, a manufacturer such as Canon adopts a multi-segment strategy by targeting small, medium and high volume users, whereas Kodak Copier business only concentrates on the high volume users.

2.3 Positioning

The final stage in the market segmentation process is that of positioning, which involves selecting a position and signalling it to the target market. Positioning is the designing of the company's image so that target customers understand and appreciate what the company stands for in relation to its competitors. A number of strategies are available to position business to business products:

- Position on **product features**. Toshiba portable PCs are divided into three families according to screen technology.

- Position on **benefits**. This approach is similar to the previous one though the difference can be illustrated with the adage 'don't sell the steak, sell the sizzle'. For example, IBM have an advertising strap line that states, 'At IBM the last thing we'll offer you is a computer.' The copy goes on to offer solutions to business problems.

- Position on **usage**. Apple computers are often positioned on the desk top publishing capability needed by many businesses.

- Position on **user**. This associates the product with a user or class of users. So for example, ICL produce computers for retail organisations such as Boots and Sainsburys and position on the basis of specialisation for the retail user.

- Position **against competition**. With this approach marketers make either direct or indirect comparisons between their product and competitors products. When any computer company wins an industry award this is often used in advertising to differentiate themselves from the competition.

3. Conclusions and discussion

From the examples provided it should be apparent that all three stages of the market segmentation process are important. It is true to say that much more research has been conducted into segmenting consumer markets; however there are many effective applications of the concept in business to business markets as the examples provided illustrate. Any marketing manager in this sector should ensure that she or he is familiar with and able to apply the market segmentation process.

7 Models

(a) **What are models?**

Because marketing systems are very complex it is necessary to represent them as models with a number of key elements displayed. These models are essentially simplifications of the real world but they do enable us to understand and plan the underlying processes. Although they are becoming increasingly scientific, many models used in understanding the promotional process are essentially empirical in character. Nevertheless they have proved useful.

(b) **Overall value of models**

Using models is of value for the following reasons.

(i) They simplify complex situations.

(ii) They allow postulation and measurement of actions.

(iii) They can be used to support decision making and planning.

(iv) They can be used for analysis purposes and to aid shared understanding in the marketing team.

(c) **Examples of models**

The three specific models we have chosen to use are:

- The AIDA model
- The (radio signal) communication model
- The integrated marketing communication model

(d) AIDA model

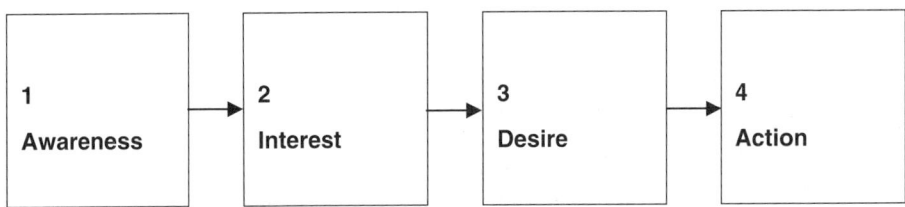

(i) **Description**

This very simple model has stood the test of time since evolved by Strong in 1925. It describes the stages of consumer's behaviour as they move towards the final action which may be the purchase of goods or services. This model reminds us that a sale is not an instant process, rather it is the result of a number of individual stages. The consumer has to firstly be aware of the product/service. Secondly the consumer needs to have some specific interest in the product/service. Thirdly before the sale the consumer has to be motivated by having a particular desire for the product/service.

(ii) **Applications**

Though simple this model can be used to analyse plans and monitor all advertising campaigns. Its very simplicity is a powerful aid in this process. To start with it is necessary to know the awareness levels of your product/service in the target market. Then it is necessary to design the advertising campaign message to interest the target audience. Next various sales promotion incentives may be used to create desire for the product/service.

(iii) **Limitation**

At the same time as being a strength, the simplicity of the four step AIDA process is a weakness, and more comprehensive models have been developed. Colley, in his 1960's book *Designing Advertising Goals to Measure Advertising Results* (DAGMAR) develops a more comprehensive response hierarchy with the following elements.

Awareness > Comprehension > Conviction > Action

(e) **(Radio signal) communication model**

The communication process

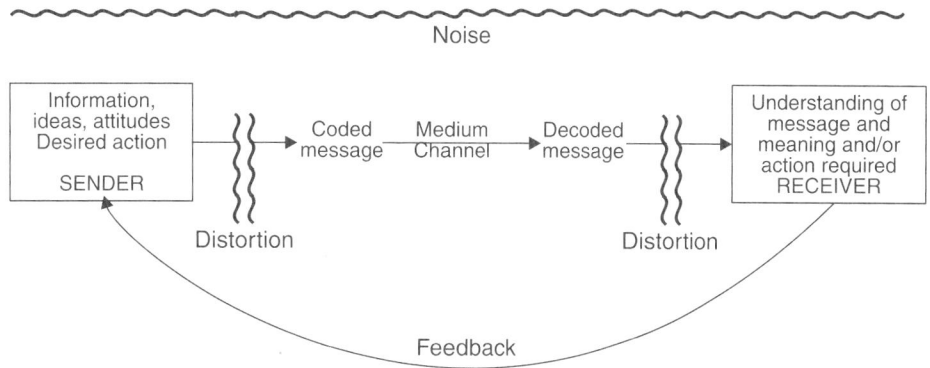

(i) **Description**

This model is clearly based on that of sending a radio or a telephone signal and can be used to emphasise that the communication process is more complex than it appears at first sight. For example, there may be 'noise' in the system. This may equate to the clutter of competing advertisements in the chosen media. The receivers (consumers) may also have to **interpret** what the message means to them. This is the 'decoding' process.

(ii) **Applications**

Increasingly sophisticated advertising is being designed, in which the messages are minimised. They may be coded very cleverly in a colour scheme or by the use of a particular actor representing the product, for example the blonde Rutger Hauer dressed all in black representing Guinness, or the puppy representing Andrex toilet tissue. The process of encoding/decoding is obvious in these examples.

(iii) **Limitations**

Like other models, the process of analysis is essentially a qualitative one which does not help with deciding on the absolute amounts of advertising spend. The model is also limited by the many other factors that it does not allow for but which are present in the market place, such as the degree of competitive reaction.

(f)   **Integrated marketing communication model**

The integrated marketing communication process

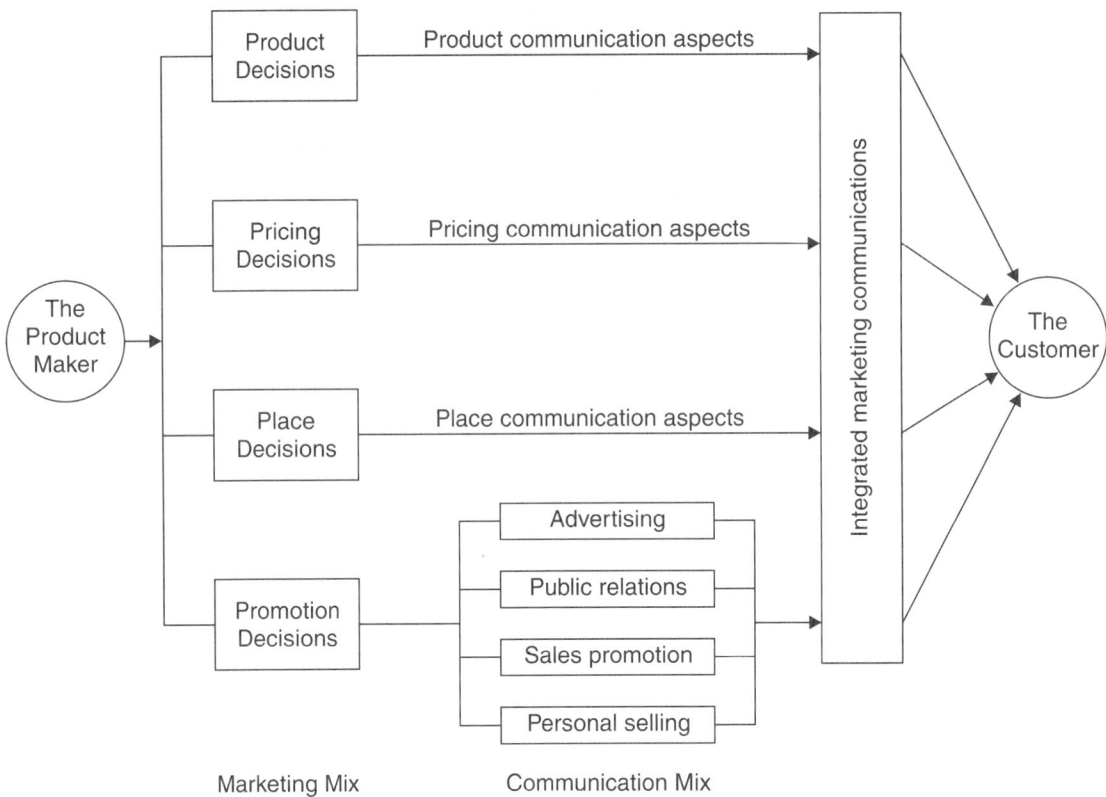

(i)   **Description**

This model attempts to depict the whole of the marketing communication process. It demonstrates that each element of the marketing mix can make a contribution to the communication process. It suggests that these elements must be integrated with the elements of the promotional mix. The whole process links the company with its customers in the most effective way.

(ii)   **Applications**

Increasingly both agencies and clients recognise the need to integrate campaigns in the method described above. Each element can have a distinct role to play in the overall process. A synergistic combination is possible if the overall result is greater than the sum of the separate parts.

(iii) **Limitations**

Historically major patterns of communication may have been established by a company (for example advertising) and limited knowledge may prevent it from using other techniques such as direct marketing. The above model, though comprehensive, does not show how to make decisions about the relative proportion of each element of the overall mix.

8 New products for growth

FOR PRESENTATION TO: THE BOARD OF DIRECTORS

Prepared by: A Marketer
Date: June 200X
Subject: Examining new and existing products for greater potential

The four year time period enables us to consider the development of new products, support for products in growth markets, and divestment or repositioning of products that are in the decline phase of their product life cycle.

New product development process

The company is unlikely to achieve its goal unless it puts in place a process of new product development. These new products must be carefully researched, developed and if possible tested in the market place prior to launch.

Idea generation. This can be systematic or by chance. My recommendation is that the company adopts a systematic procedure to generate new ideas. The company should put in place a system for scanning its marketing environment to identify new opportunities. This should be supported by a systematic process of marketing research closely linked to the research and development process. New ideas can also be generated from employee suggestions, the research and development function or simply by observing competitive activity and listening to customers.

Screening of new ideas. The new ideas generated should be systematically put through a screening process. This process should analyse each idea in terms of its potential development, the market potential, financial resources required to develop the idea, its relevance to the overall strategic direction of the organisation, likely return on investment and the organisation's overall capability to market the product effectively.

Business analysis. This analysis involves a detailed evaluation of each idea with more comprehensive marketing research and testing of the concept, a detailed competitor analysis and a full analysis of the resource requirements that will be required to launch successfully and achieve sales targets. The market analysis should determine the degree of market attractiveness: particularly the level of competitiveness, growth rates and longer term potential.

Test marketing. This is recommended, although not always possible. The product can be tested either with one customer or in a particular region. It can involve simple trial or be supported by testing various marketing mixes to see which has the most effect on sales. This stage may require considerable investment and may need to run for several months prior to a decision being made to launch the product.

Existing product portfolio

It is recommended that the company assesses its current portfolio. The BCG matrix is a model that we can utilise to assist us in this process.

The matrix will enable us to identify our products' market positions, relative to our competitors with the largest market share. It will also enable us to evaluate whether the products are in growing or mature markets. Finally, it will enable us to identify the balance of our overall portfolio of products and assess which products should be supported for growth (stars or possibly question marks), or divested to free up resources (dogs or possibly question marks). The matrix should also indicate whether the organisation's successful mature products (cash cows) are sufficient to generate the cash needed to support the other products that will help us achieve our goal of a fourfold increase in turnover.

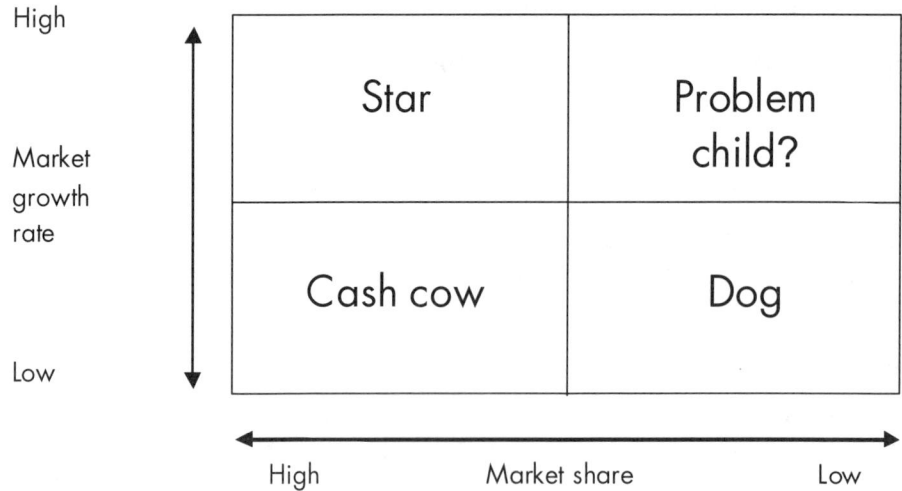

The findings of this analysis will therefore require more detailed marketing research, to identify those products that offer the most chance of growth. We may also consider the possibility of repositioning some of our products into new growth markets.

9 Pricing policy

Report

To: The management
From: A Marketer
Re: Pricing policy of a product line

A product line can be defined in terms of a 'broad group of products whose uses and characteristics are basically similar'. Such products can be differentiated by:

*   Price
*   Packaging
*   Targeted customer
*   Distribution channel used

A firm may have a line of products because it wishes to target a number of segments of the market, all of whom require different benefits. The following are the considerations you might make when detailing the influences on pricing of a product line.

(a) **Product quality**. If the firm is seeking a niche upper market segment and a reputation for quality then it may decide a high price is necessary (for example, the Caribbean cruise holiday market). This price may hold for all products in the line, yet there may be special offers for block bookings or during certain times in the year when demand falls.

(b) **Company image**. The firm may be seeking an exclusive image in the market place and may use pricing strategy in conjunction with public relations to achieve this, for example Marks & Spencer.

(c) **Costs of production**. The firm will want to meet the full costs of production and make sustainable profits, so pricing must reflect this. The bigger the operation, the bigger the scale economies available from production and marketing, particularly where products are very similar (thus permitting bulk manufacture/purchase of parts). This situation would help secure lower prices and increased competitiveness in a mass market.

(d)   **Degree of standardisation of products**. An extension of (c) above, this implies that where products in a line are quite different in order to meet consumer needs, then the costs of the product and, therefore, the price, will have to be higher.

(e)   **Desired level of profit**. A firm may willingly take losses on one line of product as long as the range of products meets the forecast profits target. It may price, therefore, to achieve this goal.

(f)   **Desired level of market share**. A firm may set or alter prices as a promotional tool to realise market share goals.

(g)   **To manage the portfolio effectively**. The firm may have a number of product lines in the market (or different markets) at the same time. Portfolio analysis may indicate that price changes to specific products in specific lines at specific times may realise more revenue; the firm is thus able to use pricing to manage profitability.

(h)   **To market diversify**. The firm may be able, through lowering or increasing the price, to take its product line into a different market (upper or lower in income grouping). Some changes to the line (apart from price) would also probably be necessary in order to do this.

(i)   **As a promotional tool**. A firm may use its pricing structure as a promotional tool to bring 'value for money' to the customer's attention. In order to increase added value it may offer 'free servicing' as an added incentive.

(j)   **To capitalise on novelty**. If the product line is new, and the market largely untapped, a firm may be able to harvest significant profits from the market over the short term by pricing up the whole line. Innovative products will command this competitive advantage until other, similar products enter the market, when the firm will need to reduce its profits to stay competitive. Such pricing up over the short term will additionally help cover the heavy research and development costs of innovation.

(k)   **Price leadership**. Where a few suppliers dominate a market (an oligopoly), price competition is most unusual. Any reduction in price by one supplier is likely to be matched immediately by the others, so no benefit accrues. Price increases which are not matched rapidly erode sales. It is common in such markets for a price leader to emerge. This is likely to be a major player with a reputation for efficiency. The price leader indicates the current appropriate level of prices without using its leadership competitively.

Please raise any queries regarding this report with me.

A Marketer

10 Physical distribution and marketing

REPORT

To: Board of Directors
From: A Candidate
Date: 4 December 200X

Introduction

The process of **physical distribution** is a key element of our marketing strategy - we must ensure that our products reach the customer in the right quantity, at the right time and in perfect condition. In marketing text books it is described as the 4th P along with promotion, price and product. This report outlines the reasons why physical distribution should become a **component of marketing** and **not** the **final delivery part of the production process**.

The customer's perspective

It is important to consider the extent to which our organisation has adopted a customer orientation. Customers of our products are not concerned with **how** the product reaches the point of sale, only that it is available in the quantity and at the quality they require. If we see distribution as the final delivery part of the production process then we are in danger of adopting a production orientation The focus of our attention will be on the efficiency and effectiveness of our production and distribution systems and not on market factors and customer needs.

Competitive advantage

By focusing our attention on the market it is possible for the organisation to identify and assess new/innovative distribution opportunities that will achieve a competitive advantage. Such opportunities will range from transforming the channel structure through to tactical activities with our distribution channel. Distribution has until recent years had the least attention of the marketing mix elements but with increasing levels of competition and commoditising of products, its importance as both a strategic and tactical weapon is now being recognised.

Service and added value

The matching of the distribution process to our organisation's service marketing activities is an important consideration. Management of the distribution channel can provide many opportunities for improved service delivery ranging from stock management, order processing to guaranteed delivery. It is also important for us to identify our customers distribution problems and provide solutions that add value to our overall product offer.

Supply chain management

Our major customers require increasingly sophisticated channel management techniques to ensure our products maintain their shelf presence. Examples of these are the increasing importance of trade marketing activities and category management techniques as opposed to traditional product management activity. We also need to establish closer and stronger relationships with other distribution channel members to ensure that we maximise the efficiency and effectiveness of the total supply chain not just our final part in the chain. Many retailers are now adopting the concept of efficient consumer response (ECR) in trying to ensure that the distribution system works in a co-ordinated manner. Similarly, information technology is playing an increasingly important role in our customers stock handling and purchasing functions.

Integration of marketing strategy

The final argument for including distribution as a component part of marketing is the need to integrate our distribution activity with our total marketing activity. We must ensure that the promises we make in our communications are met by our distribution channel activities. Similarly our distribution strategy can reinforce our brand's positioning in the minds of the consumer. It is important that distribution is part of marketing's responsibility to ensure that our organisation maintains its competitive edge in the marketplace.

11 Service marketing

Presentation Notes on Services Marketing

By: A. Candidate
Audience: Interview Panel
Equipment needed: Slides, Handout

1.   Introduction

Good morning ladies and gentlemen. Over the next 30 minutes I would like to outline a number of key characteristics of marketing any service and then relate these to the particular task of marketing an hotel. I'll be happy to take questions at the end of the presentation.

2.   Aims of presentation

(a)   To outline the distinctive characteristics of marketing an hotel service

(b)   To consider ways in which the marketing mix should be extended when marketing the services of an hotel

3.   The characteristics of services

Intangibility

A significant characteristic of services is the relative dominance of intangible attributes in the make-up of the service product. A service is a deed, performance or effort, not a product which can be seen, touched and taken away. This makes it difficult to evaluate before purchase and means that customers do not own the service.

How can the hotel manage this intangibility?

We need to use tangible cues to service quality and manage 'physical evidence'. For example, our staff should look professional, which includes a hotel uniform and attention to personal grooming. The rooms should be spotless, and follow the hotel's overall decorative identity. The food we serve should be of a high standard and offer our guest variety.

Inseparability

Services have simultaneous production and consumption which emphasises the importance of the service provider and therefore the role of our contact personnel. The conference organiser and the waiter, in our customers' eyes, is the hotel.

Consequently, selection, training and rewarding staff for excellent service quality is very important. The consumption of the service often takes place in the presence of other customers, as in the restaurant, therefore enjoyment is not only dependent on the service provider but other guests as well. It is important to identify and reduce the risk of possible sources of conflict. For example our restaurant layout should provide reasonable space between tables and smoking areas.

Heterogeneity

This characteristic can also be referred to as variability. This means that it is very difficult to standardise the service our guests receive. The receptionist may not always be courteous and helpful and the maids may not remember to change all the towels, for example. Due to inseparability a fault such as rudeness cannot be quality checked and corrected between production and consumption.

This again emphasises the need for rigorous selection, training and rewarding of staff. Evaluation systems should be established which give our customers the opportunity to report on their experiences with our staff. In addition we must ensure that our processes are reliable: for example, the way we book in guests, organise their keys and deal with checking-out.

Perishability

Consumption cannot be stored for the future. Once a hotel room is left empty for the night that potential revenue is lost.

This makes occupancy levels very important and it is necessary to match supply with demand. For example if our hotel is busy in the week but not at weekends, a key marketing task is to provide incentives for weekend use. To cater for peak demand we can employ part-time staff, and multi-skill full time staff. We can also use reservation systems in the restaurant and beauty salon to smooth out demand. If our customers have to wait, comfortable seating should be provided in the reception.

4. The extended marketing mix

The marketing mix for products is the well known 4Ps of product, price, place and promotion. For service marketing we add three additional Ps to our tool kit: physical evidence, process and people.

Physical evidence is used to manage the essentially intangible nature of the hotel service. As previously stated, smart staff, an impressive lobby and interior design for all areas of the hotel is important to establish an appropriate position and signal this to customers.

Managing processes helps to deal with the inseparability and heterogeneity characteristics. If standards and processes are adhered to a consistent level of service can be delivered. For example receptionists need to be trained to deal with demanding business people and cleaning staff need to prepare rooms to a consistent standard.

Probably the most important element of the services marketing mix is people. Hotel staff occupy a key position in influencing customer perceptions of service quality. Without training and control, employees tend to be variable in their performance which in turn leads to variable service quality and customer satisfaction.

5. Conclusions

Key professors in the field of services marketing, such as Bateson, Zeithaml and Bitner, all suggest that there are three key jobs for service marketers; managing differentiation, managing productivity and managing service quality. Should I be successful in my application today, I too would make these three issues my top priority for the hotel.

Does anybody have any questions?

12 Modes of entry

> **Tutorial note**. Candidates should be able to define each of the alternative international market entry methods included in the question and clearly explain the difference between these structure choices. The second part of the question tests the ability to suggest factors which are important in making this international operations decision.

Article: Marketing Business, UK marketing practitioners, members of CIM.
Title: International Marketing - What Level of Involvement?

Articles abound in the marketing and general management press urging managers to exploit international marketing opportunities. But how should organisations go about entering foreign markets and what are the choices?

Many market entry methods are available, each with a different level of involvement in terms of risk and control. Phillips, Doole and Lowe provide a useful ladder of options:

Levels
of
involvement

Wholly-owned subsidiary
Company acquisition
Assembly operations
Joint venture
Strategic alliance
Licensing
Contract manufacture
Direct marketing
Franchising
Distributors and agents
Sales force
Trading companies
Export management houses
Piggyback operations
Domestic purchasing

For this article we shall consider the differences between exporting, trading companies, licensing, joint ventures, and direct ownership:

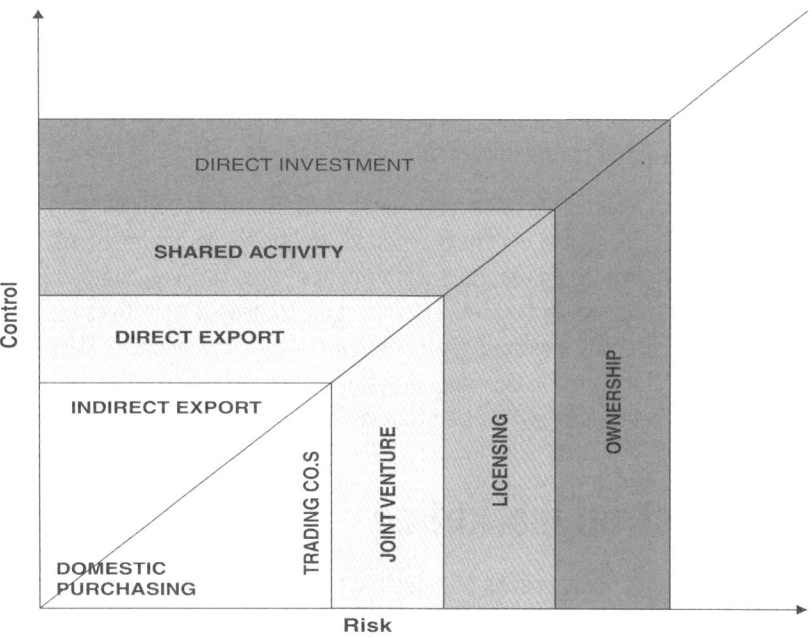

Exporting: involves minimum effort, costs and risk. Indirect exporting is the simplest and cheapest form of market entry and involves having your products sold overseas by others. This includes domestic purchasing, piggyback operations, export merchants and houses and using trading companies (see below). Most small companies start this way as costs and risks are low. However, this is at the expense of control over how the goods are marketed overseas. Direct exporting is the next step taken, where a company wishes to secure a more permanent long-term place in international markets and begin to exercise more control. The disadvantage with this is that whether using agents, distributors, franchising or direct marketing, the level of investment required increases because the marketing, distribution and administration costs are borne by the company.

Trading companies: represent a form of indirect export and involve a company selling its products to the trading company, which buys in one country and sells to buyers in another country. Much of the world's food is sold internationally in this way and trading companies are strong in managing counter-trade activities. The problem with using trading companies is the lack of control, and experience which the firm will miss out on.

Licensing: also involves relatively low levels of investment and is a form of management contract in which the licensor confers to the licensee the right to use either patents, trademarks, copyrights or product/process know-how. A lump sum and royalty is paid by companies who use one of these; for example, many Disney characters are licensed to companies who use the characters on fabrics and games aimed at children. It can be an attractive form of market entry in politically unstable countries and for medium sized firms wishing to launch a successful brand abroad.

Joint ventures: these involve the shared ownership of a specially set up new company for marketing and/or manufacture of products overseas. This can be a significant feature of licensing, but the difference with joint ventures is that each company takes an equity stake in the newly formed firm and control is usually split equally. They may be used due to government restrictions on foreign ownership in countries such as China and South Korea, and where complementary technology skills can speed up development. For example, vehicle manufacturers have initiated a number of joint ventures or the similar structural form, strategic alliances, including Alfa Romeo with Nissan and Fiat. Costs of single sourcing and strong competition encourage joint ventures. However, differences in aims and objectives and the substantial increase in investment required are the disadvantages with this form of market entry.

Direct ownership: is often the choice where commitment is high and long term and the country is politically stable. In this type of situation direct ownership becomes attractive as control and profits are highest. Direct ownership can involve assembly, wholly owned subsidiaries or company acquisition. Multinationals such as Kodak have directly owned subsidiaries in many countries and import products from foreign subsidiaries.

Factors to take into account in selection of the options

In making the market entry choice a number of factors should be taken into consideration: level of resources available, degree of control required, amount of commitment, particularly from senior management, risk of losing proprietary information, size, stability, competitiveness of overseas market, government restrictions and incentives, marketing strategy & objectives for international operations and, of course, the company's existing level of foreign market involvement. Very often the final decision is based on the risk/return equation and, in reality, related to taking advantage of opportunities that present themselves, which cannot always be planned.

13 Industrial marketing

Presentation: Characteristics of Industrial Marketing
By: Marketing Manager
To: Junior Marketing Recruits

Equipment: Slides, Handout

1.   **Introduction**

Welcome! Over the next few minutes I would like to outline a number of key characteristics of industrial marketing as they particularly pertain to our industry - moulded plastics. The aims of this presentation are twofold:

- to outline the distinctive features of marketing to major motor manufacturers
- to consider in what ways the marketing mix is distinctive for industrial plastics products.

Let me ask you a question. How quickly did it take you to decide on your last car? On the model, the colour and whether you should pay extra for metallic paint? Probably a long time, it wasn't a very quick decision. This should start you thinking about the distinctive characteristics of complex products and the type of marketing required.

2. **Distinctive features of marketing to major motor manufacturers**

2.1 Characteristically our products are bought when needed; this is known as derived demand. Our plastic dashboards are ordered when consumers buy our customers' cars. Our sales are therefore dependent on the fortunes of the car industry.

2.2 The purchase quantities are usually large.

2.3 Target marketing is simpler as there are a small number of customers and readily available SIC codes and trade directories such as Kompass.

2.4 Typically our components are technical in nature and therefore high value. This results in a high risk purchase which requires long term contracts with our customers and a good MkIS to monitor the re-buy situations of our competitors' customers.

2.5 The type of product affects the buying process our customers employ. In situations where we are tendering for new business the process is likely to take a number of months. The stages are likely to be problem recognition, general need description, product specification, supplier search, proposal solicitation, supplier evaluation and selection, order-routine specification and performance review. Later this afternoon you will meet one of the buyers from Ford, who has agreed to outline its buying procedures for you.

2.6 Purchasing departments of major motor manufacturers are large and staffed by highly professional buyers. The decision-making process outlined is not down to one individual but to what is referred to as a 'decision-making unit'. This is made up of users, buyers, approvers, influencers and deciders. When marketing to the motor manufacturers the concerns and questions from all these people must be addressed. They each have different priorities. Buyers will be concerned with how much our products cost and how soon we can deliver. An assembly manager will be more concerned with the quality and how easily it can be inserted onto the line. All members of the DMU will have opinions and they will depend upon their background, past experience of the product and their perceptions and personality.

Our marketing must address their concerns and influence their decisions in favour of this company.

3. **Marketing approach**

3.1 Relationship marketing is vital. This involves a focus on retaining customers through building trust and commitment. Communication, shared values, joint projects and building in switching costs are all factors we consider. The role of the key account manager is vital. S/he needs to be an excellent communicator, problem solver and negotiator and be able to build a number of relationships spanning the different functions of both companies. We have a very good relationship with Ford and they provide us with testimonial information to use when trying to win new accounts.

3.2 The traditional marketing mix is also very important. The product is technical and purchase involves higher risk, which means a greater use of services, for example the provision of technical advice and technical specifications. Price is negotiated and new orders are often put to tender. We need to consider legal & economic constraints, cyclical demand, administered, bid and negotiated pricing approaches. In distribution we mainly supply direct, except for a small amount of smaller component business which is handled by distributors. With the advent of Just-In-Time manufacturing issues related to production, transport, storage and inventory holding are vital concerns. Finally, promotion focuses upon personal selling through our key account managers. The remainder of the budget is spent on trade press advertising, the use of exhibitions, trade promotion and publicity.

4. **Conclusions**

I hope this presentation has highlighted a number of distinctive characteristics of industrial marketing and how these influence our approach with customers and the emphasis placed on the different elements of the marketing mix. Are there any questions?

14 Charity

Managing the marketing activities for a charity may seem radically different from that of managing marketing in a profit-orientated enterprise. However, marketing a charity may offer a more creative arena for marketers, and often considerably greater challenges.

Goals

Often goals of business organisations are formulated in quantitative statements; for a non-profit organisation, goals may be stated in contribution value terms, or in terms of levels of support over a given period.

Structure

Within business organisations, there is usually a formalised structure of operating. In charities, more of an informal approach may prevail; there may be many more 'interests', perhaps individual (rather than collective groupings as with business) with a lack of agreement about how to move the charity forward. Opinion leaders in charities may have no formal management training, or may be retired; they may possess a fixed mindset and be highly resistant to change. Hence charities may be fairly slow moving organisations with fixed norms of operating.

Results

One can measure the effectiveness of business organisations by the bottom line result - profit. In a charity, no such measure exists and it can therefore be very difficult to measure results.

Intervention

With a charity, the effects of management intervention are largely unknown, as most charities operating today are structured for social ends rather than for strategic reasons, like most business organisations. Businesses are often structured into levels of hierarchy and accountability. Charities are frequently much more informally structured.

Possible objectives for a charity

- Surplus maximisation (equivalent to profit maximisation).
- Revenue maximisation (as for businesses).
- Usage maximisation (maximising the number of users and their usage).
- Usage targeting (matching the capacity available).
- Full cost recovery (minimising subsidy).
- Partial cost recovery (minimising subsidy).
- Budget maximisation (maximising what is offered).
- Producer satisfaction maximisation (satisfying the wants of staff).

Marketing principles and charities

(a) **Strategic visioning**. As with a firm, a charity would have specific ideas of what it wanted to achieve, though these may not be as explicit or formalised as with a business organisation.

(b) **Marketing audit**. A charity would want to find out how effectively it had been operating but would probably do this in an ad hoc way, and not conform to the marketing audit procedure followed by many firms.

(c)   **SWOT and PEST**. Unless a charity is particularly well organised and led by a marketer or someone with contemporary industrial/commercial experience, then it will largely be more re-active than pro-active. It may have a knowledge of the factors constraining it, but its knowledge of itself in terms of efficiency and effectiveness may not enable quality management.

(d)   **Marketing objectives, strategy and tactics**. Although staffed by committed individuals, charities usually operate in the short term; rarely are objectives and strategies formally set. Tactics seem to evolve and staff are motivated on the basis of progress made.

(e)   **Control, feedback and review mechanisms**. Periodic committee meetings and annual reviews facilitate progress and results communication; very rarely are there clear channels or identified mechanisms for performance measurement as with business enterprises.

Pilot paper and answer plans

The Chartered
Institute of Marketing

CIM Professional Series Stage 2

Marketing Planning

Marketing Planning

Time:

Date:

3 Hours Duration

This examination is in two sections.

PART A – Is compulsory and worth 50% of total marks.

PART B – Has **FOUR** questions; select **TWO**. Each answer will be worth 25% of the total marks.

DO NOT repeat the question in your answer, but show clearly the number of the question attempted on the appropriate pages of the answer book.

Rough workings should be included in the answer book and ruled through after use.

© The Chartered Institute of Marketing

CIM Professional Series
Stage 2

Marketing Planning – Specimen Paper

PART A

Derby Cycle Corporation

The Derby Cycle Corporation (DCC) is a bicycle designer and manufacturer that holds the leading market share in Canada, Ireland, the Netherlands and the UK, and is also a top supplier in the US. Formed in 1986 to acquire Raleigh, Gazelle, and Sturney-Archer from TI Group, the company markets under those brands and others, including Derby, Nishiki, Univega and Diamondback. DCC has manufacturing operations in five countries and produces mountain, city, hybrid, British Motorcross (BMX) and racing bicycles. The company plans to expand through acquisition in the US and Europe and by offering accessories and apparel.

The UK bicycle market has seen the rise of global brands and competition on the back of different bicycles types targeted at different market sectors. In the 1980s mountain bikes from US manufacturers became popular and Raleigh became a follower rather than a leader with such products. Despite Raleigh's 98% brand recall scores with UK customers, the popular mountain bikes have US heritage, and today's parents are not necessarily buying Raleigh for themselves and their children. In addition, as the mountain bike market matures a wider product range is available, with some bikes selling for as little at £99 (40% of the mountain bike sector is below £120). Own label bikes are available from retailers, mail order and the Internet.

The Diamondback brand was acquired by DCC in 1999, and the UK bicycle manufacturer Raleigh was later appointed as the distributor for the UK and Ireland. This was significant for Raleigh as Diamondback was a global brand with consistent West Coast USA youth imagery. This gave it credibility in the BMX and mountain bike product sectors where Raleigh's older, British and family-oriented brand equity was less appropriate.

With both brands, Raleigh needed to establish distinct positions in the market. This would have an impact on new product development, pricing, distribution and communications activities. Focus groups were conducted in the USA and UK with male/female, urban/rural and serious/leisure cyclists in order to develop a detailed understanding of both the Raleigh and Diamondback brand essence and values. This would form a blueprint for all communication agency briefings in order to provide consistency and focus.

NB: This paper has been written using the case study from the Marketing Operations paper, June 2001.

PART A

Question 1.

You are acting as a marketing consultant to the DCC Marketing Manager.

a. Identify and briefly explain the components of the marketing plan for DCC.

    (10 marks)

b. Identify and critique the main challenges in the marketing environment that are likely to impact on the Raleigh and Diamondback brands in the next two years, and explain the limitations of the market information used when conducting an external audit.

    (15 marks)

c. DCC plans to expand through acquisitions in the US and Europe and by offering accessories and apparel/clothing. With reference to appropriate theory, explain these planned growth strategies and the potential associated risks for the company if they implement these strategies.

    (15 marks)

d. DCC has decided to launch a range of Diamondback clothing in your country. Recommend the marketing mix decisions for this range of clothing.

    (10 marks)
    (50 marks in total)

PART B – Answer TWO Questions Only

Question 2.

Your soft drinks manufacturing company has conducted a gap analysis.

a. Explain the concept of 'gap analysis' as used in marketing planning.

(5 marks)

b. With reference to appropriate theory, recommend how such a 'gap' could be filled by an organisation.

(5 marks)

c. The organisation has realised that it needs to identify more domestic and international segments to target when planning its market development strategy. Evaluate the concept of segmentation and targeting, including the benefits of segmentation.

(10 marks)

d. Recommend how the following variables for segmentation could be used for drinks products:

i   Lifestyle.

ii   Benefits sought.

(5 marks)
(25 marks in total)

Question 3.

Your organisation has developed a new range of cosmetic products to be targeted at the 'grey' market.

a. Explain and justify the role of innovation within organisations.

(5 marks)

b. Critically evaluate reactive and proactive approaches to new product development.

(5 marks)

c.   Explain the following terms and offer examples for cosmetic products:

   i   Replacement products.

   ii   Relaunched products.

   iii   Imitative products.

(10 marks)

d.   Explain the role of branding in relation to the development of new products and its impact on the marketing mix decisions.

(5 marks)
(25 marks in total)

Question 4.

You are the marketing manager of a low cost air travel organisation and you are currently developing the marketing plan for next year.

a.   Recommend both qualitative and quantitative techniques for forecasting which could be used when preparing the marketing plan.

(5 marks)

b.   Identify and justify the main external factors from the macro and micro-environment affecting this organisation's pricing strategy.

(10 marks)

c.   Critically evaluate the following approaches that this organisation will need to consider when setting its pricing strategy:

   i   Marginal analysis.

   ii   Breakeven analysis.

(10 marks)
(25 marks in total)

Question 5.

The marketing manager of your university is worried about service quality.

a.   Explain the criteria that affect student or customers' perceptions of service quality.

(10 marks)

b.   Discuss the role of internal marketing and explain why it is important for services marketing.

(10 marks)

c.   Recommend how the marketing mix for this university might be adapted for full-time international students who wish to attend the university.

(5 marks)
(25 marks in total)

1

(a) **Situation analysis**

> **Tutorial note.** The setting gives a brief summary of the intended marketing strategy, which is to target two different segments: the youth and young adult market with the street-credible Diamondback brand and the family oriented segment with the Raleigh brand. We have omitted an executive summary as the question is only worth 10 marks and the answer needs to be concise.

Entry of global brands - increasing competition. Decline of Raleigh brand leadership - widely available, cheap mountain bikes.

High Raleigh brand recall.

Marketing strategy

Two brands, Diamondback and Raleigh, aimed at distinct market sectors.

Raleigh - traditional, for the older person, image of quality and reliability.

Product - largely traditional but with read-across of components for scale economies.

Price - value for money/small premium for established brand.

Promotion - largely traditional, in-store, via personal selling.

Place - traditional bike distributors such as Halfords.

Diamondback - global brand with street-cred, aimed at the mountain bike market.

Overall position is mass market but not economy – should have genuine mountain bike status and realistic cost.

Product - technically sound - need for up-to-date, athletic outdoor image - paintwork and transfers very important - possibility of range of complementary accessories and clothing.

Price - value for money.

Promotion - wider advertising featuring image as above. Promotion to specialist dealers to persuade them to stock brand as value for money but credible product.

Place - as for Raleigh plus more specialised bicycle dealers.

Numerical forecasts

It is not possible to give any specific numerical forecasts as we have no data to work with. However, we would expect to see realistic targets for improvements in turnover and profit and realistic estimates of marketing expenses.

Controls

It is equally impossible to specify marketing controls as we have no knowledge of Raleigh's organisation, methods or expectations. However, we would expect to specify some time bounded targets and allocate some responsibilities.

(b) **Challenges in the macro-environment**

> **Tutorial note.** Your answer to this will inevitably depend on the extent of your background business awareness, and your ability to relate your knowledge to the consumer durables sector.

Some possibility of continuing concern with road safety cutting the market for children's' bikes.

Countervailing effect of green awareness of bikes' lack of pollution.

Falling interest rates making credit purchases easier.

Increasing use of cars and road congestion.

Challenges in the micro-environment

Continuing competition from highly targeted brands.

Falling costs of basic components such as less exotic frame tubing allowing increased cost competition.

Lack of overall growth in the essentially saturated UK market.

Demographic change – rising population for whom car travel is the norm, falling population of fit older people for whom the bike is a friend.

Falling prices of small and used cars creating more attractive substitutes to the bike.

Market information

Easily available secondary information may be out-of-date or irrelevant.

Obtaining primary information is expensive and time consuming.

Detailed information on competitors' policies and practices is very difficult to obtain.

Feedback from sales staff may be coloured by their inherent tendency to optimism.

(c) **Expansion by acquisition**

Gives rapid market expansion.

Probably brings experience and expertise in the market concerned.

Can be expensive and may require large amounts of cash (as opposed to eg shares) though under-utilised assets such as real property can often be disposed of for cash

Detailed investigation must be made of current market success and future prospects – it is in the vendor's interest to paint a rosy picture.

Integrating staff, where this is necessary can be very difficult because of cultural differences.

It is rare that all the aspects of the two marketing mixes involved are fully complementary. Adjustments will be needed to eg product portfolios, distribution networks, price and credit policies.

Accessories and clothing

Ansoff – product development – new products for old customers.

Exploit existing brand equity and distribution channels by selling new products in existing markets.

Low risk strategy – less so than entering new markets with existing products and much less than diversification.

Advertising synergy – bikes, accessories and clothing can be shown in the same ads and can use the same strapline.

Challenge will be sourcing new products – will they be bought in? Implications for quality and reliability of sources.

Financial commitment should be lower than expansion by acquisition, especially if new products bought in.

(d)

> **Tutorial note.** The question gives you no details of what the range contains so you are free to use your imagination. The only proviso is that it should probably be linked with bikes and the outdoors in some way.

Overall market position to reflect Diamondback bikes – see (a) above.

Product

Integrated range of outdoor activity clothing with bias to mountain biking - incorporate Diamondback logo and colourways.

Fleeces, jerseys, t shirts, underwear and tight pants in 'technical' wicking moisture control fabric. Rainproof cycling jacket, hat, overtrousers overshoes and gloves, using modern high breathability fabric.

Clothing to be of good acceptable quality.

Accessories to include bike tools, puncture repair outfits, pump, saddlebags, panniers and small frame bags.

May be largely bought in and rebranded.

Price

Price to reflect Diamondback bike prices – not economy, but accessible to teenagers.

Promotion

Ads in cycling magazines.

In-store displays.

Initial get-one-free promotion with upscale Diamondback bikes – nb aim is to promote accessories not bikes!

Place

Cycle shops as for bikes.

National chains of 'sports' clothing distributors eg JJB Sports.

2

(a)   Forecast gap between profits/revenue from existing or planned operations and required level of profits/revenue.

Diagram

(b)   New product market growth strategies (*Ansoff*).

Market Penetration

Product development

Market development

Diversification

(c)   Nature of segmentation and targeting - mass market approach no longer valid - consumers no longer grateful for anything they get - increase in accuracy of focus of marketing mix - increase in customer satisfaction.

Segmentation has potential to increase profitability by increasing customer satisfaction -

- Product features closer to customer needs and wants.
- Increase in customer choice by generating variety of desirable products.
- Can also identify segments most likely to buy thus allowing greater focus of promotion.

(d)

> **Tutorial note.** As always when a question is set within the context of a particular industry, you must be prepared to extemporise from common sense and everyday experience. There should always be some marks to be gleaned from correct use of general theory.

Lifestyle (psychographic) segmentation – based on values, interests, personality, habits and so on.

For soft drinks segmentation variables could be activities and interests.

Games playing and even watching professionals - 'energy drinks'.

Pub–going – mixer drinks and non-alcoholic beer substitutes.

Work - 'energy drinks' - drinks packaged in sizes suitable for box lunches.

Voluntary activities – refreshment drinks in bulk packs – 6, 12, 18.

Foodies – fruit and vegetable juice drinks with a minimum of 'E numbers' and other additives.

Benefits segmentation based on benefit sought by consumer.

For soft drinks segments might be based on -

- flavour
- social cachet (cost, endorsement)
- 'healthiness' - vitamin and mineral content
- price
- caffeine content

3

(a) Innovation is a major source of competitive advantage when it adds customer-pleasing features to the marketing mix - not just the product.

Even in commodity markets eg grain, crude oil, innovation can be used in non-product aspects eg price, credit, delivery, stock holding, packaging.

Must be controlled to avoid value-destroying effects stocking up with an unpopular new product.

(b) **Reactive** – respond to competition's innovation.

Proactive – innovate independently

'First to market' not historically a successful strategy for smaller companies – technical innovations require careful management and significant financial resources to overcome almost-inevitable teething troubles. Larger companies that have taken up troubled innovations have typically had the greatest success with them.

A reputation for innovation can be a source of competitive advantage among customers interested in the latest thing.

Low risk of reactive approach must not become excuse for unimaginative followership.

Reactive approach uses competitors' innovations as a kind of market testing activity - when competitor has successful new product, this indicates imitation will probably be profitable.

Some new products legally protected by patent/registered design - allows innovator to skim market and gain high profits for several years - when imitation possible, price falls markedly eg Black and Decker workmate - clones now available at fraction of original price.

(c)   Provide definitions of the terms (and examples as the question requires).

(d)

> **Tutorial note.** Branding is a huge subject and the temptation here will be to write too much. Stay focused and remember this part is only worth 5 marks!

Branding – form of product differentiation.

Brand values/promise - tangible and intangible aspects of products create a complex whole in consumer perceptions.

Using existing brand for new product should give immediate identity and market positioning.

Brand based promotion in past has created existing market for new product.

Brand value must not be eroded by poor or inappropriate new product!

Marketing mix expectations created by existing brand values must be exploited and reinforced by mix chosen for new product eg prestige brand should not be undermined by economy price of new product .

4

(a)   General economic forecasts from eg Bank of England, US Federal Reserve, DTI.

Air transport forecasts from eg International Air Transport Organisation (IATA).

Holiday industry forecasts from trade associations.

Business travel forecasts from eg National Business Travel Association (NBTA) (US).

Surveys of large organisation travel managers.

Focus groups formed from regular air travellers of all kinds – the airline's frequent flyer programme would be a good starting point, if one exists.

Air traveller surveys carried out by British Airports Authority (BAA) staff.

Volume of forward bookings especially those made on-line.

(b)   **Macro-environment**

General economic confidence as reflected in GNP, interest rates and unemployment figures. Can affect prices both ways – people on low incomes may be tempted to fly more by availability of low cost fares – more prosperous people may choose to trade up to full fares.

Prospect of further deregulation of routes.

Micro-environment

Cost of aviation fuel – depends largely on oil price generally.

Cost of landing fees.

Any introduction of newer, more economical aircraft.

Prospect of changes in burden of personnel costs.

Potential for price moves by competitors.

Potential for market entry by full-cost airline subsidiaries.

(c)

Marginal analysis -

Supply and demand

Any change to supply or demand will exert pressure on market clearing price – practical implication – will low cost airline industry carrying capacity rise or fall in the coming year?

Analysis of costs – possible implication – diminishing economies of scale when hours flown start to reach practical limit and aircraft and crews must be hired on short term basis.

Breakeven analysis

Nature of breakeven – importance of contribution – C/S ratio .

Difficulty of establishing a simple measure of output – seat/mile? Cost depends on sector length, landing fees, aircraft used.

Can probably establish an overall breakeven volume in terms of seat/miles per month, say.

5

(a) Quality only definable by customer perception - *Grönroos* service quality model - comparison of expected quality with perception of actual quality.

Two principal components of perceived actual quality – technical (what) and functional (how).

Overall organisation image can influence perception of service quality and even reverse judgement.

Parasuraman et al suggest gap between expected and perceived actual influenced by 4 other gaps.

Consumer expectations/management perceptions of quality.

Management perceptions/specified standards.

Service standards/ service delivery.

Service delivery/external communications – what is promised.

(b)

Internal marketing - define here as internal promotion of high aspirations for service quality.

People and process - important features of service marketing mix – people at all levels of hierarchy come into contact with customers and can sour relationship/impress- people operate processes.

People must understand their importance to high quality service and be motivated to provide it.

Leadership by supervisors and managers important - all staff should internalise need for high standards.

(c)   **Product**

Nature of academic courses largely a matter for academic staff.

But - enhanced product includes study facilities, premises generally, domestic accommodation, catering, availability of student finance and financial advice – special needs of overseas students should be considered eg dietary requirements, accommodation advice.

Promotion

Overseas advertising in appropriate media and website and in appropriate languages.

Price

Room for manoeuvre on credit terms, welfare funds?

Place

Use of website to deliver introductory or pre-course material?

People

Internal marketing to promote need to make overseas students feel welcome.

Register of staff language skills.

Process

Disorientating effect of studying overseas and possibly in foreign language to be specifically acknowledged in design of processes and provision of support.

Physical evidence

Link with promotion in provision of brochures and other informative material - graduation ceremonies and degree parchments.

Further reading

Adcock, D (2000), *Marketing Strategies for Competitive Advantage*. John Wiley and Sons Ltd. (Chapter 8)

Ansoff, I (1987), *Corporate Strategy* (revised ed). London: Penguin. (Chapter 4)

Cowell, D (1995), *The Marketing of Services*. Butterworth Heinemann. (Chapter 8)

Dibb, S, Simkin, L, Pride, W M, Ferrell, O C (2001), *Marketing: Concepts and Strategies* (4th European edition). Houghton Mifflin. (Chapters 1, 5, 11)

Grönroos (1984), Strategic Management and Marketing in the Services Sector. Kriger. (Chapter 8)
Gummesson, E (2001), *Total Relationship Marketing: Rethinking Marketing Management*. Butterworth Heinemann. (Chapter 8)

Howard, J A & Sheth, J N (1969), *Theory of Buyer Behaviour*. Wiley. (Chapter 10)

Kotler, P (1991), *Marketing Management*. Prentice Hall. (Chapters 1, 4, 5, 8)

Kotler, P (2002), *Social Marketing*. Sage Publications. (Chapter 8)

McDonald, M (2002), *Marketing Plans: How to Prepare Them, How to Use Them*. Butterworth Heinemann. (Chapter 1)

Porter, M (1996), *Competitive Advantage*. Simon & Schuster. (Chapters 3, 4)

Porter, M (1996), *Competitive Strategy*. Simon & Schuster. (Chapters 3, 4)

Smith, P R & Taylor, J (2001), *Marketing Communications: an Integrated Approach*. Kogan Page. (Chapter 5)

Wilson, R M S & Gilligan, C (1997), *Strategic Marketing Management: Planning, Implementation and Control*, Butterworth Heinemann. (Chapter 3)

Zeithami, V A, Parasuraman, A & Barry, L L (1990), *Delivering Quality Service: Balancing Customer Perceptions and Expectations*. The Free Press. (Chapter 8)

List of key concepts and Index

REVIEW FORM & FREE PRIZE DRAW

All original review forms from the entire BPP range, completed with genuine comments, will be entered into one of two draws on 31 January 2009 and 31 July 2009. The names on the first four forms picked out on each occasion will be sent a cheque for £50.

Name: _____   **Address**: _____

_____

_____

How have you used this Text?
(Tick one box only)

☐ Self study (book only)

☐ On a course: college_____

☐ With BPP Home Study package

☐ Other _____

Why did you decide to purchase this Text?
(Tick one box only)

☐ Have used companion Kit

☐ Have used BPP Texts in the past

☐ Recommendation by friend/colleague

☐ Recommendation by a lecturer at college

☐ Saw advertising in journals

☐ Saw website

☐ Other _____

During the past six months do you recall seeing/receiving any of the following?
(Tick as many boxes as are relevant)

☐ Our advertisement in *Marketing Success*

☐ Our advertisement in *Marketing Business*

☐ Our brochure with a letter through the post

☐ Our brochure with *Marketing Business*

☐ Saw website

Which (if any) aspects of our advertising do you find useful?
(Tick as many boxes as are relevant)

☐ Prices and publication dates of new editions

☐ Information on product content

☐ Facility to order books off-the-page

☐ None of the above

Have you used the companion Practice & Revision Kit for this subject?   ☐ Yes   ☐ No

Your ratings, comments and suggestions would be appreciated on the following areas.

	Very useful	Useful	Not useful
Introductory section (How to use this text, study checklist, etc)	☐	☐	☐
Introduction	☐	☐	☐
Syllabus coverage	☐	☐	☐
Action Programmes and Marketing at Work examples	☐	☐	☐
Chapter roundups	☐	☐	☐
Quick quizzes	☐	☐	☐
Illustrative questions	☐	☐	☐
Content of suggested answers	☐	☐	☐
Index	☐	☐	☐
Structure and presentation	☐	☐	☐

	Excellent	Good	Adequate	Poor
Overall opinion of this Text	☐	☐	☐	☐

Do you intend to continue using BPP Study Texts/Kits/Passcards?   ☐ Yes   ☐ No

Please note any further comments and suggestions/errors on the reverse of this page.

Please return to: Kellie Vincent, BPP Learning Media Ltd, FREEPOST, London, W12 8BR

REVIEW FORM & FREE PRIZE DRAW (continued)

Please note any further comments and suggestions/errors below.

FREE PRIZE DRAW RULES

1   Closing date for 31 January 2009 draw is 31 December 2008. Closing date for 31 July 2009 draw is 30 June 2009.

2   Restricted to entries with UK and Eire addresses only. BPP employees, their families and business associates are excluded.

3   No purchase necessary. Entry forms are available upon request from BPP Learning Media Ltd. No more than one entry per title, per person. Draw restricted to persons aged 16 and over.

4   Winners will be notified by post and receive their cheques not later than 6 weeks after the relevant draw date. List of winners will be supplied on request.

5   The decision of the promoter in all matters is final and binding. No correspondence will be entered into.